Elisha Benjamin Andrews

Gospel from Two Testaments

Sermons on the International Sunday-School Lessons for 1893

Elisha Benjamin Andrews

Gospel from Two Testaments
Sermons on the International Sunday-School Lessons for 1893

ISBN/EAN: 9783743393356

Manufactured in Europe, USA, Canada, Australia, Japa

Cover: Foto ©Lupo / pixelio.de

Manufactured and distributed by brebook publishing software (www.brebook.com)

Elisha Benjamin Andrews

Gospel from Two Testaments

GOSPEL FROM TWO TESTAMENTS

SERMONS

ON THE

International Sunday-School Lessons

FOR 1893

EDITED BY

REV. E. BENJAMIN ANDREWS, D.D., LL.D.,

PRESIDENT OF BROWN UNIVERSITY

PROVIDENCE:
PRESS OF E. A. JOHNSON & COMPANY.
1892.

PREFACE.

THE gentlemen who have taken part in the preparation of this volume are not on this account to be considered champions of Sunday School study according to the more or less definite method which has become associated with the International Lessons. Other systems may be better. We simply found this one in far more common use than any other, and wished, if possible, to promote its efficiency. One unfortunate impression cultivated by this mode of biblical study we have done our best to dissipate: the impression, namely, that the various portions and books of the Bible are all of the same importance. While no verse of the Sacred Volume is without value, not all is pure gold, as so much is. To assist in correcting this mischievous error of reducing all Scripture to one and the same level in respect to edifying power, the expositions in this volume have been made honestly historical. The Old Testament has not been forced to anticipate the New, but has been left to voice naturally, in its own way, such instruction as it has to give. By this procedure, it is believed, much is gained, not only for biblical scholarship, but as well in depth of religious impression.

The aim of these sermons is to promote a sound and cool understanding of Holy Scripture, always the primary purpose of good Sunday School teaching, at the same time keeping up a pronounced homiletical interest. The book is thus intended to aid two classes of biblical students, teachers in Sunday Schools and ministers engaged in preaching. It is never quite easy to further both these interests in the same discourse, though all genuine expository sermons attempt this; and in some of the passages discussed upon the following pages the difficulty has proved so far insurmountable that the keen reader will think one intention or the other more or less subordinated. Critics may perhaps be willing to account for such and all other shortcomings in our work by the refractoriness of the scriptural passages on which the sermons thought faulty are based. At any rate we are sure that judges of expository preaching will find in the volume many rich and model specimens of this.

Minute exegesis we have entirely avoided. Commentaries, Bible Dictionaries and the innumerable Sunday School Lesson Helps furnish enough of this. We seek to perform a much more important service, that of placing the lesson for each Sunday in its proper historical setting and of exhibiting its thought in its wide and general relations, doctrinal or practical. How far we have succeeded in such a purpose readers will judge for themselves. We shall be surprised if these sermons are not found exceedingly helpful in this respect.

The lessons of each quarter form a beautiful unity. Those of the first quarter are historical, sketching in a most interesting way Israel's career after the captivity. The studies of the second quarter present some of the Old Testament's finest moral teachings. The third group offers an entertaining *resumé* of Paul's missionary labors after his call to Europe. The fourth, more doctrinal, is taken up with fresh studies in the epistolary parts of the New Testament.

Interest in the book and in the scriptures which it treats will be greatly increased if the whole matter, or at least that for each quarter, is read through rapidly. The detailed study of each lesson will afterwards be not only easier but far more profitable.

May this volume do much to stimulate love for the Bible and to further the christian graces in all who read it.

THE EDITOR.

BROWN UNIVERSITY, August 8, 1892.

TABLE OF CONTENTS.

First Quarter.

ISRAEL AFTER THE CAPTIVITY.

LESSON			PAGE
I.	January 1.	RETURNING FROM THE CAPTIVITY. Ezra i: 1-11 . . . . Rev. Professor S. Burnham, D.D.	3
II.	January 8.	REBUILDING THE TEMPLE. Ezra iii:1-13. Professor Shailer Mathews.	10
III.	January 15.	ENCOURAGING THE PEOPLE. Haggai ii: 1-9 . . . . Rev. Professor Philip A. Nordell, D.D.	19
IV.	January 22.	JOSHUA THE HIGH PRIEST. Zechariah iii: 1-10 . . . . Professor George Rice Hovey.	28
V.	January 29.	THE SPIRIT OF THE LORD. Zechariah iv: 1-10 . . . . Rev. E. M. Poteat.	37
VI.	February 5.	DEDICATING THE TEMPLE. Ezra vi: 14-22 . . . . Rev. A. S. Coats.	46
VII.	February 12.	NEHEMIAH'S PRAYER. Nehemiah i: 1-11 . . . . Rev. Frederick L. Anderson.	54
VIII.	February 19.	REBUILDING THE WALL. Nehemiah iv: 9-21 . . . . Rev. Thos. S. Barbour.	62

LESSON			PAGE
IX.	February 26.	READING THE LAW. Nehemiah viii: 1–12 . . . . Rev. Thomas E. Bartlett.	71
X.	March 5.	KEEPING THE SABBATH. Nehemiah xiii: 15–22 . . . . Rev. Edward Holyoke.	80
XI.	March 12.	ESTHER BEFORE THE KING. Esther iv: 10–17; v: 1–3 . . . . Rev. F. W. Ryder.	89
XII.	March 19.	*Temperance Lesson.* TIMELY ADMONITIONS. Proverbs xxiii: 15–23 . Rev. George E. Horr, Jr.	98
XII.	March 19.	*Missionary Lesson.* THE VANITY OF GRAVEN IMAGES. Isaiah xliv: 9–20. Rev. W. S. Ayers.	104

Second Quarter.

OLD TESTAMENT TEACHINGS.

I.	April 2.	THE AFFLICTIONS OF JOB. Job ii: 1–10 . Rev. F. E. Dewhurst.	117
I.	April 2.	*Easter Lesson.* THE RESURRECTION OF CHRIST. Matthew xxviii: 1–10 . Rev. Professor D. F. Estes.	125
II.	April 9.	AFFLICTIONS SANCTIFIED. Job v: 17–27 Rev. H. H. Peabody, D.D.	134
III.	April 16.	JOB'S APPEAL TO GOD. Job xxiii: 1–10 . Rev. George E. Merrill.	142
IV.	April 23.	JOB'S CONFESSION AND RESTORATION. Job xlii: 1–10 . . . . Rev. Edward Judson, D.D.	150
V.	April 30.	WISDOM'S WARNING. Proverbs i: 20–33 Rev. B. A. Greene.	158

LESSON			PAGE
VI.	May 7.	THE VALUE OF WISDOM. Proverbs iii: 11-24 Rev. Professor J. R. Sampey, D.D.	167
VII.	May 14.	FRUITS OF WISDOM. Proverbs xii: 1-15 H. C. Vedder.	176
VIII.	May 21.	AGAINST INTEMPERANCE. Proverbs xxiii: 29-35 The Editor.	184
IX.	May 28.	THE EXCELLENT WOMAN. Proverbs xxxi: 10-31 Rev. C. H. Watson.	192
X.	June 4.	REVERENCE AND FIDELITY. Ecclesiastes v: 1-12 Rev. E. P. Tuller.	201
XI.	June 11.	THE CREATOR REMEMBERED. Ecclesiastes xii: 1-7, 13, 14 Rev. J. F. Elder, D.D.	209
XII.	June 18.	MESSIAH'S KINGDOM. Malachi iii; 1-12. Rev. R. H. Pitt, D.D.	217

Third Quarter.

LESSONS FROM THE LIFE OF PAUL.

I.	July 2.	PAUL CALLED TO EUROPE. Acts xvi: 6-15 Rev. Professor B. O. True, D.D.	229
II.	July 9.	PAUL AT PHILIPPI. Acts xvi: 19-34 Rev. E. K. Chandler, D.D.	238
III.	July 16.	PAUL AT ATHENS. Acts xvii: 22-31 Rev. C. J. Baldwin.	246
IV.	July 23.	PAUL AT CORINTH. Acts xviii: 1-11 Rev. Professor Rush Rhees.	255
V.	July 30.	PAUL AT EPHESUS. Acts xix: 1-12 Rev. W. W. Everts.	263

TABLE OF CONTENTS. ix

LESSON			PAGE
VI.	August 6.	PAUL AT MILETUS. Acts xx: 22-35 Rev. J. R. Gow.	271
VII.	August 13.	PAUL AT JERUSALEM. Acts xxi: 27-39 Rev. Professor J. M. English, D.D.	279
VIII.	August 20.	PAUL BEFORE FELIX. Acts xxiv: 10-25 Rev. Thomas E. Bartlett.	287
IX.	August 27.	PAUL BEFORE AGRIPPA. Acts xxvi: 19-32 Rev. H. M. King, D.D.	296
X.	September 3.	PAUL SHIPWRECKED. Acts xxvii: 30-44 Rev. W. S. Apsey, D.D.	305
XI.	September 10.	PAUL AT ROME. Acts xxviii: 20-31 Rev. John H. Mason.	313
XII.	September 17.	PERSONAL RESPONSIBILITY. Romans xiv: 12-23 Rev. T. D. Anderson.	321

Fourth Quarter.

STUDIES IN THE EPISTLES.

I.	October 1.	THE POWER OF THE GOSPEL. Romans i: 8-17 Rev. James T. Dickinson.	333
II.	October 8.	REDEMPTION IN CHRIST. Romans iii: 19-26 The Editor.	342
III.	October 15.	JUSTIFICATION BY FAITH. Romans v: 1-11 Rev. George B. Gow, D.D.	351
IV.	October 22.	CHRISTIAN LIVING. Romans xii: 1-15 Rev. Wm. M. Lawrence. D.D.	360

LESSON			PAGE
V.	October 29.	ABSTINENCE FOR THE SAKE OF OTHERS. I Corinthians viii: 1–13 . . Rev. Professor R. S. Colwell, D.D.	367
VI.	November 5.	THE RESURRECTION. I Corinthians xv: 12–26 . . . . Rev. Charles A. Reese.	376
VII.	November 12.	THE GRACE OF LIBERALITY. II Corinthians viii: 1–12 . . . . Rev. Clark M. Brink.	384
VIII.	November 19.	IMITATION OF CHRIST. Ephesians iv: 20–32 . . . . Rev. C. R. Henderson, D.D.	392
IX.	November 26.	THE CHRISTIAN HOME. Colossians iii: 12–25 . . . . Rev. C. C. Brown.	399
X.	December 3.	GRATEFUL OBEDIENCE. James i:16–27 Rev. President B. L. Whitman.	408
XI.	December 10.	THE HEAVENLY INHERITANCE. I Peter i: 1–12 . . . . Rev. Professor Wm. N. Clarke, D.D.	417
XII.	December 17.	THE GLORIFIED SAVIOUR. Revelation i: 9–20 . . . . Rev. J. V. Garton.	425
XIII.	December 24.	*Missionary Lesson.* THE GREAT INVITATION. Revelation xxii: 8–21 Rev. Prescott F. Jernegan.	433
XIII.	December 24.	*Christmas Lesson.* THE BIRTH OF JESUS. Matthew ii: 1–11 . . . . Rev. H. W. Pinkham.	441

THE FIRST QUARTER.

ISRAEL AFTER THE CAPTIVITY.

LESSON			
I.	January	1.	"Returning from the Captivity." — Ezra i: 1-11. REV. PROF. S. BURNHAM, D. D.
II.	"	8.	"Rebuilding the Temple."—Ezra iii: 1-13. PROF. S. MATHEWS.
III.	"	15.	"Encouraging the People."—Hag. ii: 1-9. REV. PROF. P. A. NORDELL, D. D.
IV.	"	22.	"Joshua the High-Priest."—Zech. iii: 1-10. PROF. G. R. HOVEY.
V.	"	29.	"The Spirit of the Lord."—Zech. iv: 1-10. REV. E. M. POTEAT.
VI.	February	5.	"Dedicating the Temple."—Ezra vi: 14-22. REV. A. S. COATS.
VII.	"	12.	"Nehemiah's Prayer."—Neh. i: 1-11. REV. F. L. ANDERSON.
VIII.	"	19.	"Rebuilding the Wall." — Neh. iv: 9-21. REV. T. S. BARBOUR.
IX.	"	26.	"Reading the Law."—Neh. viii: 1-12. REV. THOS. M. BARTLETT.
X.	March	5.	"Keeping the Sabbath."—Neh. xiii: 15-22. REV. EDW. HOLYOKE.
XI.	"	12.	"Esther before the King."—Esth. iv: 10-17; v: 1-3. REV. F. W. RYDER.
XII.	"	19.	"Timely Admonitions."—Prov. xxiii: 15-23. REV. G. E. HORR, JR.
XIII.	"	19.	"The Vanity of Graven Images." — Isa. xliv: 9-20. REV. W. S. AYRES,

Lesson I. January 1.

RETURNING FROM THE CAPTIVITY.

Ezra i: 1-11.

BY REV. PROFESSOR S. BURNHAM, D. D.

WITH the book of Ezra begins the history of the New Israel. Fifty years had passed, fifty weary years of exile, since, in 586 B. C., the army of Nebuchadnezzar, king of Babylon, had given the holy city of Jerusalem to the flames, and had broken down its walls. Then Nebuzoradan, the general of the Babylonian monarch, had carried away captive all the nation except the very poorest of the people, whom he left to till the land as the servants of his sovereign. (2 Kings xxv. 8-12.) All these years Israel had borne the yoke of captivity in a strange land. The promised inheritance had lain desolate and waste, without temple or altar. Pious souls among the exiles were sorrowing over the desolation of the nation, and were praying, "O Lord, let thine anger and thy fury be turned away from thy city Jerusalem, thy holy mountain." (Daniel ix.16.)

At last, the time to set the captives free and to found the new commonwealth had come. The discipline of the captivity had done its work. A purified and pious remnant had been prepared by the woes and lessons of the exile, that might serve for the beginning of the new state and for the foundation of the kingdom of God. Far below what their God desired them to be, were they, indeed. Never did they rise to realize the ideals that, according to the prophetic hopes and teachings, were possible for them. Nevertheless they were a better Israel than the Israel of old; and with at least many of them a new covenant could be made. (Jer. xxxi. 31.)

The historical event that made possible the release of the Jewish exiles, was the overthrow of the Babylonian power by the Persians under the leadership of Cyrus, their king. Scarcely had Cyrus added the Babylonian empire to his territory, when, in the same year, he issued the decree for the release of the Jewish captives, of which we have an account in the first verses (vv. 1-4) of our chapter. It is scarcely to be supposed that we have in these verses the exact words of the Persian king. Formerly it was thought that Cyrus, being a monotheistic Persian, recognized in the Jehovah of Israel the true and one God whom he worshipped, and therefore spoke as a believer in the sovereignty of Jehovah. But late discoveries of tablet and cylinder inscriptions seem to show that Cyrus was an Elamite rather than a Persian, and therefore, presumably, a polytheist. If this was the case, he would hardly have used the terms in which his proclamation is given in the chapter we are considering. It is not impossible that Daniel, who, as we read (Dan. vi. 28), "prospered in the reign of Cyrus the Persian," may have shown to the king out of the book of Isaiah (Isa. xlv. xlvi) that he had been divinely appointed to set Israel free; and that Cyrus, who was tolerant of all faiths, and claims, in his own words, to have been ordained by the gods of Babylon to execute their wrath upon the king of Babylon, may have accepted the commission as a divine trust. Even in this case the words of his decree, we seem obliged to suppose, have come to us colored by the thinking and vocabulary of the Jewish historian. But so we get only the more clearly set before us the great truth to which the historical events narrated in the chapter bear witness, and which it seems to be the author's aim to teach us. Nor is there any violence done to the real meaning and force of the royal decree. Its polytheistic coloring, or its imperfect monotheism, is simply replaced by a shading that attributes events to that Source to which alone an inspired man could be content to allow himself or his readers to refer them. In this way, he accomplishes most surely his purpose to lead men to read history aright. For he will teach us, in this chapter, that the noisy and complicated machinery of history does not find its motive power in itself. An unseen but omnipotent hand guides all the complicated motions to secure the end for which it furnishes the power. History, in our author's view of it, is but the working of a Present, Living God.

So he shows us:

First, that God is present and active in history.

To him, the downfall of Jerusalem, the long years of exile, the rise of the Persian empire, the overthrow of the Babylonian power, the decree of Cyrus, are only the means by which the word of the Lord is made true (v. 1). These are the works of God, wrought that history may reproduce his word and his thought. God, to our author, is no philosophical abstraction, no remote first cause having nothing or little to do with the daily life of the world. But he is an actual presence, a real power, an "immanent" personality. What is done in the life of the world, he does. He leads to victory the nation that conquers. He tramples underfoot the power that is overthrown. He releases the captives; he wipes away tears from weeping eyes. How wisely our author sees; how like a soul touched from on high he reads. For life and history have no meaning unless they are the creation of a present, living God. There is no enduring. of the burdens and woes of the world by a soul that thinks, except as seeing in them him who is invisible. But not less real because unseen. For always and everywhere the things unseen are the most real things.

Secondly, our author would teach us that God is present and active in the history of *all* nations.

It is not alone in Judah that God abides; but he dwells in Persia as well. The heart of the king of Persia is in his hands no less than the heart of David or Solomon (v. 1). Nor is even this the limit of the divine presence and working. His power and his life are felt in all the nations of the earth, although men do not always recognize the power that shapes their destinies (v. 2). This truth it is harder for men to receive than even the fact of the real presence in history of a living God. Israel was taught it in vain. From the time it was announced to Abraham that all the nations of the earth should be blessed through his seed, God strove to make Israel understand that it was the elect nation for the sake of all nations, his servant to make him known to the world, and to bring the world to recognize him as the God of all the earth. But the divine choice was only made the occasion of a false national pride; and divine blessings were transformed into the occasion of a national ruin. Were the men of Israel sinners above others in all this? Do not we also too often fall into the same blindness, and the same false pride of race? It is so easy to think that our land is more than all other lands "God's country," and that the Anglo-Saxon race is, in a special sense, the darling of heaven. It is so easy and so natural to suppose that God has less love and less care for other lands and other races than for ours. In fact, is it not this false pride of race, and this blind assumption of God as all our own, that often and largely stand in the way of victorious missionary effort? Are we not remiss in sending the gospel to other nations just because we do not believe that it can be to them the power of God as truly and mightily as it was to our savage and acorn-eating ancestors? Let our chapter remind us anew that God has made of one blood all nations, and that, in all, he dwells and works, loving all with the same fatherly love out of the same great, divine heart.

Thirdly, our author would teach us that God is present and active in the souls of individual men.

To him God is not simply a general presence and force in life. He does not merely work the great movements and mighty catastrophes in the history of nations. The desires and purposes of individual souls are as truly his work as the events of history. In fact, it is by his work in individual souls that he causes the great historical movements of the world's life. It is he who creates in Cyrus the willingness to let the captives go free (v. 1). It is he who creates in the exiles the desire to return to the ancient land and to build again the house of God (v. 5). Whatever is best and noblest in our thoughts and our desires, our author would have us understand, is but the echo in our souls of the voice of God. How comforting and encouraging is such a view of life! We all may be the channels of the divine power, the hearts and hands by which God will touch and move the world. If we will but open our souls to him, he will use us as the beginnings of new and better things among men. He will stir up within us new desires and new purposes, that shall issue in acts by which he will create a new world, and bring to pass his own great purposes. Thus shall we be, in the truest and best sense, workers together with God.

Our author, however, is not content with setting before us this truth of a present and acting, a living God, in these varied ways. He wishes us to see why God is thus ever present and working. So

Fourthly, he teaches us that God is thus present in history and in the souls of men, for the sake of the Kingdom of Heaven.

Cyrus is charged to build the house of the Lord which is in Jerusalem (v. 2). Men volunteer, and gold and silver are contributed, with the same end in view (vv. 5–12). But the temple at Jerusalem was the earthly centre and symbol of the Kingdom of Heaven. Poets had sung of it as the earthly abode of Jehovah. Prophets had depicted the coming kingdom of God as encircling it and making it the centre of its life and blessedness. In the prophetic vision it stood upon its lofty mountain raised above all the high hills of the country, while to it the nations were streaming as the source of their peace and their joys. Rebuilt, and forming the centre of the life of the new state, the glory that it should have would exceed all the glory of the magnificent temple erected by Solomon. However, their new state was to be no merely earthly power, but the Kingdom of Heaven itself. So, the exile occurred, and Cyrus set the captives free; Babylon fell, and all the kingdoms of the world came into the power of Cyrus, that the Kingdom of Heaven might be set up in the world. was in the world, and in the souls of men, because his kingdom was to come. Even so is it to-day. Only now the kingdom of heaven is among us, and it is its perfection that come. The King is ruling on earth from his throne in heavens; and God among men puts down one and sets up another, that the coming perfection may be hastened. For this, armies march, and navies sail; for this, wars are made and peace is declared. It is nothing that men do not what God is doing among them. They have always been blind to his presence, have always been saying of his Christ, " Is not this the son of Joseph?"

Such is the teaching of our chapter. The great truth it sets before us of the presence and activity of God in history and in the soul of man, cannot be too much or too often emphasized in the day in which we live. Our age is materialistic and believes far too much in the sole reality of the things that can be seen or felt. To it, money, armies, fleets, machinery, are actual and acting powers; but not God. Or, if not materialistic, it is too philosophic; and, with its multitude of second causes, it feels no need of the presence of a first and final cause. God is not in all the thoughts of men of this age, scarcely in any of them. The fact of God's real presence in history and in the soul, as the true cause of all that is good and

[Lesson I.] RETURNING FROM CAPTIVITY. 9

gracious in life, needs to be more clearly seen and more firmly believed in, if life is to be saved from sordidness and littleness. Nothing will make men generous, brave, strong, and self-forgetful, like the sense of a present God acting with and in them. Besides, only the conviction that God is in history and in the soul, will enable us to hope for the realization of the superhuman ideals of the kingdom of heaven, and make us willing to do and to suffer for their realization. The transformation of this world, foul with sin and laden with misery, where men devour one another in both body and soul, where crime, debauchery and cruelty, have, according to all in c , their own way,—the making of this world, but little aging an hell itself, into a place where all the sweetness and the and blessedness of heaven shall repeat themselves, tou shall live the life of God, is a work so tremendous hin ill never be done unless God is ever present in history d in the soul. Only as we see God present and active on can we have heart to pray, "Thy kingdom come."

Lesson II. January 8.

REBUILDING THE TEMPLE.
Ezra iii: 1–13.

BY PROFESSOR SHAILER MATHEWS, WATERVILLE, ME.

AN interest not wholly wanting in pathos, belongs to the returning settlers on the deserted and impoverished hills of Judea. Few in numbers when compared with the rich *bourgeoisie* comfortably settled in their shops at Babylon, established by a far-sighted king as a buffer between Egypt and his own empire; the re-founders of Jerusalem united the devotion of enthusiasts with the dangers of a forlorn hope. The history of the first twenty-five years of these returned captives abundantly shows how the desperate circumstances into which they were thrust quenched their religious fervor and blurred the noble purposes with which they re-entered the promised land. But in the first few months of their struggle with poverty their life was marked by an energy that has made the world forget those later years which had need of the drastic reforms of Ezra.

It was in the first flush of this early enthusiasm that the new settlers undertook the great object of their return—the re-establishment of their national faith. Nourished on the visions of Ezekiel, themselves the holy remnant, bearing as national vicars, the sorrows and grief of their entire people, their thoughts centered less on their political than on their religious future. The altar and the temple, not the walls and the palaces, were the first objects of their care. Before they had been more than a few weeks in their new homes, the great altar of burnt sacrifice was rebuilt, with foundations double the dimensions of its predecessor. In October, 536 B. C., it was consecrated, and thereafter the morning and the evening sacrifices were offered regularly.

Something less than a year later the foundations of the new Temple were laid. It was a moment of supreme anticipation. The old men might sob at the thought of the sanctuary of their past, but the young men saw only the nobler future when their suffering people should see of the travail of its soul and be satisfied. It was the enthusiasm of inexperience. The years of struggle with jealous neighbors and official delays, the coarsening of religious devotion, the poverty, the sin, that were all to come before the roof should close over the foundations, were hid. To their excited minds the religion of the patriarchs, of Moses, of the glorious kings, was to live again in the renewed Israel. The burst of song brought back their Psalmist; the priests clothed in the sacred robes, brought back their Lawgiver. Like the Phenix from his ashes, the new Judaism was springing from the old, and the shout drowned the weeping.

The returned captives of Judah are commonly likened to the Puritans in Massachusetts Bay. The comparison, though by no means complete, is not inapt. The Puritans sought escape from unhealthful religious surroundings in a new land; the Jews sought the same in an old. The Puritans transplanted, the Jews re-established political forms. But—and this is fundamental—both Puritans and Jews alike in seeking to reintroduce a plan of worship, turned to the distant past as the repository of religion pure and undefiled. The faith that took root in New England and the faith that took root in New Judah were not new, but renewed. Both maintained a continuity of religious life.

The desire to authenticate reforms by appeal to the past is

universal. Periods of revolution, at least in their earliest stages, are periods of restoration. Louis XVI. of France, before he became citizen Louis Capet, was the restorer of French liberty. The American colonies began revolution by demanding early privileges. The visionary of to-day declares that society and government are usurpers. Every nation has had its Golden Age, just as it expects its Golden Age. And, usually, too, this Golden Age lies in the distant, not in the immediate past. Reform adopts the political principle of the mediæval republics of Italy, "Hate your neighbor, love your neighbor's neighbor." We are told to find models not in our fathers, but in our grandfathers—preferably in their grandfathers.

In nothing does this recurrence to an authoritative past oftener and more decidedly show itself than in matters of religion. The Catholic Church may appeal to an infallible contemporaneous Pope, but the Pope himself will look to the inspired fathers. The devotee of the Church of England looks not to Henry VIII., but to a primitive episcopacy whose rights the Roman curia has usurped. Calvin and Luther looked back to Augustine and thence to Paul. Denominations appeal to their creeds, Christendom to an ancient Bible. And, to crown all, comes the man without religion, who looks back over church, creed and teacher, to find religion purest in the pre-historic man who trembled at the thunder and his own strange dreams.

Of course there are mistakes in all this. The past was not purer than the present. The nineteenth century is not nearer millennial goodness because more under Satan's control. He is a blind interpreter who sees only good in the past and only evil in the present. But, after all, this desire to bring the present into connection with the past and to make the worship of to-day reproduce the worship of yesterday, is not so much a tribute to the blind veneration of mere age, as it is the outcome of the law of religious development. There is not one of the great religions in the world to-day that has not passed through a period of reform when the cry has been, "Back to the simplicity and purity of our fathers' faith." India has had her Guadama and her Chesub Kunder Seb; China, her Confucius; the Jews, their Hezekiah and their Ezra; Arabia, its Mahomet; the Roman Church, its Döllinger; Protestantism, its Luther and its Maurice. Each one of these reformers has endeavored to purify, to rejuvenate a corrupt and decrepit faith by the infusion of forgotten spiritual truth.

A study of the renewal of the Jewish religion under Jeshua and Zerubbabel discloses two characteristics that belong to all similar periods.

First :—Periods of religious renewal are destructive. Reform is the outgrowth of abuse. The Jews went into the captivity emasculated by idolatry. They returned extreme Monotheists. No Jew took that four months' journey across the deserts without strong love for Jehovah. The influence of the captivity had been to consolidate and intensify the national faith in one Supreme Being. Idolatry and idolaters thereafter were sporadic growths. The spirit with which they re-laid the foundations of the altar was not the spirit of Zedekiah, but the spirit of Abraham.

But it is worth our notice that this apparent leap over a thousand years was no real break in the religious life of the Jews. Idolatry, not the renewal of the true worship, marked the break. The true and continuous religious life of the Jewish people is not to be found in the annals of the prophets of Baal and idolatrous kings. It lay in the hearts of unnoticed thousands who kept alive the faith that their rulers had forsaken. The real history of God's church lies not in the succession of councils and bishops, in the struggles of Popes and Emperors, in Papal corruption and Spanish inquisitions—but in the hearts of the mass of worshipers, in the actual Christianity of every age, as often in sects as in the Church. If a man will find the true Christianity of the Middle Ages he must look through the ambitions of prelates into their purposes, through an imperial Church into worshiping races. There is a cleavage line in religious history. On the one side is the essential Christianity; on the other are the local and adaptive teachings and forms. Seldom is this line wholly invisible. Sometimes it can be detected running through an organized faith, and we have the permanent element represented by the schismatics—the seven thousand who had not bowed to Baal: the returning Jews, the Donatists, the Waldenses, the Non Conformists, the Puritans. Occasionally we see it running across individual experience, as in the career of a Bernard of Clairvaux, a Hildebrand, or an Innocent, in all of whom the profoundest Christian spirit was joined to an intensely worldly ambition. When reformation or conversion discovers this cleavage line, strikes manfully along it, and splits off the abuse, that which remains is the true religious life. The untrue, the ephemeral alone is lost. The destruction of abuse is not the destruction of a faith. If the Jews left their idolatry in Persia, they brought back the songs of David.

Especially to-day do we need to remember this distinction. Criticism is the Babylon of traditional belief. It will separate the essential from the accidental. It is true that, in his zeal for truth or his desire for originality, the critic may attack the permanent, and it may seem more than once that it is not the abuse or the extra-belief that is threatened, but the truth itself. But such apprehension is needless. The microscopic criticism of this century in New Testament fields has already resulted in strengthening faith. It is not too much to expect that the present equally severe criticism of the Old Testament will result in a more rational understanding of its profound religious teachings. That everything which the past believed will remain, is impossible. The past overloaded its faith. But to fear that the final outcome of a search for truth will be the loss of anything that is true, is to believe in the eternity of lies.

After the scalpel has finished its work, it will be sun-clear that the life is left, that nothing but parasitic growth has been removed.

If it should be proved that the book of Jonah is legend, that the composite book of Genesis contains myths, that the Mosaic legislation does not entirely antedate Ezra, that the second half of Isaiah was written generations after the first, that Chronicles is much later than the exile: in a word, if the results upon which the more conservative higher criticism has united should be shown to be true, the spiritual teaching that lies in the experience of the Jewish race, the deep religious inspiration that breathes from its songs, the lessons of the immanence and love of Jehovah—all these, the real nexus of the Christian and the Jewish faith, would remain. A destructive criticism, so far as its processes are governed by a desire for truth and corrected by time, can only cleave the untrue from the true, the transitory from the eternal elements of our faith.

Second:—Destruction is simply preparatory. Its mission is to give freer scope to a developing religious life. Periods of religious renascence mark stages in religious growth. The permanent element in religion is not a statue whose limits are set by the removal of the encasing marble; it is an organism, demanding and permitting the removal of parasites, because it is itself developing and is able to replace the diseased with healthy tissue. The old truth that re-appears after the removal of abuse, is not unchanged—it is a developed truth.

The Jewish church of the return sought to re-produce the church of the early kingdom, but accurate re-production was impossible. Waiving all discussion as to how much of the traditional Mosaic legislation is post-exilic, the simple historical fact remains that the church of the return, as it was developed under Jeshua and Ezra, marks a new stage in the religious life of the Jews. The worship inaugurated when the foundations of the temple were laid, was marked by a punctilious ceremonial, a developed ritualism, an enthusiastic monotheism, a systematic theology, a codification of law, and a devotion to the national faith, to which the Jew of David's and Solomon's time was utterly unaccustomed. The system of Ezra was that of Moses, but developed. The enlarged altar and the re-modelled temple were typical of an enlarged and a re-modelled system.

The history of every religious reformation is similar. A man first awakes to the fact that abuses have been sanctioned which have been paralyzing a truth once mighty. He attacks the abuses; he lays bare the truth that had nerved men of old to martyrdom and sainthood; he attempts, by handling this re-discovered truth, to accomplish similar results in his own time. And the very first application of the old teaching to the new problem, the very first attempt at re-stating the old truth, shows to him that absolute identity between the truth as it was in one age and as it is in his own age, is out of the question. It is not simply that the times have changed and that the needs are new. The religious instincts and conciousness of men—the real content of religion—have been developing. Truth as it exists in God is unchangeable and unchanging. Truth as it incarnates itself in human experience is ever developing, for religious truth is the correlative of religious experience.

It is a truism that the formulas of one age must be re-adapted to a new. But the grounds for this need more careful attention than they commonly receive. Too often has attention been centered upon the standards and creeds—the secretions of the religious life,—rather than upon the life itself. It is of course, in a way, easy, by a comparison of the decisions of various councils, to trace the development of some central Christian doctrine like that of Christ's divinity. But it is an exceedingly difficult, if not an impossible task to trace the developing Christian consciousness that lay back of and found its expression in these decrees and articles. Yet the dynamic history of

Christianity lies in the developing religious conciousness. To compare the religion of the nineteenth century with that of the eighteenth century, we do not need to go to the minutes of religious bodies or the decisions of synods and councils—the precipitates of the theological chemistry. The religious history lay not so much in the formulations which the best Christian thought and Christian experience could make, as in that experience, in men, in religious society that gave rise to these formulations.

In times of reformation, this religious life is momentarily evident. For a few months or years the processes that have been going on slowly and unnoticed—processes which must ever remain untraceable—burst into light. The nerve centres of the Church, relieved from the paralysis of abuse, suddenly leap into intense action. It is the old life and yet the new life :—old, because it found its beginning in the far distant past; new, because it re-appears at the end of a period of development. It will, it is true, in its turn soon bury itself in attempted deliverances and formulations of its newly awakened self-consciousness. It will itself lose something of its first fresh vigor. It will itself need future renovation. But the advance it marks will never become retrogression. From the days in which the Church poured itself northward into the German forests, and leavened the wild conquerors of Roman Europe with the teachings of Christ, there has never been an ebb in the great tide of religious life. Some waves have run farther up the shore, some, farther towards the sea, but the tide has ever risen. Even periods of apparent reaction are periods of consolidation. The eighteenth century with its Diderot, and its Hume, and its Voltaire, gave rise to the nineteenth century with its Christian philanthropists and Christian catholics.

It may be objected that the Christianity of Christ antedates the Christianity of to-day, and that, in comparison with his supreme holiness, all modern religious life is poor and mean.

The objection is a fair one. But it is simply new testimony to the truth of the law of Christian evolution. So far as science has been able to formulate the law of physical evolution, the most perfect representatives of a genus often come far in advance of the genus itself. They are the type to the likeness of which, after a long period of slow evolutionary process, the genus at last attains.

The Christianity of Christ is the type of the Christianity of the race. The life of Jesus is the typical expression of the religious forces of humanity. Thus far he stands unique, but the growth of the divine forces in humanity which in his one case found their perfect and typical embodiment, are working out in the race an ever approximating Christian genus. The period is long; the process is painful; but the time is coming when we shall be like him. Each new phase of the application of Christianity to the race,—Charlemagne with his Franks, the Church with its monks, the Crusades, the Reformation, the Methodist revival, the humanistic struggles of the Christian missionary and social reformer, mark corresponding stages in the process by which Christianity is bringing men and society into an ever increasing likeness to its type. The end already is clear to the eye of faith. We know only that we are now the sons of God, and though it does not yet appear what we shall be, yet we know that when he shall appear, we shall be like him.

Looked at in this broader horizon, the re-establishment of the Jewish faith by the returned captives, grows full of suggestions. With them the period of renewal showed alike the destruction of unhealthy religious tendencies, and a new stage in the growth of the healthy. So far as an isolated historical fact may teach anything, the re-building of the Temple may teach us alike courage in the face of the present war of scholars, certainty as to the growth of a purer and more Christlike Christianity.

Lesson III.   January 15.

ENCOURAGING THE PEOPLE.
Haggai ii: 1–9.

BY REV. PROFESSOR PHILIP A. NORDELL, D. D., CHICAGO, ILL.

THE recovery of the Jews from the disasters attending the Babylonian captivity was necessarily slow and painful. The handful of patriots who returned with Zerubbabel were poor, weak, and despised. They found Jerusalem and the temple heaps of ruins, covered with weeds and rubbish. The first two years witnessed the rebuilding of the altar, the re-establishment of the burnt sacrifices, and the laying of the foundation of the second temple amid the liveliest conflict of emotions—uncontrollable outbreaks of joy and praise from the young, and of sobs and tears from the aged, who contrasted the insignificant present with memories of the resplendent past. The enterprise, which was speedily obstructed by their enemies, was not resumed until nearly fifteen years later, at the inspired call of Haggai and Zechariah. The Samaritans, who hoped again to check the work, were themselves ordered by the king of Persia to render prompt and generous assistance.

In point of literary style, of freshness, sublimity, and strength, Haggai touches the low-water mark of Old Testament prophecy. His oracles are narrow as to both time and scope. The former is limited to four months in the second year of Darius, the latter to the rebuilding of the temple. His first oracle stirred the rulers and the people to begin this task anew. Only three or four weeks elapsed, however, before fresh discouragements threatened to terminate it permanently. Just at this point a second oracle, full of divine encouragement, came to Haggai. Weak hands were strengthened, timid hearts were cheered, religious faith and patriotic zeal were kindled into a glow of enthusiasm that never failed until the work was done.

We note four considerations by which the prophet wrought this happy change in the temper of his people.

I. JEHOVAH'S ABIDING PRESENCE.

Regarded from a merely human point of view there were many and cogent reasons either for an abandonment of the work, or for its postponement until a more auspicious time. The hostility of the neighboring peoples showed itself in persistent plots to harass the returned exiles, in fomenting discords among them, and in discrediting them at the Persian court. In comparison with the number, wealth and influence of their adversaries, were not the Jews themselves weak and contemptible? Only a few years had passed since their return to a ruined city and a desolate land. In their poverty and distress would it not be audacious folly to undertake the rebuilding of a structure that had taxed the resources of the kingdom in its meridian glory and power? Would not those who in their childhood had seen the magnificence of the former house look with derision on the present comparatively puny result of their most heroic sacrifices? Had not this generation borne burdens enough without being crushed under another? Why not relinquish this enormous load to a better equipped posterity? Moreover, since they returned from Babylon, had not the Lord withheld the legitimate increase of the fields and vineyards? Had they not sown much, and brought in little; drunk, and yet not been filled with drink; clothed themselves, and yet not been warm; earned wages, only to put it into a bag with holes?

In these straitened circumstances did not the care of their families demand all their time and substance? It might be a pardonable, but was it not a rash enthusiasm in the prophet that had incited them to waste a month of labor on this hopeless task? Religious leaders are always unreasonable! They imagine that common people have nothing to do but to work and give for the advancement of visionary projects. These discouraged Jews could have invented a hundred excuses for abandoning the work. Self-justification is easy when one is eager to recede from an unwelcome task or duty.

All human objections, however, are as chaff before an explicit divine command. The voice of prophecy, re-awakened after long silence, had spoken the authoritative word. The accomplishment could not be obstructed by the arrogance of outside foes, or by the conscious weakness of Jehovah's people. However sore the discipline to which their sins had subjected them, they were his people still, a "holy seed," a "very small remnant" indeed, but one over whose preservation he had watched with jealous care. In his wrath at their backslidings he had dispersed them among the nations, but in everlasting kindness he had gathered them together from the four corners of the earth. Had he not promised by the mouth of his prophet that "they should build the old wastes, that they should raise up the former desolations, and that they should repair the waste cities, the desolations of many years?" Not, however, in their own strength, nor by reliance on their own resources. With loving reiteration Jehovah exhorts them to forget their own weakness in joyful recognition of his omnipotence; to assure themselves that "the hope of Israel, the Saviour thereof in time of trouble, is not as a sojourner in the land, nor as a wayfaring man that turneth aside to tarry for a night." As he covenanted with them when they came out of Egypt, so "his spirit abideth among them,"—that spirit which in the Old Testament was not yet revealed as a distinct person in the Trinity, but was conceived as a divine energy immanent in the world at large, but manifesting itself in extraordinary measure among Jehovah's chosen people. "Be strong and work, saith the Lord of Hosts; for I am with you, and fear ye not." There is no better ground for victorious confidence than that. His presence is infinitely more desirable than unlimited worldly wealth and power.

We, likewise, face the depressing problems of our own day, grappling with them as we can, only to be overwhelmed by the consciousness of our inability. Through repeated failures we learn that without divine help we can do nothing. We are overmatched in the battle. Weary, wounded, ready to die, we turn at length to One who has already won the victory, and who most graciously invites us to repose confidence in him, for he assures us, "All power is given unto me in heaven and on earth; and lo, I am with you alway, even unto the end of the world."

II. JEHOVAH'S INEXHAUSTIBLE RESOURCES.

What if Jehovah's people are poor, insignificant, despised? He who is in the midst of them is the rightful owner of the world's treasures. The silver and the gold are his. Though for the moment they have been seized by others, he will provide for their return to his own people. He will "shake all the nations, and the costliest things* of all the nations shall come" into his sanctuary.

Now, see, when the people really trusted the Lord and went

---

*"The desire of all nations," A. V., has no reference to Christ. A glance at the original shows this traditional and still popular idea to be a misinterpretation. (a) The context is altogether against it; (b) the word "*chemdah*" means here a thing desired because of its costliness; (c) the verb "shall come" is plural, and shows that "*chemdah*" is a collective and means "desirable things," as the R. V. rightly renders it.

to work (Ezra vi. 3-9), how wonderfully the prophet's word was fulfilled; how the expense of rearing the massive walls, and the cost of the wood-work were defrayed from the treasury of the Persian empire; how the priceless vessels of silver and gold, that Nebuchadnezzar had carried to Babylon for his own glory, as he thought, but really for safe keeping during the exile, were all restored again; how the adversaries of the Jews, who had plotted against them, were compelled by the royal decree to furnish them day by day with young bullocks, rams and lambs for sacrifices, and with wheat, salt, wine and oil as the priests had need. Not only this, but from the very day (Hag. ii. 19, 20) when the rebuilding of the temple began, Jehovah would bless their land with affluence, instead of smiting it with blasting, with mildew, and with hail.

God's work never stops for lack of means when men are willing to obey him, and to launch out confidently on his promises. The silver and the gold are forthcoming, not by miracle, but through natural channels, as surprising sometimes as actual miracles. Is the time ripe for carrying the gospel into the heathen world? See how the millions are poured every year into the Lord's treasury. Does he inspire a Müller or a Spurgeon to build orphanages? At once he sends the means, and continues sending as fast as needed. Would he see a great onward movement in Christian education? Million follows million without stint from the most unexpected sources. If men will not give spontaneously, as did Darius, to the furtherance of God's purposes, he compels them to bring the best of their substance, as the Samaritans were forced to do.

God scatters his resources neither extravagantly nor in conformity to the whims of men. The law of parsimony withholds him from giving so freely as to make unnecessary the discipline of anxiety and struggle. Even when social and moral reformations are greatly needed he does not purchase transient success by lavish expenditures. Moral results are not permanently secured by material agencies. God could have supplied the early Church with means enough to have freed every slave in the Roman empire. Instead, he projects into humanity two lofty ideals, the fatherhood of God and the brotherhood of man, confident that these ideals will ultimately and forever accomplish what neither gold nor force can do. Nor does he waste his resources in perpetuating institutions that have survived their usefulness. Local churches, as well as individual saints, are but temporary factors. He does not endow moribund remnants of churches, any more than he preserves in jeweled caskets the mouldering bones of saints. "Holy relics" he suffers with absolute indifference to moulder into common dust.

III. JEHOVAH'S GRACIOUS PURPOSES.

Haggai prophesied in a transition period. The older men who heard him had witnessed the wreck of the Jewish monarchy. The return of the captives to Jerusalem was the glimmering dawn after a dark and stormy night. The glory of the past was a memory, that of the future a dream. Transition periods are always charged with doubts and fears, with peril and pain. No mother-life renews itself without the pangs of travail, but they are sustained by a great hope, and forgotten in the greater joy over the child that is born. The sorest trials are alleviated by an assurance that they lead to higher and richer experiences. And yet men would often forego these if they could thereby escape the trial. They cling to long cherished errors because they dread the effort and pain of adjusting themselves to new truths. Hoary abuses linger in the community, in the state, in the Church, because men shrink from the sharp but transient evils attending a crisis. Modern science, philosophy, criticism,—the forces that are continually precipitating these crises—are not enemies but friends. God's purposes do not move backward. A new and better world always emerges from the chaos of the old. So long as God's hand directs the development every transition will be, not toward darkness and anarchy, but toward truth and order.

Haggai encouraged his people with the assurance that their sufferings were not meaningless. Painful as their national discipline had been, it was but an unavoidable step in the evolution of a sublime purpose. Not only did he assure them that Jehovah, their covenant-keeping God, was still in the midst of his people; not only were his resources inexhaustible, and ready to be poured out in their behalf; but he had also a purpose of grace concerning them and the whole world, immeasurably exceeding the brightest memories of the past. Despicable as this new house might appear to those who had seen the splendors of Solomon's temple, the new would nevertheless outshine the old. "Greater shall be the latter glory of this house than the former, saith the Lord of hosts." Observe that it is the "latter glory," R. V., and not the "latter house," A. V., for, whatever be its material condition, Jehovah knows of but one abiding dwelling on his holy hill of Zion. In a little while he would "shake the heavens, and the earth, and the sea, and the dry land," overturning the long established order of things in the world, and introducing a new, divine order in which his house would be the centre of revelation and worship. Haggai's vision of the messianic time resembled Isaiah's vision of the ideal Jerusalem: "It shall come to pass in the latter days that the mountain of the Lord's house shall be established in the top of the mountains, and shall be exalted above the hills; and all nations shall flow unto it. And many peoples shall go and say, Come ye, and let us go up to the mountain of the Lord, to the house of the God of Jacob; and he will teach us of his ways, and we will walk in his paths: for out of Zion shall go forth instruction, and the word of the Lord from Jerusalem," (Isa. ii, 2, 3). In that magnificent future, whose gleaming light was seen from afar by Israel's prophets, the kingdom of God will include all the kingdoms of the earth. Jerusalem will be the seat of empire, and Jehovah's temple the point unto which the gentiles will look for a world-embracing manifestation of his truth and grace. Into it they will bring evermore the choicest of their treasures, and the noblest of themselves.

That messianic day, moreover, will be characterized by universal peace. For "in this place will I give *peace*, saith the Lord of hosts." Peace, first of all, between man and God, that which every true heart yearns for supremely, but which is not found in the world. Upon the tossed and weary heart, into the troubled conscience this ineffable peace will come, and this implies salvation in its fullest, richest sense. Peace also between man and man. International rivalries, the ambition of conquerors, royal greed of power will no longer hurl nation against nation in bloody strife. Smoking ruins, trampled harvests, vultures gorging on the slain will be seen no more. The groans of the wounded and the dying, the agonized cry of widows and orphans will be heard no more. For Jehovah "shall judge between the nations, and shall reprove many peoples; and they shall beat their swords into plowshares, and their spears into pruninghooks: nation shall not lift up sword against nation, neither shall they learn war any more," (Isa. ii. 4). Peace, finally, between man and the wild beasts of the field, (Isa. xi. 6–9). The distrust between them will cease. As nature has shared in man's curse, so it will share in the benefits of man's redemption.

The glorious messianic import of this passage is independent of any actual coming of Jesus into the temple. This misinterpretation has been projected upon it by later readers. Haggai does not specify it as the "latter glory of this house." This may have been in the mind of the Spirit who prompted the utterance, but it cannot be pressed in a strictly historical interpretation.

IV. JEHOVAH'S "LITTLE WHILE."

Some of the despondent ones might have retorted, "Such glowing pictures were painted by the older prophets, but they are as far from realization as ever." "No," says Haggai, "it is only one period more, a very brief one, and then Jehovah will work signs and wonders among the nations to arouse them from indifference, to turn them unto himself, and thus prepare for the golden age." In a measure his utterance was fulfilled at once, but in its larger signification it still awaits complete fulfilment. The centuries after the exile were really a brief preface to the messianic period which began with the coming of Christ into his temple, and which still continues.

Men are impatient at the moderate pace of events in the kingdom of God. They wonder why he does not force men into swift obedience by stupendous displays of power. Because love and obedience are not wrought by force. Love conquers the kingdom of hatred only inch by inch. Viewing these things by and by from the side of eternity men will see that earth's longest periods are only Jehovah's "little whiles." The world is ripening faster than we think. Events are moving with accelerated velocity. Who knows but that the full glory of the messianic time may be close at hand? Whether near or far, every man's supreme duty to God and to his fellow-man is so to live, by the Holy Spirit's help, as to make the world better, and thus to hasten the advent of that golden age which lies not in the past, as men have sadly thought, a reminder of eternal lapse and loss; but in the future, which is still ours, a divine goal and beatific hope toward which the weary world is slowly toiling upward in the night.

Lesson IV. January 22.

JOSHUA THE HIGH-PRIEST.
Zechariah iii: 1–10.

By Professor GEORGE RICE HOVEY, Richmond, Va.

THIS chapter contains a direct prophecy of the Messiah. What a wonderful hope of a future deliverer that was which God inspired in his ancient people! Age after age it is cherished. It is the theme of loftiest song, the motive to noblest endurance and endeavor. And yet it occupies very little space in the writings of the prophets. How rarely did Moses, Samuel or Elijah refer to it! And when later prophets told more frequently of the coming king, it was never done to gratify an idle curiosity about the future, but always to awaken hope in present darkness, or to raise a true ideal for present admiration and imitation. The future was revealed for the sake of the present. Prediction was only incidental. A prophet was not one who "foretold," so much as one who "told for." He spoke for God. He was not a diviner, but a preacher. He brought God's messages concerning sin and righteousness, judgment and mercy, to people who needed instruction and encouragement in their daily life. We can therefore understand his message only by understanding his times.

But whether the prophet's words were history, exhortation or prediction, he dealt not with isolated facts, but with facts which were the expression of universal truths about God and man; truths whose application is more extensive than he knew, and whose meaning is deeper than he imagined. If then we would learn as nearly as possible the full thought of God for us, we must look at the germinal thought of the prophet as involving the deeper meaning with which Christ filled it full. These two principles must be borne in mind in the study of Zechariah.

In the midst of Haggai's short prophetic career, Zechariah began to prophesy; and apparently but two months after the last recorded utterance of the older prophet, the younger saw the vision of our lesson.

The walls of the temple were hardly yet begun. The people were still absorbed in their worldly occupations. They were a feeble remnant closely watched by neighboring peoples, who were ready to thwart them by force or intrigue. Beyond, but ever within sight, the mighty empires of the Nile and the Euphrates were now and again spreading dismay among the weaker states. The shadow of their recent captivity was still upon the returned exiles, and the future was dark with equally calamitous possibilities.

Zechariah, like Haggai, was sent to encourage the people of God. The vision of the four horsemen reveals God's constant watchfulness. The dangers which threaten shall never overtake his holy city. "My house shall be built in it; . . . my cities through prosperity shall yet be spread abroad, and Jehovah shall yet comfort Zion and shall yet choose Jerusalem." The next vision foreshows that the conquerors of Israel under the symbolism of horns are doomed to utter overthrow by mighty smiths. And then the prophet sees the city stretching out on all sides without walls, "by reason of the multitude of men and cattle therein," and because Jehovah says, "I will be unto her a wall of fire round about, and I will be the glory in the midst of her."

After these glowing promises what more can be needed to give Israel hope and joy? One-half is lacking yet. Israel is unprepared. The best gift of heaven or earth brings no enjoyment except to one who is able to receive and appreciate it. "Cast not your pearls before swine." A grand symphony only wearies him who has no ear for music. Heaven would be intolerable to one who is at enmity with God and hates righteousness.

Sin in act or in heart takes all the meaning and joy out of God's richest promises and gifts. So it prevented the Israelites from appropriating the former gracious words until its baleful influence was removed by the fourth vision of our lesson. It is a vision of free forgiveness for the nation. Joshua, the high priest, represents Jerusalem and the people. His filthy garments are symbols of their sins, and his clean raiment is a pledge of their pardon. The vision includes glimpses of the Adversary, of Pardon, and of Subsequent Life.

I. THE ADVERSARY.

Who was the great opponent of those afflicted Hebrews? Was it the nations around? Or was God himself against them? The vision reveals their true enemy. It was neither of these, but the great adversary of souls; he who tempted Christ; the prince of darkness.

The foe of man is Satan, not man; much less God, who so loved the world that he gave his only begotten son to save it.

The very names of this enemy betray his character. The Hebrew word Satan means "adversary." And here, exemplifying his name, he is standing at Joshua's right hand "to be his adversary." When did he ever do a deed or suggest a thought really to help or bless a man? The Greek name devil, "slanderer," "calumniator," is equally characteristic. Perhaps in this very vision it was by accusing Joshua before the angel that he purposed to resist him. Adversary! slanderer! how often these English equivalents of Satan and Devil fitly describe a moralist or a professed Christian, and what a relationship in character is suggested by these synonymes!

The assaults of Satan are well timed. It was when Joshua stood in foul raiment, symbol of the moral uncleanness of the people, and when the bright hopes of the returning exiles were fading away, that Satan seized the opportunity to accomplish their ruin. The days of sin, failure, despair, find him at hand to do his fatal work. In such days God alone can help.

There is solid ground for the belief that he will not fail us. David argued from God's love and goodness to him that he would not suffer him to see corruption. Jesus reasoned that because God had cared enough for Abraham, Isaac and Jacob to call himself pre-eminently their God, he would not let them perish. And in rebuking Satan, God uses the same argument. Those whom he hath chosen and has plucked from the fire ot captivity, he will not now forsake.

God's past dealings with us are a pledge of the future, an assurance of final victory. In spite of our selfishness and forgetfulness of him, he has filled our past with abounding mercies. We may say, with Paul: "He that spared not his own son, but delivered him up for us all, how shall he not also with him freely give us all things?" "I thank God . . . being confident of this very thing, that he which began a good work in you will perfect it."

II. PARDON.

The long exile, the unfulfilled hopes of the return, the temple and city insignificant compared with those of earlier times, the small number of those willing to leave Babylon, the insolence and hostility of once despised neighbors—these things, the result of disobedience to God, ever reminded the people of their national sin. And yet the chief transgressors were no longer present to be punished. They had died long since; or were far away in contented exile.

Joshua and those who had returned were the chosen remnant—men who had given up fertile fields, lucrative employments, and exalted station for the love they bore to their God and his chosen city. They may not have realized that they themselves were sinners. But in the vision Joshua finds himself in the very presence of Jehovah clothed in filthy garments. In the sight of God he himself and those about him were defiled. What all their sins were we do not know. But they had neglected God's house, while they beautified their own dwellings; they had served mammon rather than God. Surely with them as with all, the supreme law of love to God and to man had been overidden every hour by thoughts of self interest. " None doeth good—no, not one." The defiled raiment revealed their sins. It is a long step forward when the self-satisfied man learns as Joshua did the truth of Isaiah's words: " All our righteousness is as filthy rags."

How vivid and repugnant sin must have become under such a symbol. The garments were not coarse, or old, or worn and soiled with use, but filthy. By such striking symbolism God taught his chosen people to hate sin. This was no euphemistic language softening and covering the wrong doing, but rather a proclamation of it. Sin masked under the forms of fashion or elegance is doubly dangerous. It entices the weak; it warps the judgment even of the good. Far better is it by our language and treatment to associate wrong doing with those things which men detest, until they learn to abhor sin also wherever found and however clothed.

With garments so filthy but one thing can be done. They cannot be covered up. The blackest spots cannot be sponged off—as men try to do with their guilt,—for every thread of the clothing is defiled. Moreover the wretched man seems powerless to remove the unclean garments. In fact, they are part of him, they are his life, his character, himself, God must work the deed which shall free him from the burden of his sins. " Take away the filthy garments and clothe him in fair raiment," "I have caused thine iniquity to pass from thee." The burden has rolled from Pilgrim's shoulders.

III. SUBSEQUENT LIFE.

This was not the end of Pilgrim's journey; it was hardly more than the beginning. Pardon was never intended to be the end of effort or of progress. It is the breaking light after darkness, which only reveals new duties and gives greater ability to perform them. It is the divine cleansing of a daubed and disfigured canvas in order to call out the artist's best effort which shall result in a portrait of nobler beauty. Pardon is the man's entrance into paths of duty, and hope, and joyful fruition, which stretch out far beyond his vision when a just forgiven penitent.

Accordingly, the angel of Jehovah does not pardon Joshua and dismiss him; but rather pardons and then hastens to declare solemnly: "thus saith Jehovah of hosts: If thou wilt walk in my ways, and if thou wilt keep my charge," then thou shalt have the honor of priesthood with its authority and its free access into God's presence.

After pardon comes obedience. The order cannot be reversed. Joshua's previous efforts to obey were vain. The inevitable alienation of a sinner from God, whom he has wronged, prevents whole-hearted service. Only with the consciousness of forgiveness can there be full and unconstrained obedience.

But after one is pardoned, walking in God's ways is the condition of further blessing. Not that God who has forgiven once is unwilling to forgive again. He is love, and his mercies are everlasting. But a man cannot wilfully and constantly transgress God's law, and continually and lightly seek forgiveness. An earthly father may be glad to forgive a wayward son a thousand times, but how many times will that son have heart to seek forgiveness? So sin at last prevents prayer for renewed pardon. And furthermore, all the higher gifts of God, joy and peace, deep knowledge of his truth, nobility of character, by the very laws of human nature and of the kingdom of God are the result of obedience. Pardon is the prerequisite, obedience the necessary consequence.

Upon the high priest there was an especial obligation to careful obedience. He was in a sense God's representative. His office carried with it wide influence for good or evil. Before God, indeed, all are under the same supreme law of right. But towards their fellowmen, some are under heavier obligations than others. The obligation rests most heavily on the representative of God, the teacher or preacher whose influence is wider than that of one in a humbler sphere, and whose opportunity to help and guide is greater. Our opportunity to serve man is the measure of our responsibility to man. Hence to every leader in the Church the instruction to Joshua comes with especial force; he must walk in God's ways and keep his charges; his personal life and official conduct must meet God's requirements.

A larger promise limited to no man or family is now introduced by the emphatic words, "Hear now, . . . for behold." It is an old promise renewed. From earliest ages the hopes of all godly Jews had centered about one dim future figure ever expected, ever receding. Moses spoke of him as a prophet, the highest ideal in his mind. David sang of him as a righteous king, the loftiest conception of man in that age. But when the family of David became almost extinct, and its remaining members were insignificant among the great ones of the earth, when the people of God and even his prophets were afflicted and exiled, then the nobility of patient, lowly suffering and service, was learned, and the faithful, afflicted servant of God was taken as the truest type of greatness, the character most like the divine. The coming one was pictured as the servant of Jehovah, and as a sprout growing up out of dry ground from the stump of the fallen house of David. But still he was the hope of Israel. The lowly names by which he was known became transformed into titles of honor and glory. No more inspiring message could be proclaimed than the renewed assurance that this hope was about to be fulfilled. So Zechariah arouses Israel to courage and effort by the word from God " Behold I will bring forth my Servant, the Branch."

That promise has been fulfilled to us. And when we, like Zechariah, would urge as a motive for action God's greatest gift, we must speak of that same Servant, of his life, and death and resurrection. Wonderful power in human life ! His name brought fresh zeal and courage into the feeble remnant under Joshua and Zerubbabel twenty-five hundred years ago. It has never lost its power. His past life on earth, his unseen presence with us, his future appearance, inspire the Christian to nobler life and service than any other motive.

This great promise of the Branch, pledge of the continued care and favor of Jehovah, is naturally accompanied by more definite promises of immediate help. The seven eyes of Jehovah, which run to and fro through the whole earth and are the symbol of perfect watchfulness, shall be directed to each stone of the temple now building under great difficulties. More than that, he will "engrave the graving thereof," he will give the stone its beauty. He will both watch and work with his people.

Man's work is ever incomplete. He may turn up the sod, and level the ground, making it less unsightly than before ; he may plant the seed, but God alone can give the increase. In spiritual matters, no less than in temporal, our work needs and certainly receives its vitalizing and beautifying power from him who transforms the elements into flower and fruit.

Peace and prosperity complete the picture of the future of the forgiven people. Every one shall call his neighbor to come and sit under his fig tree. Righteousness and peace with God were doubtless included in this favorite Hebrew thought, but temporal peace, with all its glorious blessings, was the chief element in the anticipated reign of the Messiah.

Some of the loftiest conceptions of the Jewish religion are found in these verses. Each is a shadow of a vastly greater and more inspiring truth, which is familiar to the Christian. The priest as mediator between the people and their God, as one who represents the nation, bearing its sins and receiving its blessings, faintly pictured our mediating high priest. But how great the contrast between the two! The access of the Jewish high priest to God in the holy of holies once a year shadowed forth, but how dimly, the Christian's free approach to the throne of grace! The vague hope of some temporal deliverer, a prophet, king, servant, fell how far short of the Saviour of the world! The peace beneath the fig tree was how different from the peace of God which passeth understanding! Those old ideas and hopes had marvellous power over men; how much greater should be the power over our lives of their grander fulfilments!

Lesson V. January 29.

THE SPIRIT OF THE LORD.
Zechariah iv: 1–10.

BY REV. E. M. POTEAT, NEW HAVEN, CONN.

IT was the mission of Zechariah to stimulate the courage of God's people, to kindle again the enthusiasm for the temple and the theocracy with which they had set out from Babylon. Opposition from their foes, the enormity of the task of restoring the temple, and the necessity of providing homes for themselves, had broken their courage, and diverted them from contemplation of their great spiritual destiny. They must be brought again to the deep theocratic feeling cherished among their fathers of old.

The Lord's message to Israel through Zechariah was communicated to the prophet in a series of eight visions. It would be interesting to trace the progress of thought through all these, but this would lead us too far from the present purpose. We must content ourselves with setting forth the meaning of the fifth of these visions.

The prophet sees a seven-pronged candlestick, all of gold. The seven prongs bear seven lamps. These are supplied with oil by means of pipes, from a bowl or reservoir resting upon the top of the stem of the candlestick. An even flow of oil to the seven lamps is secured by a series of pipes connecting each lamp with every other. On either side of the lamp-stand is a luxuriant olive tree, "one upon the right side of the bowl, and the other upon the left side thereof." These two trees pour a steady supply of constant, self-produced oil through golden spouts into the reservoir at the top of the candlestick. Such was the vision*—a great candelabrum perpetually agleam with golden light, perpetually replenished with living oil from living olive trees. It is to be noted that there was no need of ministering priests to keep the lamps ablaze.

When the prophet asked the angel: "What are these, my Lord?" The angel replied: "This is the word of the Lord unto Zerubbabel, saying, Not by might, nor by power, but by my Spirit, saith the Lord of Hosts." It is difficult to carry through all the details of the vision any one interpretation of it. The clearest application of details is given us in verse fourteen, according to which the two olive trees are the two sons of oil, *i. e.*, anointed ones, viz., Zerubbabel and Joshua, or more broadly, the prince and the priest. Being interpreted, this means that the restored Israel will carry forward the work of revealing God—will shine on the darkness of the world—by virtue of the vital relation of God in his spirit to the heads of the community, viz., the Prince and the Priest. "And the most sacred mystery to which these visions point is the consummation of this relation."† This will be effected in the man whose name is The Branch, who will unite in himself both the royal and the priestly dignities, and upon whom the Spirit of God will be bestowed without measure.

It will be seen that the vision of Zechariah was a reinforcement of Jehovah's pledge to his people in Egypt. "Yet now be strong, O Zerubbabel, saith the Lord; and be strong, O Joshua, son of Jehozadak, the high priest; and be strong all ye people of the land, saith the Lord of Hosts, and work: for I am with

---

*The enterprising teacher will make a drawing for his class of what the prophet saw.

†Orelli, O. T. Prophecy, 439.

you, saith the Lord of Hosts, according to the word that I covenanted with you when ye came out of Egypt, and my spirit abideth among you: fear ye not." Long previously had Hosea pleaded with the people not to rely on armies, but upon God. "I will have mercy upon the house of Judah, and will save them by the Lord their God, and will not save them by bow, nor by sword, nor by battle, by horses, nor by horsemen." After that word was spoken, the people were dragged away to grace an eastern monarch's triumph. Jeremiah when only a handful of miserable paupers had been left with him in Jerusalem had yet persisted in believing that the Lord was on his side. The Syrians, the Assyrians, Egyptians, Scythians, Chaldeans, Persians, had all made their conquests by their armies. Yet a messenger comes to the governor just beginning to re-establish the theocracy, saying, "Thou shalt not gather an army for defence. Not by might, nor by power, but by my spirit, saith the Lord of Hosts." God will be a wall of fire about the city, and a glory in the midst of her.

This noble appeal to a heroic trust in God is preserved to us in a Psalm of the period, viz., the 118th:

The Lord is on my side; I will not fear: What can man do unto me?

The Lord is on my side among them that help me.

. . . .

It is better to trust in the Lord than to put confidence in man.

It is better to trust in the Lord than to put confidence in princes.

All nations compassed me about: in the name of the Lord I will cut them off.

They compassed me about like bees: they are quenched as the fire of thorns: in the name of the Lord I will cut them off.

Thou didst thrust sore at me that I might fall: but the Lord helped me.

The Lord is my strength and my song, and he is become my salvation.

It was a hard lesson for these returned exiles, this lesson of implicit trust in God. The nation was just awaking out of a long night, in which God seemed to have abandoned them. They were little practiced in seeing the invisible. Like Elisha's servant, they needed to have their eyes opened to perceive the mountains of Jerusalem "full of horses and chariots of fire" round about the Lord's chosen. But the men of insight among them saw in Zechariah's assurance of the presence of God's spirit in the leaders of the nation, the pledge that the new city was to triumph over all the obstacles created by the hatred and scorn of neighboring peoples,—the pledge of a completed temple and kingdom of God.

The tendency of our times is away from all special reliance on the spirit of God. Relatively, we have too great faith in secondary causes. To build a temple, you need only a competent architect, a good contractor and a good force of masons. If opposition is threatened, simply provide yourself with a sufficient police force. Such is men's creed now. We glorify organization. We deify law. We apotheosize the practical. We are witnessing a revival of the heretical belief in salvation by works. If it was necessary for James to say, "Faith, if it hath not works, is dead, being alone," it is necessary for us to say, Work if it hath not faith is dead, being alone. We give up our inspiration for institutions. We lose the Spirit of God in elaborately designed methods for his operation. The intellectual, the practical, the spiritual; this is the order of importance according to the judgment of many contemporaries. Given intellect and the genius for work, people in effect say, and a church will succeed, Spirit or no Spirit. Here is matter for grave concern to the Church of Christ. In proportion as we trust in method, eloquence, and work, we are tempted to distrust simplicity, spirituality, and prayer,

Few things, therefore, could be of more importance to the religious life of to-day than this message of Zechariah to the returned exiles. However truly and clearly seers and prophets may still apprehend God, the life of thousands goes on now-a-days in practical atheism. A competent observer, speaking of New York City, recently said: "I can at any moment take a city pastor into sets at two social extremes, where the Christian Deity is not only dead but has been buried with cynicism and contempt." A distinguished philosopher who has been seeking to purge the conception of God from vulgar anthropomorphisms has good reason to think that the result has been to "defecate the conception to a pure transparency." So by no thought and by misguided thought, the belief in a living God and Helper has lost its influence upon many minds.

And the infection has spread to the churches. Witness the almost frantic efforts of some among them to keep themselves alive. Having insensibly withdrawn from the sources of vital piety their only recourse is the process of artificial respiration. We need schooling in the science of Spiritual Dynamics and Economics.

That this thought may assume greater definiteness, let me specify some of the lessons which the vision of Zechariah has for us. I mention, out of many, three:

1. *The proper relation of God's Spirit to the Church is a vital one.* Philosophically considered, the main conceptions of God which have been current in the religious progress of the race are two: God as transcendent above the world, and God as immanent in the world. The one erects a throne for the Ruler of the Universe somewhere above the sky, and worships him from afar. It reached its extreme form among the Deists of the last century, who denied all interference on the part of God in the affairs of the world. It was the dominant, though not the only conception of God among the Jews before the coming of Christ, which helps to account for the formality and

barrenness of their religion. Nothing so robs religion of its transforming and sustaining power as the drawing of its sanctions from some distant sphere, and the deferring of its rewards to some future age.

The other conception—that God is immanent in the world—finds its best exposition in the literature of Pantheism, and has had expression and adherents ever since the time of the Vedic hymns. It reaches its extreme form in the view, still current, which denies to God personality and identifies him with the forces which upbear and impel the world.

Both these conceptions are found—though not in their extreme forms—in the Bible. The New Testament doctrine of the Holy Spirit may be regarded as the evangelical counterpart of the philosophical doctrine of immanence. The New Testament teaching here is summarized for us in the fulfilment in Acts ii. 17, of the prophecy of Joel. Joel had predicted a universal outflow of the Spirit which should reach all flesh; a dispensation of power to be marked by wonders in the heavens above and in the earth beneath. The prophet foretold a time when young men and maidens should see the visions he had seen, when the whole of life should be invested with the divine Spirit; when, therefore, no one place, as the temple, should be sacred, and no one order of men, as priests, be honored above another, because all were to be filled with all the fulness of God. God would no longer be confined above the sky, or by the walls of a single building, or by the lines which separate the nations. He would come out into the open, so to speak, and be seen everywhere. He would make every place sacred by his presence. The universe, and no longer a booth of skins or a house of cedar, would be his dwelling place. This dispensation of the Spirit began on the day of Pentecost. In it the Gospel assumes its universal character and function. But the New Testament does not say that the Holy Spirit abides in the world and world forces in such a sense as to become *one with* them. In the ministry of the Holy Spirit God is still a person different from us and from his world, but he is no longer remote. With Paul we are thrilled with the awe of a great, tender reverence when we reflect that " He is not far away from any one of us ; for in Him we live and move and have our being." We sympathize with Julius Müller when he says : " The wide distance between God and the world exists only in the imagination of a piety utterly emasculated, and of a theology merely intellectual and barren." I know of no more blighting heresy than the practical denial among us of this New Testament and Old Testament teaching concerning the presence of God's Spirit in his world, in his Church, as a vital, blessed and mighty equipment for life's battles and duties. Could I do but one thing for Christians to-day, I would give them the sense and the vision of a very present God ; so that while Mr. Spencer is defecating the conception of God to "a pure transparency," men might know their Father in heaven, on earth, and in the hearts of his children—the life of their life, putting the infiniteness of his being to their finiteness, to their folly his wisdom, to their restlessness, his rest.

2. *God's Spirit is the Church's only proper equipment for service.* The presence of God's Spirit for defence and for aggression was the burden of Zechariah's message to Zerubbabel. God is our defence. It is said that William Penn was the only colonist in America who left his settlement wholly unprotected by fence or arms, and that his was the only one which was unassailed by the Indian tribes. The first Christians depended in a peculiar manner upon the Holy Spirit for protection and leadership, and with the result that they were delivered from the hands of persecutors. They had courage to meet obstacles and power to overcome them ; they had new light on old truth, especially new light in the interpretation of the prophets ; they had new truth as they were able to receive it, or as their exigency required it. In three centuries, spite of their own

poverty and the prestige and power of those who opposed them, they overspread the Roman Empire, and the religion of the humble Nazarene became the religion of the emperor. Thenceforward, the Church leaned less on the Spirit and more on the ally she had found in the State. Before the end of the fourth century missionary work, as a means of suppressing Paganism, had given place to imperial edicts. After Augustine, who died A. D. 430, the history of the Church is barren of great preachers and aggressive evangelic effort, till the great crusading movement in the eleventh century. Precisely in this period the monstrous mechanism of the Church of Rome shaped itself as the fitting embodiment of a piety which had become formal, and of a worship which had been lost in ritual. History affords no more striking enforcement of Zechariah's message: "Not by might, nor by power, but by my Spirit, saith the Lord of Hosts."

3. *God's Spirit, appropriated by prayer, is now intended to operate through all believers.*

In the time of Zechariah, God's Spirit wrought his will by means of special representatives. The olive trees supplied the oil to the candelabrum. Only the anointed ones were in full measure supplied with the Spirit. But when Joel's prophecy was fulfilled, the Lord poured out his Spirit upon all flesh. It was a new epoch in the spiritual progress of mankind. God wills now to operate directly, without mediation, upon the hearts and minds of all believers. He speaks no longer to the company exclusively through leaders especially endowed and appointed to receive and transmit his revelations, but to each one separately, and to all at the same time. "It sat upon each one of them; and they were all filled with the Holy Spirit." In this blessed dispensation the priest has lost his function, since all are welcome to come into immediate, vital relation to God.

What matters it, however, if while we are within reach of

strength, we elect to continue in all our old weakness? The nearness of God does not insure that we shall, in spite of ourselves, personally feel the thrill and joy of his strength. Prayer is a condition to this. Through prayer, the very air about us may be charged with God, so as to bear us up like eagles in electric clouds. Closer than our breath is God with his Almighty Spirit and grace. Before Franklin's experiment for harnessing the lightning, the air was as full of electricity as it is to-day, but men did not know how to appropriate it. A battery may be charged with electric fire, but you must make your connections to get the power. We need to gear our personal lives and our Church work on to the Power which moves the world. Then shall we see a revolution in spiritual commerce and economics, which will speedily bring in the completed kingdom that was the hope of Zechariah and the inspiration of his message to Zerubbabel. We make this connection by prayer. Pray in faith, and there shall quiver along every fibre of your being a thrill of the life, light and might of God.

Lesson VI.   February 5.

DEDICATING THE TEMPLE.

Ezra vi: 14-22.

BY REV. A. S. COATS, PAWTUCKET, R. I.

THE facade of the great Church of the Escorial in Madrid is adorned with six colossal statues of the kings of Judah. They were placed there by order of the dark-souled Philip II. in token of the fact that his Church found its architectural inspiration in Solomon's temple. They represent the kings of Judah who bore the chief part in that temple :— David, the proposer; Solomon, the founder; Jehoshaphat, Hezekiah, Josiah, Manasseh, the successive purifiers and restorers.

The first five lessons of this quarter have had to do with the erection of the second great temple of the Jewish Church. Our lesson to-day is an account of its dedication. If some future king in Europe, or uncrowned son of the virgin soil of America, grown richer than any European sovereign, shall venture to build a Church, Philip-like, to commemorate his victories, a Church that finds its architectural inspiration in the second temple of Jerusalem, whose shall be the statues to adorn its facade? Shall they not be those of Cyrus and Darius, who proposed it and furnished funds from the royal treasuries for its erection; Zerubbabel and Joshua, who built it; and Haggai and Zechariah, who gave the people no peace of conscience till they finished it? If, indeed, this future European potentate or American millionaire shall order nine instead of six colossal statues for his Church, whose shall be the remaining three but those of Isaiah, who foresaw through the mists of one hundred and fifty years its coming glories, and by the vision splendid kept the hope of it burning in the hearts of the captives in Babylon; Jeremiah, who foretold, almost to the year, yet two generations away, its completion, and thus encouraged the people in making his dream a reality; and the rapt Ezekiel, whose vision of the ideal temple, "fourteen years after the city was smitten," played no small part in the erection of the real temple some fifty years after the vision was granted?

God fulfils himself in many ways. He never hastens. He never tarries. He works through a multitude of agencies, many of which, to all human seeming, are directly opposed to his purposes. When Zerubbabel brought forth the headstone of this temple with shoutings of "Grace, grace unto it," he was but consummating a work for which all history had been a preparation, and all time a condition. We pause, however, to glance a moment at the men and forces more immediately concerned in making possible this joyous occasion.

In Isaiah xliv. 28, God saith of Cyrus: "He is my Shepherd and shall perform all my pleasure, even saying of Jerusalem, she shall be built, and of the temple, thy foundation shall be laid." Prophecy in general differs from history as the ideal differs from the real, yet at times the minute accuracy of its fulfilment surprises us. Cyrus doubtless pictured himself as more than laying the foundation of the temple when in the first year of his reign he issued his decree to the captive Jews to return to Jerusalem, "and build the house of the Lord the God of Israel, (he is God) which is in Jerusalem;" but only the foundation was laid during his reign. Then, as now, every great and good cause found a few active friends, a few active foes, and a multitude of indifferent but idle well-wishers.

The active foes to the building of the temple were the semi-heathen semi-Hebrew Samaritans, whose hired counsellors in the Persian court for many years greatly hindered the progress of the work. The indifferent friends were the rank and file of the returned captives themselves, who, sent by Cyrus expressly to build the house which God had charged them to build him in Jerusalem, soon grew weary in well-doing and contented themselves in the erection of fine dwellings to shelter their own heads. Precisely here comes in the work of the prophets Haggai and Zechariah. "Is it," exclaims Haggai, "a time for you yourselves to dwell in your ceiled houses, while this house lieth waste? . . . Go up to the mountains and bring wood, and build the house, and I will take pleasure therein, and I will be glorified, saith the Lord." Zechariah, in referring to the mountain of difficulty that active foes and lukewarm friends were interposing to the completion of the temple, exclaims: "Who art thou, O great mountain? Before Zerubbabel thou shalt become a plain!"

Thus reproved and encouraged, the people, led by Joshua the priest and Zerubbabel the prince, begin anew the work largely abandoned soon after the laying of its foundations. A new obstacle is now interposed by those jealous tribute-collectors "beyond the river," Tattenai and Shethar-bozenai, who in hot haste dispatch messengers to Darius suggesting that at least a search be made in the royal archives to ascertain if indeed, as the builders declare, the great Cyrus had made "a decree to build this house of God at Jerusalem." Zeal in blocking the cause of progress often results in adding a new impulse to the same. So here. The search was made. The decree of Cyrus was found. A new decree was issued by Darius: "Now therefore . . . be ye far from thence; let the work of this house of God alone."

From this time forth we hear of no active opposition on the part of foes; no selfish indifference on the part of friends. The work on the temple, which we are not to believe had ever

entirely ceased since its foundation was laid some twelve or fifteen years before, no longer languished
> "through dim lulls of unapparent growth,"

but
> "mid good acclaim,
> climbed with the eye to cheer the architect."

At last, in the sixth year of the reign of Darius, B. C. 519, four years after they began with new enthusiasm upon the magnificent structure, larger, if the plans of Cyrus were carried out, than was the temple of Solomon, the prediction of Zechariah was fulfilled: they brought forth the head-stone with shoutings of "Grace, grace unto it." Since the decree of Cyrus, looking to its construction, was issued B. C. 536, the erection of the temple had consumed seventeen years of time. Some scholars make the interval two and twenty years.

Of the temple's cost we know but little. Ezra mentions the fact that at its inception the people themselves "gave of their ability into the treasury of the work three score and one thousand darics of gold and five thousand pounds of silver." This would equal nearly six hundred thousand dollars of our money. We must not, however, forget that both Cyrus and Darius decreed that "for the building of this house of God, of the king's goods, even the tribute beyond the river, expenses be given with all diligence unto these men, that they be not hindered." Doubtless its cost in money would have to be reckoned in millions rather than in hundreds of thousands of dollars. Who shall estimate its cost in labor, anxiety and tears?

The time chosen for the dedication of Solomon's temple, five hundred years before, was the feast of Tabernacles. With a fine insight into the meaning of history, that ever repeats itself, the Passover festival was chosen as the fitting time for the dedication of the temple that now took the old one's place and carried on its mission. Had not God in great mercy again passed over his people in bondage, as a thousand years before in the land of Egypt? It was "the children of the captivity" who kept the Passover on the fourteenth day of the first month.

The "two hundred bullocks, two hundred rams and four hundred lambs" that were now offered in sacrifice, seem but a small number as compared with the "twenty and two thousand oxen and an hundred and twenty thousand sheep," offered by Solomon at the dedication of his temple; but he had to provide a feast for a nation, while Zerubbabel had to feed but a handful of the tribes of Judah, Levi and Benjamin.

But their brethren yet remaining in captivity were not forgotten in the midst of this general rejoicing; nor were even the lost tribes of the children of Israel—lost even then to history for two hundred years. Did they not offer "for a sin-offering twelve he-goats, according to the twelve tribes of Israel?" Thus they testified in sublime faith that though lost to history, their brethren of the northern kingdom were not lost to God. Thus they expressed their conviction, abundantly justified in the vision on Patmos, that the children of God are ever to be numbered in twelve tribes. Indeed, the thought and care of these exultant worshipers for others did not stop here. They were missionaries to Judah as well as captives returned to their own land; and so we read: "All such as had separated themselves unto them from the filthiness of the heathen of the land, to seek the Lord, the God of Israel, did eat the feast of unleavened bread seven days with joy, for the Lord had made them joyful." Thus those zealous monotheists, the returned Jews, proved that it was no narrow bigotry, but a wise insistence upon unity of heart in the worship of the one God, that lay at the basis of their refusal of help in the building of the temple, at the hands of those religious eclectics, the Samaritans.

It is impossible to over-estimate the importance of the part played by the temple of Zerubbabel in the history of the Jewish Church.

As the temple of Herod was but an enlargement and adornment of that of this prince and ruler in Israel, this temple may be said to have withstood the assaults of time for six hundred years, till its final destruction by Titus, A. D. 70. During all these years it was the centre of the political, intellectual and religious life of the Jews. More than any other institution or agency, it kept the Jewish Church sound and loyal in heart to the worship of Jehovah. In spite of all the hypocrisy and corruption that disfigured Jewish civilization, it nourished many a bright consummate flower of devotion and piety, of which the priest Zacharias and the prophetess Anna were shining examples. Through all the fierce wars, defensive and internecine, of the Jewish people, this temple stood in silent protest, the smoke of its sacrifices ever ascending to heaven in mute pleadings for forgiveness, its cloisters guarding from all mutilation and corruption the oracles of God once for all delivered to the saints.

The lessons which this ancient dedication may be made to teach us are many and profoundly important.

Among them we mention these:

I. The importance of wise leadership in God's work. "Now the prophets, Haggai the prophet and Zechariah the son of Iddo, prophesied unto the Jews that were in Judah and Jerusalem. Then rose up Zerubbabel and Joshua and began to build the house of God which is at Jerusalem, and with them were the prophets of God helping them." God ever inspires the many through the few. The world will never outgrow the need of prophets—men born of God and filled with God, who see the needs of his Church and refuse his people rest till these needs are supplied.

II. The importance, the profitableness, even, of following wise leadership. "Ye looked for much, and lo, it came to little; and when ye brought it home, I did blow upon it. Why? saith the Lord of Hosts. Because of mine house that lieth waste, while ye run every man to his own house." To turn a deaf ear to God's call, to let his house lie waste, or his cause languish for lack of men and means vigorously to push it forward in all the earth, is in deepest truth to repeat the experience of this ancient wealth and pleasure-loving people, of whom the prophet Haggai said: "Ye have sown much and bring in little; . . . And he that earneth wages earneth wages to put it into a bag with holes."

III. The indispensableness of the rank and file in every great work for God. Cyrus and Darius, Zerubbabel and Joshua, Haggai and Zechariah, Isaiah, Jeremiah and Ezekiel—these are the names we mention as having a prominent part in the building of the second temple, though none of them hewed a timber, or squared a stone, or wrought with plane or hammer in its construction. But God takes account of the unnamed toilers as well as of the honored captains of his hosts. No honest, self-sacrificing work for him in any sphere of life, however lowly, shall fail of its full and blessed reward.

IV. The ultimate success of every great work undertaken for God. To the children of the captivity returning to Zion, with singing, as Isaiah had predicted, many dark days were in store. The weight of the Persian yoke still rested heavily upon them. Jealous neighbors, disease, famine and death were their portion. Mountain-high were the obstacles to the erection of the temple. They felt that they could never overcome them. But they did. There is no such word as failure in the vocabulary of him who works for God. Ever can we say of him:

> "Thine was the prophet's vision, thine
> The exultation, the divine,
> Insanity of noble minds,
> That never falters nor abates,
> But labors and endures, and waits,
> Till all it foresees, it finds,
> Or, what it cannot find, creates!"

V. God is the greatest factor in every work for God. "They builded and finished it according to the commandment of the God of Israel." This God had said of Zion by the mouth of Isaiah: "Kings shall be thy nursing fathers, and queens thy nursing mothers. . . . The glory of Lebanon shall come unto thee." We may well doubt that the returned captives in giving "meat and drink and oil unto them of Sidon and to them of Tyre, to bring cedar trees from Lebanon to the sea, unto Joppa," were aware of the fact that thus they were fulfilling God's prophetic purposes. We may well doubt if the entire history of this finished temple, seeming to us so plainly providential, seemed more so to the toilers upon it than do the common affairs of our every-day lives to us. God, however, was in it all; and consciously, or unconsciously, all who wrought for it and all who wrought against it were but advancing the purposes of him who makes even the wrath of man to praise him.

VI. Finally, we may well learn from this ancient dedication that we must build for God, with God, upon God, if we would have our work endure. One greater than the temple, who drove from its courts the dealers in oxen, sheep and doves, says to us: "Every one therefore that heareth these sayings of mine and doeth them, shall be likened unto a wise man which built his house upon the rock." In echo and interpretation of these words his greatest apostle says: "Other foundation can no man lay than that is laid, which is Jesus Christ. But if any man buildeth on the foundation gold, silver, costly stones, wood, hay, stubble; each man's work shall be made manifest."

> "Build thee more stately mansions,
>   Oh, my soul,
> As the swift seasons roll !
> Leave thy low vaulted past !
> Let each new temple, nobler than the last,
> Shut thee from heaven with a dome more vast,
>   Till thou at length art free,
> Leaving thine outworn shell by life's unresting sea."

Lesson VII. February 12.

NEHEMIAH'S PRAYER.

Nehemiah i: 1-11.

BY REV. FREDERICK L. ANDERSON, ROCHESTER, N. Y.

THE seventy years' captivity in Babylon was over. Taking advantage of the kindly decree of Cyrus, a remnant of Israel, numbering about 45,000, had returned to the blackened and desolate ruins of their once proud city, under the leadership of Zerubbabel; and after vexatious delays, due to the malice of jealous foes, they had succeeded in re-establishing their national life and rebuilding the temple of their God. It was the new birth of the Jewish people, and was hailed by the godly with sacred joy. In the words of the Psalmist, "Then was our mouth filled with laughter and our tongue with singing: then said they among the heathen, 'The Lord hath done great things for them.'"

But the joy soon turned to sadness, and the praise to supplication. "Turn again our captivity, O Lord, as the streams in the south." The resuscitation of a nation was found to be no easy task. The returned exiles were indeed only "a remnant," a pitifully small proportion of the whole people, who, for the most part, linked to the land of their exile by local, social, and commercial ties, were loath to leave their abundance, for what must have seemed to many a sentimental pilgrimage which could end only in disaster. These "few feeble Jews," inhabiting a city much too large for them, a city, too, which had lost all political and mercantile prestige, and was surrounded by an unproductive wilderness, sank gradually into poverty and despair. The walls of the city, which they had failed to rebuild, remained as Nebuchadnezzar had left them, dismantled and broken, the gates burned with fire, the taunt and reproach of their enemies, and a perpetual menace and source of weakness to the miserable inhabitants. Even the temple which had risen again on the old site could not, so felt those who remembered that, compare in glory to "the former house." Eighty years after the first return, Ezra succeeded in inducing some six thousand more to leave the land of their captivity for Jerusalem. But this small contingent, although they brought with them large sums of money, and were backed by all the influence of the Persian crown, was unable to infuse new life into the depressed body politic, and the revival of religion inaugurated by Ezra during his governorship of eight months seems to have effected little of permanent value.

Twelve years more dragged their slow length along before God's set time for the salvation of Zion arrived. But when that time did arrive, God had a man ready, a man with shoulders broad enough, a mind clear enough, and a piety deep enough to undertake and carry through the great work of the redemption of the chosen city. This man was not found at Jerusalem, but, strange as it may seem to some, was occupying high position as royal cup-bearer in the palace of the Persian king at Susa.

Let us consider this man whom God had brought into the world, and carefully prepared to do a great work for him.

His name was Nehemiah. He was a Jew, perhaps of the royal line. God had given him great wisdom and executive ability, and, in all probability, a handsome and commanding person. By means of these accomplishments and adornments he had commended himself to the great king, Artaxerxes, the son of the Xerxes who had so ignominiously failed to conquer

Greece at Salamis, and had been given the confidential post of king's cup-bearer. Thus God had advanced him to a position of immense influence, and had most richly endowed him with natural gifts, just in order that he might use that influence and those gifts in his service.

Dear reader, if God has given you any physical beauty, any social grace, any force of character, any intellectual power, any little influence in this world of ours, it is that you, too, may use all in his service and for his glory. Furthermore, if you do not so use God's gifts, but employ them simply to feed your vanity, and to increase your own pleasures, or indeed, simply forget that they were given to you for a great purpose, you not only waste them, but miss the end for which you were born, and never, in any true sense, even begin to live the life which is life indeed. Here, too, we discover the only right motive in seeking wealth, influence, beauty and social power. Every Christian man ought, with all his might, to strive for these things, that he may the more largely glorify God and bless his fellowmen. But, beware, O friend, beware, lest you seek them that you may consume them upon your worldly and selfish desires. This is naught else but to live for self, and he who lives for self is dead while he lives.

But God had prepared the heart of Nehemiah, also. The evidence of this is most beautifully set forth in the opening verses of our chapter. Nehemiah's own brother, Hanani, accompanied by some others, came from Jerusalem to Susa on a mission unknown to us, and they, of course, called on Nehemiah, if they did not lodge at his house. Notice now the great interest of Nehemiah in God's chosen people. He does not wait for his friends to volunteer information, but he asks them concerning the remnant " who had escaped," as though this was the matter which most interested his heart. Their reply is merely summarized in our account of this conversation. We must believe that they described at length and with much particularity and pathos the "great affliction and reproach" of the Jews and the ruined state of the city wall. These facts Nehemiah must, in a general way, have known before, but now he hears them from men who have been eye-witnesses of the desolation of Zion, and who naturally recount to him the bitter taunts of the enemies of God's people. Just as the graphic and burning words of the missionary kindle the hearts of those who before had a general conception of the heathen's lost estate, so the words of these friends roused the heart of Nehemiah. The intensity of his grief shows the intensity of his love for God's kingdom. It is not a subject for superficial condolence or momentary dejection. The iron enters his very soul. There is no record of any answer on his part. It is a grief too deep for words. The heart knows its own bitterness. He turns aside to the solitude of his secret chamber, where he may commune with God. When the door is shut, he sits down dumb with sorrow. By and by the tears come to relieve the pent up emotion of his heart. He cares nothing for his food. He mourns before Jehovah and prays to the God of heaven.

Reader, have you such an interest in God's kingdom as Nehemiah had in those dark days so long ago? Do you so love it that you seek diligently to know of its prosperity, or are you one of those who, caring too little about God's kingdom even to take a religious newspaper, wonder how anybody can be enthusiastic over missions? Is the news of a triumph of Jesus in this world a real joy to you? Is ill news touching his kingdom a real sorrow? Is it painful to you that so few are converted? Does the prevalent spiritual death drive you to secret meditation and earnest prayer? Happy the man who, like Paul, carries such sorrows, knows what it is to have "anxiety for all the churches," and triumphs in the victories of the Prince of Peace. His is the spirit of Christ.

We have traced so far as we could the hand of God as it prepared a great man to do a great work. Let us now watch the man as he prepares himself to do it. This preparation is made in the secret place, in prayer, true prayer, the prayer of faith and consecration. The rest of the book shows how the Father who seeth in secret rewards his children openly.

The prayer begins with an acknowledgement of the power and faithfulness of God. All true prayer must begin with God. "He who cometh to him must believe that he is." "Have faith in God," says the Saviour, in the same sentence in which he promises the great "whatsoever" to believing prayer. Our weakness in prayer is largely due to our unbelief. Oh! that God might ever be to us the most real fact in all the Universe, that we might abide in him, and know the peace and the solidity of purpose which spring from true faith. The trouble is that he seems to many a God afar off, dim, misty, vague; or if real, then hard, cold, and mechanical. We scarcely believe in him as the living God. Too often we think of him as bound hand and foot by his own laws, as powerless to help as the idol which grins at the heathen worshiper. In this unchristian frame of mind we fall to belittling, modifying, and explaining away the exceeding great and precious promises of the Bible, till they are in reality exceeding small and worthless. We need a revival of true belief in God, the Living God, for whom the human heart cries out and whom, to secure real life, it must have, the God who upholds all things by the word of his power, the great and almighty God, who is able and willing to keep all his covenant promises, doing for us above all we are able to ask or to think. The reason why Nehemiah was able to accomplish such a marvellous work was that he believed in such a God. God honored that faith, as he always will, supplying all the believer's need, through grace.

> "Have faith in God; what can there be
> Too hard for him to do for thee?
> He gave his Son. Now all is free.
> Have faith, have faith in God."

To this God of might and faithfulness Nehemiah now confesses his own sins and the sins of his people. When God is exalted, man begins to recognize his true littleness. The divine faithfulness ever reminds men of their own faithlessness. Nehemiah comes to God as a sinner, pleading for a sinful people. He does not strive to excuse or palliate. He acknowledges that their sin is great, very great. "We have dealt very corruptly," he says. They had sinned against light, for they had the commandments, the statutes and the judgments which God gave them by the hand of Moses. Nehemiah identifies himself with the people. He bears their sins before God and confesses them. So thoroughly does he love his fellow Israelites that he stands before God for them, like Moses in the breach. No man can truly pray without a sense of the inexcusableness and the ill-desert of sin; and we incline to add, no man can truly pray without such love for sinners that he would willingly suffer great sacrifices for them. And now the intercessor is ready to plead God's promises. He reminds God of his word. It is a word at once of judgment and of mercy. "If ye trespass, I will scatter you abroad among the peoples." O Lord, thou hast done this. Thy word is sure. Fulfil to us now the promise as thou hast the warning. "Yet will I gather them thence and will bring them unto the place that I have chosen to cause my name to dwell there." And still he recognizes the condition and quotes it. "If ye return unto me and keep my commandments and do them." How many fail just here! They pray to God. They confess their sins, at least with their lips. They repeat the promises, but they forget the condition. Repent! repent! No man has any right to claim a single one of God's promises unless he repents. The exhortation now-a-days is, "Only trust him." The exhortation is a good one if we remember who only have a right to trust. "Christ receiveth sinful men," but only when they turn from their sins and seek his face with all their heart. Nehemiah knew the place of repentance and only on that condition claimed the promise of God.

One more thing he pleads: God's past mercies. God has deigned to grant his people great deliverances. "Thou hast redeemed them by thy great power, and by thy strong hand." If God has done so much for them, surely he will not forsake them now. If he has lavished so much love on them, he will surely love them still.

> "His love in time past forbids me to think
> He'll leave me at last in trouble to sink.
> Each sweet Ebenezer I have in review
> Confirms his good pleasure to help me quite through."

"While they are yet speaking, I will hear." In this prayer, the great promise is fulfilled. Even while he yet pleads with God, a plan takes shape within his mind: he is enabled to offer himself as the medium through which his own petition shall be answered. He will go to "this man," the king—the informality of the reference marks the quickly forming resolution, which cannot wait for words. He will crave his favor. He will ask to be sent to build the walls of Jerusalem himself, and, " God, prosper thy servant, and grant me mercy in the sight of this man."

How many lessons press upon us here! We offer true prayer only when we are willing to do our utmost to answer the prayer we offer. "How much do you want this thing?" God might well ask, "do you want it enough to work for it, to suffer for it, to sacrifice for it?" O, how this searches us and reveals to us the hypocrisy, the shallowness and unreality of a great many of our prayers, and also the reason why they are not answered. We pray for prosperity in this world. Are we willing to toil and sacrifice for it? If not, our prayer will not be answered. God is not going to be the lazy man's helper. Let us rouse, bestir ourselves and go to work. Then God will help us, not only through the operation of natural law, but by a real, direct and supernatural strengthening. "God helps those who help themselves." We pray for the conversion of a friend, but we have no reason to suppose that friend will be converted, unless we are willing to do all we can for his conversion. We must desire his conversion enough to work for him patiently, wisely, lovingly, to speak the word in season, to live before him the spiritual life which shall commend to him the power of the gospel to save men—then God will answer our petition. But what shall we say of the bald hypocrisy of the man who prays for his own salvation, yet refuses to repent; who prays for the kingdom, and puts less than a hundredth of his income aside for missions; who pleads for the spiritual prosperity of the Church and then stands in the way of all spiritual progress by living an unconsecrated life! Nehemiah would have missed the blessing if, while he pleaded for a deliverer of his people, he had not been willing to heed the whisper of the Spirit, "Go yourself." Prayer leads to consecration. The lazy and timid Christian should be careful how he engages in real prayer. He may have some work to do straightway. This is what is meant by the saying, "It is dangerous to pray for foreign missions, if you do not want to go." And yet all other prayer is worthless, "vain repetition," foolish straining of emotion, an empty form. Does any one say, "How few answers there are to prayer!" I would say, "How few true prayers!" Lay your body a living sacrifice on the altar, and you will soon be praising God for the answers you receive.

The great lesson is the lesson of true prayer. True prayer brings its answer. True prayer is the only proper and all-sufficient preparation for any great work. "Lord, teach us to pray."

Lesson VIII. February 19.

REBUILDING THE WALL.

Nehemiah iv: 9-21.

By Rev. THOS. S. BARBOUR, FALL RIVER, MASS.

THE purpose indicated in the concluding words of Nehemiah's prayer is soon carried into effect. An opportunity is afforded the royal attendant to present his suit to the king. His cause finds favor. And, thirteen years after Ezra led his great caravan across the desert, Nehemiah is making his way to his fatherland, commissioned governor of Jerusalem, with authority to restore its walls. Our lesson finds the governor in the Jewish capital. He has perhaps stood on Mt. Olivet, upon the spot where the feet of so many a pilgrim have been arrested in later times, and has looked with contending emotions upon the glory and the desolation of the scene revealed across the deep ravine. The night-watches have found him moving slowly about the circuit of the demolished walls. And now, fully informed as to the requirements of the projected task,—his plans definitely determined, he enlists the coöperation of his countrymen and the work is begun.

I. THE NATURE OF THE ENTERPRISE.

Nehemiah's purpose, unlike the aim which brought Ezra to Jerusalem, was not distinctively spiritual. It had to do primarily with the material well-being of his people. But the layman's mission, as truly as the priest's, is of commanding claim upon the interest of the thoughtful observer.

1. The work was vitally related to the perpetuation of the national life of the Jews.

It is not surprising that the colony planted by Zerubbabel had led but a languishing existence. An unwalled city was an anomaly in ancient times. The Jewish capital was at the mercy alike of the unfriendly peoples who had found a home in the land, and of every wandering band of marauders. Moreover, privacy was a first essential, if the distinctive spirit and civilization of the Jew were to survive. As Nehemiah, in his Persian home, had listened to the story of the depressed fortunes of his people, his sagacious mind had recognized at once the need that was most urgent. Let Jerusalem be surrounded with strong fortifications as of old. Then would security return. Then might the national spirit revive. Then city and nation should hold once more an honorable place among the peoples of the earth.

2. The work was vitally related to the divinely-appointed mission of the Jews.

> "When falls the coliseum, Rome shall fall,
> And when Rome falls,—the world."

What Roman vanity is represented as alleging as to its shrine of pleasure, Jewish faith might truthfully affirm of its temple of worship. We may believe that Nehemiah was neither blind nor indifferent to the deeper significance of his work. We know his attachment to the religious faith of his people. His foreign training would tend to make him responsive to the prophetic voices which, with ever-increasing clearness, were speaking of a vital relation between the faith of Judah and hope for mankind. But whatever may be true as respects Nehemiah's thought, we at least know well that with the preservation of the Jewish national life, there was involved the accomplishment of the supreme purpose of divine grace. The Jewish State was as a great chrysalis-case, guarding a life infinitely precious, a life which one day, grown to fulness of strength, was to fly forth into the world with healing in its wings.

3. The work was the accomplishment of a divine decree.

So the prophet Daniel, taught by the angel, assures us. And certainly, at the present day, it is not difficult to discern in the work the moving of the Hand that is stretched out upon the nations. Very wonderful is the story of that strange city which, outlasting more than twenty sieges, its soil twice given up to the ploughshare, still survives. The Chaldean king, like the Roman general in later days, had declared that such a centre of revolt must be blotted from the earth. His wrath did its utmost. But, in due time, the city rose from its ashes. It rose because the mission, for which a greater king had chosen it, was as yet unfulfilled.

II. THE DIFFICULTIES ENCOUNTERED.

Nehemiah's project was one for which no spirit less resolute than that which he brought to the task would have availed. The work was heavy. There was much rubbish to be cleared away. And many a huge stone must be raised from the debris, newly-dressed, and fitted to its place in the massive masonry. Not a few of the people soon grew dispirited. But more serious than these incidental difficulties was the opposition offered by neighboring peoples. These alien races were as one man in the determination that the Jews should never again have a fortified capital in the land. Three men, each an official of one of the hostile peoples, were unresting in their bitter resistance to the work. As they learned of the new governor's purpose, they were satisfied at first to greet it with a mocking laugh. As the task was entered upon, they broke out into contemptuous derision. But when the work was seen to be rapidly advancing, their rage knew no bounds. What their ridicule had failed to effect, force of arms should now accomplish.

Is it not singular that the opposition encountered by Nehemiah should have sprung chiefly from a people who had professed themselves worshippers of Jehovah? The Samaritans had offered to join in the work of rebuilding the temple. Doubtless they justified their present antagonism to Judah. Their offer had been refused. Their daughters, too, having intermarried with the Jews, had been put away. Regarding the case from their point of view, we may be inclined to think their indignation not unnatural. But what verdict that any other could pronounce upon this people would be severe as that which they pronounced upon themselves? They had acknowledged that Jerusalem was the seat of Jehovah's worship. Yet they ceased not to oppose its welfare. Clearly their zeal for Jehovah was largely mixed with baser metal. It is to be feared that there may be in the world to-day something of fancied piety which, if well sifted, would be found to contain a large admixture of self-love. It is a severe test of devotion which sometimes comes to men in the crossing of their preferences and the humbling of their pride. But it cannot be called other than a trustworthy test. The piety which curdles under the influence of personal disappointment or humiliation, can hardly be regarded as genuine devotion.

Strange, too, that these troublers of the Jews should have pursued their vindictive course in the face of signal evidence that they were warring against God. The Samaritans were familiar with the writings which had foretold the return of Judah from her captivity. And the marvelous fulfilment of the prophecy was revealed before their eyes.

Our lesson finds the difficulties of the work at their culmination. For some time, rumors have come in of the hostile purpose of the enemy. And soon, in the very hour when the discouraged workers are declaring themselves spent, and pronouncing the work hopeless, tidings are brought from many quarters of a proposed attack by which it is designed to surprise and massacre the exhausted laborers.

III. THE PLAN PURSUED.

Is it possible to imagine a wiser procedure than that by which the people of Judah met the exigency that was upon them?

1. They prayed. Perhaps they took up the strains of a song they had often heard their Levites sing,—"Except the Lord build the house, they labor in vain that build it. Except the Lord keep the city, the watchman waketh but in vain." And so he, who through recognition of dependence upon him, giveth his beloved sleep, gave tranquil calm to these beleagured men.

2. They armed themselves and watched. Observe that the conjunction is *and*, not *but!* "We made our prayer unto our God *and* set a watch." There is no want of harmony between reliance upon God and employment of the resources which God puts into our hands. Prayer and activity have a common source in genuine desire; and if the one be real, the other will not be wanting. And let none suppose that to recognize the honoring of human activity as God's more common method of answering prayer, in any wise detracts from the greatness and beneficence of his working. What other good gift which the Heavenly Father can bestow upon his children is so greatly to be desired as increase of personal purity and strength? The supreme value of a prayerful life, whatever may be the incidental good obtained, is found in the refining work accomplished by association with God. But, if this be so, shall we wonder that God has chosen to put high honor upon the personal effort by which the soul is uplifted and made strong?

The imperilled Jews were unremitting in their watch. Their plans changed somewhat as the situation altered. At the first indefinite rumor of danger, sentinels were posted. When warning was given of the imminent assault, the whole company were furnished with arms; and, encouraged by the cheery voice of their leader, they stood ready to repel the attack. And when the immediate danger was averted, they were watchful still. Happy the man who, in the field of moral combat, displays a like wisdom! So often, a first repulse of the enemy, mistaken for a final victory, has led on to ultimate disaster. How important then the lesson taught us by the Jew. One company of the governor's personal retinue was at hand with full supply of weapons for their comrades who toiled upon the wall. The nobles rendered a like service for the people. Each laborer retained a weapon. And provision was made for a quick concentration of forces in the event of a sudden assault.

3. They persisted in the work. The disheartened found new strength, and the work was pushed on. In this again, the men of Judah were wise. It would have counted for little that they prayed and watched, had the days gone by leaving the work no farther advanced. A religious life devoted solely to watchfulness and prayer would be largely a wasted life. For the world is more than a battle-field. It is a harvest-field, where the laborers are few. With these Jews, prayer and watchfulness were but tributary to the work before them. So they persisted in their labor. Only at the time of imminent peril was the work for a little interrupted. Then they toiled on.

The conditions indeed were unfavorable. The peril was real. And single-handed work was difficult. But it is those who *will* work, whatever the difficulties under which they labor, who win. Profoundly significant is the advice given by Paul to Timothy, as he bids him to labor "out of season." Alike in building a wall, in gaining an education, in competing for success in business, in doing the work to which Christ calls us for the redemption of mankind, it is one's "out of season" work that is likely to determine the measure of his success.

Such was the noble group of devices with which the men of Judah met the problem facing them. Praying, watching, toiling, they resolutely confronted all difficulties.

IV. THE TRAITS OF CHARACTER DISPLAYED.

Rarely has there been seen a finer illustration of the qualities belonging to genuine manliness. The traits revealed were primarily those characterizing the leader, as shown by the whole story of his life. The spirit of Nehemiah lived on.

How attractive the display of these qualities which we are wont to associate with distinctively practical character! Observe the commander's self-restraint. Mockery cannot affect the calmness of his spirit, or disturb the balance of his mind. He is prudent. He takes no needless risk, omits no wise precaution. He has a faculty for prompt decision. Swiftly, decisively, his plans are formed. And see too his never-relaxing determination,—the same revealed in the reply with which afterward he baffles the craft of his enemies,—"I am doing a great work so that I cannot come down." His courage, as well, is invincible. And note withal the splendid energy of the man, which supports him through the day's toil and the night's unresting vigils, which throbs in every effort, which communicates itself to his dispirited followers, and bears the work irresistibly on.

Not less inspiring was the revelation of those qualities pertaining distinctively to personal piety. Observe the leader's never-faltering faith,—the faith which had affirmed at the beginning,—"The God of heaven, he will prosper us,"—and which, to the end, never once lost its sublime confidence. See the devoutness of spirit which recognizes God's hand when deliverance is given,—"Our enemies heard that God had brought their councils to nought." Observe again the personal attachment to Jehovah, less definitely revealed indeed than in later scenes of Nehemiah's history, but betrayed even here in the title that seems to spring involuntarily from his loyal heart,—"*Our God* shall fight for us."

Such was this man whom God sent across the desert for the help of his people. If to the qualities here disclosed, there be added the princely generosity which marked the ruler's dealings with his fellow-countrymen,—his intense scorn of injustice, his strict fidelity to his earthly sovereign,—must it not be owned that even the gallery opened for us in the Jewish Scriptures has few nobler portraits than that of this high-minded, large-hearted, intrepid official?

> "This shows, methinks, God's plan
> And measure of a stalwart man."

The traits of character shown in the work we have said were primarily those of Nehemiah. But so resplendently did these heroic graces shine in the person of the commander, that the dullest-souled in all the company of his people seemed for a time to reflect the glory. The restored national life of Judah is at its best as the Jews are seen rebuilding their wall.

V. THE RESULT.

There is scarcely need to speak of the issue of the story which we have been following. Of course the enemy was repulsed. It was a bloodless victory. The adversary struck not a single blow. In conflicts with foes of flesh and blood, the record of the most valiant will sometimes be different as respects this feature. But in spiritual warfare the result is always such.

The wall rose. In less than two months, the work was ended. And, in due season, about the restored fortifications of the capital, the triumphal procession passed. The harps awoke. The cymbals clashed. Choirs of singers raised triumphant songs. The whole city joined in one glad outburst of exultant praise. "And the joy of Jerusalem was heard even afar off."

CONCLUDING LESSONS.

The story is thick-strewn with lessons,—lessons of cheer,—lessons of admonition. Some of these we have remarked. But two suggestions of a more comprehensive character we should not fail to note before turning from the spirited scene. The two lessons, in truth, are but reverse sides of a single thought. The qualities which here are joined together ought never to be put asunder.

The one greatest need of the so-called secular life of the people of God is that the hallowed principles which Nehemiah bore to the work of building a wall, shall be brought to our daily tasks. Faith in God, recognition of God's relationship to all things, devotion to God, let these things always be in us and abound, and the "secular" shall become sacred, transfigured even as by the glory of God.

Not less important is the second suggestion. The one greatest need of our religious service is that we shall bring to it the sturdy qualities which give vigor to secular enterprises. Self-restraint, prudence, decision, the ambition to do, the fixed, determined will and courage "never to submit or yield,"— these are supreme needs of Christ's Church, alike for individual service and for united achievement.

So let our lives find in this exalted alliance a noble unity. Then, though the work which they accomplish be less imposing than that revealed when, through Nehemiah's fidelity, the walls of the Holy City rose from the debris of the hill-side, yet of this we may be confident: Our lives shall yield results acceptable to him who called us to his service. And in that enduring structure which the Great Architect is raising through the centuries, it may be found, at length, that we have builded of gold and silver and precious stones.

Lesson IX. February 26.

READING THE LAW.*

Nehemiah viii: 1-12.

BY REV. THOMAS E. BARTLETT, PROVIDENCE, R. I.

IN any age of Israel the scene portrayed in this chapter would have been deeply significant. A multitude composed of men, women and youth listens from daylight to high noon to the Book of God, while men distinguished for their learning, their piety, their rank, direct the teaching. Had such an assembly met for such a purpose in the dark days of the Judges we should have looked for the speedy discomfiture of the Ammonite or the Philistine. Had it occurred in Hezekiah's reign when the might of Assyria was pressing hard against every fortress of Western Asia, and even the stronghold of Zion was mapped for assault, we should have been prepared for the angel's flight to the Assyrian camp, the overthow of Sennacherib's pride and the deliverance of Jerusalem's imprisoned myriads. The scene before us is placed in a later age, in the dire emergency of enfeebled Israel, when a poor fragment of the nation was making an attempt to rise above the great national disaster. The Babylonian has executed God's decree against Jerusalem. The Persian has given the

---

* The sermon for this date was to have been written by Rev. R. M. Martin, who unfortunately became ill before he could prepare it.

word for the sons of Israel to return and rear again their fallen altars. Caravans from the east have come to the desolate hills of Judah. While Israel's millions are scattered among the gentiles and, except by their offerings, take no part in the return, Israel's thousands, pensioners of a foreign master, colonists beset by enemies, are striving to build again, amid the memories of their nation's greatness, a little Jewish state.

I. THE SCENE AND ITS SIGNIFICANCE.

We are in the Jerusalem of the Restoration. Yonder is the temple of Zerubbabel, an impoverished imitation of Solomon's splendid work. The profuse gold, the artistic workmanship, the cloud of glory are absent, and behind the veil, instead of ark and cherubim, only emptiness. Yonder is the protecting wall; it is new, and it is done. It is the product of sacrifice and courage, a visible proof that the spirit of the Hebrew race is yet alive. Jerusalem is a city again; its reproach in the eyes of the heathen is rolled away. Self-respect revives behind those ramparts. In sympathy with this heroic people, look around and call the place Jerusalem; but notice that it is still little more than an enclosure, its palaces heaps of rubbish, made to seem more desolate by the growth of thorns and briars upon them, its ancient streets obliterated or grass-grown, its sloping acres still half covered with the debris of the former city, a place so ruinous that even Jews deemed it a sacrifice to dwell there. Here the congregation of Israel, gathered from village and farm of Judea, is assembled for worship. Temple and sacrifice do not rivet their attention now. As by a common impulse they turn their thoughts from their manifest poverty and weakness to their single bright possession, unmarred by national calamity, their solace in captivity, the inspiration of the return, the peculiar glory of the rising nationality. It was the revelation given to their fathers. The Sacred Books had been confirmed by the ruin of the kingdom; they were now commended anew to the children's faith by the revival of Jerusalem.

Two great reformers are present, Ezra the scribe and Nehemiah the civil ruler; but neither of these needs to prompt the demonstration of reverence for the word of God. A widespread desire to hear the very words of the ancient Law, moved the assembly, and Ezra with the sacred roll but responds to this longing. The writer gives ample materials for a great historic painting. Impressed that this was one of the great days in the national history, he lingers to make events vivid before the eye. The locality where the Book was read was memorable, "the street that was before the water gate." The month and the day must be noted. Even the names of the six men who stood at Ezra's right, and the names of the seven who stood at his left, are given; then the opening of the book, the spontaneous rising up of the congregation, the prayer of Ezra, the people's response with hands raised to heaven, the band of interpreters who were making the reading clear to a generation losing its hold on the national language, the tears that filled all eyes as the meaning of God's word became plain; then the quick resolve of Nehemiah and Ezra that this people, at the dawn of national hope, amid scenes which would often enough start irresistible tears, must now be diverted from grief and turned rather to joy in view of such manifest grace from God as had brought them to that hour and that spot—is not the scene put vividly before the eye? See this fragment of a ruined nation, in hope of a better future, rallying around that law for breaking which the fathers hàd brought destruction upon the kingdom. See this assembly, on the site of Israel's former power, trying to prove worthy of the best part of their people's wonderful history, giving reverence to the written revelation which was the glory of the past and contained the hope of the future. Read this chapter and the two which follow; hear the touching and noble confession of the nation's inveterate sin; witness the making of the covenant henceforth to keep God's law; mark the leaders signing and sealing their pledge, on some great roll, in the presence of the whole assembly. That written covenant was but an attempt to give expression to the convictions wrought by the reading of the Law. Oh, those eighty-four names of the chiefs of the Restoration! The list is dreary enough for perfunctory reading. But those signatures tell us that the restored nationality has read aright Israel's history, has discerned its hope of perpetuity, has interpreted with insight its mission on earth; and, feeble as the nation is, has seriously addressed itself to its commission as trustee of a divine revelation. Such was the spirit of the multitude that listened to the reading of the law.

Point now, if you must, to the city of Nehemiah as a poor shadow of the Jerusalem of the Kings. Tell us to look in vain for material magnificence in the rising city. Remind us that the Temple can never recover its lost glory, and must be content to wait for Haggai's spiritual hope to be fulfilled, when Christ should walk that Temple's floor. Call the prince of Jerusalem a mere Persian officer. Our interest is not lessened. We still see a more thrilling spectacle than temporal greatness could ever furnish. We see these descendents of Abraham, but lately come from the land of the enemy, standing there in conscious weakness, yet knowing well that they represent a people which received promises from heaven, and now kindling their hope that a gracious God will yet through them bring about a glorious fulfilment. They have come back not merely to build again the city of their fathers. A high religious motive was the impelling power in their arduous enterprise. Leaders such as Ezra and Nehemiah had glimpses of the invisible and, while building up a nation on the soil of Canaan, looked forward in dim hope to the far away hour when there should be in Bethlehem a birth of David's great Son. Earthly power, a great population, national independence were not theirs; in their poverty they prized the more their spiritual treasures, the heavenly wisdom, the far-reaching hopes, which had been given to Israel.

II. THE OUTCOME IN LATER TIMES.

I have given an ideal coloring, it is true, to this historic painting. The chronicler is not the historian of a nation. The bare facts do not fully represent the truth. Hopes, aspirations, purposes which move a people in a crisis of their career, results which no contemporary could clearly foresee, give moral grandeur to great historic movements; and these must find place in any faithful portrayal of an epoch-making scene.

The prosaic critic will needlessly remind us that a covenant in writing, signed and sealed, may have no more power over wayward hearts than a covenant made with spoken words; that this solemn compact was not kept, that evil did not disappear from Jerusalem, that the reformer was often needed there in subsequent days. Having eyes he sees not. Generations must pass before the power of a great reform will come out in mighty manifestation. Is it indeed so blameworthy to stand over a rippling brooklet, whose swelling current will become a river and bear the commerce of cities, and be respectful as in the presence of greatness?

1. This was "the birthday of Judaism," and Judaism was great. Henceforth the heart of Israel bowed in supreme, if sometimes in fanatical reverence before the law of Moses. The scribe took the place of the priest; the pulpit took the place of the altar; scripture and prayer and teaching, the comfort of the exile, made a new religious service in Jerusalem, and one more popular than the restored ritual of the temple; congregations became participants and not merely spectators in meetings for worship, the synagogue even in Judea was not overshadowed by the temple, in gentile cities the synagogue was a light in the darkness. In a nation which had such a priceless literature, the elevation of the scribe was natural and

fitting. The synagogue service gave opportunity for continual preaching. The inauguration at the second founding of Jerusalem of the public reading of the sacred books was prophetic of better days. From that day the public reading of the scriptures has not ceased. Five centuries later, looking backward toward that day of Ezra, James in the early church said, "Moses from generations of old hath in every city them that preach him, being read in the synagogues every Sabbath." The synagogue, the beloved institution of Judaism, became the model of the local Christian church, and its simple service, taking to itself the bright supplement of the new revelation, passed with little change into Christian assemblies, and the sound thereof, echoed from one land to another and from age to age, will not die away.

2. The Maccabean age with its martyrs and heroes was another outcome of this turning of the nation to its sacred law. Read in I Maccabees the story of Jewish woes under the heel of the furious Syrian king; how the religion of Israel was assailed with malignant hate, how the sacred books were appointed to destruction, how Jews fell before the persecutor in city and hamlet as martyrs for the word of God; how the spirit of the nation kindled to meet the terrible crisis. Jews were willing to suffer for their law; they could not endure the sight of Bibles defiled, torn asunder and burned before them. When but a leader appeared they were ready to hazard battle with overwhelming odds in defence of their law, and they were able to conquer in its name. Syrian persecution and fierce Maccabean vengeance met as angry seas, and the people of the Book prevailed. The work of Ezra had not been in vain.

3. The preservation of the Hebrew Bible is another of the momentous products of forces set in motion by Ezra and Nehemiah. Scribes stepped to the front in the great historic scene. From that day the order of the Scribes had a foremost place in the nation. They received a precious trust and they magni-

fied their office; they served their nation and the world by the will of God; they taught the unlearned the Scriptures of their fathers; they laid the wisdom of heaven upon the nation's heart. They did, indeed, copy the Sacred Books with scrupulous care, and they taught coming generations how to revere even the letter of the Law; but copying was not their chief service. Books cannot long survive simply as material things. The thoughts they contain must be respected and loved if the books are to live; and Israel was taught by the Scribes for generations to revere its chief treasure, and the nation, devoted to the Book, kept that Book safe for all later times.

III. LESSONS.

First, *Some things are settled.*

People and leaders alike recognized a final authority in a book. Coming to the Pentateuch they felt that they were reaching the court of last appeal. When they should hear its voice and understand it, controversy must end. A text of Scripture, in their judgment, would be the signal for debate to cease. Every generation needs to take a fresh hold upon the truth that the Bible is a book of conclusions, and infinitely precious on that account.

We begin life in blank ignorance. When but a few years pass we are facing responsibilities. Must we meet them with wisdom acquired by experience, or by the unaided mind of man? I know how eager we are to learn by experience. But there are some things which, if learned in this way, will cripple our earthly life or end our experience on earth. If the silence of the sky had not been broken, we could not have forced its secrets. Who could have whispered to his own soul, "I am living now under the care of a kind God, with a charge to do his will, and shall pass at death into higher joys," and had assurance of the truth of his words if no voice had given God's thoughts? We needed to know some things about the hereafter, that we might bring thoughts of endless life and peace into our brief days of pain. We needed some definite answers to the ever-recurring questions prompted by the mystery of human life: Whence? And why? And whither? The Scriptures answer with authority and not as ancient or modern scribes. The Scriptures give us a canopy of fixed stars. In our voyage across the sea of life, we fix our eyes either on some dim lantern hung at the mast, moving with every movement of our vessel, or we take our reckoning by the stars of a divine revelation, which storms cannot obscure or passing ages dim.

The Bible, with its clear disclosures, its fixed precepts, its inspiring promises, is the true guide of man. Our doubts and fears cannot change it. It was here on earth when we came; it will remain when we are gone. It will bless others if we refuse its blessings.

Second, *The Scriptures richly deserve the homage of mind and heart.*

Those men in the days of old, rose up at the sight of the Sacred Roll. They performed an act that day so expressive of the nation's quickened reverence, that it was repeated for ages in Israel. Tell us, wise men, did they not revere the fairest wisdom known in any part of the ancient world? All subsequent ages have not produced books which can render obsolete those treasures of the Hebrew race. In elevation of thought, in solemn grandeur, in beauty not dependent on the witchery of words, in self-evidencing authority over the conscience and the heart of man, the Scriptures are unapproachable. What intellectual greatness can they not instruct and thrill? What mental weakness can they not comfort and quicken? The power of a thousand national reformations lies sleeping there. For nations as for individuals, its words are spirit and life.

When opposed to this authority, what is the trustworthiness of the so-called church, or that of the poor infallibility of a

Roman pontiff, or the equally presumptuous and not less pitiable opinion on mysteries which angels cannot pierce, of the next man you meet? "I have dreamed, I have dreamed," said the false prophets to Jeremiah. Their successors in later times change the formula a little, saying, "I think, I think," and the canopy of the ancient stars is assailed. Is there eternal life? Is there a heaven for man? Is God love? "Perhaps, perhaps," says the unwearied and unthinking echo of stouter unbelief. But what is the chaff to the wheat? Men know the difference, and they know which is the wheat.

Whether we examine the Bible itself, or any offered substitute for its lofty conceptions, we are almost equally assured that our homage given to the Book is not misplaced. The people of Ezra's day passed their life in a dim age; they were poor, and they were beset with hardships; but in their reverence for the Book of God, they stood "in the foremost files of time."

Lesson X. March 5.

KEEPING THE SABBATH.

Nehemiah xiii: 15-22.

BY REV. EDWARD HOLYOKE, PROVIDENCE, R. I.

THE Sabbath of the Jews was at once a religious ordinance and a national institution. This double authority of a theocratic state rendered the work of Sabbath reform peculiarly simple. The pious cup-bearer to Ahasuerus, having elected himself ruler, rebuilder and reformer, coolly gives the order and the city gates are closed each sixth day eve; sacrilegious venders and victuallers are left to lodge before the walls or be driven away altogether, and the profaned Sabbath is avenged. "Excellent," says our modern sabbatarian. Our Sunday, too, is haunted by luxury-venders, paper-hawkers, ball nines, steam-engines and even "ship-wrights," such as Hamlet's, "whose sore task does not divide the Sunday from the week." So we sometimes cry, "Oh, for a Nehemiah and his legal wall of protection to shut them out of the city!"

Such a proceeding might be effective, but would it in our day be legitimate? Can a nation which maintains utter cleavage between state and church have recourse to a theocratic method and policy? Must a people who glory in liberty of conscience be remanded to the yoke of Judaic bondage? If not, what help can the example of Nehemiah give us? If none, shall we relinquish the Lord's Day to total desecration?

Or is there some eternal and universal principle by which we may truly "keep the Sabbath" on the Lord's Day?

The question is a pressing one. Whether or not we can solve it as Nehemiah did, his problem is ours, thoroughly modern, like most of those brought before us by ancient Scripture. It is not abstract, not merely religious or moral, but profoundly practical. Of this the cry for and against opening the Columbian Exposition on Sunday is but part of the proof. The laboring masses, Christians or not, are interested in the fate of Sunday, and already begin to clamor for their lost day of rest. Society owes it to them, yet acts more and more against their interest in the matter. The work performed on Sunday is less than is commonly supposed, but in our country it is increasing, labor required by luxuries being continually added to "works of necessity."

While our American Sunday is slowly relaxing its traditional severity, the tide of agitation for Sunday is rising in the most unexpected quarters, and in a signal manner. Leon Say, the eminent political economist, president of the strong society in France for the propagation of Sunday observance, writes: "Our society unanimously recognizes that a weekly day of rest is indispensable to the working classes. Two years ago we numbered twenty members, to-day we count over 2,500, republicans, monarchists, Catholics and Protestants, bishops and free thinkers. In the post office we have got the hours shortened on Sunday, and we are now laboring with the railroad companies." A similar movement has begun in Germany.

The balance of power, as well as the burden of responsibility, concerning the treatment of the Lord's Day rests with the Lord's people. Sunday is the heritage and charge of the Church. No external foe can break it down without help from religious people. What is our duty? It is of small use to petition for the Sunday closing of the World's Fair against the poor, and take no further action. The entire question of Sunday keeping suggested by the episode from Nehemiah, needs candid discussion.

It must be conceded that the Jewish Sabbath, as such, does not constitute sufficient foundation for obligation in this department of conduct. Its law was given to an infant race, as a preliminary and provisional rule, a garment for temporary protection to be cast aside as a swaddling band when outgrown. For that people it was a positive ordinance, a sign of the Old Covenant, and ending with that. The New Testament contains more argument against the perpetuity of the Jewish Sabbath than in favor of any Sabbath. In fact, the obligation perpetually to observe it is there both expressly and impliedly denied. The foundation of sabbatic practice is the Fourth Commandment. But can the Decalogue or any part of it, as distinguished by the Christ from the spirit of it, which is undoubtedly moral and so perpetual, be binding on the Christian world? Has not the letter of all Old Testament command been abrogated by the higher law of Christ? The political and ceremonial element in the Sabbath law was temporary; the eternal and moral element was recognized, rescued and reestablished by him. The Jewish Sabbath, as such, has passed away; the divine Sabbath of rest and worship remains for a higher and freer development in the Christian world.

For this reason it is difficult to see how the duty of observing Sunday can rest on the Fourth Commandment. Such a position proves either nothing or too much. All that may be proved from Scripture for the perpetuity of the Sabbath holds good for Saturday. If we will have the literal Sabbath, we are driven to the seventh day, in accordance with the strictest sabbatarianism; there is no valid middle ground.

The letter killeth; the spirit giveth life. The spiritual principle shadowed forth in the old abides as a foundation for the new day of the Lord. There is a divine Sabbath. "There is an element of rest in the divine nature itself." Six days of work and one of rest is the authoritative rule. Failure to distinguish between the sacred, voluntary rest of the Creation and the enforced inactivity of the Jew is fatal to any satisfactory theory of a Christian rest day.

That divine Sabbath which was the foundation of the inferior institution of Judaism is also the basis of the higher institution, which is distinct from the Jewish Sabbath and peculiar to Christianity. The first day of the week, called by the Apostles the "Lord's Day," not only enshrines the typical rest of God as exemplary for his people, but it is still further divine in that it is pre-eminently Christian. Jesus himself kept the old day, because be recognized the divine foundation which underlay the temporary superstructure of Judaism. Yet he taught the deep significance of the old, to be herald and prophesy of the new ordinance, which should be not for one but for all peoples. The new Sabbath is to be an element of a Christo-centric faith. The difference is not simply a change of day; it is a change of dispensation, of divine method in redemption. The precepts and usages relating to the Sabbath must not be transferred to the Lord's Day. The new is builded on the ruins of the old. The last seventh is the sepulchre's sleep; the first day of the week is the risen Lord's.

The divinest thing about Sunday is its Christianity. Could any cause less than the risen Christ have produced a world-Sabbath? Christianity is the religion of the resurrection; Sunday is the resurrection day. So it was to the Apostles and so should it ever be to us. Their inspired example and the great fact it commemorates, constitute our authority for the observance of Sunday. And there is no other. The Apostles never cite the fourth commandment. The early fathers never refer to it as a reason for the Sunday rest. For two centuries the Lord's Day was never confounded with the Sabbath, but was always sharply distinct from it, kept with a larger liberty and in a totally different spirit. The Sabbatarianism through whose glasses colored with prejudice we look, was a growth mainly later than the fifth century. The reasons which we now give for Sabbath observance, borrowed from judaizing and puritanical influences, were abhorrent to the early Church, especially to Gentile Christians.

For the man of faith the chief benefit from Sunday is its worship. "On a Sabbath morning in New England," says Hawthorne, "the air is meet for mankind to breathe into their hearts and send it forth again as the utterance of prayer." To God's people this is so of Sunday everywhere. Of course, time is merely subjective and relative. All times alike are sacred to time's Founder. If Sunday is sacred, Monday is not profane. Yet for the Christian, Sunday is a specially consecrated day, the centre of most hallowed associations, and the channel of most precious spiritual blessings. Its worship suggests not "workshop" but the "worthship" of the living God.

The Christian's faith touching Sunday finds expression in the Latin sentences of an early writer, freely translated thus: " Day of the Lord's Resurrection,—sacred to so many and great mysteries of the divine dispensation that whatever is fixed as worthiest by the Lord may be observed in the excellence of that day. On this day the world began. On this day, through the resurrection, death received its ruin and life its true beginning. On this day the Apostles received the trumpet of the gospel that is to be preached to all nations, and the sign of regeneration to be borne throughout the world. This day, the doors being closed, when Jesus had entered into the midst of them, he breathed on them and said, 'Receive ye the Holy Ghost.' On this day the Holy Spirit promised by the Lord came to the disciples. So that we have learned it as a divine rule, given by example and handed down to us, that the mysteries of sacerdotal blessing should be celebrated by us on that day in which are gathered all the gifts of grace."

For the keeping of Sunday, or if any one will, the Christian

Sabbath, we in vain seek exact or direct precepts, even in the gospel. "The omission of particularities is characteristic of the New Testament," says Dean Stanley, and in this instance it is also a strong guarantee of the universality of the Lord's Day observance in the primitive church. As authority for Sunday keeping we should expect a broad and enduring principle, carrying in it a universal "ought," and where shall we find such but on the lips of the Lord himself? His teaching as to the old day is our best guide touching the new. For what was the Sabbath given? "The Sabbath was made for man, not man for the Sabbath." The welfare of humanity; this is Christ's universal category of command, under which Sabbath observance is a particular item. Human weal is both physical and spiritual; it unites in itself the human and the divine. A partial view of religious duty has led to "over-statements and over-strictness solely from the divine side, and to under-statements and laxity solely from the human side." But as to Sunday duty, are there two sides? Sunday is not for souls alone, or for bodies alone; it is for both. At present there is great disagreement as to what ought to be done on Sunday. But in the principle enounced by Jesus the divided opinions of clergymen and the varying practice of laymen may converge. The Lord's Day is meant for a means of grace and health to body and soul. Human good is the aim and test of all. Sunday is but a means. The end is perfected humanity. "Man exists as an end in himself," says Kant. "The true Shekinah is man," says Chrysostom. "The Son of Man is Lord of the Sabbath," and the rendering of humanity divine is the goal at which the new Sabbath aims.

How to apply this standard Church and state must each be its own judge. How shall the Church remember the Lord's Day to keep it holy? What makes anything holy? The law? That is but the broken mould in which the image of holiness was cast. Sunday is more than an institution, it is a new creation. The Son of Man is Lord,—all that leads to him and furthers his humanity is law keeping; all that leads away from him is law breaking. Not feeding the animal in the pit, but lifting humanity out of the pit sanctifies Sunday. Pleasure-hunting is frivolous and desecrating; search for good works and bringing deliverance from trouble are sanctifying. "Is it lawful to do good, to save life?" said Christ, and his accusing plotters were dumb. Sunday is dedicated to the worship of God and to the promotion of happiness and goodness in a lost humanity. The best interpreter of Sunday law is love.

If the Church exists primarily for religion, the state stands for health and morals. Sunday legislation for a Christian commonwealth finds its standard not in Mosaic ritual but in Christian sentiment. A judaizing judiciary will still stone to death the wilful Sabbath breaker; a practice which John Cotton actually proposes in his prospectus of laws for the Colony of Massachusetts. Legislation cannot rest on the ground of religious duty. That is Papacy, unendurable in a state whose divorce from Church is too complete ever to be annulled. We cannot ask the world to keep our Lord's Day in our way save in so far as it believes in our Lord. We cannot expect the Jew to accept our Sabbath until he accepts our Saviour. Yet, as the Church's gift of Sunday has proven, on moral and economical grounds, a vast boon to the state, the state owes the Church in return ample protection for freedom of worship. The state may regulate morals and protect the Church, though it cannot create or administer a religion.

The Christian Sunday is a divine gift, coming with an apostolic benediction. If it be made a yoke and a burden, it ceases to be Christian. It knows no such intolerable rules as stoning to death for lighting a fire, punishment for gathering sticks, climbing a tree, or killing a flea on condition that it doesn't actually hurt. Let these sabbatarian virtues be remanded to the scholastics and Puritans. The humorous suggestion that the Puritans hated bear-baiting not for the pain it gave the bear but for the pleasure it gave the spectators, would seem not unfitting if applied to the advocates of Sunday blue-laws. Do we wish back the spirit under which Washington was arrested and detained in Connecticut for Sunday travel? Would it make Sunday the day of resurrection joy? Take joy from the children, giving them a catalogue of "don'ts," and they will hate the Sunday with all that pertains to it. Plants must grow and lungs dilate on Sunday. It is easy for those who can come and go at their leisure all the week, to condemn shop-worn and kitchen-stained drudges for getting a breath of pure air at the only possible time. Let us in reasonable charity remember that for every man and woman the highest attainable welfare of the whole being is an imperative law. The individual or corporation that helps make Sunday to the poor and sick in hovel and garret, the healthiest and happiest day in the whole week, is, if its motive is right, honoring the Lord's Day as truly as the preacher in the pulpit or the fashionable worshiper in a cushioned pew.

But the ideal Sunday is certainly no day of sports or revelling. Holiday dissipation is wholly foreign to its spirit. There is no more fertile source of Sunday desecration than the craze for artificial pleasures which possesses this generation. Not one of the rich and varied delights which Nature directly affords, as walking, riding, botanizing, sketching, music, etc., but may be as innocent and helpful on this day as at any time; while few, if any, of the so-called social amusements or national games can be considered germane to the character of the Lord's Day. Encroachments on Sunday time by gamblers, theatre and base-ball players, saloon-goers and revelling parties, make discrimination a necessity. But let us discriminate rationally and justly.

Then we have to remember the principle of christian liberty. "One observeth the day,—another observeth it not, but both to the Lord." That is, two men equally good and equally obedient to Christ's law, may keep Sunday quite differently in detail, in which case, if both are conscientious, neither is justified in condemning the other. Only the keeping must be to the Lord, else your liberty is sheer license. Let us, in our reaction from Puritanism, not sing too lustily, " Free from the law, O, happy condition." Within the limits of spiritual law alone is there true liberty. Freedom of holy days was an apostolic principle. The early Christians did not censure or punish either non-observers or downright breakers of the Lord's Day. They simply loved the day into respect. The same love for Christ and men which they showed, and their courtesy for all, will enable us to re-establish what they established.

In conclusion, then, let not Christians abuse their liberty in relation to Sunday. If a given use of the day by me, legitimate in itself, leads unbelievers to disregard it utterly, I will use it otherwise. Not to do this were to degrade my liberty, of which Scripture makes so much, into a laxity altogether unscriptural. The day demands, in such cases, a spirit of voluntary sacrifice that shall be to the world unquestionable evidence of the value we put on the Lord's Day.

A slave comes fleeing in the darkness of midnight to a western home, appealing for a night's protection from pursuing blood-hounds. "The town is full of friends," said the father of the narrator. "I don't need friends," was the reply, "I need a defender." "You shall have it," said the old man, and loaded his gun.

No doubt the Lord can defend his day from all profaners, but he will do it through the loyal fidelity of his followers. In his name, let Book and bells summon us to keep the Holy Day of the Lord inviolate, as the Type of Creation's Rest, the Memorial of Redemptive Grace and the Pledge of Human Blessedness in the eternal Sabbath of God.

Lesson XI. March 12.

ESTHER BEFORE THE KING.
Esther iv: 10–17; v: 1–5.

BY REV. F. W. RYDER, LAWRENCE, MASS.

AMONG the Scriptures of the Old Testament the Book of Esther stands alone. Almost every feature of it that can be named is unique. Isolated in locality, peculiar in style and matter, it presents to the Bible scholar a study at once difficult and enticing. It is well even for the general reader to get a view of the essential characteristics peculiar to this volume. The old idea of the Bible, which attributed to its varied literature an identical quality, as though it had all been made on the same machine or handed down from heaven like the Two Tables of the Law, is rapidly and rightly passing away. We see that many elements and influences blended in the making of these books. Time and place, national and personal feeling, each writer's political and religious environment, the particular end which each author had in view and the special impulse that set his pen in motion, all are concerned and are therefore to be fully and devoutly investigated. This we see without abating one jot of our faith that these volumes took shape under the superintendence of God's Spirit.

Esther is the distinctively Persian book of the Bible. The glow of the far Orient is on every page. In it we tarry for a season by the home of the Magi. Says Stanley, "Even more than the Book of Job is Idumean and the Book of Daniel Babylonian, is the Book of Esther Persian. It is the one example in the sacred volume of a story of which the whole scenery and imagery breathes the atmosphere of an Oriental court as completely and almost as exclusively as the Arabian nights." It is plain that the book marks an episode rather than an epoch. It makes no attempt at a continuous account of the Persian period in Hebrew history. We have merely the narrative of one exciting event. This short story, it should be noted, contains all that we know of the vicissitudes of the chosen people for a whole generation. The book presents an entirely new set of *dramatis personæ* on a new stage. Throughout the entire narrative there is no mention of any person who had been prominent in national affairs previous to the reign of Ahasuerus, or of any who appear later. Nor is there any effort to connect the events recounted here with what has been or is to be. The book is, in fact, a bayou alongside the stream of sacred history, from which we may look out thereupon, but no part of the stream itself. Yet, far the most difficult and exceptional feature of the volume is its total lack of religious quality. The failure of the book's unknown author to mention the name of God has often been severely commented upon. That omission was nearly fatal to its standing in the canon of Scripture. But this almost unaccountable fact is not the book's most serious fault. The story is wholly lacking in the pious flavor that characterizes the other parts of the Bible. From beginning to end there is no mention of any religious act, unless fasting is so to be considered, nor does any sign of devoutness, or dependence on supernatural aid emerge anywhere in the narrative. The lovely idyl of Ruth, which is likewise an historical "aside," is fragrant with a piety and faith that is entirely missing in Esther. The narrative moves on the level of ordinary history. Plot and counterplot, patriotism, courage and self-sacrifice, with happy fortuities which are not referred to divine Providence, tell the unvarnished tale. Yet this strange suppression of religious feeling in the book is a cogent argument in favor of its historic character. Had the author's purpose been, as many think, to justify a spurious festival by a fictitious account of its origin, it is inconceivable that he should have left out the most forceful plea which he could possibly have made. He must have been writing the history of actual events.

THE SITUATION.

Jerusalem had fallen. The Hebrew tribes, torn from the soil in which they had rooted for six hundred years, and deported to a foreign territory, dragged out a servile existence as strangers in a strange land. But Babylon had fallen also. The huge fabric of Nebuchadnezzar's empire was crushed to ruins in a single night. Now, over the vast territories once ruled by the conquerer of Judah, the Medo-Persian was sovereign. One hundred and twenty provinces, from India to Ethiopia, composed this magnificent realm. What effect the conquering of their conquerors had on the fortunes of the captive nation we do not know. Probably little or none. The Hebrews seem to have lived on in peaceful subjugation, slowly rising in the esteem of their neighbors and spreading through the Persian domain, till the farthest of Persia's six score provinces had its Jewish colony. On the throne sat Ahasuerus, that Xerxes of Greek history whose army of a million shields met its first check at the glorious pass of Thermopylæ, and fought in galleys under the cliffs of "seaborn Salamis." This prince displays all the usual traits of an oriental despot. Vain, voluptuous, capricious, cruel, yet mingling with these qualities an unhesitating courage, great administrative skill, and military genius of no mean order, he stands a representative monarch of his race and time.

A curious providence had elevated to his side a young Jewess, Hadassah by name, the cousin and foster-child of one

Mordecai. Toward the close of a prolonged festival, the king, excited by wine, had commanded Vashti, his queen, to unveil her beauty before the festal throng. This was a flagrant violation of immemorial etiquette, as shocking to Asiatic modesty as an order to the president's wife to disrobe at a state reception would seem now. Vashti refused and was promptly divorced. To the oriental mind one thing is worse in a wife than immodesty, and that is disobedience. Her successor was chosen by competitive examination among the beauties of the realm. The choice fell on Hadassah, who is better known by her Persian name, Esther, "the star." About the same time Mordecai appears to have been promoted, presumably by Esther's influence, to the rank of court chamberlain. It so came to pass that in the hour of its deadliest jeopardy, the Jewish nation had two noble representatives in positions of power near the person of the king. Such things do not fall out by chance. "In time of peace prepare for war," is a principle of God's providence not less than of man's sagacity. When storm and peril are far from popular thought, he is quietly putting his servants where they will be needed. The man or the woman for the emergency is forthcoming, because God, who foresees the emergency, makes ready for it. Many a strange conjunction of history is to be explained by this divine provision.

> "Behind the dim unknown
> Standeth God, within the shadow,
> Keeping watch above his own."

Christianity had its Paul, Protestantism its Luther, English freedom its Cromwell, American liberty its Washington, each in the very hour when he was indispensable.

CRISIS AND DELIVERANCE.

A malignant plot, begotten of a petty quarrel between two courtiers, an Agagite and a Jew, menaced the Jewish race with annihilation. The nature of the feud we only conjecture. Also we cannot explain Mordecai's rashness in defying the king's command. His course could have but one termination. Sooner or later, it must work his destruction. One point, however, over which difficulty is raised, is perfectly clear. Haman failed to wreak summary vengeance on his adversary, because he meditated a more magnificent stroke. Bulging with injured vanity, he planned a revenge proportionate to his own importance. The scheme was nothing less than the wholesale slaughter of the race to which Mordecai belonged. Haman scorned a small reprisal. He would wipe out the insult in a nation's blood. What mighty matters turn on trivial circumstances! Desolating wars spring from questions of court etiquette. National history is the equilibrium of diplomatic intrigue. The payment of old grudges is still one paramount function of the statesman.

The plot was well laid and almost succeeded. By a specious plea, a decree from the king was obtained. The edict of doom had gone forth, and the day of slaughter was fixed. Consternation spread through the realm. Between the captive people and their doom stood one frail life. The fate of a race and the religious future of the world hung on the patriotic daring of a young and untried woman. Would she be equal to the occasion? Mordecai, as he now saw the consequence of his temerity, saw also the single hope that remained. Some one must entreat from the king the life of the nation. Who so likely to gain that favor as the beloved queen, chosen for her goodness and beauty from among the daughters of the land? Yet what a slender chance! Every approach to the monarch was barred by armed guards, whose duty was to smite without warning or mercy the unbidden intruder. The king had not summoned Esther for thirty days and might not do so for twice thirty more. Even her connection with the doomed people appears to have remained unsuspected. Moreover, the laws of the Medes and Persians change not. An edict once issued must stand forever. The king himself could not annul it. A dubious prospect indeed on which to risk one's life! Yet it was the only hope. Sometimes God opens a door for us, and sometimes he leaves us to force it open. It was the supreme hour in Esther's history. The tide that leads to fortune was at its flood. A nation's fate trembled in the balance of her fortitude. Perhaps she had come to the kingdom for such a time as this. The sterner stuff of which men are made had often quailed and failed in easier passes. Was this tender woman sufficient for a venture so deadly? On her decision her people's future hung. But Mordecai's confidence was rightly placed. Esther rose grandly to the occasion. Dressing herself in festal robes, whether for enthronement or burial, who could tell? she made her way into the royal presence.

There is in all history no more thrilling scene. A queen, young, beautiful, famous, with life before her and everything to live for, staked all on a single throw to save her people from destruction. By her patriotism, her high daring, her noble self-abnegation, Esther deserves a place second to none in the annals of human heroism.

Evidently the guards recognized her. For one dreadful moment they hesitated to strike. Small wonder if she felt the blood curdling about her heart; if her sight grew dim, and the solid earth under her feet seemed to quake. But the vision of her beauty awoke the old love in the king's heart. While she stood and the sentries delayed, Ahasuerus stretched a gracious scepter toward her—and the cause was won.

A few swift touches complete the story. The exposure and overthrow of Haman, the proclamation of the second decree, neutralizing what it could not revoke, the gallant stand of the Jews against their assailants, the execution of Haman on the very gallows he had built for Mordecai, are told with graphic power in the book itself. They call for neither recital nor comment here.

Out of this exciting episode arose the great Feast of Purim. It commemorated the nation's deliverance in Babylonia, as the Passover marked the deliverance from Egypt. The name is derived from the Persian word, Pur, "a lot," because when Haman cast lots to determine the day of slaughter, the date fell so far off as to give ample space for redemptive effort.

Philologists make some difficulty over the word, and critics pick flaws in the texture of the narrative. But as to the place and importance of Purim in the post-exilic history of Israel, there is no debate. National institutions, however, do not arise from romances. The Feast of Purim must have had an origin. For two thousand years it has stood before the world, unaccounted for in any other way. It is therefore an eloquent witness to the veracity of this account. It proclaims the Book of Esther a real record of a terrible crisis and an heroic rescue.

REFLECTIONS.

What are the lessons of the story? First, we have here a striking illustration of God's way of working out great plans through the ordinary affairs of men. No miracle is mentioned in this book. No angels walk in fiery furnaces or stop the mouths of lions. No dreadful plagues afflict a stubborn land. Seas do not divide or manna fall from heaven. No withering lightnings blast the oppressor, or rocking earthquakes unhinge prison doors. There is only the familiar movement along the familiar lines of human action. "But God's works are here though his name is not." Jehovah, who had a thousand times interposed by signs and wonders, did not desert his people now. The open eye beholds him here not less clearly than in the miraculous displays by which he is presented elsewhere. The fortune that lifted Esther to the throne, and seated Mordecai at the king's gate, the headlong wrath of Haman and his inflated pride, the sleeplessness of Ahasuerus, the delay of the lot, and Esther's desperate venture,—these, with all the incidents of the drama, seem like the common run of history. So they are. But God usually publishes his revelation and his will through common history. Miracles are rare things. Divine Providence is constant and unfailing. God works more largely and not less visibly in the daily life of the world than in those startling exhibitions by which his power makes itself known at long intervals. The thing to be expected is that he will continue to do so. Through the machinations of politics, through the unrest and striving of noble souls, through social evolutions, national vicissitudes and ethical experiments he will lead our race to its grander future. All the mighty and irritating problems of our day will be solved along these lines. We should work with God unto their solution. The Book of Esther has the special value over the other parts of the Bible, that it addresses us on the same level of divine Providence where, most likely, we must ever work with God.

The career of Haman exemplifies another great principle of the divine government. Evil reacts on its perpetrator. Curses come home to roost. Into the pit dug for others the digger falls. He that doeth wrong shall receive for the wrong that he hath done, and there is no respect of persons with God. Haman plotted the slaughter of a nation and brought destruction on his own house. He built a gallows for Mordecai and himself hung thereon. By wrong-doing no one is so severely injured as the wrong-doer. The victim deserves less commiseration than the oppressor, on whom the rebounding retribution of crime surely falls. Men do not comprehend this law, though the pages of history teem with illustrations of its operation. The story of Esther should impress its inviolability on our minds.

Decision and self-sacrifice are the strong elements of Esther's character. Not beauty, rank, or fame, but the prompt willingness with which she risked all for the saving of others is the sure basis of her renown. To step unhesitatingly into the place of dangerous duty betokens a nature of heroic mold. No warrant to fame is surer. Mr. Ruskin, in an essay on "The Roots of Honor," discusses at some length the question why it is that regiments of men organized for peaceful industry get less praise than regiments of men organized for violence and slaughter. As to the fact there can be no doubt. The military hero is still the hero. The commercial world rears few monuments to its captains of industry or its merchant princes. The reason, according to Mr. Ruskin, is that the soldier's trade is not slaying but being slain! "All kinds of bye-motives may have determined his choice of a profession and may affect his conduct in it. But put him in the fortress breach with all the pleasures of life behind him and only duty and death before, and he will keep his face to the front and die for the nation." It is this element of sacrifice in the soldier's career that gives him universal fame. We who look admiringly on Esther's heroic action should not miss its central lesson. Nor should we think that opportunity is lacking us in these piping times of peace. To stand with righteousness on the unpopular side, to speak out against shams, conventionalities, demagoguism, debauchery, formalism, bigotry, or any sort of wrong or hypocrisy, will tax the stamina of the bravest. The path of self-denial and sacrifice seems drear and dusty as we look adown it. It is, nevertheless, the road by which all must walk who would come at last to a renown that fadeth not away.

Lesson XII. March 19.

[TEMPERANCE LESSON.]

TIMELY ADMONITION.

Proverbs xxiii: 15-23.

BY REV. GEORGE E. HORR, JR., BOSTON, MASS.

THE Scriptures do not follow the method, which is somewhat prevalent in our public school temperance instruction, of minimizing the attractions of strong drink. On the contrary, the Bible writers portray the delights of the cup in the very language which a profligate man might use. Their descriptions, however, are not to make wine attractive, but to show that, in spite of its allurements, there is peril in it. Take, for instance, the language of the last part of this twenty-third chapter of the book of Proverbs. The writer speaks of wine as "red," as "giving its color in the cup," as "moving itself aright," or "going down smoothly." He dwells upon the tempting qualities of strong drink, yet, he does this, not to win us to the cup, but to enforce the truth that the pleasant invitation is really an insidious temptation. "Its end—like a serpent it bites, like a basilisk it stings." The child who is taught that wine is not pleasant to drink, when he comes to taste it, will be apt to conclude that all his temperance instruction was untrustworthy, and the well-meaning but narrow-minded teachers and writers from whom he learned, will find that they have indirectly helped to form the habits they sought to prevent. Nothing is so wise as to follow the method of the Scriptures and teach the whole truth, without covering up or twisting the slightest circumstance for the sake of making a point. Let us frankly acknowledge that it is a pleasant thing to drink wine, that the attractions of the cup are very considerable, and then like reasonable men let us see why it is that, in spite of its tempting qualities, wine is an indulgence to be foregone, so that the more atttractive it is to us the more we should be on our guard against its fascinations. Everyone must see how greatly the exhortations to temperance in the passage before us are strengthened, because the writer is so open-minded in considering the facts, and so candid in his admissions as to the attractions of the cup. We feel that it is not a fanatic, seeing but one thing and without any sense of proportion, who is dealing with us, but a broad-minded man who has considered all the facts, and who, in view of them all, gives to us this urgent advice against indulgence in wine.

The writer supports his exhortation to temperance by three considerations, which have as much weight to-day as they had in that distant age in Palestine.

I. INDULGENCE IN WINE LEADS TO POVERTY.

"The drunkard and the glutton shall come to poverty, and drowsiness shall clothe a man with rags." There are facts in abundance to verify this strong statement. The organization of charitable work has done much to throw light upon the causes of poverty and of failure to succeed in life. The visitors of the Associated Charities, in Boston, have learned that one of the first inquiries to be made, when a family is found upon the borders of destitution, is in regard to the habits of the bread-winner as to strong drink. It is doubtless true that intemperance is an effect of poverty as well as a cause of it. But when one engaged in philanthropic work meets day after day those who might be earning a respectable livelihood were it not for drink, and who lose the employment furnished for them because of their intemperance, he comes to believe that while men often fly to drink because of poverty, yet in the majority of cases, intemperance is the direct cause of their failure to earn a decent living.

In our American life, the competition in gainful callings is rapidly increasing. It is not quite so easy as it once was for a young man to secure a foothold in industrial, commercial or professional life. Whatever we may think about the abstract right or wrong of indulgence in mild stimulants, the fact remains that a young man who wishes to rise in the world, seriously discounts his own chances by acquiring the drink habit. Other things being equal, it is the abstinent man who keeps his place in times of commercial depression; it is the abstinent man to whom promotion comes. The position of trust and the larger salary belong to him. The merchant who drinks is apt to lower his commercial rating; the lawyer who drinks alienates his clients; the physician who drinks loses patients. It is the duty of every man to get on in the world, to rise, by all honorable means, to a high place in his calling, to be a successful man among men. But whoever, to-day, would make the most of his powers and opportunities, must run the race with no unnecessary weights. In the competitions of life a glass of wine may keep the doors of opportunity double-bolted; an occasional glass of beer may be the clog which prevents one from reaching the highest success. The young man who affects to despise the confidence of others, or the clear head and the ready command of every faculty that are associated with abstinence, jeopardizes his own future. The economic consideration for temperance may not be the highest in the scale of motives, but it is high enough for the Scriptures to enforce, and high enough to lead every self-respecting man to the practice of the virtue.

II. INDULGENCE IN STRONG DRINK DISHONORS THE FAMILY.

"Hearken unto thy father that begat thee, and despise not

thy mother when she is old." Filial obligations do not cease when the child has reached his majority and age has stricken his parents. Regard for parental wishes and feelings, for the home traditions and standards, still binds the dutiful son. He realizes that his parents suffer not less but more from his misdeeds as a man than from his waywardness as a child.

We see the operation of this motive of filial regard when a young man of christian training is thrown into temptation. In spite of himself he thinks: How would my father and mother regard this thing? How would they feel were I to do it? Perhaps the temptation appeals to him very strongly, perhaps he does not for himself feel that he would take great harm from yielding to it, but the thought of the pain it would give to his father and his mother enables him to resist it. He realizes that the most cruel blows are not necessarily physical. They are against the sentiments and moral standards of those whose lives are bound up in ours. If there is any temptation about which wise parents are anxious, it is the fascination of strong drink. They know the peril of it. And even if the son does not see the evil of it himself, it is a cruel and dishonorable thing to affront the love of those whose lives and interests are all involved in his conduct.

But still further, in the Scriptures the family is regarded as a unit, and its honor is in the keeping of every member of it. " Honor thy father and thy mother " means more than that children while in the home should obey their parents; it implies that the family's honor should be sustained by every member of it. The misdeeds of one member of the family inflict an injury upon the whole household. A son deems it a curse if his father has committed a crime; he is right in thinking that his family name is stained, and that a father can leave his children no better legacy than that of a good name; but a child's evil deed stains the family honor in a like way. It is one of the best signs of our times that there is an increasing disposition in this country to regard family honor as something to be greatly prized. It is a sentiment which is allied to some of the noblest promptings of our nature, and may serve as an invaluable support and incentive to virtue. One who enters into this deeper meaning of the fifth commandment will be slow to put himself under the dominion of a master who may blast his name with indelible disgrace. No man with his eyes open can fail to see that strong drink is doing as much as anything to drag down noble names and tarnish the lustre of honorable parentage.

III. INDULGENCE IN STRONG DRINK ROBS LIFE OF ITS HIGHEST WORTH.

"Buy the truth and sell it not; also wisdom and instruction and understanding." Life means opportunity to exchange lower values into higher. In one of our Lord's parables he represents a steward as turning the opportunities of his position into friendship. The story typifies the use to be made of life. With our days, energies, and opportunities we may buy the lowest or the highest things. In one sense it is not true that we carry nothing out of the world. We carry out of the world all we ever had in it, transmuted into nobility or degradation of the spirit. The supreme test to be applied to any habit or course of conduct is its relation to our power of turning the things of the earth into "the true riches." It is by this test that indulgence in strong drink is decisively condemned. The best medical authorities, and those not committed to any total abstinence theories, unite in saying that one of the principal psychological effects of alcohol is to loosen the delicate and firm grasp of the will upon the passions. It gives a slack rein to the lower nature. It is only through holding the forces of the lower nature in absolute subordination to reason and conscience that it is possible to turn life into truth, into pure affection for the excellent, into the service of man and the worship of God. The control of the lower nature by spiritual forces in most of us is too fitful and unsteady; we do not sit on the throne of our own souls, masters of ourselves, and any indulgence of any kind that gives the forces of the lower life a freer rein assails the mastery through which alone there is the possibility of transmuting earthly life into the values of eternity. There is no more certain way to lead one to part with his divine heritage more cheaply than Esau sold his birthright, than to weaken the spiritual restraints upon the lower nature through strong drink.

The root of intemperance is the love of pleasure. All these considerations upon which we have dwelt are verified in the larger truth that life has another end than the satisfaction of the body. We have duties to ourselves, duties to others, duties to God. Wine is pleasant. No one acknowledges that more frankly than the author of this book of Proverbs. Its fascinations appealed to him as they do to us. But there are other things in life of more worth than sensual gratification. An honorable career as a man among men is worth more. A filial disposition and an honorable family name are worth more. And above all, the power to use life so that its energies and opportunities may be transmuted into the solid substance of character, into "truth in the inward parts," into pure affections, into personal conformity with the law of righteousness, is worth immeasurably more than the tickling of the palate or the exhilaration of the brain.

But we must not forget that temperance is not everything. A man may be temperate and be unkind, malicious or pharisaical. The temperance of the gospel is one of the nine "fruits of the spirit." The vital force that blossoms in the glorious cluster of the Christian virtues—personal faith in Jesus—is the source of a self-controlled, temperate life. This faith co-ordinates all the forces of the soul to the service of Christ, and overcomes the love of pleasure by the constraining love of a Divine Saviour and Master.

Alternative Lesson XII. March 19.

[MISSIONARY LESSON.]

THE VANITY OF GRAVEN IMAGES.

Isaiah xliv: 9-20.

By Rev. W. S. AYERS, Portland, Me.

THIS lesson takes us back a little, back to the days of Israel's thraldom. The prophet sees the people of God either discouraged under their long captivity, or else satisfied with their foreign home. He endeavors to awaken both classes with a view of the greatness of the God whom they serve, and of the mission to which they are summoned. Not only are they called to preserve among themselves the knowledge of a living God, but they have a world-wide mission to the Gentiles, consisting in the extension of this knowledge. To arouse them to the importance of that mission, to keep them from satisfaction with heathenism, to encourage them to prepare themselves for their sovereign work of rebuilding and universalizing the theocracy, the prophet presents before them this picture of the vanity of idolatry in contrast with the glory of Jehovah. The contrast extends over several chapters, growing sterner and more vivid as it advances, till here it reaches its climax. God is, and there is none beside. Idolatry is not only sinful, but infinitely absurd.

The words are addressed not to the heathen to show them the unreason of their worship, but to God's own people to awaken them from unfaith and lethargy. The prophet's purpose is to quicken the confidence of his people in Jehovah by showing the imbecility of looking to idols. A great catastrophe is overhanging the nations. Cyrus is sweeping all before him, and guardian deities long trusted are proving powerless. Yet Israel need fear nothing. Jehovah has foretold all this though idol gods could not do so. Nay, the approaching overturn of the world is to be Israel's new birth of glory. These words, displaying the absurdity of idolatry, are only part of the argument by which the prophet would inspire the people to look to God for deliverance. The entire chapter is involved. It is a lesson in God's method of training the nation that is peculiarly to bear and manifest his name.

God's people must be prepared for their divine mission to the world by being deeply convinced of his reality as the only living and true God, and of the superiority of a religion based upon such monotheistic faith. While they stood in fear of gods many and lords many, and seriously compared them with Jehovah, it was impossible for them to be "a light to the Gentiles." As we only appreciate the darkness by its contrast with the light, so men could never feel the fatuity of heathenism, save as they realized the verity and the unity of God.

Substituting homely prose for glowing poetry we may, after a fashion, reduce the prophet's thought to propositions like the following:

I. Neither the idol nor its god knows anything, while Jehovah knows all.

II. Neither the idol nor its god can do aught, while Jehovah is almighty.

III. Neither the idol nor its god is aught, while Jehovah is the living God, God of the entire universe, and a God of love, in a word, the perfect Personality.

IV. The worship of idols or their gods is degrading, while that of Jehovah exalts and saves the soul.

I. The prophet holds up the good-for-nothing idol over against his vision of Jehovah, that we may the better realize the glory of God's omniscience. In his opening sentence he shows the folly of trusting the heathen gods for deliverance, because they are senseless. They see not nor know. Those who trust them are like them. They know not, they consider not. Their eyes are shut that they cannot see, and their hearts that they cannot understand. Their deceived hearts have turned them aside, so that none of them can deliver his soul, or say, Is there not a lie in my right hand?

But Jehovah, God of Israel, is a living God. He is a Person, not only having knowledge, but truly universal in knowledge, bound to no date or time, seeing the end from the beginning. To the simple mind prediction of future events is the clearest proof of divine power. Only God can tell what is to happen to-morrow. The prophet therefore reminds Israel that God had of old foretold the captivity, and now foretells the victories of Cyrus and Israel's own triumphant return to Zion. Who shall hesitate to trust a being like this! Though far from Zion they are safe. One is their Guide, whom their craftiest foe cannot baffle, to whom no event is dark.

II. In the same way the prophet pictures the vanity of idols to make more real the power of God. This magnifying of Jehovah is, as we have seen, the marrow of the whole discourse.

The weakness of these gods and the absurdity of trusting them have their fit analogue in the fact that the idols are the mere creations of men, weak men, whose strength is consumed with hunger, and who faint with thirst. Whereas the everlasting God, Jehovah, the Creator of the ends of the earth, fainteth not, neither is weary. He giveth power to the faint, and to him that hath no might he increases strength. So that they who wait upon Jehovah shall renew their strength; they shall mount up with wings as eagles; they shall run and not be weary; they shall walk and not faint. All kingdoms and all kings are in his hand. He says to Babylon, Come down and sit in the dust, sit on the ground without a throne. Cyrus the Great is his anointed, through whom he subdues nations, looses the loins of kings, breaks in pieces doors of brass and bars of iron, all for Jacob his servant's sake.

"Thus saith Jehovah thy Redeemer, I am Jehovah, that maketh all things; that stretcheth forth the heavens alone; that spreadeth abroad the earth. Who is with me? that frustrateth the tokens of the liars and maketh diviners mad; that turneth wise men backward and maketh their knowledge foolish; that saith of Jerusalem, She shall be inhabited; and of the cities of Judah, They shalt be built and I will raise up the waste places thereof; that saith to the deep, Be dry, and I will dry up thy rivers; that calleth Cyrus, My Shepherd who shall perform all my pleasure; even saying of Jerusalem, She shall be built, and to the temple, Thy foundation shall be laid."

Who can measure the power of such preaching as this in stimulating God's people to great deeds? It nerved captive Israel to rend his chains and return to Zion. It was soul and fire to the Maccabees. It kept faith alive in the dark period just before Jesus came. It has heartened for his task every great reformer and revivalist in the history of the Church. God's sovereignty: God's almightiness,—we need more faith in it now. The timidity we sometimes feel in facing the almost unlimited work committed to the Church, the fear, for instance, that we are wasting our forces on such an immense empire as China, arises from the fact that we do not fully believe Christ when he says: "All power is given unto me in heaven and in earth." No faint-hearted missionary ever reaped a harvest for God. No half faith in God's power can kindle in our churches zeal to execute the great commission. How long before a truer faith in the almighty shall inspire us to undertake afresh at his command that task which unbelievers will forever count hopeless, the conversion of the world! Let us not be discouraged by the years we have waited. God moves slowly now, for his people do. Let them duly believe in him and he shall cut the work short in righteousness and nations shall be born in a day.

III. The idol, or its god, is nothing, but Jehovah is all and in all, the one and only God of the universe, personal and benign. Thus saith Jehovah the king of Israel: "I am the first and I am the last, and beside me there is no God."

The Jews were fitted by their captivity for a larger mission. Their view of God was widened and spiritualized. Earlier they had thought of Jehovah in a half heathenish way as confined to a particular temple, a special land and a peculiar people. Some of them feared that in captivity they were beyond his care. Separated from their temple and from all else that had before forced upon their religion a local character, at the same time filled with a sense of the reality of their religion which no vicissitudes could shake, they opened their minds to the truth that "God is Spirit," and gradually acquired the ability to worship him "in spirit and in truth." This was the discipline by which it pleased God to evolve a pure monotheism in the earth. Even his chosen people had never, as a whole, risen to a truly spiritual view of him before. Usually they had called upon him as "Jehovah, God of Israel," with hardly a broader thought than that of their heathen neighbors who invoked "Baal-zebub, god of Ekron." Now, they simply believe in God. He is indeed still "*God of Israel,*" but he is Lord of all being besides.

Inseparable from God's universality or metaphysical perfection, so to speak, is, in the prophet's thought, his love, or moral perfection. This is the strongest point of contrast between Jehovah and all heathen deities. The forgiving love of God, blotting out the trangressions which brought his people into exile, this moral trait of the supreme being, which was Israel's hope, was precisely the one most foreign to the thought of idolaters. Heathen have sufficiently vivid conceptions of the awful wrath of their offended gods, and strive in every way to appease that wrath. Of love in the world's Ruler they know nothing. Their thought is that sin must work out its penalty, grind and crush as it may. Forgiveness, if they could think the thought at all, they would set down as proof of weakness. This central notion of Christianity is one which every heathen people has despised. No other element of heathen's ignorance is so sad as their ignorance of the love of God. To teach them to commit themselves, in all their desolation of heart, to his compassion, to convert their fear into humble confidence, to lead them to cast aside every offering by which they would placate God's wrath, and expectantly to whisper each want into the ear of a Heavenly Father, to help them realize his tender individual care,—all this is our privilege. It should inspire us to any sacrifice. Yea, it will inspire us to all needed sacrifice provided we ourselves realize the blessedness of the divine love.

IV. We turn from the contrast of deities, so to speak, to the contrast between the effects which their worship has on the worshippers. Over against the glorious future to come to Israel as possessing the true religion, we have a vivid picture of the degrading influence of idolatry. The knowledge of the degradation proceeding from heathen worship is intended to work as a powerful motive in the minds of God's people to appreciate and accomplish their mission. We have a right to judge a religion by the men it is capable of making. The curse of idolatry lies in this, that it not only robs a man of every high conception of his destiny, but degrades the present life.

There are those who see so much beauty in heathen religions that they think it useless to carry the gospel abroad at such immense sacrifice. No doubt darkest heathen possess certain elements of valuable truth. Nowhere has God left himself without a witness in men's bosoms. But he who would regard such faint glimpses of divine wisdom as worthy to be compared with Christianity, or even with the religion of the prophets, cannot himself have received more than isolated rays of light from the Sun of Righteousness.

Heathen worship degrades the understanding, because, so long as minds are taken up with low, material conceptions, no very large expansion of them is possible. One of the first things heathen do when they begin to acquire enlightenment, a prime help in breaking away from the tyranny of idolatry, is to give their old theology a spiritual meaning. Having gone so far they almost uniformly renounce it entirely.

Heathen worship is made so absurd in this picture which the prophet has painted us, that we wonder how any rational being could ever be held by it, and from that day to this, evidence has been multiplying to prove its inability really to satisfy the understanding. The intelligent Hindu protests that his idol is only a symbol of the supreme spirit to which he bows. Even the Chinese have a temple to the Most High in which is to be found no idol. The argument that idolatry is necessary for the ignorant is like the kindred argument against the wide distribution of the Word of God. The intellectual expansion necessary for the interpretation of that Word will come only with the effort to interpret it, and the high spiritual conception necessary to the worship of a spiritual God will come only when every material image is taken away and the mind forced to grasp God directly. So far as idolatry is concerned, the notion that heathen religions are a preparation for Christianity is absurd, if for no other reason than that it is a reversal of nature. The intellectual thraldom of idolatry is incompatible with that expansion of mind which is necessary in order to grasp the thought of God. The heathen need schools of the best type, but all educational and other civilizing agencies will prove disappointing if we depend on them alone. Idolaters must be delivered from the mental slavery which idolatry imposes before it will be possible for them to make any considerable progress even in secular things. This mental emancipation the gospel of Christ alone can affect.

Idolatrous worship also degrades the moral sense. It is a fact which none can deny, that desperate vices characterize all heathen communities. Human life as such they little regard. They have but a feeble sense of human brotherhood. Bloodiest cruelties occur in them unheeded. It is only as men apprehend the fatherhood of God that they recognize in other men their brothers, and begin sedulously to cultivate the truly human virtues. So long as a religion gives its devotee no thought of a life larger than the present, it will be found powerless to elevate for him his present life.

Heathenism may boast some noble thoughts, but a system of idolatry capable of giving its constituency a high moral and spiritual sense, the world has not yet produced. The reason is that idolatry does not have in it the means for properly educating the conscience. We are the images of the deities we serve. A degraded religion necessitates a low idea of man. So long as the idolater is inspired by no ideal outside of himself, the sinful tendency of his own bosom drags him and his god to a base level. There is, in such worship, not only no power of educating the conscience, but the souls of such worshippers lose their moral insight. The drift of every religion, till Christianity, has been downward. Their beginnings show traces of a worship truly devout, but their later developments are usually associated with loathsome vices.

Instead of being changed by the best conceptions of their religion, heathen are wont to change their religions, making them vehicles for the grossest passions of human nature. The heathen deplorably need morality, but it is useless to teach them our moral code unless we can give them the inspiration which makes it practicable. So long as they worship their base gods they cannot feel the beauty of such a code, or come into living sympathy with it.

Never before or since has the world received such a moral code as that which Jesus gave, because no other teacher ever entertained or taught so rational or lofty a view of God as was that of Jesus. He plants morality on the right basis when he insists that if we truly love God the love of man must follow. We cannot injure man without offending his Maker, whose sacred image he bears. For this reason Christianity alone among religions has in it the power of properly educating the conscience. It gives every moral act a definite relation to God. It presents God as possessing every conceivable moral perfection. It bids us rise to these perfections. The nearer we come to God, the keener our perception of right and wrong. The nearer we come to the light, the more of our own blemishes and imperfections do we see. And because God is perfection, there can be no end to this educating process till we have reached the perfection of the Divine Being. How completely does Christianity satisfy the progressive nature of man, and how ignobly has every other religion failed in this! Christianity is the final religion. It is in perfect wisdom as well as in perfect love that our Lord and Master commands: Go ye into all the World: disciple all the nations.

THE SECOND QUARTER.

OLD TESTAMENT TEACHINGS.

Lesson			
I.	April	2.	"The Afflictions of Job."—Job ii: 1-10. Rev. F. E. Dewhurst.
I.	"	2.	"The Resurrection of Christ."—Matt. xxviii: 1-10. Rev. Professor D. F. Estes.
II.	"	9.	"Afflictions Sanctified."—Job v: 17-27. Rev. H. H. Peabody, D. D.
III.	"	16.	"Job's Appeal to God."—Job xxiii: 1-10. Rev. G. E. Merrill.
IV.	"	23.	"Job's Confession and Restoration."—Job xlii: 1-10. Rev. Edward Judson, D. D.
V.	"	30.	"Wisdom's Warning."—Prov. i: 20-33. Rev. Benjamin Greene.
VI.	May	7.	"The Value of Wisdom."—Prov. iii: 11-24. Rev. Professor J. R. Sampey, D. D.
VII.	"	14.	"Fruits of Wisdom."—Prov. xii: 1-15. Mr. H. C. Vedder.
VIII.	"	21.	"Against Intemperance."—Prov. xxiii: 29-35. Rev. John Humpstone, D. D.
IX.	"	28.	"The Excellent Woman."—Prov. xxxi: 10-31. Rev. C. H. Watson.
X.	June	4.	"Reverence and Fidelity,"—Eccles. v: 1-12. Rev. E. P. Tuller.
XI.	"	11.	"The Creator Remembered."—Eccles. xii: 1-7, 13, 14. Rev. J. F. Elder, D. D.
XII.	"	18.	"Messiah's Kingdom."—Mal. iii: 1-12. Rev. R. H. Pitt, D. D.

Lesson I. April 2.

THE AFFLICTIONS OF JOB.

Job ii: 1-10.

By Rev. F. E. DEWHURST, Burlington, Vt.

THE treasure-house of Hebrew literature contains no nobler product than the dramatic poem which unfolds the spiritual experience of Job. On literary grounds alone it ranks with the immortal works of the Greek dramatists and with the dialogues of Plato. Like all the great literature of the world it is dominated not by the esthetic purpose, but by a motive deeper than beauty. Life in its joys and sorrows, life in its mighty struggles, life beset with its problems and enigmas, life beating its way out into the knowledge and mastery of its conditions, has been the theme of the world's greatest seers and singers. Saga, epic and drama are the record of heroic deeds, of sublime achievements, of the love that "hopes and endures and is patient." They are interpretations of life, and we miss their meaning and message unless we come to them to find light upon our way. In addition to this the drama of Job has that distinct spiritual quality which has come to us from the Hebrew life. It has that serious earnestness, that freedom from merely speculative interest in its problem, that urgency toward some solution of life which shall satisfy not only the reason but the heart, that we are accustomed to find upon the Hebrew page; and because it has these qualities it is of more than Hebrew significance. It is truly "all men's book."

Let us briefly note the literary structure of this epic. The introduction, or prose prologue, gives a graphic account of Job dwelling in all the splendor of eastern prosperity; describes him as an oriental millionaire, the owner of flocks, lands and children; indicates him in one emphatic phrase as "the greatest of all the children of the East;" and relates also his conspicuous devotion to the religion of his people, a devotion scrupulous as well as conspicuous. After the merry-makings of his children he offers extra sacrifices, for he says: "It may be that my children have sinned and renounced God *in their hearts.*" He is, in a word, the perfect man, the man therefore upon whom according to the current religious doctrine, the divine blessing must come in amplest measure.

It is upon this man, prosperous, happy, faithful, righteous, that disasters fall, as Shakespeare says, "not singly but in battalions." One fateful day sweeps from him all his earthly possessions with his sons and daughters. Yet, though he is bent under the blast of the tempest, his faith does not succumb. "In all this Job sinned not nor charged God with foolishness." At last he himself is touched with the most loathsome form of leprosy, thought to be the uttermost curse of man, the sure sign of the wrath of the Almighty.

The prologue closes by introducing the three friends of Job, who by appointment have come "to bemoan him and to comfort him." Then in poetic form ensues the action of the tragedy. There are three cycles of dialogue, in each of which the three friends speak and Job answers them in turn. Then Elihu, a younger man, who has waited for his elders to speak but who is out of patience with the inadequacy of their discourses, undertakes in wordy form to set forth the cause of God. Last of all, God speaks, first brushing aside his youthful advocate with a word. Then in majestic language he challenges Job, asserting the tokens of his presence and power, while Job listens in a silence that grows every moment more significant, until, all teachable and humble once more and with a new light shining down upon him, he makes the answer which is at once the literary climax of the drama and the spiritual crisis within his soul: "I had heard of thee by the hearing of the ear, but now mine eye seeth thee."

Such is the frame and body of this wondrous piece. Let us see now what a throbbing heart beats within it. Let us see what truth of universal experience is working itself into expression in the dialogues between Job and the friends who come to comfort him. We must remember that a fundamental postulate of ancient religion made prosperity the direct result and reward of faithfulness to God. It was a radical conviction. The current religious evidences presupposed it and built upon it. The righteous man must be a prosperous man, and the prosperous man was known by that fact as a righteous man. But the day was sure to come when some one would see that this doctrine was an inadequate interpretation of the facts of life; that the inference from the traditional belief was too sweeping and too terrible. The conviction must have begun to force its way into the minds of men before the book of Job was written, but in this book for the first time the new faith gets a clear and triumphant establishment. Naturally then the writer seizes upon a typical case; upon a case which shall be fit to prove the inadequacy of the current belief. The problem thrust out for solution is that of a representative man in point both of prosperity and of religious fidelity. It is Job the most prosperous of the children of the East, Job over-scrupulous in his service of God, who sits there in the ashes, bereaved, smitten, afflicted, and from whom his friends turn their faces.

Here then is thrust upon us in the person of Job a flat contradiction of the traditional theology. It is as difficult an instance as could be cited. It is the case of an afflicted, wretched man who seems to be also a righteous man. A few days before and no one could have been found to impugn his goodness. Job himself would have been the first to say that there must be something wrong, some reason for pain and punishment for any man who was found in the estate to which he now had come. See what a terrible strain therefore is put upon the reigning theology! See what a dilemma that trio of friends is in! It is little wonder that upon their friend with the mark of the divine scourge upon him they gaze for seven days in silent dismay before they dare speak. They must believe that this good man is no longer good or they must be disloyal to their faith. It is a struggle between friendship and orthodoxy; but when at length Job breaks forth in his impetuous way they reach their decision and instantly become champions of the traditional idea. Eliphaz, Bildad and Zophar,—they are the mouth-pieces of conventional religion, but in different ways. Eliphaz has seen visions and is in touch with the supernatural; Bildad is the quoter of maxims and sayings of the fathers; Zophar, ignorant bigot that he is, is the mere zealot of a formal orthodoxy and blurts out his angry protests at Job who can dare doubt or complain.

After the first passionate protest of Job the three friends are aroused to a sense of their duty. They must not let this impious tendency go unrebuked. Eliphaz speaks guardedly and considerately; Bildad less so, and when Zophar's turn comes his bigot nature is aroused to such a pitch of fury that he launches forth into denunciation: "Should a man full of talk be justified? Oh, that God would speak and open his lips against thee! Know that God exacteth of thee less than thine iniquity deserveth."

When these defenders of conventionalities have had their turn Job begins to face a new issue. He sadly realizes that these men have no light or comfort for him. Their threadbare common-places, their pious remarks yield no consolation to his troubled spirit. Is this all that you can say, he asks them. This is an old story. "Who knoweth not such things as these?"

As Job realizes that his friends by the stress of their religious position must believe that he is undergoing punishment for his sins, he rises up in the splendid consciousness of his integrity and says :—I too will face this issue. If it comes to this then I abandon once for all the religion and the God of these men, for *I know* that I am innocent. I will take what comes from such an unjust God. I can hope for nothing good. "Though I be righteous mine own mouth shall condemn me. Though I be perfect it shall prove me perverse. *I am* perfect; I regard not myself; I despise my life, yet it is all one; therefore I say he destroyeth the perfect and the wicked." Let us not miss the significance and the grandeur of this issue, for here is the tragic collision of mighty forces. It is a man pitting his integrity against the belief in God which is forced upon him by the traditional faith, daring to walk out into the darkness of doubt rather than give the lie to the integrity of which he is conscious. It is the array of the deep and primal instincts of the soul against the so-called revelations of God in objective ways. There is no moment in the whole drama more full of awful consequence than the moment when Job dares to take that attitude. There is no moment more full of consequence to human destiny anywhere than the moment when the sure instincts and intuitions of the soul come face to face with some dictum or doctrine hitherto regarded as the authoritative word of God. It is indeed a day of "judgment and of burning" when the ethical and spiritual insights of man confront the received traditions of religion and condemn them as untrue. But it is by that very fact a day of promise for religion, a day in which it shall begin to rise to higher flights.

Here then was the crisis for Job. It flashed upon him that these friends of his were not only bringing no light and comfort to him, not only deserting the place of friendship, but were actually saying what was not true in order to justify their religious assumptions and maintain their orthodoxy. "Hear now my rebuke," he says, "and listen to the charges of my lips: Will ye speak what is *wrong* for God? and will ye, for him, utter deceit?" From this moment the path of Job is determined for him. He has let go the last feeble hold upon the traditional faith. If he must make the choice between truth and God he will choose truth. He will give up God rather than love a lie.

> "Behold he may slay me; I may not hope;
> But my ways will I maintain to his face."

Thus our hero has reached what Carlyle called "the Everlasting No," when he says: "My whole ME stood up in native God-created majesty and with emphasis recorded its protest. The Everlasting NO had said, Behold thou art fatherless, outcast, and the universe is the devil's; to which my whole ME made answer, *I* am not thine but free and forever hate thee."

How like these are the words which Job addresses to God!

> "Is it beseeming to thee that thou shouldest oppress;
> That thou shouldest despise the labor of thy hands,
> While thou shinest on the counsel of the wicked?"

It is a long way from the everlasting no to the everlasting yea, and Job has that journey now to take. Out into the darkness of doubt and denial he goes. He has abandoned the only God he yet knows, because that God can be defended only by a lie. With bruised and bleeding hands he must beat his way through the thicket. He must carry his sad heart with him and the consciousness that his friends have utterly forsaken him; that there is no light above him; that in all the universe he is alone. There is only one sure thing, the compass of all his wandering; it is his integrity. The sense of truth and right within him he cannot surrender. This he says must now " be to me for salvation."

The remainder of the book tells us the story of the perilous passage of the soul of Job "between two worlds, one dead, the other waiting to be born." He must tread the wine press alone. He must hammer out his destiny with fear and trembling, "and the triumphant issue to which he came is a strange forecast of those later words of Paul: "It is God that worketh within you to work and to will of his good pleasure." "Worketh within you!" That was the one thing to which Job clung, the sense of truth in his soul, the inner light. That was all he saw at first. He could not yet identify the inner conviction with the outer fact; could not yet see clearly that

> "Nothing can be good in him
> Which evil is in me."

But when the protests of his friends grown more feeble and inapposite are all over, when Elihu the youthful champion of orthodoxy is through his wordy harangue and God speaks, then Job begins to come out from the thicket through which he has beaten his way, out from the dark cloud which has hidden every light except the single ray within him. God says to Job,—

> "Gird up thy loins now like a strong man
> And I will ask thee and inform me thou."

Thus at length Job is to get his hearing and his justification from God himself. Yet there is no formal vindication of Job; there is little light shed upon the dark problem of pain and suffering. To our surprise at first the drama yields no general theodicy. Job simply receives the theodicy his soul needs. God asserts himself and declares to his anguished servant "the perpetual self-justifying course of a harmonious universe." The great majority of those who, spite of all its pain, believe our life to be after all somehow good, cannot tell you why. Like Job, they see God and it is enough. In that presence Job grows tender and humble and courageous. He does not retreat from his position. He does not surrender the sense of his integrity or reaffirm the traditional faith. No! the old world of his faith is forever dead, but the new world of a larger and clearer faith at length is born. He asks no vindication when God is done. His whole soul utters itself in one triumphant exclamation,—

> "I had heard of thee by the hearing of the ear
> But now mine eye seeth thee."

Now he knows that the God in whom he once believed and about whom his friends still babble on, is only a *hearsay* God. Their revelation corresponds to no deep reality in the soul itself. They can even belie the deepest facts of consciousness in order to defend their doctrine of God. But Job by his fidelity to the deep and indisputable facts within him has found their correspondence with the facts without him. There has burst at length upon him the blessed revelation that God and truth are one. By maintaining the integrity of his own deepest nature he has at last found the ground of an invincible faith; no longer a hearsay God, but a God "whom mine eye seeth."

If we have caught the spirit of this wondrous book we shall love it with a deeper love than ever and shall begin to see how in truth it is "all men's book." And when the days come, as come they will and must to some of us, that knock away the props of tradition, when the God of whom we have been told seems only a hearsay God, when we must choose between truth and tradition, we shall find comfort and courage in the story of Job. Moreover, it may reflect new light on the path of the great Servant of Jehovah, who, because he also maintained his integrity before God and walked in the light of his soul, "was despised and rejected of men while we esteemed him smitten of God and afflicted." It will disclose the deeper meaning of his words in the face of death,—"I came to bear witness to the truth," and will establish in our hearts the unshakable conviction which the cross of Christ forever demonstrates, that God and Truth are one.

Alternative Lesson I. April 2.
[EASTER LESSON.]

THE RESURRECTION OF CHRIST.
Matthew xxviii: 1-10.

BY REV. PROFESSOR D. F. ESTES, HAMILTON, N. Y.

IN the interval between the crucifixion and resurrection of Jesus there were many individuals and groups in Jerusalem whose feelings and behavior we may try to imagine. Did no single sting of conscience trouble the Sanhedrim in their hour of triumph, when the Galilean prophet had been executed at their demand, and the tomb where the lifeless body lay had been secured with seal and guard? How felt Pilate and his wife, when she eagerly questioned as to the result of her dream-prompted message, and he described to her the man of Nazareth, mocked, wounded, condemned, but more than kingly in his silent dignity, and more than human in his righteousness and patience? Of Judas we know. The swart face of the suicide in his ghastly death-pallor was buried in the field which the wages of his treachery should buy, this brief possession his sole reward.

From the foot of the cross, John, the beloved, led to his own house Mary, the mother of Jesus, through whose soul a sword had indeed passed. Was Peter in his sorrow and penitence with them through all the Sabbath hours as he surely was at Easter dawn? How fared it with the household at Bethany? Were they who had made such proof that Jesus is the resurrection and the life as hopeless as all others? Did the twelve and the rest of those who had hoped that it was he who should redeem Israel, shrink from each other in their disappointment and their fear, or did they, like frightened sheep, huddle together, finding sympathy at least in each other's sorrow?

The women who had been drawn together by their desire to serve Jesus in his life, were, we are assured, still drawn together by their desire to minister to him in his death. During his work in Galilee, Mary of Magdala, and Joanna, the wife of Chuza, Herod's steward, also Susanna, and many more accompanied him, grateful for healing, providing for his needs from their possessions. With little chance of error, we may add two more names to the list of those known to have been of this company: Salome, the sister of Mary the mother of Jesus, the wife of Zebedee and the mother of James and John; and "the other" Mary, the wife of Alphaeus and the mother of James and Jude. This company had come to Jerusalem to be near Jesus during the Passover season. Three of them, the two Marys and Salome, are named among the many who had followed from Galilee and who stood by the cross, and the two Marys with Salome and Joanna were among those who, in the dawn of the first Easter, sought the tomb to find it empty.

Sorrowful and anxious must have been the vigils of these women, "last at the cross, first at the tomb," as daughters of Eve fitly first to know that the promise made to their mother had found complete fulfilment in the triumph of Jesus, precursors and types of the host of christian women who have since enriched earth with their watching and weeping and praying and serving. We may well fancy that after John had led Mary from "the place which is called The Skull," the others had watched with straining eyes amid the unnatural gloom, had marked the head dropping in death, had beheld the spear-thrust, and at last, as the sun, nearing the horizon, cast the shadows of temple and palace along the slopes of Olivet, had seen Joseph and Nicodemus tenderly taking the body from the cross, wrapping it hastily in linen, heaping it over with spices, reverently leaving it in the tomb which had never known occupant before, and closing the door with a stone whose weight taxed their united strength; and then they had gone to their abiding place to weep and plan and prepare to serve when the dawning first day should permit.

The Sabbath was spent in enforced inaction. In their privacy the women do not seem even to have heard of the seal and the guard. Their only fear as they approached the tomb, was that they should be unable to remove the stone. When the sunset of the Sabbath allowed business to be done, we may suppose that they hastened to purchase the spices and ointments which would be necessary for the completion of the embalming which had been scarce begun on the late afternoon of the crucifixion day. Hours of patient night toil in their preparations followed, and as soon as it began to dawn toward the first day of the week, the women were ready to set out for the tomb. With good reason we may think that the party was not a small one. It was not unnatural that it should break into groups. While some followed heavier burdened, the two Marys pressed on before in their impatience to reach the place in the garden where their thoughts had been abiding.

Going as they supposed to sorrowful service, they were unwittingly hastening to joy of which they had not dreamed as even possible. Death had given place to triumphant life. The lately crucified and buried one was now the Risen One. Within the garden tomb the power of God had wrought more mightily and gloriously than anywhere else in human history. But of all this we can not know the manner, we can only know the fact. All the gospels tell us that Christ rose from the dead, none tells us how he rose. Doubtless the Evangelists knew no more than they told. How by divine power the quickened spirit came to the incorrupt body, re-animated it, transformed it so that it was no longer merely that which is sown, but became that which shall be, first fruits of the harvest, conformed to the spirit and fitted for its service,—how this was wrought we are not told, because almost certainly no man ever knew or could be told. Matthew confines himself to such of the attendant circumstances as most nearly concerned the women whose feet sorrow made eager to fly tomb-ward.

First, there was an earthquake. Earth which had shaken when the spirit of Jesus left his body, now shook again as they were re-united. Earth which shall quiver amid the terrors of the resurrection to the last judgment now trembled at the resurrection of him who shall himself be judge. How extended this earthquake was we have no means of knowing. It may have centred about the tomb, reaching little farther, finding its chief purpose in shattering the seal of Rome, which in vain pomp had been set upon the stone. "He that sitteth in the heavens shall laugh, Jehovah shall have them in derision." He but lifted his finger, he but willed, and the quaking earth crumbled Rome's imperial seal to dust.

Then came a messenger of the Lord, doubtless one of those beings for whom we have no name but angelic, because we know their office but have no idea of their nature. He rolled away the stone which lay, heavy and sullen, against the door. The women, as they came, were anxiously questioning how they could find entrance through the passage which it barred. Many an anxious soul has drawn comfort from the story, how an angel rolled away the stone and made their anxiety needless. Its assurance ought to sink into every soul and give it peace, so that we shall no longer be questioning, "Who shall roll us away the stone?" when God's power may already have removed the difficulty, surely can and surely will remove it, so that we can go straight forward in every path of duty.

We may also remind ourselves that from every tomb was the stone rolled when it was rolled from Christ's tomb. Heavy, stern, immovable, lay the weight of hopelessness before the burial-place of every dead one, until Christ came forth from Joseph's opened tomb, but now the stone is everywhere rolled away. To be sure the graves of earth are not emptied yet, their tenants still occupy, but as we gaze upon them, as we go down toward them, we know that there is no stone of doubt and hopelessness resting upon them. When the angel rolled away the stone from that garden tomb early on that Easter morning, it was rolled from every tomb, and the dead have but to hear the trumpet to come forth.

Having rolled away the stone, the angel seated himself upon it. His appearance was gloriously brilliant, so that the eye could no more bear it than the very light itself, and his raiment was dazzlingly white as the snow. Is it any wonder that before such a being, the soldiers, rude, earthy, sinful, shrank back in terror? It may be that they had stood undaunted while the earth trembled beneath their feet. A Roman soldier stood, unshaken, at his post while the falling ashes buried Pompeii and himself, to be a martyr and monument of duty. But before God's angel the very Roman guards lay prostrate, faint and swooning in terror.

The mission of the heavenly messenger, or rather messengers, for there were more than one, may be in some respects a matter of question more than of assertion or knowledge. Did they fold the grave-clothes of Jesus? Why was the stone left for them to roll away? Had they any message for the terrified soldiers? Were they visible all the time or to all persons? We certainly know that they had a message for the women, fulfilling thus their great office of ministering to those who shall inherit salvation. To them, trembling still at the earthquake if themselves had felt its power, naturally startled at the prostrate forms of the guards, if they had not yet shrunk away into the city, certainly awestruck at the displaced stone, the open tomb, the form majestic in whiteness and light, came the gentle tones of comforting address.

"Fear not *ye*," with an emphasis on the "ye" which impliedly contrasted the loving seekers with the guards. "Fear not *ye*, for I know that ye seek Jesus the crucified." They had nothing to fear from the servitors who came from heaven to assist in the resurrection, and to announce it first. They had no occasion to fear anything. Stone, seal or soldiers, earthquake or angel, nought should harm those who lovingly sought the crucified, even though they knew him not yet as the Risen One. The message which soothed them may not unfairly be turned to our own comfort. At Christmas time we sing:

> "O ye, beneath life's crushing load,
> Whose forms are bending low,
> Who toil along the climbing way,
> With painful steps and slow;—
> Look up! for glad and golden hours
> Come swiftly on the wing;
> Oh, rest beside the weary road,
> And hear the angels sing!"

At Easter time, as well, we may listen, amid all doubts and fears, to find that the tones of the angels spoken so long ago in other ears, echo still to ours, if only we would see Jesus: "Fear not *ye*, for I know that ye seek Jesus."

The message to the women mounts from encouragement to comfort, from comfort to joy: "He is not here, for he is risen, even as he said." The first announcement of this stupendous, crowning fact, the most significant, not only of the gospel story, but also of all history, falls from the lips of an angel, such a one as strives to read the sense of these stories and scenes and transactions of earth, and yet must forever fail in this endeavor. How could one who has never known the heartache and the tear, the shadow of death long preceding far following the agony of the closing coffin and the dull sounding clods; how could such a one sound the depth of the meaning of the message which he was the first to utter, "He is risen?"

"He is risen, as he said." Then a divine seal is set on his every claim and saying, and our faith is valid. "He is risen;" then we have a living Saviour, declared to be the Son of God with power. "He is risen;" then death is vanquished, and the uniform victory of the universal victor has been broken, the beginning of his complete and eternal defeat. "He is risen," the first fruits, the promise, the power of universal resurrection. "He is risen," then we too shall rise.

The wonderful message has a confirmation. The women may see the place where he lay. Doubtless, awe-struck but eager, the women pressed to the door and saw what John and Peter later saw, the grave-clothes lying in order, and the handkerchief which had bound his face carefully laid by itself, and doubtless, as Peter and John, so the women needed but a glance to be convinced.

Scarcely pausing at all to hear the messages of comfort and of truth, the angel adds a message of duty. The women must go quickly to the disciples. Delay does not befit the errands of the Lord. They must tell them of his resurrection, and must remind them that he would precede them into Galilee. It was not asserted or implied that he would not manifest himself at all at Jerusalem, and to the disciples in general he did not show himself till the great company came together upon the Galilean mountain.

They turn to go, those women of whose names or even number we can not be fully sure. Mary Magdalene surely was not with them. At first sight of the displaced stone she had hurried away to notify Peter and John, then to follow them back, and to have herself the vision of angels and the first sight of the risen Lord. The rest now, with intense emotion, fear and joy inextricably interwoven, with eager feet run as bidden to bring the disciples word. It may be that they scattered into groups as they went, seeking the different quarters where disciples might be found, and that Joanna and Mary the mother of

James were not with the rest when Solome and the others saw Jesus. However it may have been, to those women who had taken the message from the lips of the angel and were hurrying to deliver it, came Jesus himself, with kindly greeting, "Hail."

Curiously but vainly do we question as to the details of the appearance of Jesus. Of some things however we may be assured. Jesus stood before them not in unsubstantial vision, but in veritable personality. He was re-embodied, and it was not a form temporarily assumed, but his own body, through which he was manifested. This was the very same body which had been nailed to the cross and laid in the tomb, although we have no right arbitrarily to make this identity to consist in any particular fact or relation. Though the same body, it was also the same body transformed, to use St. Paul's distinction, no longer a "psychical" body but a "pneumatic" body. Perhaps the very completeness of the fitness thus implied to serve and to manifest the spiritual nature, was the reason why he so often was, for a time at least, unrecognized.

Now, however, he is recognized, and the women, grasping his feet with reverent touch, prostrated themselves in adoration. They did not doubt, they believed, and yet their hearts were thrilled and stirred with an awe that was close akin to fear. Accordingly from the lips of Jesus fall the same encouraging words which they had heard from the angel but a few moments before, "Fear not." He also repeats the message of duty, but makes it wonderfully more tender as he repeats, "Go tell my brethren that they depart into Galilee," and crowns the whole with the promise that there they shall see him.

Suddenly as he had come, he disappeared from their sight, and the women hastened on their errand to the disciples. There is no reason for limiting the word "brethren" either to the kinsmen of Jesus after the flesh or to the Twelve. "Whosoever shall do the will of my Father who is in Heaven, he is my brother." What Jesus had condescended to say in the days of his flesh, when he was like us, this his word repeats after resurrection has made him for a time at least unlike us. Even now the believer's uplifted eye and longing heart may recognize in him on the heavenly throne none other than a brother.

The message of the women to the brethren was soon performed. Twelve days after, they were in Galilee, soon five hundred of them at once saw Jesus, forty days and he was taken from the sight of men till the end. Thus the message has lost its original force by fulfilment, yet the loving heart delights in what it suggests. The risen Lord has gone beyond Galilee. Heaven has received him. Whither he has gone before, we too shall follow, and there we shall see him. Easter is memory less than promise, promise of rent tombs and opened graves, promise of corruption putting on incorruption, and of death swallowed up in victory, promise of Christ receiving us to himself. "And so shall we ever be with the Lord."

Lesson II. April 9.

AFFLICTIONS SANCTIFIED.
Job v: 17-27:

BY REV. H. H. PEABODY, D. D., ROME, N. Y.

THIS lesson describes an old-time attempt to console one overtaken by calamity. The speaker is Eliphaz, one of the three friends in the religious drama who, hearing of Job's afflictions, had come to comfort him as he sat disfigured in his leper-house. He and Job had talked together before. Eliphaz we may think of as older than Job, with a reputation for wisdom; one whose tone was that of certitude, as if he had been a prophet. Like Job he was a non-Israelite, for he dwelt in Teman, a district of Edom.

Who and what was Job, and what occasioned this "seance of sorrow?" While the book is not to be taken as literal history, Job was probably more than an ideal, some popular hero or prince having actual existence in the land of Uz, "greatest of all the sons of the East." So pure was his virtue that the Lord pronounced him the least blemished of mortals. As in the belief of that day prosperity was supposed to follow righteousness, the writer makes his hero rich in thousands of sheep and camels, and surrounds him with happy sons and daughters. Strength and tenderness blend in him in ideal proportions. He has indestructible integrity, yet is far removed from over-confidence. His is a real humility, closely allied to the reverence with which he looks up to God. He is not self-righteous but righteous. His power he uses not for selfish advancement, but chivalrously for the defense of any weak party. His love moves irresistibly to relieve distressed humanity; and so far is he from the Oriental despot as to allow all men, even slaves, to call him brother. Truly "there is none like him on the earth."

Sent forth from the "celestial council" Satan is to test this man with dreadful severity. At once his misfortunes begin. Disaster follows disaster in swift succession. The Sabæans in the south, the Chaldeans in the east kill his servants and his grazing flocks. Fire falls from the sky, equally destructive. Finally the whirlwind, striking in its fatal course the house in which his children are met, in a twinkling bereaves him of them all. In appalling climax, yet calling out no word of complaint, a most loathsome form of leprosy is added to the list of his calamities, in consequence of which Job is sent to the leper's abode, away from the dwellings of men. Here his three friends find him, and try to comfort him. Mystically brooding, like true sons of the eastern desert, they sit for a long time, awed by his grief, till at last Job opens his mouth and curses his day.

The lesson is part of Eliphaz's reply to this outcry of Job. Job's plaint is that of bitter despair, not reckless in the sense of irreligious, but desperate and vehement, as when the heart is bruised, and faith, confused and darkened, loses her way. His cry is that of one whose spiritual vision is eclipsed. The whirlwind has struck the house of his faith, and all its beams are trembling from the shock. The question: "If man needs be born why should he not pass at once to the grave?" evinces that Job's philosophy of suffering has suddenly failed, and that earth presents itself to him as a vast and cruel torture chamber. There is rebellion within. He cannot brook outrage even from his Maker, and outrage it seems, since his heart sees no divine intent in the suffering. Yet his rebellion is rather from defective light than from wilfulness.

As with all men in deep trouble, Job's only possible comfort is what the truth can give. Job is in distress for some spiritual interpretation of his recent experience, which may save to him the divine beneficence, and so save him from what to his earnest nature would be the worst conceivable disaster, the wreck of his faith.

All men when at their best wish to be ministering spirits. Few there are who do not try their hand at comforting their fellows. But Eliphaz deemed himself a master in the art. What large and tender consolation had he then for his friend? He gave what he had, as do we all, but the limits of his insight tended to defeat his attempt. He fails to throw any interpretative light across the field of Job's experience, the only way really to comfort him, but instead, implies that it betokens guilt. He states the general truth, than which nothing is more consoling, that the interior life is meant to be advanced by suffering divinely imposed. "Happy the man whom God correcteth." Yet, spite of Job's piety, and he had felt its strength and sweetness, he thought—his theory pressed him to this—that even in so good a man, covered up in some corner of his life, were guilty things which accounted for the curses of marauder, lightning, cyclone, disease and death. Eliphaz views these calamities as direct penalties from God for definite sins. Logically he demands repentance. Let Job sorrow the sorrow which reforms the life and back will come the old prosperity. Then nature will lose its power to harm Job: "He shall deliver thee in six troubles; yea, in seven there shall no evil touch thee." "Destruction when it cometh," flood, fire and storm shall pass thee harmlessly by. That is, by this theory, moral perfection makes physical evil an impossibility. Repent, and you will be a millionaire. This was the comfort that Eliphaz proffered Job. It was the best he had.

Job casts it aside with indignation. It was at best only a half truth, and a half truth can be more cruel than a lie. Intended to relieve, it only intensified the poor man's distress, since it tended to destroy what comfort remained in the midst of his sorrow, the consciousness that before and since his troubles he had preserved the central integrity of his heart.

His experience gave the theology of Eliphaz the lie. It is not true that physical evil passes the righteous by unharmed. It is not true now and it was not then, that such calamities as the volcano, the tornado and the electric discharge bring, are agents of the divine wrath. A cyclone is no respector of persons to be brought on or warded off by bad or good conduct in men. John Winthrop, who thought that a great tempest in Connecticut, occurring the same hour when Margaret Jones was executed for witchcraft, was stirred by Satanic influence, was a true disciple of Eliphaz in misinterpreting God's ways. Formerly every potato rot, drought and epidemic was looked upon as God's emphatic censure for some particular sin. It was the well-nigh universal primitive belief that prosperity and adversity meant the good will or the ill will of the gods, and that earth-quakes, noisome pestilences and storms were their enginery of retribution, brought to bear upon sinners with unerring accuracy. That the sun should shine alike on good and bad, or that the tower of Siloam could fall upon any but sinners, was too much even for the marvel-loving Jew.

In this belief of Eliphaz and of his times, Job, too, shared. The two saw eye to eye, yet the philosopher did not comfort Job for the reason that he was conscious of no guilt. Could he have found the soot spots on his heart, he might easily have accounted for his calamities, but they were not there. He denied with indignation the hidden sin which his friend surmised. While agreeing to the general trend of the Temanite's argument, he warmly rejected its personal application. Evidently he had observed that good men, devoid of special guilt, often suffer from outward calamity; he now stood facing the same truth in his own experience. A single intractable fact brought straight home to a man's business and bosom, will do much to disabuse him of a pernicious theory.

The problem that Job struggled over is ever new. There are ills not arising from our sins, from which no care-taking will insure us exemption. Nature still holds on to her destructive ways. Every prophet's work is largely one of consolation. Men accept their sin-punishments in mute acquiescence; would indeed mistrust the divine beneficence did they not befall. But the cyclone which spins the settler's cabin into ruins, the outbursting volcano depopulating some sunny land, the storm at sea that dresses in black so many families along the shore, the awful conflagration which licks up with its tongues of fire the blood of a frantic multitude,—these we cannot trace to anything the sufferers have done. In the light we now have touching nature, to talk about them in the Eliphaz strain would be blasphemy. The laws of retribution within us and of physical nature without us we understand better now, and we do not so easily confound the two. The God who pays the wages of sin for the breach of moral law we accept more and more, only to query over inflictions which have no such meaning.

What then shall we say to correct the Temanite's false notion that all pain is penal? Why should the good suffer? If these calamities of Job were not wages of sin what were they, and what is signified when Satan is represented as arbitrarily imposing them?

In our day we think perhaps too little of calamities as punitory. The boy who thrusts his finger into the candle does not figure it as sent to burn him but to give him light. Pestilence and whirlwind have no selective power. No saint of to-day, at all intelligent, would think of asking exemption from either on account of his saintliness, if he put himself in their way. Now and then one will be found talking of such misfortunes in the old Eliphaz strain, but to most they are accepted as consistent with divine love, because affording beneficial discipline in the school of life. Here is the truth after which Job was vaguely feeling.

The true "sources of consolation" for life's non-punitory ills are higher up than Eliphaz could see, in a more comprehensive vision of God, where all semblance of cruelty forever disappears, —a vision widening the field of the divine beneficence, covering the very calamities which so threw Job's cheer into eclipse, and revealing the Father's love both in punishment and in his general discipline of his children.

Sometimes when reports of calamities cast their mystery-shadows upon us, we would fain retire to some land where they might never come. But think what would be involved in the absence of dangers and losses. From infant days perils are around us. Childhood is continually tormented by them. The whirlwind, the lightning, and numberless pettier perils had been about Job as a boy—the wasp to sting, the leaf to poison, disease to prostrate him. Could he not see that if his childhood had been cushioned in perfect security, he had enjoyed no growth of character? Fear is developed early. The child is startled at the ocean's roar and the shriek of the midnight wind. What endless bumps and bruises a boy gets before he becomes properly on his guard against physical evil. This is hard but beneficent, since without such experience in smaller perils one could gain no fit cosmological training. More: In this "institute of danger" childhood begins building character in the invaluable forms of courage, patience, and prudence.

The same is true touching the childhood of the race. Had there been no peril, no trial, life would have been stagnant and drowsy. Under the stimulus of danger, art, science, industrial civilization, all are spurred to perpetual advance. We got our first schooling as a race in overcoming the foes of our physical life and peace. By energy, fortitude and heroism, races mount to material security, and they maintain this only by a vigilance kept alert through the sense of danger. To banish the perilous and the trying would be to close the door of the school in which we receive our best education and character, our best outfit both for ordinary and for the highest sort of life.

To this we add the consolation which comes from seeing the vicarious use of suffering, from vision of the benefit to some one from your deprivation. Many a pang to the utility of which we are blind will, when looked upon from some more spiritual altitude, console us, in that it has told upon the corporate good.

The aged and dependent craftsman regards as a calamity the invention of the machine which will displace him and force him into idleness and penury. It should, however, comfort him that this machine is finally to cheapen goods for the poor, to increase the wages and lighten the toils of multitudes. In this way one sees himself a sufferer for the common good, and is at once made braver, coming verily to rejoice in the cross. Even the man who suffers from pestilence and storm may glory in the inexorable as being the merciful, since all past calamity tends to make the present safer. For, meantime, no fate befalling us in the material world can in the least injure our immortal part. Drown the body in the sea, crisp it in the fire, mangle it in the wreck; if this is all, it is yet well with the essential man, and if his death has bettered others' life, he has gained. Not all the whirlwinds brewed upon the deserts of that East where he had his home, could have brought loss to Job's spirit like a single act of wrong.

Still higher does consolation rise if we welcome the truth that innocent suffering is, for all we know, as intrinsically necessary as merited punishment. We cannot exactly demonstrate this necessity, but the harmony which the assumption of it brings to the moral world, gives it a certainty which demonstration could scarcely increase. Job was not perfect. Ideals existed which were unopened to him, or opened yet unreached. The most perfect characters reveal imperfections under the moral search-light of Christ, and men called good wonder that any one ever thought them ideals at all. Job was the best among many, though far from absolute excellence. Why he should bear undeserved suffering is answered in what he came to be. Suffering always adds quality to character, toning down the harsh and coarse, lifting up common-place piety into distinctly fine and heroic character, cooling the heat of sensuous ambition and starting unquenchable aspirations. Life's best wine is not pressed from the vintage of prosperity. It is a fact that without suffering men do not rise, but sink, while under afflictions properly borne life tends to greater richness, fulness and power.

Job's worst loss was his loss of faith in the power of righteousness to insure prosperity. This, too, had its consolation higher up. Real heroism is known by the way it strips itself of material good in loyalty to the duty-call. If it be true that righteousness usually tends to prosperity, it is also true that it may limit the same. Let us not, carried away with the romance of virtue, ascribe to it more of material victory than actual life warrants. If we do, the awakening is disastrous, for honesty is on occasion seen to be poor policy. In competition with unrighteousness the good man often fails and is driven to the wall. Not but that righteousness benefits in many ways, yet many forms of virtue, carried beyond the conventional to the ideal, certainly involve sacrifice of lower good. What can console us then? This, that, looked at from the interior, honesty is not policy at all, but a law of spirit's life. Virtue is all the more virtue since to maintain it sacrifice is required. If it were not so, if virtue opened at once upon a paradise of fat things, then there need be no struggle on the way to perfection. Every surrender of the lower good for the sake of righteousness yields a stronger hold upon all the elements of christian life—more peace, joy, strength. Here in the realm of the spiritual we find ample consolation for all the material losses that virtue brings.

So we take up the note of trust spoken by Eliphaz, "Behold, happy is the man whom God correcteth," and lift it to a richer music in Christ. Not for Job, certainly not for us though in our fuller light, has the mystery entirely withdrawn. But a condition of calm trust is possible for us, where the unsolved shall cease to perplex. We are not to be dandled into quiet, like a broken-hearted child, but treated so as to develop life and power. We need not ask for comfort but for life. God cannot comfort us in any comprehensive measure except by leading us on into more real life. So Job was won back to trust and set face to face with the old integrities. So may we be won. Then, if mystery remains, we will carry its secret exultingly within.

Lesson III.   April 16.

JOB'S APPEAL TO GOD.
Job xxiii: 1-10.

By Rev. GEORGE E. MERRILL, Newton, Mass.

THE tide of trial often sweeps so heavily over a man's faith, that it survives only with struggle. For the time, reason is wholly submerged; light-winged imagination and airy hope are snared like a butterfly in the waters; only faith shows its superiority, and holds on to life until the trial is overpast. Then reason is re-born; hope leaps up again; fancy once more sketches its beautiful and not always illusive pictures, and we are sane and whole, living with that "abundant" life of which St. Paul speaks, making the happy present rich with the treasures of both past and future.

Such a time of trial is before us in the drama of Job's life. His words are those of perplexity. His friends, who have tried to console him by telling him that they know all about it, have made the matter worse. There is no task more delicate than consolation, and the failure is always miserable, when, in place of simple, heartfelt sympathy, the would-be consoler brings an easy philosophy of the ways of the Most High, and expects his diagnosis of your case to be taken as its remedy. Even if the Book of Job had no other purpose than to teach us how to comfort the sorrowing, it would be one of the most valuable books in the world.

In the fifth chapter, Eliphaz has spoken feelingly with Job of the uses of affliction, and in beautiful and doubtless true language has set before him the value of pain as a correction from the Lord. But it may be doubted whether a child ever felt the rod any the less from being assured that his punishment was wholly for his good. The assurance itself only brings an additional pang in the thought of the personal vileness that breeds such dire necessity. To a sensitive soul, chastisement may be harder to bear than punishment would be to a soul less delicate. The words of Eliphaz, beautiful as they are and hopeful of a brighter future, have not solved the problem for Job. And so he cries out here: "Oh, that I knew where I might find God, that I might come even to his seat!" It is the last cry of a believing soul. Earthly friends fail us. Not one knows the bitterness of the cup. No reasonings cover the case. Men throw out their little cantilever spans, like poor inch-worms feeling for the next place for a foot-hold; but the space is infinite, and no resting place is found. The bridge is impossible. God is ever beyond, and the heart still cries out after him, who alone can reveal himself by his own act of grace. God can help. He can console. We feel sure of this all the time. If we can only find him, we shall find what we need. And so we cry out as Job did: "Oh that I knew where I might find him, that I might come even to his seat!"

To find God! This is the greatest problem in all humanity's search. "Show us the Father and it sufficeth us," said Philip to Jesus. Well it might "suffice" them! Such a revelation would have satisfied the craving of all ages in all the world. The growth of the idea of God in the human mind affords subject for study of the most interesting and important kind. To some it seems that all ideas of God, however various, are corruptions of an original revelation of God's true nature to the soul of man, so that all the heathen mythologies retain traces of truth, and are witnesses to man's struggle to keep some belief in deity. To others the growth of religion seems more natural, beginning with the crudest notions of a power beyond and above our own life to which we owe allegiance, while from these crudest ideas the mind has been led on to monotheism at last, to the One God as the First Cause, the Ever Living Spirit from whom all things proceed. But whatever view is taken, it is manifest that to all men in all time the greatest problem has been to find God. It would "suffice them" if they could "come even to his seat." They have longed as Job did, "to order their cause before him." If they have not been able to discover the secret of his Presence, they have resorted to every expedient, however childish or awful, to substitute for that Presence something that might represent God: they have sought out "a tree that will not rot" and "set up a graven image that shall not be moved." Or, if not content with this deity of their own manufacture, they have thought of God as a far-off God, dreadful in his almightiness, an omnipotent tyrant to be appeased by gifts or placated by bloody sacrifices of themselves or their children. Sometimes men have come very near to God, and their thoughts of his goodness and righteousness have been strangely close to the revelation made of him by Jesus Christ at last. But all their strivings, all their failures have proved one thing beyond controversy: that there is a spirit in man, and that it is inevitable that man should reach out after God, the Author of his being, the Sustainer of his life, the Lord of his conscience, and the End, to whom all things tend. God is the Alpha and the Omega of the soul's alphabet, within whose limits lie all the possibilities of human thought.

But in the lesson before us now, there is no vague speculation with regard to God. Job's search for him was not that of mere philosophy; it was the longing of an ardent faith. Long ago this patriarch had got beyond the point of questioning God's existence. The drama does not anywhere present him to us as a doubter, a scoffer. From the first he was a man of faith, though on that very account a man to be tested. Satan does not pursue those who are already his own with the pertinacity with which he followed Job. The patriarch longs to find God, but it is the longing that springs from need, and that is justified by a firm belief that "God is, and is the rewarder of all such as diligently seek him." Job belonged to God, and he knew it. But he failed to find him now. And this was really the greatest test of Job's piety. Pain had not shaken his faith. But pain apart from God could not be borne. We often think that suffering is irreconcilable with a belief in God. But is it not even more impossible to understand it if we do not believe in God? Pain without God can have no explanation. Pain with God, with him to sustain, to overrule, to deliver, and out of all to bring to pass the glories of righteousness and the perfection of his eternal purposes of spiritual life, can have many explanations. If we have God and can reason with him, much of our darkness disappears. In his light we see light. If we cannot find God, and if there is no eternal purpose, no intelligent end to be reached by and by, however remote, then there seems to be no refuge from the most gloomy pessimism, when we consider the awful realities of this world. No man needs to find God so much as he who fully appreciates, either through his own experience, or a divinely born sympathy, the woes of life. And if for a while the heavens are as brass and there comes no quick answer to prayer, no answer save the mocking echo from those brazen skies that seem to contain no God, our case is hard indeed. It is the greatest trial of all, greater than the direst pain, to be in that suffering without the consciousness of God's presence. We remember the cry even from the Cross of Calvary: "My God, my God, why hast thou forsaken me." This was the supreme proof of Jesus Christ. And this was the trial of Job, when he turned from earth and all its disappointing friendships so powerless to help, and longed after God, only to find God hiding himself where he could not see him. Could it be that God was not to be found? Maybe Job could never find him. But his faith was too strong to be shaken by his own failure. If he could not find God, God could find him. "He hideth himself on the right hand, that I cannot see him. But he knoweth the way that I take." And so the sufferer comforted himself, as the righteous man will always comfort himself, in the fact that God knows, his knowledge covering all the need of our ignorance, his grace and power supplying all the strength that our frailty demands. To the true, to the good, it is always a joy that God finds us, even when we cannot find God.

And now we come to a most interesting fact in Job's experience. He did not think aright in all respects, as we shall note, but of two things he was sure: If he could find God, he believed that he would find him to be perfectly just on the one hand, and on the other perfectly loving and merciful. With respect to God's justice Job was right, though his belief that he himself would find perfect acceptance with that justice was wrong. Job went too far in his self-confidence. It was a pardonable fault. It was natural enough under the exasperating circumstances. He had been forced in his suffering to defend himself. He had been wrongfully accused by his three friends. When in the commonest courtesy they ought to have passed over his faults in silence, if indeed he had really sinned as they thought, they had proceeded to charge him with unrighteousness as the only cause for his present evil case. They had assumed that all his sufferings were in the way of retribution. Job knew they were not, and was forced to defend himself. If in his indignation he went too far, we can hardly wonder. But as we read his words we say to ourselves: What! had this man got beyond the need of praying for the forgiveness of sins? Was he so pure that he needed not to utter the cry of David: "Cleanse thou me from secret faults!" He is so sure of his own righteousness that he will reason with God, he will fill his mouth with arguments, sure that God will justify him. He knows God's mind. If Eliphaz has made the mistake of assuming to know too much about Job's case, Job makes the mistake of knowing too surely the mind of the Almighty. He, too, "darkens counsel by words without knowledge." And so Job would be bold to talk with God. But if we turn to the last chapters of the book we find that God came to Job. God spoke, but not as Job anticipated. Every sentence fell upon Job's ear to teach him that he had failed to realize his own imperfection and God's perfection. And then what did Job do, this child of God who had longed for a chance to reason with God and show him the rights of the case? In the first verses of the fortieth chapter the patriarch speaks. This man, strong in his own righteousness, bold in his confidence that he is just in God's sight, resolved to fill his mouth with voluble argument if only he could find God,—this man says: "Behold I am of small account; what shall I answer thee? I lay my hand upon my mouth." And in the forty-second chapter: "Then Job answered the Lord and said: I know that thou canst do all things, and that no purpose of thine can be restrained. Who is this that hideth counsel without knowledge? Therefore have I uttered that which I understood not, things too wonderful for me, which I knew not. . . . I had heard of thee by the hearing of the ear; but now mine eye seeth thee, wherefore I abhor myself and repent in dust and ashes!" Ah, to see God is the end of controversy. We hear of him now; we see as in a glass darkly; we listen for his stately goings, but we cannot tell, for he is as the wind, that bloweth where it listeth; we may think we know, or we may murmur and complain in darkness; we may do, as Job would not do, rebel and defy and blaspheme; but the time will come when God shall find us and reveal himself to us. Then the hand will be put upon the mouth! Then we shall be still, and know that he is God. Happy if we now are wise reverently to acknowledge him and to wait patiently and truthfully for his salvation.

For he has salvation for us. I said that Job was sure of two things, God's justice and God's love. He found God perfectly just, but that justice condemned him. He also found God's love, and that love forgave him, justified him, and restored him to life more abundant and satisfying than ever. He believed that God would "not contend with him in the greatness of his power." God would show him the mystery of his pain, and out of it all would bring forth good. Job knew his sufferings were not mere punishment. What they were for, he could not as yet understand. We know that they were to test him, and so they were to show the power of God's indwelling grace, the undying energy of faith and the righteousness that comes by faith. The enemies of God were to be silenced. Satanic sneers were to be put to shame. All these things were in the purpose of God in suffering his servant to be troubled. And thus it is always the rare privilege of suffering, to prove the soul superior to circumstance, if God upholds it and if his life is in it. "Who knows," said the adviser of Queen Esther, "if thou didst not come to the throne for this very purpose," and the words strengthened the beautiful queen to do her duty by her persecuted people. "Who knows," the righteous man may say to himself in any adversity, "who knows but this very pain may be my one greatest opportunity to prove that faith can withstand trial, to honor God by my steadfast endurance, and to show the world that its direst evils cannot pluck me out of his hand. "Go tell your master," said a beleaguered general, who was summoned to surrender, "that I will show him how an Englishman can die!" The hero of this splendid drama made similar answer: "Though he slay me, yet will I trust him." And that trust was not put to shame. Job's heroism failed not of its reward. If God's truth could not admit Job to be perfectly righteous, yet God's love could redeem him and give him victory. The sufferer had fought a good fight, he had kept the faith. He had come forth like gold, purified from alloy, proved to be gold by surviving the fire. Now he could see God's purpose, see that love was all the time holding him and making him the conspicuous, the chosen and heroic example of its power. No wonder then that the drama ends with Satan foiled, and God's supremacy securing Job's felicity!

To find God! The ancient patriarch found him and gloried in his love. Do we suffer, and in our pain long to find God? "He who hath seen me hath seen the Father," are words that come from the one divine voice that we can hear. Let it "suffice us." "Let not your heart be troubled," said the same Saviour at that same time. Oh let us put away all doubt and all fear. We can afford to leave ourselves in the hands of him who was the God of Job, the Father of Jesus, and of whom Jesus was the perfect revelation in the flesh. "For this is life eternal, to know God, and Jesus Christ whom he hath sent!"

Lesson IV.   April 23.

JOB'S CONFESSION AND RESTORATION.

Job xlii: 1–10.

By Rev. Edward Judson, D. D., New York City.

IN the philosophy of suffering the book of Job is the world's greatest classic. In all his thinking about pain man has never advanced beyond this book. Its theme is the old enigma,—the bitter cud which thoughtful and serious men have chewed from the beginning: Why does one sorrow after another submerge the righteous man? Rhetorically the book consists of prologue, a first dialogue, a monologue, a second dialogue, and an epilogue.

I. The statements of the enigma take up the prologue, chapters i–iii. What force any philosophic thesis has when couched in a story! Here a metaphysical disquisition assumes the form of a dramatic poem. The artist throws upon his canvas a titanic figure, Job. He is an Arab Sheikh of the ancient regime—a man whose righteousness was indubitable, yet whose sorrows were without precedent. He may very well have been an historic character, belonging to the patriarchal age. The story had become part of the folk-lore prevalent in the poet's time. People were perhaps in the habit of saying, "as unlucky as old Job." The artist takes this character as his stuff, just as Shakespeare took Julius Cæsar, and he proceeds to weave out of it his philosophic drama.

Job was a righteous man, perfect and upright, one that feared God and eschewed evil. A bad man would not have answered as the subject of this poem, for then all readers would instinctively feel that when trouble came upon him it served him right. The central figure must be a man of exemplary character in order that we may appreciate the pinch of the mystery.

He was at the outset a most prosperous man. This also the art of the piece requires. It would not do to make the great sufferer one who had never known better days. A man is really not capable of the deepest suffering who has never had his fill of happiness. How keen the distress which we experience when we feel the good things of this life slipping through our reluctant fingers! It is possible for well-to-do people to over estimate the misery of the poor, imagining themselves, with their standard of comfort, to have lost all. Were those of us who are used to luxuries and have never had a chance to become callous to hardship, actually to sink into poverty, we should suffer far beyond what most of the poor suffer. Job must take this bitter headlong plunge from happiness into misery. For

> " A sorrow's crown of sorrows is remembering
> happier things."

This is the personage, so prosperous and so deserving, whom misfortune singles out as the target for her sharpest shafts. He experiences, first, loss of property. All his possessions are swept away. His sheep are killed by lightning. Bedouin Arabs swoop down and drive away his oxen and camels and asses. He who had been a millionaire, a prince of plenty, is reduced to absolute want. How many a man prefers death to endless contention with the disabilities of poverty! The rich have their troubles, to be sure, but their money certainly enables them to purchase many kinds of alleviation and diversion.

Then came loss of family. What parent but would prefer to bear anything rather than this! We should not mind being stripped of all else we have, if only the dear ones of our home-circle could be left us. But a cyclone comes, and at one stroke Job's seven sons and three daughters are hurried into eternity. His wife, indeed, was spared, but, through the keen irony of Providence, she was left only as a thorn in his side. She enhanced his wretchedness by her sneers, and Job might well have breathed Wordsworth's sigh:

>"The good die first, and they whose hearts
> Are dry as summer dust,
> Burn to the socket."

But this rich and rare cluster of miseries was not yet complete. To cap the climax, disease must be added. "I can endure any misfortune," many a man says, "if only I have my health." This boon was denied Job. Leprosy attacked him, and that in its worst form, elephantiasis. His ailment was both painful and loathsome. His limbs swelled to monstrous proportions. His skin became hard, rough and tuberculate, so as to resemble an elephant's hide. First came hideous sores, and then, unless the malady was stayed, the finger-joints and limbs even would slough off. Save from God's intervention, there was no hope until death came and set the prisoner free.

It is thus that in the prologue of his poem, the author of the book of Job places before our eyes in concrete, graphic and colossal form, the righteous sufferer, and suggests the profound enigma: Why does sorrow upon sorrow submerge the innocent? In this way "he makes palpable," as Renan has it, "the mysteries which one feels within one's own heart, and to which one has been painfully endeavoring to give tangible shape."

There are, indeed, many saccharine elements in human life.

>"The Guide of our dark steps a triple veil
> Betwixt our senses and our sorrows keeps;
> Has sown with cloudless passages the tale of grief,
> And eased us with a thousand sleeps."

It is a peculiarity of human nature to pass over our mercies unobserved, and, on the other hand, to remark and to exaggerate every trouble and pain. All our commonest physical experiences, as breathing, eating, drinking, falling asleep, are accompanied by pleasures which, like snow-flakes, fall silently and unobtrusively into our lives. Such pleasant sensations are taken as a matter of course, and do not arrest our attention. Trouble, on the contrary, makes a deep dent in our consciousness. In this way life seems to many of us sadder than it really is. But back of all this there still remains the hard, angular fact of the suffering inflicted upon the undeserving, and causing many of our best minds to doubt either the power or the benevolence of the Christian's God. The pains endured by the lower animals with uncomplaining patience, the fears that haunt the steps of childhood, the rigors inflicted upon their tender offspring by improvident and cruel parents, the hidden sorrows of the

"Hearts that break and give no sign
Save fading lips and whitening tresses,"

the vast accumulation of sordid miseries that would be unfolded before our eyes if all the opaque brick walls of our tenement-houses were suddenly to become transparent,—these are only a small part of that great problem of evil with which the Book of Job has to do, setting all our best literature to a minor key, as when it extorts from the lips of Byron the pathetic line,

"Smiles form the channel for the future tear."

II. We have seen that in these first three chapters, which constitutes the prologue of his poem, our author offers a concrete statement of the problem of suffering. This is worth a great deal. If we can once fairly state a problem and let its difficulty assume in our minds definite outlines, we are on the way to a solution of it. But the author of Job is not content with a strong and impartial presentation of the mystery of evil, he makes an attempt to solve it. The prologue is therefore followed by a long and stormy dialogue between Job, the righteous sufferer, and three sages, Eliphaz, Bildad and Zophar, who endeavor to comfort him. This dialogue occupies chapters iv-xxxi. Job's friends account for suffering on the score of retributive justice. They represent the orthodox church of the poet's age. Suffering, they say, is graduated to sin. Pain follows transgression as the cart-wheel follows the ox. The bad man is sure to suffer, and the good man to be happy. If a man is in trouble, we can safely say that he has done wrong. So they keep reiterating, "Come, Job, own up. You have been on the sly a great sinner, or else you would not be such a great sufferer." Their speeches weary us with their monotony and repetition. As they go on they harp more and more vehemently on the same old string, while poor Job complains bitterly of his sufferings, denies their charges and insinuations, and holds fast to his integrity. But while his opponents become more heated as the discussion proceeds, Job grows calmer. Like one who climbs a dark and difficult mountain, he once in a while emerges upon a sunlit eminence. As in that noble passage, woven by the church of England into her majestic burial service, "I know that my Redeemer liveth," he voices the expectation, not that prosperity will come back, not even that justice will be done him in this life, but that a glorious posthumous vindication will be his portion. His Defender or Avenger will assuredly some day appear upon this earth, and dreadfully rebuke those who now too readily chide him. He almost arrives at the hope expressed in Bryant's exquisite hymn:

> "Nor let the good man's trust depart,
> Though life its common gifts deny;
> Though, with a pierced and broken heart,
> And spurned of men, he goes to die"

> "For God has marked each sorrowing day,
> And numbered every secret tear,
> And Heaven's long age of bliss shall pay
> For all his children suffer here."

III. Having stated the enigma in his prologue, and having in the dialogue between Job and his three friends, as an inadequate solution, suggested the principle of retributive justice, our author introduces a new character, Elihu, who in a monologue, which occupies chapters xxxii–xxxvii, brings forward the thought of the disciplinary character of suffering. In pain is heard the voice of God. But he openeth the ears of men; he sealeth their instruction; he withdraws man from wrong purposes; he hides pride from man; he gives songs in the night; he teaches us more than the beasts of the earth can learn. Who teacheth like him? The sufferer should meekly respond: "I have born chastisement, I will not offend any more; that which I see not, teach thou me; if I have done iniquity I will do so no more."

We have in Elihu's discourse a glimmer of the truth so familiar to Christians: "Whom the Lord loveth he chasteneth." Every branch that beareth fruit, he pruneth it, that it may bring forth more fruit. The fruitful branch it is worth while for the wise gardener to pay attention to, and to cultivate even with the keen pruning-knife. As I heard a musical director of rare artistic insight say to his choir, "The better you sing the more fault I will find with you."

Suffering quickens our moral perceptions, toughens our spiritual fibre, develops within us the capacity to soothe and sympathize, makes us more Christ-like. As delicate calicoes are passed rapidly and deftly over hot rollers, so that the fuzz may be scorched away and the pattern become clearer and more conspicuous, so the spirits of God's people are exposed to sufferings, that worldliness may be burned off and the image of Christ brought strongly out. This truth, suggested by Elihu, is so much in advance of the rest of the book that it seems almost an anachronism, and hence is supposed by some scholars to have been added to the poem by a later hand.

IV. Elihu's monologue is followed by a dialogue between

Job and the Almighty. This begins with chapter xxxviii, and ends with the sixth verse of chapter xlii. It contains a sublime description of God's power as manifested in the creation of the universe, the earth, the sea, the constellations, the light, the rain, the snow, the wild goat, the wild ox, the eagle, the horse, the hippopotamus, and the crocodile. The passage suggests a spirit of reverent agnosticism. It contains no intellectual solution of the great mystery; no theodicy; but it suggests, without working out, a solution for the honest heart, far better for men's practical use than all the formal theodicies which men have so laboriously written. The problem of evil transcends finite intelligence. We are a small part of a very large plan, and our sufferings are mysteriously required in the rounding out of the divine purpose. We are wrong in placing ourselves at the centre of the universe, and in expecting to fathom its mysteries by reasoning out from the relations which things bear to us. From the finite standpoint all seems confused and chaotic, just as the mosaic in St. Peter's dome, when seen near at hand, looks ugly and meaningless. "This world," according to Longfellow, "is but the negative of the world to come, and what is dark here will be light hereafter." President Dodge's words, inscribed on his tomb, are the best commentary on Job: "The soul is the enigma; God is the solution."

V. The epilogue of the book, embracing the last eleven verses of the closing chapter, describes the return of happiness to Job. The Lord rebukes the three sages for their harsh judgments. They ask Job's forgiveness and Job prays for them. The Lord turns his captivity. His wealth is restored to him twofold. He has again seven sons and three beautiful daughters, and he lives to a good old age, surrounded by his kindred, friends and acquaintances.

This is not mere poetic justice. The great truth is suggested that character is the parent of comfort. There is such a principle at work in human life. The Psalmist sings: Trust in the Lord, and do good; so shall thou dwell in the land, and verily thou shalt be fed. And again, I have been young and now am old; yet have I not seen the righteous forsaken, nor his seed begging bread. Christ says: Seek ye first the kingdom of God, and his righteousness; and all these things shall be added unto you. This broad principle is operating all the time in human life. But the individual career is sometimes too short to enable it to work itself completely out. Its operation is more clearly visible in the history of the family, the state, or the nation.

To the individual man there seems often to be left only the consciousness of his integrity and the hope of Heaven. After all, these Old Testament guesses point to Christ, who brought life and immortality to light. In him we reach the solution of earth's darkest enigmas. Through simple faith in his resurrection, we learn to wait in patience for the explanation of life beyond the grave, and to entertain the hope that breathes in Tennyson's lines:

> "Oh yet we trust that somehow good
> Will be the final goal of ill,
> To pangs of nature, sins of will,
> Defects of doubt, and taints of blood;
>
> "That nothing walks with aimless feet;
> That no one life shall be destroyed,
> Or cast as rubbish to the void,
> When God hath made the pile complete;
>
> "That not a worm is cloven in vain;
> That not a moth with vain desire
> Is shrivel'd in a fruitless fire,
> Or but subserves another's gain.
>
> "Behold, we know not anything;
> I can but trust that good shall fall
> At last—far off—at last, to all,
> And every winter change to spring."

Lesson V. April 30.

WISDOM'S WARNING.

Proverbs i: 20-33.

By Rev. B. A. GREENE, Lynn, Mass.

EVERY nation has its proverbs. Whether it possesses an elaborated philosophy or not, there will always be found current among any people, short, pithy sentences, summing up the experience and observation of generations. They are partly the sayings of sages, partly expressions born out of the ripened intelligence of the common people. According to old Howell, they are marked by "sense, shortness and salt."

The wisdom of all the ancient and of all the oriental peoples partakes largely of the proverbial type. The deep, perplexing problems of life called of old for solution as loudly as now. Men then gave close observation and showed keen insight, but they did not have the extended view and logical grasp of later times. They saw things in the concrete and spake in sententious forms. The proverbs of a people note the high water mark of its intellectual and moral enlightenment.

The Book of Proverbs, from which our lesson is taken, was a growth. To it were gathered, from time to time, the accumulating maxims of the generations. David did not write all the Psalms; Solomon did not write all the Proverbs; but each of these authors is typical and pre-eminent in his sphere.

The theme of the Book of Proverbs is wisdom. In Hebrew literature, the book is to be grouped with Ecclesiastes and Job; while the theme, wisdom, is regarded as belonging to a trinity:

the law, prophecy, wisdom. The law was first, preparing the soil of the human mind with theistic and monotheistic conceptions, giving "the commandments and claims of Jehovah." Prophecy was a progressive interpretation of God's will, as it was unfolded in the life of the people through judgments and increasingly clear disclosure of his purposes. Wisdom was a resultant growth of thought, which, in time, came to assume the character of a Hebrew philosophy.

I. Who is the Wisdom represented as uttering the words of the lesson?

Manifestly, it is the highest Hebrew wisdom personified. This is exactly according to the oriental manner of speaking. Indeed, we ourselves practice it; we represent religion, philosophy, art, statesmanship, each, as lifting up a voice and calling upon man to look above the material, the low, the temporal, the selfish and the narrow. It is natural to personify.

Wisdom here, as also in the ninth chapter, where it is pictured as building its temple of seven pillars, is grammatically in the plural number, "wisdoms." This fact may refer to its superior excellency, but it more probably shows, as Oehler remarks, "that the Divine Wisdom includes all kinds of wisdom, and therefore especially the moral forces by which human life is directed." Wisdom is undoubtedly intended to be understood as the mouthpiece through which the wisest known judgments of men shall find deliverance as to special phases of private, domestic, social, business and public conduct.

It should be carefully noticed that the wisdom we are considering is not a kind of retiring, meditative philosophy. She does not have in mind the few, the elect. She goes into the broad thoroughfares, lifting up loudly her voice of warning and instruction. "In the wide streets," amid the thronging multitudes, "at the head of the bustling places" where business is transacted, "at the openings of the gates" where tribunals meet and public questions are discussed; yes, throughout the city at large as well as in these prominent places, she makes her proclamation and utters her fitting words. What can be intended here if not the wisdom of "all the wise men and teachers and prophets," pointing out to their brethren the way of duty, privilege and life?

If it be asked what the sources of this wisdom were, the reply is that they were the experience, observation and insight, which came to richly endowed men walking in the light of a revealed personal God.

The beginning, the very alphabet of this wisdom is the fear of the personal God who has revealed himself as Jehovah. In response to such reverential recognition, God said to Solomon: "Lo, I have given thee a wise and an understanding heart." While Solomon had penetrating discernment in a pre-eminent degree, it is true also that "there is a Spirit in man as man, and the breath of the Almighty giveth them understanding." Wherever it possesses thoughtfulness and reverence, "the spirit of man is the candle of the Lord, searching all the innermost."

But not altogether from this spiritual intuition, by itself considered, is Wisdom able to speak. It is evident that a large portion of her utterances come from such intuition as reacting on men's experience and observation. Elihu was right in saying that "Days should speak, and multitude of years should teach wisdom." Youth is advised to attend to the instruction of a father, and forsake not the teaching of a mother. Inexperience is to sit at the feet of experience. The gem pictures in the Book of Proverbs are so realistic as to prove that the materials for this ethical sketching were given by views of actual life.

Let us turn now to the message which Wisdom brings. It is a message of warning, but it is also the message of a friend. Neither the severe nor the final word is pronounced at once. Consider, therefore:

II. Wisdom's reproof tempered with the kindness of gracious promises.

At first the warning is implied rather than expressed: "How long will ye love simplicity? . . . Turn ye at my reproof, and I will pour out my spirit upon you." The reproof consists in calling things by their right names. To name an act is, sometimes, its sufficient condemnation. How often is the soul gradually drawn into a sin which is progressively blinding the eyes to its real nature and outcome. A young man enters city life. Its novelty fascinates him. He comes into contact with practices which he was once taught to abominate; but, someway, in the glamour of the new environment, they do not seem so very bad. He yields to the fascination. By and by, if he is fortunate, he is awakened by some friend who, not mincing matters, gives the right name to the downward course he is pursuing: "You are in the path which drunkards tread; your feet are perilously near the harlot's door. Turn from these ways or you are lost." Would not that be the voice of Wisdom to-day as truly as in ancient times?

Wisdom addresses her words to the "simple," those who are blinded by sin and so lack moral discernment; to the "scorner," him who speaks slightingly of truth and virtue, making sport of that which should command his most serious attention; to the "fools," those who have reached a state of almost total insensibility and obduracy touching moral things. It is thus seen that attention is called to the natural progressiveness of sin as well as to its intrinsic character. As all these dupes belong to one class, Wisdom has reproof alike for each of them.

Wisdom appeals to their moral self-respect. There must be a spark of it left. She will give them credit for that. "How long will ye love simplicity?" In your heart of hearts you know that it is wrong. Oh, turn, turn! I speak words of reproof, but behold! if you give heed to my voice, I will cause my spirit to gush forth upon you: you shall feel a mighty energizing influence working helpfully in your souls. I will make you to know my words. Now they may appear empty or forbidding, but if you turn, they shall flash forth new, rich meanings of blessing.

Would that we were not called to press on into the darker portion of Wisdom's message. Why may not Wisdom, having spoken so plainly, so tenderly, stop there? Will not man recognize kindness when it is shown him? Will he not give heed to the voice of Wisdom when he cannot mistake it? Facts say no. Some men, multitudes, rush on in their ways of selfish delight in spite of all such reproof. Then there is nothing left for Wisdom but to lift up a sterner voice, charge the tone of it with a ring of finality, overtake men further on in their mad careers and shout in their ears with a prophet's indignation startling lessons from the Book of Doom. And so we are compelled to consider:

III. Wisdom's portrayal of the irretrievable calamity awaiting the persistently disobedient.

Two phases of the calamity are depicted: one in which Wisdom is represented as being deaf to all calls for deliverance, and giving expression to the "highest and most contemptuous indignation;" the other, in which their punishment is set forth as due to the working out of relentless natural law.

"Because I have called and ye refused." Wisdom has been speaking for a long time, and in the face of repeated refusal, lifting her voice louder and louder. She has repeated her invitation through months and years. And her words have not been the unfeeling utterance of official tutorship. She adds, "I have stretched out my hand;" I have besought you with all tenderness and compassion. No pains have been spared on the part of teacher and prophet; no forms of appeal have been overlooked by the yearning heart of father and mother. Wisdom, the wisest and best of all that can be uttered, is personified and made to appear before man in the attitude of kindliest entreaty. We, in these days, have no need of personification; in the person of Jesus Christ, we have the actual incarnation of wisdom, and blending with it the divinest of love. "Come unto me," he says, "all ye that are weary and heavy laden and I will give you rest."

Because of all this, inasmuch as you have persistently refused and would not listen, since you are resolved to have your own way, roughly pushing aside all that is dearest and best, the end is drawing nigh, doom's day is approaching. And I, even I, who have so lovingly called you, will stand one side and let what you have to fear come upon you as a destructive tempest. I will no longer protect you, no longer interfere when your calamity sweeps down upon you as a whirlwind. I, who have spoken, entreated and urged, who have dinned your ears day by day with my sorrowful pleading, even I shall then be compelled " to treat you as enemies who deserve contempt ;" your overthrow will be as complete as when a besieged city rallies and puts to rout the loud-boasting and sneering soldiery of the besieging hosts. Then laughter and triumphant rejoicing is on the other side. The city that was to be the spoil, the helpless prey of feelingless, bloodthirsty invaders still stands, intact, calm, and serene, looking down in triumph upon the field of her enemy's disaster. It was undoubtedly through some such imagery as this that the strong language "I will laugh at your calamity and mock when your fear cometh" found its way into the mouth of Wisdom. The intention is that the actual fact of impending doom, and the terribleness of the final overthrow, sure to come, shall be made to reflect back fame and glory upon the Wisdom who predicts. In the second Psalm the same thought is found. When kings, rulers, and the wicked, even all the strong men of the earth, set themselves against the Lord's anointed, "He that sitteth in the heavens shall laugh: the Lord shall have them in derision." A time is coming when the scoffer and the scorner shall reach their limit, and when judgment shall begin. Alas! to all the wicked a time will come as it did to the city of Jerusalem, the beloved capital of God's privileged people, when even a tender-hearted Jesus, One willing to be crucified for his enemies, shall be compelled to say: "Behold, your house is left unto you desolate."

How often does it happen when men unskilled yet foolishly venturesome thrust their vessel out into a stormy sea along a rocky coast, being presumptuous in the face of kindest warning, and sneeringly offering to take their chances, that the following morning dawns bright and fair, the sunshine smiles, and the waves clap their hands, in the very presence of a stranded wreck and of lifeless forms upon the shore! Go to nature, thou sneering, scoffing dupe: consider her ways and be wise.

Wisdom also declares that the time of entreaty and of choice will at length be past. "They shall call upon me, but I will not answer; they shall earnestly seek me, but they shall not find me." Do these words seem harsh and forbidding? They are indeed terrible; but they are as clear and unmistakable as any words that Wisdom has ever spoken.

What does warning mean if there is no danger actually ahead? Is the holy, wise and powerful God like a foolish, over-indulgent father who often threatens and never intends to punish? Is the day of judgment a fiction of the imagination? According to Isaiah, iniquity, persisted in, will separate between man and God, will make God hide his face that he will not hear. We find such words as these in the very heart of the Gospel: "When once the master of the house is risen up and hath shut to the door, and ye begin to stand without, and to knock at the door saying, Lord, open unto us; he shall answer and say, I know you not—depart from me all ye workers of iniquity." We are not to modify or tone down what we are pleased to call the early, crude harshness of the Old Testament religion, to make it comport with an over-tender interpretation of the New Testament. Both Testaments are thoroughly agreed in the two-fold teaching of their wisdom. Their universal testimony echoes and re-echoes down through all the ages, to the effect that moral character persisted in fixes itself in evil if it is evil as inevitably as in good if it is good. The truth is not that a genuinely penitent cry for help would then be inefficacious, but that sin will so harden its subject that real penitence will never come. The cry which will be refused will be no penitent but a selfish cry.

The disobedient man himself, in his heart of hearts, has a premonition of this impending doom. "When your fear cometh," that is, when that which you feared breaks upon you. There is in the soul of sinful man in startling flashes if not in an uninterrupted daylight of conviction, "a certain fearful looking-for of judgment and fiery indignation." One and the same God who inspired the teachings of Scripture has ordained nature to her service of parabolic instruction and inwrought in the moral structure of man laws in accordance with which "the invisible things of the world are clearly seen, even his eternal power and Godhead."

In all this warning of Wisdom there is nothing arbitrary, sudden, the result of an indignant afterthought. Sin's destiny is part and parcel of the world's universal justice. So, Wisdom still further emphasizes her warning by adding, as a second consideration, that the scorner's punishment will be due to the working of relentless natural law. "Because they have hated knowledge and despised all my reproof, therefore shall they eat of the fruit of their own way." What the farmer plants in springtime and cultivates in summer, that, in kind, and that alone, may he gather in autumn. If there are inexorable laws in the universe this is one of them. In the first chapter of Genesis everything was created to be "after its kind." This stands among the foremost laws of the natural world. And as we read on into the body of Bible history we find this "Natural Law in the Spiritual World" also, and as much at home as it is in nature herself. In the last chapter of Revelation are pictured two kinds of life; the blessed, belonging to those who do God's commandments and have right to the tree of life; and that of such as are unjust, filthy, idolaters, lovers and makers of lies. Two kinds of moral estate at last: each old probationer in his own place. Whatsoever a man soweth that shall he also reap. Sow to the wind and reap the whirlwind; sow to the flesh and reap corruption.

Wisdom is not content simply to state spiritual consequences in the language of natural law. She would make specifically clear the issue of the punishment out of the wrong-doer's own acts. "They shall be satiated with their own counsels and devices." If evil men are determined to have their way and live after their own desires, they shall be satisfied to the full. "Wherefore, God also gave them up to uncleanness." When the Almighty leaves scoffers to their own devices, distress and anguish are not far away. What else can a man expect who has run his course of riot till his flesh mortifies, and poured alcohol into his blood till it would ignite if exposed to a lighted match! What more terrible punishment can we imagine than for a corrupt man to be given over to his own evil!

One of the most vivid pictures in my memory is that of the wreck of a man in a poor-house. He had prospered in business, had hosts of friends, occupied a high place in society, had a beautiful wife. In the midst of his prosperity he, as a town officer, selected a site for the poor-house and fitted it up for occupancy, little knowing that it was destined to shelter his own last days on earth. He was tempted and fell. He deserted his wife for a mistress, fled the town, and revelled in his sin and in speculation for a few years. The mistress was brought back a maniac. A little later the man returned, well-nigh helpless with paralysis, and utterly penniless, to spend his few remaining months as an inmate of that poor-house, and one of its most abject and miserable occupants. That man was simply "filled with his own devices."

Lesson VI.   May 7.

THE VALUE OF WISDOM.

Proverbs iii: 11-24.

By Rev. Professor JOHN R. SAMPEY, D. D., Louisville, Ky

WHAT is wisdom? Let us at the outset carefully consider the import of this most exalted term. There is in it no hint of evil, no suggestion of weakness. By it we are lifted to the loftiest plane of human attainment, and from this height we look upward to the perfection of the divine nature; for "wisdom" is not only connected with the most exalted achievements of the human spirit, but includes the most sublime processes of the divine mind.

But what, in particular, does the inspired penman mean by wisdom? Is it in his mind identical with shrewdness, sagacity, brilliancy? From these terms it takes what is good, and rejects what is bad, being far more comprehensive than either or all of them; for while these words suggest the wisdom of the serpent, they exclude the innocence of the dove. Is wisdom synonymous with discretion, good judgment, common sense? It has much in common with these lofty terms, extracting from each all its strength and sweetness. A more important and fundamental inquiry still remains. Is wisdom related to righteousness, purity, piety? According to the Book of Proverbs, there can be no true wisdom apart from religion. "The fear of the Lord is the beginning of wisdom." The confirmed atheist is a fool. A recognition of God's existence lies at the basis of all right thinking and correct conduct. This may not be the prevailing opinion now, but it certainly was the thought of the sage who gave to his contemporaries three thousand proverbs.

Let us bear in mind then that there is a moral and spiritual as well as an intellectual element in the wisdom of which our text treats. We might with propriety, in certain verses, substitute *piety* for wisdom.

The text emphasizes the value of wisdom by six considerations.

I. Though piety does not deliver us from all disappointment and pain, yet it transmutes punishment into loving fatherly correction (vv. 11, 12).

There is a great gulf between the punishment of a rebel and the chastisement of a son. One is an act of vengeance, the other is prompted by love. What a blessed privilege for the Christian to be assured that his stripes are for his own profit, that he may become more like his Heavenly Father. Let this commonplace of christian thought be ever fresh to us. "The fining pot is for silver and the furnace for gold, but the Lord trieth the hearts." We may rest assured that his divine alchemy will achieve the best results. Even when the furnace is at its hottest, let us have courage and stand the test, remembering the words of the wise, "If thou faint in the day of adversity, thy strength is small." Afflictions, by making our hearts tender and trustful, may become a most gratifying evidence of our sonship. The reality of our communion with God, the certainty that he has heard us and helped us, the sweet peace that follows upon submission—these personal experiences become to us the strongest evidence of our acceptance with God. When we think of the blessed fruits of affliction, we are almost prepared to carry out the Apostle's command to count it all joy when we fall into divers temptations. If wisdom does not wholly banish pain, she graciously converts the bitter enemy into a helpful friend.

II. Wisdom without wealth is of more value than wealth without wisdom (vv. 13, 15).

May not the superiority of wisdom over wealth, as here set forth, remind us of the dream of Solomon at the beginning of his reign? His first and sole request of Jehovah was for wisdom in ruling the chosen people, but God added to him riches and honor. No man ever put a higher estimate on wisdom than did Solomon. All the more do we marvel at his lapse into folly and sin.

But how many of the young people of our day would choose wisdom in preference to wealth? Is it not an accepted doctrine in many quarters that money will atone for the lack of everything else? "Put money in thy purse." "Wealth is the principal thing, therefore get wealth; and with all thy getting, get rich." Even those who preach against avarice often show a keen appreciation of the worth of money. Now it is useless to attack money. Let us rather emphasize the value of character, of a pious and holy life. When we employ gold and rubies as a standard of value, we grant to them by that very use a value of their own. But we may show to the young the supreme excellence of piety.

> "Better is a little with the fear of Jehovah,
> Than great treasure and trouble therewith."

III. True wisdom leads to health, wealth and happiness (vv. 16, 18).

We are not shut up to the alternative of choosing between happiness and wisdom, for if we follow in wisdom's ways, all these things shall be added unto us. If we set our hearts on pleasure as the chief good, she will coquette with us, always eluding our grasp, while wisdom waits for our embraces, being richly able to crown us with chaplets of glory.

Let us inquire more carefully into the correctness of this central proof of the supreme value of wisdom. Is it true that to live wisely means to live long? Does piety lengthen one's days? Ask the insurance companies. Why do they besiege preachers and teachers, while they shun the frequenters of the bar-room and the brothel? These latter are living for pleasure only, and earnestly wish to live a long time. Yet the facts all go to show that their lives of folly will subtract largely from the numbers some day to be placed on the slabs, marking their graves. A life of piety, other things being equal, will be longer than a life of sin. The healthiest persons are those who keep all God's laws—those which regulate the mind and soul, as well as those which govern the body. Oh, for good health, that we may be strong to do the will of God!

But what shall we say of wealth? "In her left hand are riches and honor." A wise man is industrious and frugal, and therefore secures the respect of his neighbors. He is honest, and thereby secures their confidence. For such a man the door to success stands open.

The Bible emphasizes the importance of cultivating those traits and habits which tend to the steady accumulation of property. It may be safely said that the young man who will take as his business manual the Book of Proverbs, will achieve success in life, if only he has any natural ability to begin with. The only permanent success comes along the path of industry, honesty and frugality. The gambler or the man who employs the tricks of trade can never purchase a good conscience or the favor of God. The wealth which is most enjoyed and most wisely employed, is that which flows through channels approved by the Word of God. "Honesty is the best policy," but it is neither pious nor politic to obey the Scriptures as a mere matter of policy.

"Her ways are ways of pleasantness, and all her paths are peace."

The devil tries to make every new generation believe that piety is the dullest, most stupid and intolerable thing in existence. He arrays against it the good cheer and gaiety of youth. He insists that the necessary alternative is to choose a dry, morose, impossible something called Christianity, or to give up one's self without restraint to the pleasures of this life. But let us keep prominent before the world for all time the fact that the happiest persons on earth are those who are most fit for heaven. Religion makes one happier by ridding him of all anxiety as to his future well-being, by sweetening all his sorrows, by deepening all his joys, and by opening to him new and blessed experiences which no unbeliever can share. Holiness and happiness are joined together in a heavenly union.

IV. The possession of wisdom links man with God, who, by wisdom, created and ever sustains the universe (vv. 19, 20).

It is in his mental and spiritual nature that man shows the image of his Maker. The divine Architect planned and built the heavens and the earth with consummate skill, and wherever man attains the noblest ends by the wisest means, he shows his kinship with the Creator. A feeble reflection of the divine Wisdom is still found among men, and it should be our constant aim to improve our minds by all healthy educational processes, and to discipline our spiritual natures by the use of the means appointed by God.

The poem which we are studying contains a very beautiful passage, in which Wisdom is represented as pressing upon men her claims by a description of her joyous existence with Jehovah before the creation of the world. The personification is of such rare beauty and power that we cannot refrain from quoting it, as translated by Professor Conant:

"Jehovah possessed me in the beginning of his way, before his works of old.

From everlasting was I anointed, from the beginning, from times before the earth.

When there were no deeps, I was brought forth; when there were no fountains abounding in water.

Ere yet the mountains were sunken; before the hills was I brought forth.
While yet he had not made the earth nor the fields, nor the first clods of the habitable world.
When he founded the heavens, I was there; when he traced a circle on the face of the deep; when he established the clouds above; when the fountains of the deep became strong; when he gave to the sea its bound, that the waters should not pass his command; when he appointed the foundations of the earth; and I was one brought up at his side; and was day by day a delight, sporting always before him; sporting in his habitable earth, and my delight was with the sons of men."

How full of joy is Wisdom in the presence of Jehovah! She is a playful child, happy in the Creator's smile, taking delight in the works of his hand, and feeling a peculiar interest in the sons of men. We cannot help thinking of the mystery of the God-head, and of the Divine Wisdom who became incarnate for the purpose of restoring the fallen sons of men to their original purity and bliss. But for the development of the poet's argument, let us remember that Wisdom is of supreme excellence because she connects man with God, being the friend and servant of both.

V. True wisdom is not only life to the soul, but an ornament to the person (vv. 21, 22).

How often does the author picture wisdom as a tree of life! Shut out as man is from Eden, he may yet partake of this tree of life. His soul cannot die, if wisdom dwell therein.

But Wisdom is not merely useful, she is also ornamental. She is beautiful in herself, and will add new attraction to the soul that retains her.

In the East ornaments are prized even more highly than in our own country. They are placed on all parts of the body that are exposed to view. What a rich necklace does wisdom make! Here is no cheap or gaudy toy, but an adornment corresponding to the meek and quiet spirit which the Apostle recommends to the christian women of a later day. Let us all seek to be beautiful in person, in speech, in action. Wisdom can teach us the secret.

VI. The value of wisdom is next shown by two pictures of security (vv. 23, 24).

Traveling has always been attended with more or less of danger. Even in our own time, when the comfort and safety of travel have been wonderfully improved, we still have fearful accidents on land and on sea. Probably journeys through mountainous districts have been attended with more of danger than any other kind of travel. In Palestine robbers have from the earliest times infested the dens and caves west of the Dead Sea and the Jordan valley. Besides, there is the constant danger that comes from poor roads through a hilly, broken country. Narrow paths border on yawning chasms, where to stumble is to be lost.

The orators and poets of the Bible are fond of depicting danger under the figure of stumbling. It is well for us to remember how full of meaning the image is. But if Wisdom is our guide, we shall go safely through steep and slippery defiles, and Jehovah will keep our feet from being taken. Think, christian mother, of the pitfalls that encompass your boy in the midst of life's fierce competition, and pray God to give him an understanding heart. Pray that your daughter, whether she be in ease or one of life's toilers, may be a woman of knowledge and discretion. O young man, let the command in the golden text become your rule of life. "Trust in Jehovah with all thy heart, and lean not on thine own understanding." Then you can journey through trying places with perfect safety.

The second picture of the wise man represents him as sweetly sleeping after the labors of the day. He is not wrapped in the heavy slumber of the sluggard on a poorly kept bed, nor is he nervously clutching his purse like the gambler or the conscienceless speculator, but he sleeps sweetly like an infant; his mind at peace with God and men, and his conscience at rest.

It would be evident from these pictures of security and peace, even if there were no other proof, that wisdom in the Book of Proverbs includes piety. The wise man is the godly man. He displays the highest knowledge who best obeys the will of God. No beginning in sound philosophy can be made without faith and obedience to God.. Religion is neither impracticable nor impractical. It is the first thing and the last.

Shall we not take away with us two practical lessons?

1. Judged by the standard commonly accepted even among the irreligious, piety yields larger returns than impiety, so that the impartial judge must pronounce piety to be wisdom, and impiety to be folly.

Compare godliness and lawlessness as to the improvement of health, the amassing and employment of wealth, the comforts of home—in a word, let us take happiness as the standard, and inquire in the light of universal experience, whether the pleasures of piety do not exceed those of sin. I verily believe that they do. "Godliness is profitable for all things, having promise of the life which now is, and of that which is to come." It is all a delusion of the devil to think that God robs his people of all joy until they get within the pearly gates. We do not forget the cross, or the losses, or the persecutions, which every true Christian must bear, but we remember the sweet consolations that take away the bitterness from our afflictions, and we also think of the keen pangs that pierce the sinner's heart, and the thorns that infest his pillow. Even the earthly rewards of piety commend it as of more value than a selfish life. Hence the Old Testament saints, who lived before the coming of God's Son to bring life and immortality to light through the Gospel, bravely resisted the assaults of the tempter, being confident that it was the part of wisdom to fear and serve the living God. They had glimpses of immortality, but they were not constantly sustained by the glorious thought that the rewards of heaven would atone a thousand times over for the privations of earth.

2. Let us thank God that we have now other motives, mightier still, for leading a life of righteousness. The love of Christ and the rewards of Heaven draw us away from sin with cords that can never snap. How can anyone be so foolish as to continue in sin? No longer does wisdom, merely as a beautiful abstraction, invite men to a life of holiness, but the Son of Man, the living Embodiment of wisdom, with pierced hands and feet, pleads with us to be reconciled to God. He knocks at our doors, bringing an urgent invitation to the heavenly feast. Is it wise to turn him away?

Lesson VII.   May 14.

FRUITS OF WISDOM.

Proverbs xii: 1–15.

By H. C. VEDDER, New York, N. Y.

CHARACTER is not a creation but a growth. The christian life begins with the new birth, but no more spiritually than physically are we born in the full stature of a man. Growth of character, like growth of sinew, is always a slow and often a painful process, demanding daily exercise, proper nutrition and patient continuance in well-doing. The fruits of wisdom are not to be gathered at will; they are of slow growth, and ripen only in the sunshine of God's grace. He who with impatient hand seeks to reap where he has not sown and to gather where he has not scattered, may fill his hands with leaves and chaff, or tear his flesh among thorns and brambles, but he will assuredly bring home nothing of value to himself or others. Whoso would pluck wisdom's ripe fruit must be content to produce it according to the laws of the heavenly husbandry. Some of these laws are contained in the scripture that is now to be our meditation.

At a hasty reading, these fifteen verses will no doubt seem to many a hap-hazard collection of sayings, more or less unintelligible as they stand in our common English version, with hardly a connecting link of thought. With study of the verses the difficulties lessen and finally vanish. We shall find in this scripture, if we look closely and somewhat re-arrange the order of the verses, a well reasoned, logically ordered, and aptly expressed lesson on the essential nature, the outward marks and the rewards of wisdom. Contrasted with these, the nature, manifestations and results of folly are described in stinging, caustic phrases.

I. The essential nature of wisdom consists in a disposition of the heart. Our lesson begins and ends with the statement of this basal truth: "Whoso loveth correction loveth knowledge," and again, "He that is wise hearkeneth unto counsel." It is the same truth taught elsewhere in the Proverbs in the words, "The fear of Jehovah is the beginning of knowledge." It is the fool who hath said in his heart, "No God;" it is the fool who proves himself akin to the brutes by his hatred of reproof; whose folly is incorrigible because his way is ever right in his own eyes. The foundation of wisdom is reverence toward God, respect for God's law, readiness to be led by God's providence, to be chastened, disciplined, reproved, corrected. The wise man is perfected by this discipline, as a diamond is shaped and polished in the grinder's hand; and though he finds his chastening for the present not joyous but grievous, in the end it bringeth forth the peaceable fruit of righteousness. But the fool learns nothing from such experience; though he were brayed in a mortar with the wheat, says the Wise Man elsewhere, yet will not his folly depart from him. Discipline has no magic power in itself to transform character. The same fire that melts wax bakes clay; and the correction that softens the wise man's heart and turns him from the error of his way only hardens the fool's self-will and confirms him in folly. The humble, teachable spirit is the first requisite for the gaining of knowledge, and especially the knowledge of the deep things of the spiritual realm. May God make us as little children, that we may enter into his kingdom, and be filled with the knowledge of his will in all wisdom.

II. But assuming the existence of a discipline-loving spirit—and in the case of every Christian we are assuredly entitled to do this—what does this scripture tell us of the outward manifestations, the cognizable marks, the perfected fruits of wisdom? In the first place, wisdom will be manifest in right thoughts. "The thoughts of the righteous are just, but the counsels of the wicked are deceit." There is no vice more hateful to God and man than lying, but back of the deceitful lips is a false heart. Moral rectitude is the condition of all other virtues whatsoever. Unless a man is honest with himself, honest with man, honest with God, there is no hope for him in this world or in the world to come. The voice of religion and the voice of the world are at one in this matter. Like dry rot at the heart of a tree, like quicksands underneath a foundation, falsehood makes strength and stability impossible. Society is bound together, not by laws or by force, but by mutual trustfulness, and trustfulness is possible only when the mass of men are men of just thoughts regarding the ordinary affairs of life. The streams of commerce would be dried up and grass would grow in the streets of our great cities, if the time should ever come when men find each other unworthy of trust. It is crass folly that attempts to make its way by falsehood and deceit. Honesty is not the best policy merely, but the only policy by which mankind can keep itself above barbarism and anarchy for a single decade.

But high as is the ideal that the Proverbs set before us, the highest note is not struck in this verse. The wisest of men did not reach the moral height of Him who spake as never man spake, and it was reserved for Jesus to point out the ripest fruit of wisdom, as manifest in the inner man: "Blessed are the pure in heart, for they shall see God." Purity of heart connotes rectitude, and all other virtues, for it is the reflection of him who is absolute holiness, and higher than this no goal can be set for our attainment.

The natural sequel of right thoughts is right speech, which is accordingly named as the second manifestation of wisdom. "A man shall be satisfied with good by the fruit of his mouth," and though the transgression of the lips is a snare to the evil man yet the righteous shall come out of trouble (v. 13). In no way are wisdom and folly more easily discovered than by the use of speech—the greatest blessing and the greatest curse known to man. The sins of the tongue are as numerous as they are deadly: swearing, lying, slander, tale-bearing, quarreling, flattery, filthy communications. No sins are so insidious and so frequenty committed. Then there are what we may call the vices of the tongue: discourtesy, exaggeration, rash and inconsiderate speech, vulgar and silly speech. Excessive speech is in itself a vice, for it must needs be that one who is forever pouring out words is often pouring out folly. We cannot stop to examine these fruits of folly in detail, but if further word of warning be needed against the serious nature of these transgressions and the difficulty of overcoming them, let the Apostle James furnish that word. "The tongue," he says, "is a little member, and boasteth great things. Behold how much wood is kindled by how small a fire! And the tongue is a fire: the world of iniquity among our members is the tongue, which defileth the whole body, and setteth on fire the wheel of nature, and is set on fire by hell. For every kind of beasts and birds, of creeping things and things in the sea, is tamed and hath been tamed by mankind: but the tongue can no man tame; it is a restless evil, it is full of deadly poison. Therewith bless we the Lord and Father, and therewith curse we men, which are made after the likeness of God: out of the same mouth cometh forth blessing and cursing. My brethren, these things ought not so to be."

Shall these things be with us? Shall we not rather learn the beautiful and helpful uses of speech? A word fitly spoken, we are told, is like apples of gold in a frame of silver filagree; let the occasion frame the word and each will set off the other. The lack of a little tact often spoils the best-intended effort to speak a helpful word. Bearing this rule in mind, we may learn to use the tongue wisely and nobly, in the reproof of the erring, in the instruction of the ignorant, in giving honor where honor is due, and in speaking words of truth and soberness at all times, as those who expect to be called into judgment for every idle word. This use of speech is one of the richest fruits of wisdom, but also one of the slowest to ripen yet skilful and patient husbandry will not miss its reward in due season.

With right thought and speech, right action goes hand in hand. "A virtuous woman is a crown to her husband, but she that doeth shamefully is as rottenness in his bones." All womanly virtue, not chastity merely, is here praised as the fruit of wisdom. "He that tilleth his land shall have plenty of bread" (compare also v. 9). Industry is here, as everywhere in the Proberbs, exalted as one of the chief attributes of a wise man. "A righteous man regardeth the life of his beast, but the tender mercies of the wicked are cruel." Kindness to man and beast is another characteristic of the wise man, as inconsiderate and indiscriminate cruelty is characteristic of the fool who lives for self. These specifications of the fruits of wisdom are somewhat lacking in breadth and inclusiveness, it is true, but the elements of virtuous character in man or woman are included or implied in them. They are rather specimens of the fruits of the tree of wisdom than an attempt at exhaustive enumeration. The virtues are generally found in groups, not separately. With industry will usually go temperance, frugality, patience, and a whole troop of the more useful qualities in the workaday world. With kindness will be found associated all those unselfish graces that enoble life and make it worth living. With chastity go fidelity, honor, and the loftier virtues that lift men above the things of sense and promote human progress in the knowledge and love of the good, the beautiful and the true.

III. This scripture also holds forth the rewards that come to him who cultivates the fruits of wisdom. The truly enlightened man finds the pursuit of wisdom its own sufficient reward, but all men are not to be moved by the noblest motives. Something that appeals to self-interest, that promises an appreciable addition to possessions or enhancement of happiness, is needed to stimulate their wills to continuous effort.

The first of these rewards is prosperity. This is promised no less than three times in this brief passage: "He that tilleth his land shall have plenty of bread;" "The root of the righteous yieldeth fruit;" "The doings of a man's hands shall be rendered unto him." There may be a hint in these words of something higher than mere wordly prosperity, but that is the prominent thought. The wise man shall be increased in goods as the years go by. Wealth is not, save in exceptional cases, quickly gained by some lucky stroke—and in these cases is seldom honestly come by—but is the result of forethought, frugality and industry, patiently continued through a series of years. These virtues, we are assured, shall not miss their due reward. In their haste to get rich, men forget the conditions under which riches may be honestly, and at the same time surely, acquired. The wise man does not undervalue wealth, but he is as far from overvaluing it; he is not willing to exchange for it, his integrity, his self-respect or his good name. He is content to be prospered in accordance with the laws of God, and seeks not his own advancement at the expense of his fellow men. Riches are not always prosperity, even according to the low standard of the world.

A second promised reward is the praise of men: "A man shall be commended according to his wisdom, but he that is of a perverse heart shall be despised." Only a fool is careless of the good opinion of others, but the wise man does not live chiefly to win this good opinion; he strives to deserve it, but if he satisfies the demands of his own conscience and of God's laws, he can live without man's praise if need be. Yet the approval of men will seldom be withheld in the end from him who walks in wisdom's path. If ambition has wrecked many souls, if it has deluged continents with blood, if it has prompted the most atrocious crimes, it is also the lever that has given the world every forward impulse in its history. The desire to be honorably distinguished, to leave a name that future generations will cherish with admiring affection, is a more powerful motive with most men than disinterested benevolence. The commendation of man is promised to the wise according to the measure of his wisdom.

Security is a third reward promised to him who pursues wisdom. This, too, is mentioned thrice in our lesson: "The root of the righteous shall never be moved;" "The house of the righteous shall stand;" "The righteous shall come out of trouble." The fruit of wisdom is righteousness in thought, speech and act, and to this righteousness, ultimate triumph is promised by the word of him who cannot lie. The wicked fool is sometimes prosperous—for the time, and as men commonly count prosperity—and he sometimes wins the applause of men for an hour, but the righteous alone is secure in his prosperity. There is a power in the world that makes for righteousness. The stars in their courses fight against wickedness. There are, it is true, cases in which the right goes unrewarded or wrong goes unpunished in this life, but they are comparatively few. Ordinary human experience, crystallized into many a pithy popular saying, confirms God's assurance to us that only the prosperity of the righteous man is secure. He has builded his house upon the rock, and all else is but sinking sand.

The righteous is secure because "A good man shall obtain favor of Jehovah." This is the last and greatest reward of the pursuit of wisdom, for it includes—makes possible, indeed—all the others. He who is favored of God shall also enjoy every other good gift. Not always to the outer eye is this promise kept, but the eye of faith pierces the surface of things and sees it to be profoundly true that all things work together for good to them that love God and are loved by him. The Christian is not more certain of his own existence than he is of the loving care of a Heavenly Father.

May God give us day by day more of this wisdom that cometh from above—a wisdom that is hid from the wise and prudent of this world, but is revealed unto babes. May he inspire us to cultivate its fruits with greater diligence, and reward us yet more richly with his favor. "The end of the matter," saith the Preacher, " all hath been heard : fear God and keep his commandments, for this is the whole of man."

Lesson VIII. May 21.

AGAINST INTEMPERANCE.*

Proverbs xxiii: 29-35.

By the EDITOR.

THE Bible gives the foes of intemperance, as it gave the foes of slavery, much trouble. Since it is incomparably the most powerful moral treatise in existence, they naturally desire to enlist it in their crusade, but in seeking to do this they find it an independent, not to say sometimes a refractory ally. In the perplexity thus caused, certain advocates of temperance renounce the Bible utterly, while others fly to almost as vicious an extreme in their efforts to make the old book teach as they wish. Of all the perversions of Scripture ever committed, if not the worst, certainly among the worst have been those to which pious men have resorted in the supposed interest of temperance. It cannot be that so good a cause and so good a book are at heart out of harmony. Perhaps in to-day's study we shall sight a mode of reconciliation between them.

The Bible is the most earnest and successful temperance book ever written, but its plan for promoting temperance is very much broader than that followed by many excellent peo-

---

* The sermon for this place was to have been from the pen of Rev. John Humpstone, D.D., but, owing to a most regrettable inadvertence, this one had to be substituted.

ple now. Its entire method in this matter does not appear upon the surface. To understand how wise this is we need to consider that while our marvellous Word of God was intended for all lands, classes and times, the precise tone and application of its message necessarily varies with centuries and circumstances, according to the moral needs of the successive generations of men to whom it comes. In studying the whole sweep of the Bible's tactics against intemperance, we have to review, first, the *prima facie* teaching of the book, its doctrine, that is, as the sacred writings must have been understood on this point in the times when they appeared, and as, moreover, those who composed them intended them to be understood; and in the second place, the application which under the guidance of the fundamental, eternal and most vitally moral principles of the Bible we are to-day to make of its temperance teaching.

Attending, first, to the *prima facie* attitude of the Bible on the subject, we notice that the book nowhere absolutely proscribes the use of strong liquors. It does not do this by explicit command and it does not do it by the example of inspired men. Our Saviour himself turned water into wine for the use of guests at a marriage festival. Good men have indeed argued that this was "sweet" wine, which would not intoxicate; but such a view has no solid foundation. It was wine which, had any drunk of it too freely, would have deprived them of their wits. So would that which Paul urged Timothy to take, for his stomach's sake and his frequent infirmities. There can be no doubt that all or nearly all the biblical worthies, like our own great-grandfathers, made more or less use of intoxicants, or that they regarded this use, so long as moderate, perfectly innocent. Excess in this habit, the abuse thereof, is what the Bible condemns, and such vice it does its utmost to repress.

It is thus the hardened drinker with whom our lesson for to-day deals. Nowhere in these verses are we told that the taste of strong drink is to all and under all circumstances sinful. Those who are condemned are such as "tarry long" at the wine and make effort to hunt up "mixed wine," both sure signs of sottishness and depraved appetite. They who have woe, sorrow, contentions, complaining, and wounds without cause, are marked by these very designations as drunkards. They are men hopelessly deep in their cups, whose "redness of eyes" unites with the redness of their noses to advertise them and their ways to all who meet them. The command here not to touch wine or even look at it, is of force, according to this scripture, not universally or unconditionally but only in certain states of the wine or of the man: viz., when the appearance or the taste of the drink makes it specially tempting. "Look not thou upon the wine when it is red, when it giveth its color in the cup, when it goeth down smoothly." If thou tamper with it then it will master thee; thou wilt be weaker the next time, falling more easily, until at the last what now seems so pleasant shall prove thy death, biting like a serpent and stinging like an adder.

No doubt it might sometimes be a man's duty even in ancient days to abstain entirely from the use of intoxicants. If this were not necessary on one's own account, probably cases might arise then as now when duty would require one to forego an intrinsically innocent pleasure on account of one's influence over others. But as a general thing, according to the plain and inevitable interpretation of this passage and of all the other scriptural teachings devoted to the subject, as the men to whom they were first delivered must certainly have understood them, moderate indulgence was in those times the only definition of temperance. It was the privilege and the usual practice of the best people. If there were any limitations to this rule, they were strictly exceptional, and each had to be justified by principles more or less aside from the ordinary course.

As we have said, the Bible is a moral guide for all generations. But that interpretation of it upon any point which is the most natural and correct for a people at a given grade of culture, is not necessarily the proper interpretation for all probationers to the end of time. There are back-lying principles of the Word of God, not meant to reveal themselves with much power, if at all, in earlier ages, which become operative and binding when the conditions of society are such as to bring them into prominence. Not only was biblical revelation, considered in itself, progressively given, but men's apprehension of it as a whole after it is all delivered, is also progressive.

If moderate indulgence in intoxicants was legitimate and right for the saints of Solomon's or our Saviour's time, it does not at all follow that this is the rule by which people are always to go. Circumstances alter cases. The immutableness of the Bible's morality does not consist in any immutable rules of conduct considered as a strictly external affair. The outward acts that are right for one age are not necessarily right for another. They may even be wrong. They are almost more likely than not to be so. There is truth in what has been called the relativity of ethical precepts as to outward deeds. So far as rules of conduct relate to external acts and not to states or acts of will, not one of them is perpetually valid.

What it is best and right to command or permit in one century it becomes best and right in another absolutely to forbid. Moses allowed polygamy and Christ forbade it; but neither was wrong in his precepts. In this rubric of morality there is no conflict between them, since each bade what was best for his day. Christ himself inculcated, by his example, the duty of fidelity to the Synagogue, knowing at the time that days would come when, in consequence of his own words and spirit, believers in him would be forced to oppose the whole Jewish polity in the bitterest manner. The old pro-slavery agitators were quite right in citing Scripture as on their side. In the "first intension," so to speak, of its utterances on the subject, the Bible is a strong pro-slavery treatise. To-day we have dug deeper into it and we find that the fundamental meaning of the divine word is, for our time and forever hereafter, hostile to all forms of human bondage. History has justified slavery quite as positively as Scripture has. The institution was anciently a great aid to civilization. This is, however, no plea for continuing it now. With these examples before us, we shall be less surprised if we find that while the Bible's temperance requirement once was only, "Indulge, but with circumspection," it now reads, "Abstain."

What is it after all which pure religion wishes to accomplish in men? Surely it is not uniformity in formal behavior, but holiness and righteousness in life, which may consist with much variety in good men's outward acts. The aim of God's truth is to produce character, not such or such modes of action irrespective of character, however excellent such modes of action might intrinsically be.

It is because it seeks to build character, not conformity to an external model, that Scripture employs to direct us the power of argument. The inspired writers persistently refuse to treat us like brutes or children, to be guided by dead or blind commands, the reasons for which we cannot understand. They appeal to us as rational beings, laying before us the reasonable considerations which ought to govern our acts. "Come and let us reason together," says God's Word. Every child of God is expected, on occasion, to give a reason for the hope within him. All conduct under the influence of divine revelation is meant to flow from rational self-determination, not from impulse or compulsion.

It requires no very deep regard to see that a policy of moderate indulgence which would be entirely innocuous in earlier days might now be extremely perilous and harmful. In antiquity the life of men was relatively cool, phlegmatic, dispassionate. Society as we now know it hardly existed. Men lived apart. Individuals were more and communities less important than now. There was no feverish rush for wealth or for other objects of human desire such as greet us on every hand at the present time. Men were less in danger morally from any form of social habit than they are to-day.

> "Who can see the green earth any more
> As she was by the sources of time?
> Who imagines her fields as they lay
> In the sunshine, unworn by the plough?
> Who thinks as they thought,
> The tribes who then roamed on her breast,
> Her vigorous, primitive sons?
>
> This tract which the river of time
> Now flows through with us, is the plain.
> Gone is the calm of its earlier shore.
> Bordered by cities, and hoarse
> With a thousand cries, is its stream.
> And we on its breast, our minds
> Are confused as the cries which we hear,
> Changing and short as the sights which we see."

As man's life on earth lengthens out, society suffers a progressive condensation, the rate of this progress continually accelerating. The change in this respect which has come over the world since the beginning of the present century, to go no further back, is tremendous. We do not appreciate it without considerable thought and much knowledge of history. Men now go in droves. Society is a momentous fact. The influence of man over man is enormous and inevitable. All the conditions of our modern life force men to act together, and thus to put themselves to a great extent and far more than was necessary before, in one another's power. The causes which have have swept away individualism in trade and industry make it also impossible in its old form in morals and religion. Solid godliness in a man tells as never before, and so does vice. If I use intoxicants, I cannot help being more a power for evil over my neighbor than would have been possible for a man of my character and position in the middle ages.

This thickening up of the world's population, this intensification of social influence, this habituation on the part of all of us to movement in squads and companies, of course reacts upon individual experiences, temperaments and constitutions. We breathe oftener than our ancestors did. Our pulses beat faster. Perfect self-command is a harder attainment year by year, and this not only because of the greater importunities from without but also in consequence of lessened stability within. Stability is lessened partly by the habit of acting with others, and partly by a certain nervousness and lack of equipoise which are strictly personal, modifications of our individual being, though generated by the new and peculiar circumstances amid which we are now living.

Here in America climatic peculiarities increase the difficulty in a person's maintenance of solid self-equilibrium. It is more dangerous for an American to drink than for a European. There is somewhat in our atmosphere which breeds nervousness, fever, and a quick temper, unfavorable to deliberation or mature reflection in any department of life. We draw conclusions too quickly, and are never thorough, according to the old world's standard. We are born to commit suicide, as it were, by over-rapid, abnormally intense living.

Two facts, then, rise into view as modern modifiers of a good man's moral task when facing the sin of intemperance. One is that each of us needs more care of himself under the influence of temptation, and particularly of sensuous temptation, than did the contemporaries of King David or of the Apostle Paul. We cannot with impunity venture so far with an imperious appetite as they could. The "hedge principle," *obsta principiis*, beware of the first step, is more applicable to our conduct than it was to theirs.

Meantime individual character, personal morality, is as precious as ever. The New Testament is much more emphatic in this point than the Old. A picture like our lesson, calling so much attention to the mere bodily evils of intemperance, would seem out of place in the teachings of Christ. He is too serious and spiritual. The body is indeed precious, but mainly as the temple of the Holy Ghost. One has no right to tempt himself to profane that temple. To impair the solidity of our moral standing and walk is criminal because of the infinite value of the soul, created and intended to become perfect in the image of God.

The other fact touching the duty of modern saints to be rigorously temperate is that the principle of abstinence for the sake of others of right now claims a sweep of application broader than needed to be accorded to it in biblical ages.

Suppose that we ourselves are morally strong, quite sure that regular indulgence in wine would never harm us in any manner; then, were we alone in the world, the indulgence would not be wrong. But, while the mere whims of people good or bad are not authoritative, and it may sometimes be our duty to traverse them by way of remedy, we have no right ever to gratify ourselves at the cost of real net moral harm to our fellowmen.

It follows that the scope of legitimate independence as to habits that involve outward action is more limited in modern than it was in ancient times. Nearly all the conditions of life were of old such that most men were little in danger of being overwhelmed by passion or appetite or rushed on in a path of life which was morally objectionable. Little by little, though very rapidly for the last century, reverse conditions have become prevalent, so that rules for the practical guidance of life in such a matter as temperance naturally bear a tenor considerably more stringent than their original one. To-day, instead of moderate indulgence being the rule, subject to certain limitations, abstinence is the rule, with exceptions only in cases of necessity.

Lesson IX. May 28.

THE EXCELLENT WOMAN.

Proverbs xxxi: 10–30.

BY REV. C. H. WATSON, ARLINGTON, MASS.

IN the portraiture of woman, the background of the Book of Proverbs is as dark as the pit. Upon that sombre canvas, this sharp, strong picture of the virtuous woman comes out well. Woman is, in this book, ever looking, tending and moving, either down or up, either down to hell with the men she has duped, or upward with her household toward the kingdom of God. She is either "strange," "foolish," unworthy, through folly and shame, of the natural order of life which she has desecrated, or "good," "virtuous," "excellent"—the personification of wisdom in her simple home relations. All these excellences centre in the woman described in to-day's lesson.

She is domestic. That word sets forth her various relations as by a touch of golden light. She is wife, mother, neighbor. As to what a woman should be in the first two of these relations, people are not perfectly agreed. In certain "advanced" circles, a babel of different voices is heard upon this question. Touching the glory of wifehood and motherhood, however, morally sound persons will always be of one opinion, the one based on the concordant teaching of Nature and Scripture. The best wisdom of every age will echo that belief, self-styled "progressivists" to the contrary notwithstanding. Some truths are too deeply written in law and life to be rubbed out. It is extraordinarily significant that in this book, the world's best wisdom-literature, the virtuous woman is enthroned in a home, as if there were this one sphere and opportunity for the development of the whole of woman, and only this one. In such a view, the Book of Proverbs is but the mirror of nature. God hath most wisely set the solitary in families. Man for woman and woman for man is nature's manifest law. If the two sexes are to develop each its maximum strength, realize and mature to the full each its many-sided nature, each grow the richest possible character, they must be united. It is no better for one to be alone than for the other.

True, if hindering circumstances exist, if cases arise, as they often do, where life in the estate of singleness is unavoidable, nature's aim is not necessarily defeated. Character may then be developed by some sort of devoted activity for general society, which is more important than the single family. Jesus was not a husband, foregoing this lesser relation, doubtless, that thereby he might the more savingly become Bridegroom to the whole Church of God. Nor can Paul's manner of life be adduced as indicating celibacy to be a higher law than marriage. His and his Master's example in this respect only proves the existence of cases where a man's or a woman's call to serve general humanity involves such special danger and is at the same time so urgent, that the divine blessings of companion and children must be renounced rather than beset God's servant with needless cares, or force a family circle to share his woes.

A great majority of the excuses which are made for not entering into the family estate betray selfishness if not depravity. When it is otherwise, when celibacy is enforced by hard circumstances or by some divine devotion as just pointed out, the subject of it is more often a woman than a man. Corresponding to this is the compensating fact that even involuntary independence of this sort opens a field for woman's divinest tact and power. "She spreadeth out her hand to the poor; yea she reacheth forth her hands to the needy." Though not a wife or a mother, she may still be neighbor, the compassionate, strengthening, nearest one to many a weak, ignorant, blind stumbler on the path of life. Wonderfully enriching is such a ministry. It bespeaks the spirit of Jesus, and it has in it the noblest essence of all the family relationships. In this way veritably the barren may have more children than she which hath a husband. There are women with many children who are not mothers. There are mothers many who have borne no children. These familiar pictures confront us everywhere in life: the natural relationships perverted by those who are unworthy of them, and the worthy shut out of those relationships in kind yet sharing nature's rich and abundant compensations. Nature is rarely confined to one method of securing her essential ends.

But while no woman need think her life a failure if she does not marry, nature's obvious rule is that each woman have a husband and found a family, and that in the experiences thus occasioned she grow the humanities and sagacities that shall make her "virtuous." This term as the wise man used it suggests a large endowment of common sense, moral strength, and various general practicalness. The characteristic begins with the exquisite sensibility that is specially womanly, and broadens out into heroic qualities, bodily strength, mental grasp and firmness, capacity for wielding power, all still compatible with the delicacy and purity out of which they spring. To have been a faithful wife and mother makes possible to a woman enterprises vastly greater than those terms suggest. In sounding the depth and measuring the height and breadth of those relations, she instinctively binds to herself interests beyond her own household. The woman whose "husband is known in the gates," and whose "children arise up and call her blessed," must have been trained in a practical school. She is no balloonist; hers is no aerial philanthropy. She knows how large a task in practical compassion can be wisely undertaken, and how tasks which are assumed can be most deftly carried through. She goes outside her home with the immense skill and capacity gained there. Her tact is unerring, her insight never fails. She makes few mistakes in ordinary neighborliness, or in those more perplexing moral and social problems where men so often err. It appears certain that in many departments of sociological investigation and practice women will far excel men.

The woman on whom this family training has done its normal and perfect work, "home body" though she may be, cannot but be felt in the city hall, state house and capitol; in the gates, on the streets, through the marts. This is the kind of woman that gets to the heart of places, practices and institutions without much wear of shoes or rasping of throat. There is another kind that gads out soles and uppers to get nowhere, and continually spoils the voice in saying nothing. One bears relationships which she has wholly accepted, to the meaning of which she has attained; the other, though perhaps called by the sacred name of "wife" and "mother," has failed to be either, not knowing the divine career they suggest, or suspecting that she has missed it.

The excellent woman's relations are suggestive of her duties. Wife, mother, neighbor, are a trio of relations that open into more than a trio of duties, and bring more than a triple crown of reward.

When it is said of a woman that "the heart of her husband doth safely trust in her," that "she will do him good and not evil all the days of her life," something more than plodding, domestic dutifulness is intended. It means that her varying duties to him and his have grown fruitfully from the one root of duty to her own soul. She has not tampered with her deeper self. She began with the "fear of God," never losing it in any subsequent relation with husband, child or neighbor. Rebekah had at first a love brave and beautiful, but by fatal dalliance with truth fell into dark favoritism and deception, which breathed the mildew of fraternal hatred into the souls of her sons. How different the woman of our lesson, who continually fastens her true, clear eye upon what is due to herself as a responsible being. He who keeps himself God keeps. The character beginning in those depths comes clearly out, and every heart can safely trust it. It will do good and not evil all the days. There is no foundation for common duty like radical dutifulness of soul. It is a hidden, wide-ramifying root of moral stability and undeviating righteousness. Such inner piety becomes a great first cause in a character, virtues being only its effects, the natural outgoings of a faithful soul into all the practical duties which the relations of life lay open. The loyal soul is more than any efficiency that calls attention to it. The virtuous woman is greater than anything she says or does. Her touch gives even the trivial consequence; her contact with the commonplace makes it eminent.

How plain and ordinary are the excellent woman's activities! The description of her contains not a syllable about ideals, abstractions, philosophies; not a hint of mysticism, theosophy, transcendentalism, or over-soul. How homely, concrete, practical, unromantic and almost vulgarly busy she is! Twelve verses of the twenty-two composing this alphabetical acrostic poem relate to her diversified industries. They picture a busy woman at home, that is all. Her life-work is doing her whole duty as a wife, mother, neighbor, nothing more. Was she really right? Is she to be praised? If she is our model, some modern women, "emancipated" from those duties, are astray. Let us see how time is passed and strength used by this woman whom the Bible crowns.

John Ruskin, stern lover of reality, keeps close to the scriptural award when he says: "Woman's power is for rule, not for battle; her intellect is not for invention or creation, but for sweet ordering, arrangement and decision. She sees the qualities of things, their claims, and their places. Her great function is praise. She enters into no contest, but infallibly adjudges the crown of contest."

Along this line of influence, practical arrangement, knowledge of values and places, moral discrimination, and infallible judgment, the activities of the excellent woman run. She does not dwarf her power by seeking its public display. She is not carrying on a "reform," addressing political conventions, or straining herself to prove that a woman can do a man's work. She knows where her rule is most potent. Is there any other human sovereignty so absolute, permanent, or gracious, as the mother's? It is the dominion of love, of the love which takes her bravely and wisely through life's deep travail, pain and sacrifice, over the highway from innocence to wisdom. This process is always strenuous, and often of uncertain issue. It is not as common for woman to end wisely and strongly as it is for her to begin gently and purely. Her often rough career of suffering and subjection may bring weakness to her character, bitterness or frivolity to her intellect, or a despairing skepticism to her spirit.

When, however, an earnest and highminded woman accepts her sex, and gives her life to the exacting yet ennobling activity which it makes possible for her, she acquires from her ministry the secret joy of Christ. Her voice gains authority akin to his whose spirit she has assimilated. She does what men can never do, yet what must be done, else society will be undone.

Women are to-day everywhere doing work that was formerly reserved to man. Mostly, this is well. Our lesson teaches that the model woman has no fear of masculinity in the mere form, the external nature, of the work she does. Welcome, welcome, each newly opened door inviting girls and women to the earning of honest livings. But are men doing women's work? Nay, they cannot and will not try. No masculine crusade in that direction is perceptible. Characteristic woman's work is too holy and fundamental for the rougher sex. To brood over the beginnings of moral and physical life, to create pre-natal influences favorable to physical strength and happiness, as well as to moral character; to foresee and foreshape environments with tireless tact and self-devotion; to animate the future of souls with her own self-created present, and paint them with heavenly hues from her own blood—this is woman's work. It is more celestial than any that man has done, and requires a virtue of which he is incapable. It bespeaks a dominion beyond his grasp. It calls forth a heroism that does not exhaust itself in great public spasms, but quietly renews itself every morning, and watches its eternal treasures while the world sleeps. Earth and heaven join in this work, one as truly present as the other.

But while woman's special sphere borders so closely on heaven, and makes her co-operant with God himself, much of her peculiar activity is intensely practical. There is nothing too common, trivial, difficult, disagreeable, novel or impossible for a true wife and mother to consider her business and to master. She has a noble discontent that cannot rest until she has tested by her touch everything in near and remote relation to the interests of her household. She knows that there is nothing in the environment but is silently moulding the husband and impressing the plastic child. Nothing short of a moral and material mastery of the family surroundings can satisfy her. Every little thread of practical knowledge detected by her vigilance, gets into her hand. It is by such acquisition that wisdom comes, as also authority and power to bless.

The excellent woman's vast knowledge is hers through practical duties conscientiously done. She knows all about wool and flax. She has the discerning eye and touch for fabrics. She is aware that bodies are more than raiment, yet it is respect for bodies and the sense of their preciousness that renders her an authority in clothes.

She has unfailing taste and judgment in foods. The life is

more than meat, but she reflects that proper diet makes life happier and more efficient still. She is acquainted with the best markets. She can tell a good piece of land, when and how to buy it, and what are the most suitable means for improving it. In all sorts of merchandise she is equally a *connoisseur*. Hers is a judgment by fundamental and practical knowledge. It is begun in acquaintance with the raw material, continued in "laying her hands" to the tools of manufacture, and ended in an expert feel for its texture and in ability to fix its price in the market. Such keenness in appraising values makes her strong in those vigilant economies which improvidence always wrongly confounds with meanness. They relate to her powers as well as to her goods. She has always surplus vigor for needful deeds whether of business or of mercy. The arms stretched out to the poor are strong, the hands touching the needy deft and steady. She has learned the criminality of waste and suffers no foolish leakages of mind, spirit or force. While it is yet night she riseth to nourish the family's strength for the day and to plan and to start its work.

Evidently the excellent woman makes no main business of "society." She does not keep a *salon*, else she would not retire until the time when she now arises for the day's duties. Things are chaotic with a woman when she confounds night with day, cultivating a kind of brilliancy that flashes best in the dark, and has to hide from the old, truth-telling sun. Our noble woman's discipline includes even the unruly member, for she openeth her mouth with wisdom, and the law of kindness is in her tongue, which must be still until it is ready to move according to that law. She has the composure of self-disciplined and self-regulated strength. She has provided against more formidable visitors than "snow," hence nothing disturbs her soul's equipoise. "Strength and dignity are her clothing, and she laugheth at the time to come." With such a character, the time to come must issue out of that which now is. Hence she can calmly wait. There is no prophecy of good more sure than the present possession of a character and spirit like hers.

It is in this lofty sense that duties are connected with rewards. Just as surely as relations point to duties, duties entail rewards. The reward already lies potentially in the palm of the dutiful hand. No idle hand need attempt the seizure. If reward comes only to its own, idleness can only vainly clutch and reach out. Through good work faithfully done does character go to its crown. Its crown is thus its own. God gives it, but we fashion it. "We then are workers together with him." "Ye are my crown" said the Apostle to men for whom he had given his bodily exertions and his heart's blood. Is not this the law of life and of the more abundant life yet to come? What need of richer reward than the results worked out by our own spirits, and perfected by our own tireless and devoted brains and fingers, as we have found God, found ourselves, accepted both, and wrought righteousness in our various relations, through our duties to God, ourselves, and our children? Is not the mother's crown of glory a rich one, which she wins in firmly treading down, like the Sistine Madonna, the dark clouds, the powers of evil, the insidious allurements of selfishness and vanity, which surround her offspring, and holding high her child toward the sweet angelic influences which are borne down from God to minister to him? What better praise than in eschewing deceitful favor and vain beauty, and choosing like Michael Angelo's favorite sibyl, rather to become lowly and worn but wise in teaching little children and leading them into the kingdom of God? Does not that woman excel the many that have done virtuously, who binds herself voluntarily to her own nature and possibilities as woman, wife and mother, sees the greater in the seemingly less, and lives for it day and night, her faith failing not, but ever holding fast to the substance of things unseen?

Lesson X.   June 4.

REVERENCE AND FIDELITY.

Ecclesiastes v: 1-12.

BY REV. E. P. TULLER, LAWRENCE, MASS.

THE writer of Ecclesiastes was a preacher or debater. He was a man of experience who gave to his companions in the assembly the result of his observations in life. He had tried the various methods by which men seek satisfaction. All had failed. Money, wisdom, appetite, social delights cannot permanently please. True peace is to be obtained only in recognizing God as the Righteous One, and in obeying his laws.

The preacher, however, warns against a false idea of devotion to God. There is as little real blessing or true religion in a thoughtless attendance upon religious duties or in formal offerings of service as there is in seeking wealth or pleasure. True inward vital belief in God and reverence for him are required. They will assure you a correct relation to your fellow-men, who are, with you, God's rational creatures, living under his law and the objects of his love. If you regard him as you ought you cannot but treat them as you ought. The true fear of God is thus the basis of a righteous life, and such a life, and such a life alone, answers the deepest cry of the human heart for satisfaction.

The first section of the lesson indicates some of the specially important ways in which a truly reverent attitude toward God reveals itself, and where hypocrisy is most easily fallen into as well as most deleterious: first, in public worship, second in private devotion, third in spontaneous promises of religious charity.

Our fear of God is well tested in public worship. "Keep thy foot when thou goest to the house of God." Temple or synagogue services call for a reverent attitude of mind and heart. Reverence will doubtless manifest itself in respectful demeanor and thoughtful expression; but the phrase "keep thy foot," refers rather to the state of the soul. Guard thy heart when thou goest to worship God. How to guard it is declared. Go to offer your sacrifice with sincere repentance and a true desire to please God. Engage thoughtfully in the services. Attentively follow the minister as he offers the sacrifices. Meditate deeply on the passages from law, or prophets, or psalms in the liturgy. Impress your mind with their signification and their significance, the meaning of the sacrifices, the truth of the words. Much of this truth may be old; see if you cannot go more deeply into it than has been your wont. Do not dawdle, do not sham. And going home with new thoughts and thoughtfulness touching divine things, put in practice whatever convictions the Spirit of God may have borne in upon you. That will be true worship.

This is good gospel for the year 1893. How many thoughtlessly visit the house of God, go from mere habit, or because others go, or because they expect to see their friends there, or to hear some new thing? To not a few church attendance is literally a sacrifice, performed as a required duty, as though presence in God's house were the sum total of worship. Others look upon it as the great thing to do to keep God on good terms, and, consequently, after performing the sacrifice, return to their usual round and mode of living. By acting in any of these ways we dishonor God and offer the sacrifice of fools. We betray a total misapprehension of God's will in this weighty matter. They that worship God must worship him in spirit and in truth. God seeketh such to worship him. To be true worship sacrifice must be an expression of the immost soul. Hardly less of an evil is it when pretending worshipers hurry through the service with minds full of cares over the past or of plans for the future. Such do not profit by the truth proclaimed, and it is only an accident if they carry away from the solemn assemblage any benefit at all.

A man's fear of God is very severely tested also in those devotions which take the form of prayer and are personal instead of congregational. Such devotions may be offered in the temple or in the home, in public or in private. Wherever presented, to be real, they must be more than formal, more than mere lip-service. To chatter before God is to show little appreciation of his character or of the true nature of prayer.

Remember who and what God is. He is not a fellow-man, or a fellow-being, as an angel; but is the author of all being. In majesty, in holiness, in greatness, he is farther above us than we above the minutest forms of life. Before him we, though existing in his image, fade into insignificance; while all the significance we at any rate have, beams from him, for we are the work of his hand. Almighty, he creates and controls the universe. His knowledge is infinite. The righteous one, holy, blessed, the God of Abraham, Isaac and Jacob, of David and Solomon, before whom angels bow and whom no temple can contain, is the being thou wouldest fain invoke. And thou!—thou art upon the earth, with thy little mind, frail body, and life but a span long. Oh, "be not rash with thy mouth" if thou wilt speak to the Eternal! Use no hackneyed expressions that shall let the mind drift. Weigh thy speech, and see to it that soul goes into every word. "Let not thy heart be hasty to utter anything before God; for God is in heaven and thou upon the earth: therefore let thy words be few,"

This, too, is valuable exhortation for contemporary professors of religion. Both the evils which Ecclesiastes impliedly condemns, formality in congregational worship and listless, flabby mentality in private prayer, dreadfully re-act on character. They beget general insincerity and hollowness of heart. They create an incapacity for genuine and solid godliness. Doubtful if human beings morally more worthless anywhere exist than those whose inner life has been thus honeycombed: men who, in their way, pray easily and without ceasing, but do not tell the truth, pay their debts, give for missions, deny themselves for their neighbors, or show any other essential christian grace. This conjunction of sham piety with real godlessness brings upon religion nearly all the odium it suffers; and it founds the suspicion, almost a conviction in the minds of many fairly sensible worldlings, that all religion is a cheat.

Were the Ecclesiastes with us now he would very likely amplify this part of his sermon into particulars somewhat as follows: 1. Do not pray too long, either in public or in private. Do not attempt to tell God all you know. Imitate Christ in this, who always prayed briefly. Pray for exactly what you want, in your own way, however homely. Speak to the point, and be soon done. 2. Let the anti-ritualist beware of ritual. Do not get enslaved to set forms of supplication. Use not vain repetitions, as the heathen and many Christians, especially ministers, do. 3. Pray regularly, yet beware of regularity in prayer. Otherwise you will fall into the error of supposing that going through a certain form once, twice or thrice daily is praying, and it is not. Prayer is the spirit of prayer. This is why we can pray without ceasing yet not be always upon our knees. 4. Avoid making in prayer inordinate confessions of your own sinfulness. You are wicked enough, doubtless, but do not paint the picture so dark as to make it a solid black surface and no picture at all. Be careful and serious here. 5. If you are a pastor, do not use the form of prayer as a means for publicly castigating the parishioners who wish that you would hand in your resignation.

The tendency of loquacity and make-believe worship to render men's characters unstable seems to be the preacher's reason for noting in connection with that vice the bad habit of hasty promises, pledges and vows touching religious duty. Our scripture bluntly tells us this is the practice of fools. "When thou vowest a vow unto God, defer not to pay it, for he hath no pleasure in fools; pay that which thou vowest. Better is it that thou shouldest not vow than that thou shouldest vow and not pay." Talking too much on matters in general, habitually speaking out something or other on whatever subject is presented, we address God carelessly, and this not only in the way of adoration and petition but in promises as to what we will do for him. We then make too thoughtless covenants with men as well.

Once, in distress, you said: If God will deliver me from this trial, I will present a gift to him; I will perform such and such a service. But the danger being past, the gift appeared more than could well be paid, the service greater than could easily be performed, and your vow went unfulfilled. God had not required of you that act. You pledged it of your own accord, and you failed to do as you agreed. Such cases are not confined to prayer. In the midst of a great crowd of people, when various influences stir my emotion, I, in a moment of warmth, volunteer to perform some deed of charity. But the excitement wears off, and I find my heart unwilling to carry into effect the covenant uttered by my lips. I may in my haste have promised what it was physically impossible for me to perform; in which case, if I had reason to fear it was so, my "mouth has caused my flesh to sin" (v. 6). It is no valid excuse in such a case for me to come before God's minister and plead immunity from God's wrath, on the pretense that I made a mistake, "for it came to pass through the multitude of thy dreams and vanities and many words."

Of course we are here implicitly bidden to perform all proper promises whenever we possibly can; but the point particularly insisted on is that we have no right ever to make promises or undertake obligations of any sort without adequate reflection. Think before you bind yourself to this or that course. That it is in itself a good course does not alone make legitimate your agreement to take it. Do not be stampeded into making pledges even to the doing of good. And, obviously, if it is wrong to assume under excitement obligations which cooler judgment would have declined, it must be wrong to excite men for the purpose of securing from them such obligations, or to solicit such from them when excited. We should remember this when urging congregations of young people to sign the temperance pledge. Under impassioned appeals for money for missions or other christian work, while many are stingy and phlegmatic enough, not a few pledge more than they ought. Results on the whole would, beyond question, be better if, in such instances, we addressed ourselves more to principle and less to emotion. We should thus foster sincerity and enrich character, whereas now, according to the scripture which we are studying, some of our practices tend to dispel both. Be frank, genuine, sincere, solid, really what you seem; not frivolous, flighty, giddy, volatile, hypocritical or rash—this is in sum the message of our lesson's first section.

The second and briefer section of the lesson seeks to dispel certain illusory facts which appear to controvert some of the advice given in the first. Verses eight and nine explain the vanity of high official position; verses ten to twelve elucidate the vanity of wealth.

Do not be deceived at appearances, says the man of observation. You may think that the extortionate Persian officer who struts about his province in his fine uniform is happy and satisfied with life. It may seem strange to you that I prescribe righteousness when you are distressed. You, perhaps, suppose that the oppressor who disregards God and truth has a delightful situation and an easy time. But you are mistaken. The peace of such is only apparent. The oppressor is in turn the oppressed. Throughout that immense Persian empire there is a hierarchy of officers, grade above grade. Each higher functionary grinds the face of the one beneath, and lords it over him without mercy, while all alike are crushed for the pleasure of the king. Each is, in fact, compelled to brutality toward his inferiors in order to satisfy the demands of those over him. These slaves in high places suffer no less than you suffer. Most of them have no proper peace or contentment, but exactly the reverse; and if any chance to possess real enjoyment, it comes not from their positions, but from their dispositions, the very dispositions I am urging you to acquire. In a sense, indeed, the great ones of earth are underlings after all. Every one of them, even the king, is dependent on the fruit of the field and the labor of the masses.

The millionaire is precisely as miserable as the great official. The rich are to be pitied, not envied. Temporal wealth is a great burden. If you have it the rabble incessantly besiege you. Beggars, retainers, and servants eat up all your increase, so that the support of your establishment costs a continual struggle. After all, the only thing which large possessions bring to their owner is the poor privilege of looking about him and saying, All this is mine. Dives must spend his days in toil and fret. Night brings him no sleep, but he tosses, anxious for the morning, yet not knowing why. "He that loveth silver shall not be satisfied with silver; nor he that loveth abundance with increase: this also is vanity."

How timely is this message! The belief that the rich and great are extraordinarily happy, that they enjoy an extra share of life's good things, that their lot is enviable, and that God is very mean, or at least acts mysteriously, in so exalting them above the rest of us, is the most stupendous delusion of this age. So far as one can judge, it deceives more people now than at any preceding period, and deceives them worse. It is the darling hoax of our century. We see this alike in the airs which great people put on, and in the toadying attitude of the multitude toward them. The saddest aspect of the present labor agitation is the assumption of nearly all who plead for the poor, that their only need is a larger share of the world's wealth. They deserve this, and God grant that it may soon be theirs; but if it comes alone they will find it no true wealth. As our writer says, if one is not too poor, there are great advantages in being poor. With, perhaps, not over-much to eat, drink, or wear, yet, if a man has a decent plenty, nothing need worry or annoy him. His sleep is sweet and his conscience at rest. But at any rate wealth could not promote his joys. A man's life consisteth not in the abundance of the things which he possesseth. Bless God, the human soul is too fine and high a thing to be satisfied with the gold that perisheth. "Thou hast made us for thyself, O God," cries St. Augustine, "and restless is our soul till it finds rest in thee."

lesson XI. June 11.

THE CREATOR REMEMBERED.

Ecclesiastes xii: 1-7; 13, 14.

BY REV. J. F. ELDER, D. D., ALBANY, N. Y.

THE author of these quaint and mystic words has just been giving counsel that seems almost ironical in the freedom which it allows: "Rejoice, O young man, in thy youth, and let thy heart cheer thee in the days of thy youth, and walk in the ways of thine heart and in the sight of thine eyes." But the advice may be taken soberly in connection with the warning that certain judgment will attend any infraction of the laws of health or morals. The preacher seeks to buttress young persons' moral purpose by the injunction to remember their Creator in the days of their youth. "Now," is a word of entreaty. "Remember, I pray, thy Creator." Remember him as the tempted Joseph did when he cried, "How shall I do this great wickedness and sin against God?" The best antidote to the perils that lurk in "Let thy heart cheer thee in the days of thy youth" is "Remember thy Creator in the days of thy youth." A holy fear of God will chasten our pleasures without lessening our enjoyment.

Another reason for moderating the pleasures of youth by the fear of God is found in the stealthy but resistless approach of old age with its manifold infirmities and its flagging appetites. A well spent youth helps both to delay those evil days and to make more tolerable those years of infirmity of which we shall say, " I have no pleasure in them." Then the sun and the light and the moon and the stars—symbols of life and happiness—will be darkened often and the clouds return with scarcely an interval after the rain. The misfortunes of youth are like a summer shower to the buoyant spirit—quickly come, soon gone. But in old age " storm after storm rises dark o'er the way," and " it never rains but it pours." Happy are they who have learned so to remember God when young that the joys of religion shall compensate for all the pains and sorrows of their extreme age.

Adopting now a new figure, our writer continues to dilate on the multiplied evils of age, in well sustained imagery which presents, at points, almost insoluble riddles. To understand his analogies let us picture a lordly castle. Sentinels stand at the gates; bands of armed retainers swarm its courts; watchers in the lofty turrets espy danger from afar; in the women's quarter the ceaseless hum of the mill is heard grinding corn for the great household; the gates are thronged with coming or departing guests; huge underground cisterns give ample supply of water drawn from their cool depths by wheel and bucket; around gushing fountains the serving maids poise the full pitcher gracefully upon the head; within the lofty halls golden lamps hang from the ceiling by silver cords; and all is wealth, luxury, power, bustle, enjoyment, life. Now imagine such a lordly estate in ruins, deserted by all save a few old retainers too timid and feeble to resist attack, and you have the basis of the imagery in our lesson.

The trembling keepers of the house may well represent our hands, which have been so laborious for our body's weal, toiling for and defending it, till, palsied with age, they shake and tremble. The strong men armed, on whom feudal houses have rested as thrones on bayonets, will answer to our sturdy limbs that have supported the body for fourscore years, but totter at last. The failing grinders clearly point to the mouth, a natural grist mill, which in old age becomes sadly out of order in both the upper and the nether millstone. The lookers from the turret windows are our eyes, and their darkening is the dimness of vision that grows with years.

The closed doors are the organs of hearing through which the soul receives tidings from the outer world. In old age these doors are partially and sometimes altogether closed, an affliction second only to blindness itself. This calamity is very bitter. The writer dwells upon it as upon no other detail of the picture. He notices that the familiar sound of the domestic mill is scarcely heard; that to the old man's ear it is no louder than a sparrow's note ("the sound of the grinding," not "he," is the subject of the verb: "it shall rise, or attain to, the voice of the bird"); and that the notes of the choicest singers and the loudest songs are all too faint for him to hear or enjoy.

With the failure of his bodily powers, the old man's mind, too, loses its grip and poise. He becomes afraid of what is high, either in climbing or in other exertion. He who at eighteen gloried in putting his cap on the top of the tallest mast in the harbor, at eighty hesitates to mount the quarter deck. He is haunted, too, by imaginary fears. Calamities seem to impend. Lions are in his path, and he grows morbidly conservative.

What state of mind or body is indicated by the blossoming almond tree is one of the darkest enigmas in the chapter. Perhaps the key is in Jeremiah i. 11, 12. "Jeremiah, what seest thou? And I said, I see a rod of an almond tree. Then said the Lord unto me, Thou hast well seen: for I will hasten my word to perform it." The Hebrew name of the almond means "watching" or "early waking," because "what the cock is among domestic animals the almond is among trees. It awakes first from the sleep of winter." Hence God uses it as a sign of the speedy performance of his word. Hence, too, it is used here as a symbol of wakefulness, which is often a concomitant of old age, especially in the form of early rising.

In the old man's enfeebled condition, also, the grasshopper becomes a burden: the most insignificant responsibility or care oppresses him. And finally his flagging appetites refuse to respond to any stimulants. "Desire" should probably be "the caper-berry." The seeds of this plant are used in modern cookery, and the berries were, of old, supposed to have medicinal virtues. But even this strong spice fails to rouse the dormant appetites. Naught remains but for the worn-out probationer to seek the grave—his long home, so called because "occupied longer than any house in which he has lived"— while, after the fashion of the day, the hired mourners follow the bier through the streets with their loud cries of woe.

Regarding this mention of the burial as parenthetic, and "or ever" as equivalent to "before," we come to the man's final dissolution, in which all this gradual decay and failing function finds its inevitable end. Death is here contemplated and described under a series of symbols at once beautiful and expressive. What more significant of a human life, and especially of a masterful human life, with its cheering and radiant influence, than a shining lamp fed with unfailing oil, and held aloft that it may give light to all that are in the house—a golden bowl perchance hung by a silver cord? But now the thread of life is severed, the silver cord is loosed, the golden bowl is dashed, the oil is spilled, the light goes out in darkness. Again, how like we are to earthen vessels filled at some exhaustless fountain, as our lives are in fact supplied from the fulness of the Eternal! But when the pitcher is broken at the fountain we are, so the mouthpiece of the crafty Joab phrased it, "as water spilt on the ground, which cannot be gathered up again." Or when we look at the wondrous mechanism of our bodies and see how life courses through them, we realize how apt an emblem of death is the broken wheel at the cistern's mouth, no longer able to draw the life-giving water from its depths.

But the lamp is not the light though it helps to manifest the light; the pitcher and the wheel are not the water though they bring it to men's lips. So body and spirit are distinct in nature and, for a time at least, in destiny. Broken lamp, shivered pitcher, shattered wheel, lifeless body are consigned to earth's common rubbish heap. But the immortal spirit, like the flame and the water spilled on ground and kissed by the sun, seeks the skies. There is no materialism here. The outer man shares the fate of kindred dust; the inner, the real man, seeks the source of all spiritual life, in God. Is it pantheism? Is the returning spirit absorbed in God as the falling drop is swallowed up in the sea? Let the doctrine of a final judgment, strict, personal and minute—more than hinted at here and clearly revealed in the New Testament—be our answer.

Let us hear the conclusion of the whole matter, the sum of the whole discourse.

The conclusion here given is not that of this particular lesson merely, but of the entire Book of Ecclesiastes. Its author's "main drift and purpose, broken indeed by many side eddies, now of cynical bitterness, now of worldly wisdom, now of keen observation, was to warn those who were yet in quest of the chief good, against the shoals and rocks and quicksands on which he had well-nigh made utter shipwreck of his faith; his desire was to deepen the fear of God in which he had at last found the anchor of his soul" (Plumptre).

Yet his conclusion fits very well the particular portion of the book embraced in our lesson. "Fear God" is but another way of saying "Remember thy Creator" with the threatened judgments which follow. The one injunction precedes the other; while the infirmities and sorrows of old age so picturesquely set forth may, so far as they are premature, be a part of the very judgment against which we are warned. These considerations, then, drawn from our lesson, go to support the exhortation to early piety with which it opens.

1. The manifold infirmities of old age.

To be sure, we may not live to become old, but so much the more do we need to remember our Creator in the days of our youth. The alternative is certain: either a premature death, or the common lot of age. And what can be sadder than to feel that all the pleasure of vigorous health has forever passed away and naught is left but the contemplation of inevitable and unceasing decay, and certain death without hope. How pitiful is the plea of the loyal Barzillai to be excused from the oppressive gratitude of his king. "How long have I to live that I should go up with the king unto Jerusalem. I am this day fourscore years old, and can I discern between good and evil? Can thy servant taste what I eat or what I drink? Can I hear any more the voice of singing men and singing women? Wherefore then should thy servant be yet a burden unto my lord the king?" How sweet to those so broken, on whom every earthly pleasure has palled, is the comfort of a christian hope: to know that inasmuch as they have remembered their Creator in their youth, their Creator does not forget them in time of old age. Then, too, how small the likelihood that if one has neglected his Creator in the days of his youth he will change when he is old. Habits are confirmed, prejudices hardened, will power fixed as regards the world but weak toward God, and the whole spiritual nature shares the deadness of the body. We may repeat the question of Nicodemus, with a single added word, "How can a man be born *again* when he is old?"

2. The possible perils of a youth unrestrained by the fear of God.

Most young men are ready to fall in with the counsel "Rejoice, O young man, in thy youth, and walk in the ways of thine heart." "But know thou for all these things God will bring thee into judgment." Youth indeed is the time for joy, for hope, for love, for pleasure. It comes but once; let a man make the most of it. But mark this stern threat of judgment suspended over us like the sword of Damocles. It is not alone the final judgment that we are to fear, but the more immediate consequences of transgression as well, among which may be the premature experience of decrepitude. Every day is a judgment day. Never forget that we are made and live under law; that if we transgress in our pleasures we must suffer. Get all possible fragrance out of life's roses, but beware of thorns. Nemesis sits in every house of pleasure. Do not spend your youth so as to incur remorse and shame and pain. The surest safeguard for any young man is the fear of God. "Rejoice, O young man in thy youth" turns us out into a broad pasture of pleasures. "Remember thy Creator" is a silken tether that checks us if we approach too near the bounds of danger. "Be not deceived. God is not mocked. Whatsoever a man soweth that shall he also reap."

3. Religion is the supreme good of young men as of all. It "never was designed to make our (rational) pleasures less." "Fear God and keep his commandments; for this is the whole duty of man." "Duty" is not in the Hebrew. Religion is the whole of man, his *summum bonum*. We were made for God and never attain wholeness of being till we find it in him. Life is a partial, distorted thing apart from God. Religion is not merely something to be lived, but life itself. "The whole of man" is life, as it is the whole of God. Young man, you want to "see life." Then see God, through personal purity and fidelity to the divine commands. You will thus see life in such wise that you will hunger no more for the pleasures that only kill. You will come up from the darksome crypt to worship in the whole vast temple of your being, consecrated in its wholeness, from inmost shrine to fretted vault and gleaming pinnacle, to him who is the proper Fear of man.

4. The solemn meeting of the soul with God. "The spirit shall return to God who gave it." The very words imply an accounting for the use of what was given. What a meeting will it be: that unveiled vision of God. What manner of address will the Father of Spirits have for his returning child? O, Spirit of a mortal, I sent thee forth to achieve thy destiny immortal. I welcome thy return. How fared thy pilgrimage on earth? I sent thee to dwell in prison house of clay that thou mightest therein do me service and fit thyself for larger mansions. I gave thee arms with which to help thy fellows. Hast thou wrought only for self? I gave thee strong limbs to bear thee where thou wouldest go. Have they led thee only into paths of sin? I gave thee eyes like pools in Heshbon, wherewith my glories to behold in earth and sky and sea. Hast thou bent those eyes on vanity? I gave thee ears to hear, to drink in all sweet melodies and to hearken to my word. Have they been deaf to my entreaties? I gave thee lips to sing my praise, or voice thy prayer, or utter words of consolation to thy weeping brother. Have they been filled with bitterness and cursing, and used to set on fire the course of nature? Were thy members servants to uncleanness? Or didst thou make them instruments of righteousness to God? Thy probation in that house of clay is ended and thou hast come home to judgment. Mansions fair await thee, or a prison house more dark than that in which thy mortal clay is slumbering. Thou must abide with God if thou hast grown like God: or with the devil and his angels if they on earth have been thy guides. Thy fellow-in-the-flesh—the Nazarene—shall be thy judge. He triumphed over earth and flesh and evil spirit, and set thee an example brave, and grace to thee did proffer for thy victory. These words, or the equivalent of them, all of us now strong and blooming with youth are one day to hear. "Remember, I pray, thy Creator in the days of thy youth."

Lesson XII. June 18.

MESSIAH'S KINGDOM.

Malachi iii: 1-12.

By Rev. R. H. PITT, D. D., Richmond, Va.

THERE is something very interesting and almost pathetic in the growing intensity of the Messianic hope among the Jews. Though long deferred it seems to feed upon delay and to be strengthened by disappointment. The influence of this hope is interwoven with their history and is a potent factor in the formation of their national character. Leaving this out of view we should fail to secure an intelligent notion of this strange people and of the influential part they have borne in the world's history. There are many prophecies unmistakably Messianic, utterances that have no meaning if they are not so interpreted. We believe it can be shown that in general these prophetic utterances grow in plainness and directness in proportion to the prophets' nearness to the advent of the Messiah. Certainly the passage under consideration is not surpassed in these qualities by any other. There are predictions of the Messiah more elaborate, but none more specific, more clear in their reference to the new dispensation.

This does not surprise us. We should naturally expect that the last of the race of prophets, with whose words the canon of the Old Scriptures closes, between whom and the coming of the Messiah only four centuries intervened, would see with most unclouded vision and speak with least uncertain sound.

The earlier seers had stood in the morning twilight. They knew that the day was coming and they said so. But it was gray dawn which they saw and the chill of the night was still upon them. The sky of our prophet's vision was rosy and blushing, and stray beams of light were already coming over the eastern hills. It is Malachi who brings the cheering and comforting assurance: "Unto you that fear his name shall the Sun of Righteousness arise with healing in his wings."

THE FORERUNNER.

There are other prophetic utterances concerning that unique and admirable person who was to link together in his office and his work the old and new covenants. But in none of them is he more plainly pointed out than here. The passage at Isaiah xl. 3, is hardly so clear as this in its reference to John the Baptist. The Baptist is a singularly noble and striking figure and has scarcely received the attention to which he is entitled. This was inevitable, since he was so quickly followed by another whose peerless personality dwarfed and obscured him. He recognized his fate, and rejoiced with a loyal manliness beyond all praise, that One whom he came to announce, whose shoe-latchet he was unworthy to loose, "must increase" while the voice which made the announcement grew "faint and far." But it ought never to be forgotten that the Master himself said, " . . . there hath not arisen a greater than John the Baptist." The finest quality of courage, the best type of self-abnegation, all the virtues without any of the vices of asceticism, a rare and beautiful blending of sternness and submissiveness—these were among the features of a character which must always command our unqualified respect. John prepared the way of the Lord by direct announcement. "There cometh one after me," he said, and proceeded to describe him. And when at length he came, John cried "Behold the Lamb of God!"

But he also made preparation for the coming of the Messiah by the character of his preaching, the substance of which was a call to repentance, and the announcment of the nearness of the Kingdom of Heaven.

THE SUDDENNESS OF MESSIAH'S COMING.

It seems a little strange that, after centuries of weary watching and waiting, without bating one jot of heart or hope, despite national misfortune amounting almost at times to national annihilation, now when the day drew near, the people to whom the promises were given should be unprepared for Messiah's advent; that a special messenger should have to be sent to assure them of it, and that even he could not make them ready. The growing clearness and intensity of general prophetic utterances, and the Voice itself crying in the wilderness, were alike so unavailing that the Lord came "suddenly."

And this, too, although the prophet represents them as seeking and delighting in him who was to come—"The Lord whom ye seek" is about to appear, he said; "even the messenger of the covenant whom ye delight in." Some old commentators tell us that these expressions are ironical. They may be right. Certainly few were actually seeking Jesus when he came, and few delighted in him after he had come. For the multitude "there was no beauty in him that they should desire him," and "no form or comeliness" in him when they saw him. Seek him and delight in him indeed! From the day that Joseph and Mary fled with the Child to Egypt until that woeful day when his pursuers found their diabolical delight in standing about his tortured body, wagging their heads in scorn and hate, and saying, "Let him come down from the cross: he saved others, himself he cannot save," they only sought him to do him harm.

And yet there was and there still is in a deep and real sense a seeking for him, a delighting in him. He is rightly named the Desire of all nations. Through hardness of heart, the vision of "his own" was blinded, and "his own received him not." But "had they known it they would not have crucified the Lord of Glory." He himself said: "Father, forgive them, they know not what they do." It is not unreasonable, and it does not lessen their guilt, since their blindness was self-imposed, to think that their hatred of Jesus was due in part to a misapprehension of his character and aims.

THE PURPOSE OF HIS COMING.

He is the "Messenger of the Covenant," of the new covenant of grace and mercy. The prime object of his coming is to promulgate and to seal this new compact which is to displace the old. But following the emphasis of the prophet, let us consider the function of the Messianic office on which he lays especial stress. The fact that this particular feature of Christ's mission is more or less misunderstood and obscured in our own time, makes it all the more important that we should pay attention to it.

The prophet uses three figures, all of them familiar and significant. The coming One is like fuller's soap; he is like a refiner's fire, and he shall sit as a refiner and purifier of silver. There is probably no ground for the notion that these figures indicate various kinds of cleansing, such as outward and inward. It is, however, worthy of remark that in one figure he is the refiner's fire, and in another he is the refiner himself.

The prophet seems unwilling to figure him under the guise solely of mere material agents. But the whole passage, freed from fanciful interpretation, teaches that Christ came to purify, and to purify in part by destroying, and that this destruction was an element in the process of restoration. For this purpose was the Son of God manifest, that he might destroy the works of the Devil. This work of cleansing was to begin with the sons of Levi, the priesthood, the religious leaders and teachers. It seems to be true—and it is a solemn and startling truth—that whenever corruption of morals or doctrine prevails, the grossest immorality and the most deadly heresy are to be found among the priestly class, among the religious leaders and teachers of the time. The best type of character that any system of religion can produce, and the worst as well, will be found among the priests and the preachers. In the Jewish economy, the prophetical office, which was largely sporadic and irregular, was necessary to supplement, and also, in no small degree, to oppose the influence of the priesthood. That Jesus found the worst corruption in the priesthood is seen in the fact that his gentle spirit never waxed so hotly indignant as when he dealt with priests. Then, indeed, his righteous wrath flamed out and he was a refiner's fire ! But his mission of purification was not confined to Scribes and Pharisees, to Priests and Levites. It was for all the people and all the ages. He was not simply and merely a Saviour, to die a sacrificial death, out of which hope of forgiveness and of heaven was to come. This he was, but he was something more. He had a doctrine for the life which now is as well as for that which is to come. His religion was not mere "morality touched with emotion." It was morality based on eternal, unchanging principles, and interfused with, baptised in, the deepest and holiest emotions of which our regenerated natures are capable. Only we must not forget that it *was* morality, of the sternest, loftiest, gentlest, purest type, that character and conduct are always prominent and eminent in the view which it takes of human duty and destiny.

Be not misled by the common and thoughtless talk of an "old gospel." The gospel which does not touch and cleanse and purify every department of life is not the "old gospel." The gospel which has no helpful sympathy for those who suffer wrong, and no righteous anger for those who do wrong, is not the old gospel. The gospel that condones sin, that compromises with evil, that is guiltily silent in the presence of social, political and commercial wrongs, is a new gospel, and whosoever preaches it will be *anathema maranatha*. The Messiah whose claims the "old gospel" sets forth, and whose doctrine it records, sits as a refiner and purifier of silver. He is like a refiner's fire and like fuller's soap. The prophets themselves were never so severe in the rebuke of wrong-doers as he was. He was a swift and terrible witness against all such. And if his churches wish truly to reflect his spirit they must take his position. There are now, as in the time of the prophet, adulterers, false swearers, those who oppress the hireling in his wages, who wrong the widow and orphan, who turn aside the stranger from his right; and if they will not fear God, they ought at least to be made to regard man. That "all will be elsewise by-and-by" is a cheap variety of comfort which we ought to be ashamed to administer so long as the wrongs for which we offer consolation may be speedily remedied.

There are two errors to which the present generation of Christians are exposed, and against which we need to be warned. One is that already discussed: the assumption, much more general than we are disposed to think, that Christianity has nothing to do with the social order, with political, national or commercial life. The other is the supposition that in the attempt to purify, to refine, to reform, we have no need of Christ or his religion. The former of these is fatal to the true mission of Christ, the latter is equally fatal to the success of the attempt to purify. The source of moral defection and corruption is indicated in this prophecy: The wrong-doers fear not God. They rob God. They depart from his ordinances. The process of purification which the Messiah adopts is indicated further on. He begins at the foundation, he lays the axe to the root of the tree, he looks beyond the symptoms to the seat of the malady and calls upon the wanderers to return to

God. The fear of the Lord in the large and significant sense of this phrase, as used in the Scriptures, is not only the beginning of wisdom; it is also the beginning of moral purification.

THE MERCIFUL MESSIAH.

The Messiah is restorer as well as destroyer. The fuller's soap, in the process of cleansing, removes the soil and stain but leaves the fabric unhurt, the refiner's fire burns out the dross but leaves the silver white and shining. Jesus has always something to propose in the place of that which he opposes. He is no mere iconoclast. His denunciation of evil and of evildoers is not mere indulgence in the luxury of passionate hate. He cleanses the fabric, he purifies the silver, and both are the better and the world is the better for the process. And as the refiner watches with unflagging interest the glowing fire, the shining metal, the consuming dross, so the Lord watches the process of purification. If providential trials are symbolized by the fire, they are to be regarded as so many voices calling those who pass through them to repentance. And the call to repentance, whether it come in the form of providential dealing or of direct message from God's word or God's servant, always carries with it the promise of abounding blessing. When it is obeyed, when the people begin to fear God and work righteousness, the shadow of the curse is lifted, the blight disappears from field and vineyard, heaven's windows are opened, the founts of divine mercy are broken up, and blessings beyond the capacity to receive them are poured out.

Several practical reflections ought to be noted in conclusion.

1. May not this hasty glance at the prophet's conception of Messiah give us a somewhat more exalted view of Christ? Ought we not to regard it as a part of his mission and so of his churches' mission, to right existing wrongs of every sort? It is even now a time of great unrest and agitation. There are wrongs in the social order; there is corruption in political

life; there is national unrighteousness; wild, feverish and godless gambling is rife in the commercial world. Ought we as disciples or as ministers of Christ to be indifferent to these? Has the Messiah no message now of sympathy for the wronged and oppressed and of inexorable condemnation for the oppressors?

2. Let us carefully note and faithfully follow Christ's method of meeting and dealing with wrong doing. Call back the wrong-doers to the fear of God, the beginning of wisdom and of personal righteousness. Rebuke, entreat, exhort with all long-suffering, but remember that all is in vain so long as God is not feared.

3. Let us believe in the power of Christ to heal the hurts of a sore and weary world. Let us be sure that once the fundamental law of his gospel is obeyed, wrongs will vanish and humanity will be one vast brotherhood. For this he died.

4. And if his gospel has within it this refining and purifying influence, if it is the foe of the oppressor and the friend of the oppressed, how dare we as we honor him withhold it from the perishing nations whose need of it is so deep and who as yet have not heard of it?

From the beginning of this discourse I have not talked of the other world. This silence is not due to any sympathy with the philosopher who said impatiently, "There is no other world. Here and now is the only fact." Far from it. But I have felt profoundly that in the prophetic conception of Messiah, in the Messiah's conception of his own mission, in the gospel of Christ, this world with its wrongs needing to be righted, with its burdens waiting to be lightened, with its oppressed and down-trodden ones crying for relief, this tangible world of the "here and now," fills a very large place. And when we get our Lord's conception of what needs to be done and his power to accomplish it we shall be more anxious to give his gospel to them that are perishing without it.

THE THIRD QUARTER.

LESSONS FROM THE LIFE OF PAUL.

LESSON
I. July 2. "Paul called to Europe."—Acts xvi: 6-15. REV. PROFESSOR B. O. TRUE.

II. " 9. "Paul at Philippi."—Acts xvi: 19-34. REV. E. K. CHANDLER, D. D.

III. " 16. "Paul at Athens."—Acts xvii: 22-31. REV. C. J. BALDWIN.

IV. " 23. "Paul at Corinth."—Acts xviii: 1-17. REV. PROFESSOR RUSH RHEES.

V. " 30. "Paul at Ephesus."—Acts xix: 1-12. REV. W. W. EVERTS.

VI. August 6. "Paul at Miletus."—Acts xx: 22-35. REV. J. R. GOW.

VII. " 13. "Paul at Jerusalem."—Acts xxi: 27-39. REV. PROFESSOR J. M. ENGLISH, D. D.

VIII. " 20. "Paul before Felix."—Acts xxiv: 10-25. REV. THOMAS E. BARTLETT.

IX. " 27. "Paul before Agrippa."—Acts xxvi: 19-32. REV. H. M. KING, D. D.

X. September 3. "Paul Shipwrecked."—Acts xxvii: 30-44. REV. W. S. APSEY, D. D.

XI. " 10. "Paul at Rome."—Acts xxviii: 20-31. REV. JOHN H. MASON.

XII. " 17. "Personal Responsibility."—Rom. xiv: 12-23. REV. T. D. ANDERSON.

Lesson I. July 2.

PAUL CALLED TO EUROPE.

Acts xvi: 6–15.

By Rev. Professor B. O. TRUE, D. D., Rochester, N. Y.

THIS sixteenth chapter of the Acts of the Apostles contains the first known record concerning the advent of Christ's gospel in Europe. It is not likely that this is due to the paucity of our information. While there may possibly have been scattered Christians at Rome and perhaps at some other points in Europe before Paul left Asia, this is far from certain; while it is certain that such believers, if there were any, were very few, unorganized and unaggressive. From a human point of view, till the Apostle of the Gentiles began work at Philippi, there was absolutely no prospect that Europe would be converted to the faith of Jesus. His coming was therefore a crisis, a turning of the tide in the affairs of men.

Paul's call to Europe is one of the decisive events in human history.

Asia, Europe and America embrace the nations which represent respectively the highest civilization of the past, the present and the future. The spread of civilization from Asia to Europe and its propagation from the old world to the new, mark the most notable epochs in all history. The importance of these and similar cardinal occurrences is almost never appreciated even by historians, far less by ordinary people. Pivotal deeds in the life of mankind are often almost ignored, while an unwarranted importance is ascribed to romantic and hazardous adventures. The discovery of America, four hundred years ago, and the settlement of the colonies, later, were scarcely more significant for the new world than the contributions of the Orient to European civilization. The classical nations of Southern Europe owed much to Egyptians, Phœnicians and the ancient Aryans, but the more definitely known impact of Asia against Europe at a later date is much more impressive and far more often emphasized. In their strife for the mastery of the ancient world, great warriors and armies hold a large place in political history, yet their permanent influence upon the ruling nations of modern civilization was insignificant compared with that of the single apostolic missionary who was at Troas summoned from his work in Asia to the evangelization of Europe.

There are few places so rich in their association with human emotion, thought and action, as the shores of the water-ways which separate Southeastern Europe from West Asia. Apart from Egypt, the Holy Land and a few historic cities like Rome, no portion of the earth is in historic interest comparable with this. Hereabouts the human mind first became reflective, and here it attained the most perfect flower and fruitage of its pre-christian culture. Crœsus, Midas and Mausolus, the native kings of Lydia, Phrygia and Caria, in Asia Minor, by their fabulous wealth impressed their names upon the languages of the civilized world. The Grecian colonies which sprang up east of the Aegean were in the arts and sciences scarcely inferior to the mother country. They counted among their citizens Homer, Thales, Herodotus, Hippocrates and Apelles—princes respectively in poetry, philosophy, history, medicine and painting. A few miles from the Troas of Paul was the site of ancient Troy, where the first great conflict of Greeks with Asiatics inspired Homer's immortal Iliad, written in the tongue which, enriched by later poets, philosophers and scholars, Alexander was to carry over all the East. Pergamos, famous for its library of two hundred thousand volumes, was not far distant. Five hundred years before Paul, the fleet of Darius sailed from Samos to the bay of Marathon. A decade later the immense army of Xerxes crossed the Hellespont, proud and confident of victory, yet destined to utter defeat at Salamis and Platæa. Later, Alexander the Great passed the Hellespont with 35,000 men and began his gigantic conquest of the East, so full of importance for all subsequent history. Unconscious of his mission, he spread throughout the Orient that language more perfectly fitted for transmitting to posterity the record of Christ's words and work than any other ever known, the language in which Paul was to write his matchless letters, John his gospel of love, and Luke his book of apostolic deeds. Troas Alexandria, whence Paul set sail for Europe, was one of nearly twenty cities which bore the great conqueror's name. Nearly three hundred years after Paul's vision there, Constantine fixed upon Troas as a site for the new capital of the Roman Empire, though finally selecting Byzantium, which he named Constantinople. Here and at Nicæa, Chalcedon and Ephesus, the first general councils of the Church were held, witnessing those doctrinal discussions which agitated Christendom and the Roman Empire. Three centuries later Mohammedans took possession of these shores, forcing Christianity in self-defence to push its missions among the Teutonic tribes of Northern Europe. Constantinople, however, long saved from the Moslems and a providential conservator of Greek learning, scattered the rich treasures thereof throughout the West, thus giving to the Teutons the impetus and inspiration which at last issued in the Protestant Reformation. And when this reformation was on and the Protestants were in desperate straits, from Constantinople as a Moslem capital issued those Turkish hordes whose timely attacks upon the Catholic Emperor, Charles V, saved Protestantism from re-subjection to the Roman Church.

The deeds of these temporal conquerors were "with confused noise and garments rolled in blood," but in the obscurity and solemn stillness of a night, a summons aroused the Missionary to the Gentiles, more momentous in its results than all the marching and counter-marching of earth's armies. In fact, to the European work of Paul, so sublime as the proclamation of heaven's redemptive work for the western continents, all those other historic movements were ancillary and subordinate. For that, in the providence of God, Asia was hellenized, taught the language and the modes of thought which qualified it to adopt christian truth. For it the Roman Cæsars consolidated and unified diverse nations, while the universal peace secured by the imperial administration rendered possible the extended missionary travels of Paul and his compeers, rapidly spreading the good news of the divine kingdom through Rome's entire domain, which then comprised the whole civilized world.

As Christ was the ganglion to which all important forces in human history before him converged, and through which, clarified and corrected, they again diverged to develop the distinctive elements of christian civilization, so Paul stood at the parting of the waters between Asia and Europe, in some sense the continuator of Christ's work. About that historic boundary clashed the great antagonistic powers of the ancient world. At this tragic meeting place of Asiatic and European influences, all the decisive forces of antecedent history seem to have centered in the person of Paul. From him and from the impress of the truth which he brought to Europe, all that is best worthy of permanent preservation in human history proceeded. In the strange providence of God, who makes "the wrath of man to praise him," Christian and Turk, Romanist and Protestant, Jew and Gentile, believers and infidels, the worldly ambition of rulers, no less than the fanatical superstition of multitudes, have been compelled to subserve the proclamation and the perpetuation among men of Christ's gospel.

Paul's experience before and after his passage to Europe is typical of true and effective christian work in all ages,

Some features of this experience are particularly instructive. Paul's call to Europe was divine. After that night vision at Troas he did not enter Europe seeking God's blessing upon any work that was merely his. He went to do the work of God. "When he had seen the vision, straightway we sought to go forth into Macedonia, concluding that God had called us to preach the gospel unto them."

To Paul this, like that at his conversion, was a heavenly vision, revealing the will of God. It may have been mediated by the Apostle's previous knowledge and experience, possibly by the vivid reproduction in his memory of the dress, appearance and words of some Macedonian traveler who had described to Paul the religious destitution of Europe. Yet the agency of the Holy Spirit in the vision is clearly recognized. The Spirit of Jesus hastened the journey to Troas, not suffering delay by permitting the Apostle to turn to the right into Bithynia or to the left into Southwestern Asia. Unmistakable now was the impression that he must at once change the place of his labors from Asia to Europe.

It is an invaluable inspiration for an actor at the commencement of any great or important undertaking to be assured that he is divinely called and will be divinely guided in his work. Our personal plans and preferences may be so subservient to a supreme desire to serve others that we may of right consider ourselves as really called of God to specific places of service as we are to his general work. Paul sought and received such divine guidance. When the Jews would not hear he turned to the Gentiles. When the nearer Gentiles were obdurate and hostile, he turned to "the regions beyond."

But while Paul's call to Europe was of God it was also a call from men. One of the best proofs that God calls us to a given work is that men bid us to the same. The Macedonians did not realize how greatly they needed Paul. But God knew and Paul soon knew how greatly Pagan Europe needed the gospel, Athens with its speculative philosophy, and Rome with its luxury and worldliness. Peter and the other Apostles could bear the gospel to the scattered Jews and to the Gentiles of Asia. But there was no christian apostle in Europe, and they of Europe perished for the gospel no less surely than Asiatics.

Every true missionary is sent of God because there is some human need of his presence in the place whither he goes. The perusal of Cook's "Voyages" and the godlessness of the South Sea Islanders impelled Carey to his foreign work. Judson was drawn to Burmah by the lost condition of the great Asiatic nations. Contemporaries called these men deluded adventurers, enthusiasts; but a century of missionary history approves their devotion as rational and heroic. Like Paul, they based their action on no wild fancy, but on undeniable fact. They could afford to work and to wait. The unsupplied need of multitudes of their fellow-men, a pressing and imperative demand not met, called for a supply. That was the unanswerable economic justification of the ancient as it is of the modern foreign missionary enterprise. It was the reason for the great commission. There is nothing arbitrary or capricious in that all-embracing command. It is a recognition of the great law: where sin abounds grace superabounds.

In this light the Macedonian call is a typical cry for the gospel. It was God's call issued through men's needs and men's lips. It was a cry for help. So long as mortals dwell under the shadow of sin, misfortune and death, they will raise appeals to their more favored fellows for physical, mental and spiritual help. God pity those who steel themselves never to regard such voices! Habitual neglect, indifference and stolidity may render some who most need to cry, unconscious of their state. Men can become so discouraged or desperate that passivity and silence may take the place of demonstration. But the eloquence of a need so profound that it is unconscious of its depth has a pathos all its own.

Behold this world to-day with its marvelous resources and privileges so unequally distributed. In every land human beings are reaching out to others stronger and more fortunate, for enlightenment, comfort and healing. Yet what picture of possible material need can be so pathetic as that of either youth or age passing into the valley of the great shadow "without God in the world," with no assuring word from Christ showing unto the victims his Father and our Father! Our brothers who worship an unknown God wait for us to declare unto them the true and living God. It is the cry of the ages. God grant that it may make itself heard until every member of the race has accepted the glorious gospel.

We have seen that the call of Paul to Europe was a divine call, that it was an expression of human need and that it was a typical cry. Observe now its reception. The summons was at once recognized and obeyed. From the beginning of his christian life to its close Paul was delicately responsive to every indication of God's will. This was the chief secret of his power. The first question of his christian experience was "What shall I do, Lord?" When he described his conversion to King Agrippa, years after its occurrence, he added, "I was not disobedient to the heavenly vision." It was true. Those first hours of ready obedience were followed by further enlightenment, until habitual obedience to the will of God insured repeated heavenly visions. Paul made plans for his journeys but they were always subject to revision. They were repeatedly modified as the spirit directed. So far from being self-sufficient or self-centered Paul welcomed heavenly guidance, and in that attitude always received the blessing which he craved.

Woe be to the man who never has a heavenly vision, to whom life is eating and drinking, buying, selling and getting gain; who has no high and holy mission, whose plans begin and end with himself and his selfish interests! A double woe to him who sees across his path a work of God, beholds an open door of glorious opportunity and privilege, and, refusing to enter, is disobedient to the heavenly vision ! True men seek first of all to know and do God's will. They are less anxious to push their own plans to success than to be efficient in the execution of God's. During the darkest crisis of the civil war, at a time of solemn and almost desperate interest, a trusted counsellor said to the President, "I hope the Lord is on our side." With the reverent pathos which was characteristic of him, and with the profoundest philosophy, Mr. Lincoln replied, "I hope we are on the Lord's side." In that spirit Paul went to Europe.

With such a conviction every real missionary work must be prosecuted. Of work so undertaken the success is certain. Obstacles can only intensify the conflict, and no contingencies can prevent ultimate victory. The fulfilment of any man's private plans is unimportant, but it is of the first importance for every man to conform his life to the plan of God. The immediate results of such activity may appear humble and even discouraging; but the worker may be assured that no real work for God can fail. As God lives it will be established and its results be everlasting. Paul's first convert in Europe was a woman; but her home, Thyatira, became the seat of one of the seven churches of Asia, and very likely Lydia was instrumental in its formation. Our Lord astonished his disciples by a prolonged conversation with a woman at Jacob's well, but that noonday instruction prepared for the work of Philip the Evangelist and the great gospel joy which soon filled the city of Samaria. Paul's fidelity caused his imprisonment at Philippi, but, as with Joseph, the prison became a place of more than royal triumph. It witnessed the jailer's conversion and the Apostle's speedy release.

Little did Paul know of the future christian civilization of Europe. Yet he moved forward step by step, following daily light and daily guidance, confident that by his life and labors or by his death his mission would certainly succeed. The vision which called him to Europe revealed the tragic need of immediate help for men, but it did not unveil the centuries of christian history during which the truth declared by Paul was to move the dominant nations of the world and make them the conductors of christian truth to the remotest parts of the earth. In the sublime faith which did not "ask to see the distant scene," Paul repeated the experience of ancient patriarchs and prophets. He anticipated those moral heroes of the christian centuries —the evangelists, philanthropists and patriots—who in great emergencies have "endured as seeing him who is invisible."

These men of strong discriminating faith in what shall and must be, the men who are fellow-workers with God, are the men who accomplish the Herculean tasks in the world's advance. They work with resistless power because they work with faith. They can be patient when others are disheartened. The certainty of final success robs opposition of its chief power. Such confidence of faith inspired Wiclif to speak at the peril of his life, Huss to die for the truth, Luther to take his stand against the established Church and in favor of a movement as yet unorganized and uncertain of a future. That faith sent the Pilgrim Fathers to the New World, and sustained them throughout that dreadful winter when half their number died of exposure and want. By faith and against worldly appearances Carey and Judson planted modern Foreign Missions. Cromwell, Washington, Lincoln and Cavour had it too; that is why men remember them. Such men are the true seers and saints, the genuine statesmen and patriots of earth. Over selfish adventurers like Cortez and Pizarro, or ambitious warriors like the first Napoleon, these men tower in moral grandeur like Chimborazo over the ant-heaps at its base. There is no surer mark of greatness than the vision—which Jesus had, and Paul, shared by other prophets and saints in their measure—that this or this or this is God's way, though the world with univocal bray cries, "Fool."

Lesson II. July 9.

PAUL AT PHILIPPI.

Acts xvi: 19-34.

BY REV. E. K. CHANDLER, D. D., WARREN, R. I.

THE absorbing interest of this dramatic passage culminates at two points, which surpass all others in profound significance and deep spiritual instruction, viz. :

I. The Great Question, What must I do to be saved?

II. The Great Answer, Believe on the Lord Jesus Christ.

I. *The place.* Philippi was a place of peculiar interest to the classically educated Paul. Undoubtedly he was familiar with its monumental history, representing as it did two mighty nations, which had contended for the glory of its possession.

He had studied the records of the flaming deeds of Alexander the Great; he knew the pride of his ambitious father, Philip of Macedon, to whose sagacity the city owed its name and its glory.

The region was eloquent of heroic deeds and famous battles, which doubtless he rehearsed as he pointed out the paths by which the republican army entered, the ridge on which stood the camps of Brutus and Cassius, the marsh crossed by Antony as he approached his antagonist, the hill where Cassius died by his own hand, and other scenes rich in historic interest.

As Paul and Silas walked out beneath the triumphal arch, which commemorated the great victory of Philippi ninety-four years before, to the place of prayer upon the bank of the

Gangites, they may have spoken of these heroic memories of the past.

But no such incentive was necessary to incite them on to a grander warfare. Their mission was not that of the historian or the poet. Theirs was a nobler struggle upon the shores of the new continent, a struggle for a spiritual dominion. The weapons of their warfare were not carnal "but mighty through God to the pulling down of strongholds, and bringing into captivity everything to the obedience of Christ." They proposed to found a more enduring empire than that of the Cæsars.

The collision. The impending conflict soon began. Avarice was the principle first assailed, the stronghold first to feel the shock of attack by the soldiers of the cross. To be sure, it was clothed in heathen superstition, but the principle is the same whether in pagan or in christian garb. For unholy gain a poor Pythoness, a "female slave" who was possessed with "a spirit of divination," had brought "much profit" to her employers, by appealing to the credulity of the Philippians. Her frenzied ravings, though attesting the genuineness of the Apostles' divine commission and the truth of their message, were offensive to them and injurious to the cause they advocated. The exorcism of the demon which was supposed to control her was a bold interference with the business of her greedy employers, and a stern rebuke of the deliberate fraud by which they were getting rich. The first bolt of the conflict with paganism was hurled against dishonest money getting. This shot fired the heart of the enemy as an attack upon the pocket-book usually will. The battle was on.

Incidents. In quick succession follow the arrest, the dragging to the forum, the false indictment before the civil magistrates, an early instance of the unholy alliance of Church and State, the demand of the enraged mob, the judgment of the easily bribed court, the inhuman scourging, and, finally, the deliverance to the strict guardianship of a barbarous jailer who, in perfect sympathy with the furious persecutors, cast them into an inner, dark and damp dungeon, their feet secured in the hard, unyielding wood. The midnight has come, the lonely watchman walks his appointed rounds, quiet reigns in the prison. But not all are sleeping; some are tossing upon their hard couches, vainly trying to lose their sorrows in slumber's transient dream. Hark! from the inner dungeon come forth strange sounds. The watchman springs to the door to find it securely fastened as before. The sounds become louder, so that the prisoners not yet asleep are listening to the refrain of prayer and song sweetly echoing through the dark corridors. Suddenly a terrific crash is heard. The windows rattle, the doors creak and fly open, the walls rock, the solid foundations tremble, the shackles of the prisoners are loosed as by an electric current, confusion reigns supreme in darkness like that of Egypt. The terrified jailer leaps from his couch and in the first despair of the moment is about to take his own life, when from the inner dungeon comes forth the commanding appeal, "Do thyself no harm; for we are all here." It is the gospel call to self-preservation, which since then has been echoing around the world, warning the poor dupe of his own selfish despair, whether in gamblers' den, saloon, brothel, Sabbath-breaking excursion, or standing upon the first steps that lead the self-indulging youth down to ruin. Everywhere the trumpet peal of apostolic solicitude for the well-being of others should inspire vigorous protests against all forms of sinful indulgence that lead to self-injury.

The conviction. Quick as the flash of the lights he called for as he rushed impetuously in trembling and falling down before Paul and Silas, the jailer's perturbed conscience revealed to himself his own gross sin towards the men and their God, whose presence and power he now fully recognized in the tumultous events of that fateful night. The fervent prayer came spontaneously, as a geyser's hot eruption, from his burning heart, "Sirs, Masters, what must I do to be saved!" No more important question ever sprang to the lips of man. No young man or maiden can ask any other question of such momentous import. Its significance includes earth and heaven, its scope spans time and eternity.

Doubtless, the first overwhelming rush of conviction, on the part of the astonished jailer was wrought largely by the supernatural drama of the night, but largely also, it is our privilege to believe, by the heroic loyalty of the Apostles to the truth, by their serene endurance of hardness as good soldiers of Jesus Christ, by their unselfish solicitude for the welfare of their persecutors, and their cheerful trust in God, whose special protection they manifestly enjoyed. His own base part in their ill treatment and his cowardly attempt upon his own life might well overwhelm him with remorse. Well might he, well might any awakened sinner, standing face to face with his own sinful nature and fronting the demonstration of God's presence and power everywhere open to unprejudiced eyes, ask the great question, "What must I do to be saved?"

II. The Great Answer.

The reply to this momentous question was two-fold. It involved the two central principles of Christianity, faith and obedience.

1. Faith. The answer, "Believe on the Lord Jesus Christ, and thou shalt be saved, and thy house," was addressed to an intelligent, responsible person, capable of independent self-determination. The jailer's household was promised salvation upon precisely the same conditions as himself. The individuals of that domestic circle were instructed in the same truth and received it in the same intelligent way as the head of the household himself. Christ was presented to them as the object of their several personal faith. They were to believe on him, taking him as the ground of their religious belief, the final authority for their doctrine, practice, hopes and joys. He was

to be the object of their affections, the one towards whom their love, reverence, spiritual emotions and feelings of a religious nature were to go out in loyal adoration.

He must be the ultimate ground of their religious opinions. Their views of truth must conform to his teachings. The spiritual longings of their religious nature were to be centered in him and find their sweetest satisfaction in him alone. Towards him were to gravitate all their best and holiest desires. By their personal trust in him they were to be justified from their sins and find conscious peace with God. Through this saving faith they were to be pardoned and released from the just penalty of their sins. But relying upon Jesus for exemption from the penalty of sin would not release them from the ethical obligations laid down in the sermon on the mount. Accepting Jesus as Saviour did not imply that they were henceforth to be free from the moral law. Their obligations to obey the law were not abrogated, but rather strengthened by the profession of faith in Jesus which they eagerly and promptly made. Believing on him was the entrance upon a life of practical godliness, a testimony to the genuineness of their christian profession which the world has always recognized as its right to expect and demand. Not only were they to take Jesus as their personal Saviour from the guilt of their sins, but they were to find in him a perfect Model and Pattern of life. He alone is the ideal of human excellence. No doubt the Apostles made all this and more very plain as "they spake unto him the word of the Lord, and to all that were in his house." They probably dwelt upon the sweet simplicity of the requirement, showing the younger members, if quite young, how easy a thing it is to believe on the Lord Jesus. The scope of the answer thus explained was seen to be much larger than the anxious question of the jailer, who, in his terror, thought only of himself and his personal salvation. His whole household was included in the saving grace of God, that even then was appearing to all men. So the gospel is always larger in its rich supplies of mercy than the recognized needs of man. God's compassion in the saving truth of Jesus is broader than the cries of the race. "Where sin abounded, grace did much more abound."

2. Obedience. In unfolding to the jailer and his household the nature of faith, the Apostles could not fail to teach its twin essential of salvation, obedience. In fact it is so completely woven into the texture of true faith that separation between them is practically impossible. If one truly believes on Christ he will obey Christ.

Paul's experience at Damascus, when he was not disobedient to the heavenly vision, and his presence in Philippi in obedience to the Macedonian appeal, were conspicuous illustrations of this principle. Had this pioneer evangelist been deaf to these calls of duty the opening of Europe to the gospel might have been delayed a thousand years.

It is not strange that the Apostles, being themselves the embodiment of this principle, should so emphasize its importance in their preaching that the convert would see the absolute necessity of implicit, prompt and cheerful obedience.

Lydia had confessed her faith by immediate baptism. Her cordial hospitality to the Apostles was a welcome witness to the sincerity of her profession. It is not strange that the jailer and his living household should immediately, in the very night on which they accepted Jesus as their Saviour, request baptism at the hands of the Apostles. Delay in confessing the Lord in this ordinance is nowhere in the New Testament authorized by precept or example. Instant, loving, happy, public confession of Christ in baptism, by all who embrace him, is the universal teaching of apostolic precedent.

The jailer's prompt obedience in this ordinance was not a blind freak of a frightened man or the sudden impulse of fanaticism. It was an intelligent, free, well-considered act of the will. So should it always be, and when thus observed the blessing is always sure to follow, as day succeeds the night. Neither the towering influence of Paul's character nor the awe-inspiring events of the night were sufficient to frighten him into so solemn and responsible a confession as that which he made in his baptism. He surely was no fanatic or weak-minded sentimentalist to be dominated by a whim or transient frenzy. His prompt obedience in baptism was an intelligent act, the result of sane, deliberate reflection and definite conviction of truth and duty.

The conditions were essentially the same as regards the members of his household. That there were infants in his household or in that of Lydia, too small to understand the simple truth of the Apostles' instructions and therefore baptized upon the faith of their parents, is an assumption not worthy of serious consideration. All who were baptized were capable of the same instruction and were baptized upon the same conditions of faith and obedience. Baptism is not essential to salvation, but it is essential to perfect obedience, perfect peace, and perfect development of christian character.

Before he was baptized the jailer performed an act of symbolic interest in washing the stripes of the Apostles. Here was a forecast of that practical operation of the gospel in relieving the sufferings of humanity, for which the world had wearily waited many long and dark ages. No charitable home for orphans, no hospital for the maimed and diseased, no almshouses for the poor, no kindly asylum for the deranged, no safe retreat for the aged, no such benevolent institutions shed one gleam of comfort upon the world's tidal waves of sorrow, before the introduction of the religion of the Nazarene. Paganism and infidelity do not bind up the broken-hearted, protect the weak, comfort the unfortunate or wash the stripes of those persecuted for righteousness' sake. In spite of the progress of Christianity these nineteen hundred years, there is much yet to be done in applying its humane and beneficent principles to the solution of ominous problems that seriously confront the student of sociology to-day. The spirit of our Lord acting as an emollient in human society, prevents wounds as well as binds them up.

The gospel was not intended to touch the spiritual nature of man alone, but to shed light through all the dark places of life, to lighten up its trials, to sweeten its hardships, purify its joys, heal its wounds and minister to humanity's temporal as well as spiritual needs. The converted man should ever be ready to imitate the example of the Philippian jailer in trying to heal the wounds that are constantly inflicted by the misfortunes of our human estate. The conflicts between capital and labor, the corruptions that debase our political life, the oppresions that bring hardship and sorrow to many homes of honest toil, all these practical relations of men in society need the application of the spirit of charity that was taught by him who went about doing good.

Joy reigned in that converted household after the new experiences of that memorable night. In ministering to the temporal necessities of the Apostles, its members exhibited the spirit of practical Christianity which the world ever needs, and received the profound joy which such ministrations always bring. In the prompt, intelligent and practical obedience that was manifested in the speedy baptism, we find the source of true, lasting and sweet joy. No wonder they rejoiced greatly. Young converts who promptly obey always do. No surer fountain of perennial happiness has ever been opened than that of just such loving, ready and cheerful obedience.

To such as find perpetual inspiration in this refreshing fount, the command and promise is as of old; "Go your way, eat the fat and drink the sweet, and send portions unto them for whom nothing is prepared; for this day is holy unto the Lord; neither be ye sorry; for the joy of the Lord is your strength."

Lesson III. July 16.

PAUL AT ATHENS.
Acts xvii: 22-31.

By Rev. C. J. BALDWIN, Granville, O.

PAUL on Mars Hill had as a preacher of the gospel certain great advantages. He had no need to seek an audience: a great congregation had already sought him and insisted on hearing him preach. No effort was necessary to awaken their interest; the Athenians were the most eager listeners in the world. Spending their time in hearing and telling novelties, they were anxious to listen to the Jewish preacher. They had even given him their noblest rostrum, the chief pulpit of the nation, on the Areopagus, where Demosthenes and Pericles had delivered their classic orations.

Nor was it necessary that Paul should propitiate them with reference to his theme: they were already prepossessed in favor of much that he had to say. They believed in the supernatural, the immortality of the soul, a state of rewards and punishments after death, and in a divine government of the world. The Greeks were not an atheistic or an irreligious people. They were excessively devoted to natural piety. Indeed the matter of worship was overdone by them. Their city was crowded with statues, shrines, altars. The temple and the priest were everywhere. All the social, æsthetic and intellectual life of the people was colored and shaped by ecclesiasticism. And this Paul recognized when he said, "Ye men of Athens I perceive that in all things ye are unusually religious."

What then was their deficiency and how did the Apostle propose to supply it? He saw the point of their need and addressed himself to it when he said, "As I passed along and observed the objects of your worship, I found an altar with this inscription, 'To the unknown god.' What therefore ye worship in ignorance, that I declare unto you."

They were groping in the dark; he was able to lead them into the light. The function of Christianity in this world is to interpret men to themselves, religiously: to tell them the meaning of their imperfect moral nature and its operations. The gospel does not introduce religion to men: they are religious naturally, always and everywhere. The gospel need not urge men to believe in the supernatural; they are believers already. It is not necessary to recommend worship to them; they are all worshiping something, looking up and bowing down to somewhat other and greater than themselves. Christianity never teaches men to erect temples, build altars, offer sacrifices, for these things are already done or doing everywhere. Athens is as crowded now as of old with shrines and worshipers, and the Athenians are to-day a "very religious people."

But the trouble is that men's faith is blind, their adoration misdirected. The more altars they have the worse off they are. The religion of this world is active and powerful, but it is ignorant and misleading. Now Christianity comes as the sunshine to a world lying in darkness, not to create but to reveal, not to give to men a spiritual nature but to instruct that which they have, not to build for them an altar but to show them how to use the one already existing.

Religion may exist where it is not recognized as such. Many a person is really a worshiper who does not know that he is one. What else is he who devotes his life to gain, making of wealth his chief end? Perhaps he never goes to church or reads the

Bible or offers a prayer. He calls himself an atheist. But he is not. He has a god whom he worships. He is a regular devotee at the shrine of Mammon, the deity who is never without an altar with libations thereon, and living sacrifices earnestly rendered by selfish souls.

If religion is a re-binding of the nature to that which is apart from it, above it, or greater than it, the world is full of religion. How many a temple to the goddess of Beauty and Pleasure may be seen rising in sculptured pride along the streets of our luxurious cities! How many a sanctuary to Mars, grand and awful as the Capitol at Rome, has towered above the battlefields of earth, with its red altars smoking and its trophy-hung walls!

No religion in this world?—there has always been too much of it. The great embarrassment of the gospel is that wherever it goes it finds men pre-occupied with other faiths. There are so many temples and idols that there is no room for the cross.

Even the so-called agnostic or rationalist—we use the terms without disparagement, to denote those who object to the spiritual scheme of salvation—is really an intense religionist. Instead of discarding faith in the unseen, reverence for and obedience to higher realities than the eye of flesh can see, he is exercising those qualities to the greatest extent. He has his deity, but he calls it Nature. He has his Bible, but he terms it Science. He has his altar, but he denominates it Experiment. The student of truth who rejects the supernatural is as far as we are from regarding humanity as sufficient to itself. He believes as we do in a supreme somewhat in and by which and for which are all things. He recognizes a moral government to which all responsible beings are bound, and by which right and wrong are determined and treated in connection with rewards and penalties.

And more: he has his plan of salvation, a system of deliverance from error and evil. He calls it Evolution. He trusts in a Saviour whose name is Culture. He hopes for a Heaven to which Progress is the path.

Now here is religion although it is not recognized as such. Here indeed are many of the elements or materials that Christianity asks for. And when we see the self-sacrifice and devotion of genuine scholars to their ideals, how they humble themselves and become as little children to enter the kingdom of truth, how they deny themselves, take up their cross and follow science whither it leads them; and when we mark their patience, fidelity and love toward the systems they serve, we often wish that we believers in the supernatural had their spirit. If Christ could receive from Christians the same self-denying consecration which Truth receives from the truth-seeker, it would be all that he asks for, and much more than he receives from most of us.

What then is the great need of humanity? It is light—an illumination of the realities already around us, an interpretation of the mysteries now within us. Here is the altar ready for a sacrifice: but it is to the "Unknown God," and the world is waiting for some one to decipher that inscription.

To supply this need the gospel comes as Paul to Athens. It says to the ambitious, striving soul, so full of needs and desires and efforts, "You are right in your discontent but wrong in your means of satisfying it; your hunger and thirst are natural, but you have not the true bread and water of life. Go on then in the acquisition of riches; but let me show you the genuine treasures to secure. Go on in pursuit of beauty, pleasure, peace; but take for your ideal the charm of holiness. Go on in search of truth; but let it be the primary not the secondary, the ultimate not the proximate, the cause not the effect, that you aim at."

And having said this, Christianity proceeds to substitute the perfect for the imperfect, the true for the false. In addition to its advice, it reveals a person who is the way, the truth, the life.

In Jesus Christ dwells all the fulness of the godhead bodily. He presents to us the ideal of all good, wealth that will not perish, beauty that cannot fade, power that never fails, wisdom that is supreme. He thus answers all the soul's dumb questionings and supplies all its inarticulate needs. When the ships of Columbus touched the edge of the New World, it was in the night; and although the mariners knew that their goal was before them, they must wait for the morning to gain possession of the prize. In God's own time the morning came, revealing America. In like manner the explorer of truth can never be a discoverer, until the Sun of Righteousness arises to make known the realities that lie dimly felt in the darkness. Christ is necessary to make of man a spiritual Columbus.

Specifically, the gospel interprets to us the following blind instincts:—

1. *The yearning after perfectness.* This is one of the innate and original tendencies of human nature. It is the motive power of all religions. It is peculiar to no age or land but is among the distinguishing characteristics that separate man from the brutes—dissatisfaction with the present and a longing for something better. What does it mean? Why have men always been building temples, pyramids, columns, stretching their hands and straining their eyes upward, reaching out toward ends which they cannot see? The ideals of art, philosophy, religion, even when realized never satisfy the soul; there is always a higher height not yet attained.

> "The highest mounted mind, he said,
> Still sees the sacred morning spread
> The silent summit overhead."

These things are a mystery until the light reveals to us a grand attraction on high, a Creator who has inspired the creature with an impulse toward himself. The hunger and thirst of the spiritual nature are the witnesses which God has left in man to testify to the human need of the divine. And when the waters of the sea respond to the unseen moon, and rise and fall in rhythmic movement along the shores of life, Jesus comes and explains to us the phenomenon: "No man hath seen God at any time, the only begotten Son which is in the bosom of the Father, he hath declared him." Now we understand; the instincts of faith, prayer, reverence, aspiration —all religious tendencies, are interpreted by God in Jesus Christ.

2. *The truth respecting immortality.*

The query "does death end all" did not originate with readers of the Bible. A belief in continued existence beyond the grave is indigenous to humanity. Life always refuses to accept death as a finality. But why this persistent clinging to vitality? Why build the cenotaph and tablet and keep the memory of the departed green? To these "obstinate questionings" there is no answer from natural religion. Men go on hoping, fearing, theorizing about the hereafter, and decorating the grave with every protest that art can make against the idea of extinction. But what of it all? We are but groping among the dimly seen forms of truth, and our conjectures are at best the "blank misgivings of a creature moving about in worlds not realized," until the daystar from on high visits us. "Christ brought life and immortality to light through the gospel." The resurrection of the Lord Jesus was like the morning to them that sit in darkness and the shadow of death. It justified all the dreams and vague ideas of those who refused to die or let others die, in the sense of annihilation. It explains to us our own faith in the unknown and rebukes everyone

> "Who never sees
> The stars shine through his cypress trees,
> But hopeless lays his dead away,
> Nor looks to see the morning ray
> Across the mournful marble play."

The instinct of immortality is not misleading or irrational. It is based on fact and the nature of things. History justifies it, prophecy encourages it, experience is yet to confirm it. "As by man came death, by man came also the resurrection of the dead." "We know that if the earthly house of our tenement be taken down, we have a building from God, a house not made with hands, eternal in the heavens."

3. *Man's impulses toward deliverance from evil.*

Sin and salvation are not confined to the range of scripture revelation. They are the warp and woof of religion everywhere. Not a form of paganism but is based on the ideas that men are not what they ought to be and that they may escape from their evil plight. Hence the altar and the sacrifice, the priest and the suppliant, that every clime and age have seen.

What mean these universal and perennial realities? They may be false and corrupting in their influence. But if you could abolish them and destroy every bloody shrine and ghastly offering in which the impulse of wrong-doers has found expression, what remains? *The propitiatory instinct.* This is inseparable from human self-consciousness. It is born of the conscience and its accusing power. It is the natural effect of man's sense of justice and moral obligation. Given a conviction of sin, and the idea of sacrifice inevitably follows. Sacrifice to what? Ah, that is the question. Whom shall we appease and what shall we offer because of our wrong doing? Is it some conjectural deity, or our own ethical nature, whose law has been broken and whose authority must be propitiated?

Thus men stand beside the nameless altar on which they lay their sin-offerings of many kinds. Not one conscious wrong-doer but has rendered some sacrifice there, from the slain victims of the pagan to the self-correction and consecration of the moralist. By some means sin is always made to point toward salvation.

But how blind and futile all these efforts. How they re-act in aggravation on the guiltiness which they represent. And yet they are all useful in this sense : they serve as the shadow or symbol of the truth. For they give to the gospel its text, "Whom ye worship in ignorance that I make known to you." They show the place and need of the cross of Christ. The instinct of salvation within us points to the true Saviour without us. All the sacrificial rites of natural religion have been voices in the wilderness crying " prepare ye the way of the Lord." It is by the principle of satisfaction to justice which man's moral nature has always observed, that the atonement has been heralded and prepared for.

How blessed this office of interpretation ! To go out into a world of sin and suffering and decipher the red inscriptions on its altars of agony, to tell the self-accusing and tormenting heart the meaning of its pain, to lift from the darkened eye of gropers after peace the veil that hides their object, this is the benign mission of Paul to Athens, which has never ceased.

It is the welcome errand of every believer to-day to present the cross as the antitype of the sinner's experience in striving to escape from sin. It is the clue to all the mysteries of conscience. It will answer the questions of ethical inquirers. It will consummate and crown all the ideals of souls seeking peace and purity. For it is the divine reponse to humanity straining and striving from the depths toward the heights.

" I declare unto you " is the true motto of the christian messenger. He is sent on a mission of revelation and his words and works should be full of light. Let there be no ambiguity in his statements, no apologetic tone in his voice. He has a gospel to proclaim and he should utter it with all the clearness and confidence of a herald. The word " declare " stands in the New Testament for the " preaching " of Christ and the Apostles, and it well describes the style and effect of their treatment of truth. " I have declared thy name and will declare it " was the voice of the Messiah. " I have not shunned to declare unto you the whole counsel of God" was the testimony of Paul, and "that which we have seen declare we unto you" was that of John.

These witnesses not only made the truth known, they made it clear, bright, attractive. They so emphasized divine revelation that no one could resist it. It was to them the most real, important, blessed thing that men could hear. So they "declared" it.

This is what Christianity asks for at the hands of all its servants, and it is what the world needs in order to be convinced of the truth — something more than a revelation. There may be and should be such a bright and brilliant showing forth of divine realities as will force them on the attention and credence of men. Christ himself was not only the Light of the world. He was the effulgence of the Father's glory; and Christians are to be lights of the world in the sense that their works shall "so shine before men" that the Father may be glorified of them.

We must declare the gospel. It is essentially a bold, bright, beautiful thing. Why present it timidly or tentatively, as though it were a candidate for human favor, or must depend on the results of human experiment? Let the gospel have a fair chance at men. Let the grand self-assertions of the ancient "I am" roll their thunder through the sermon and the lesson. Let the dear, divine "Ego" of the Lord Jesus be repeated and emphasized by preacher and teacher. We have a message to declare, not a theorem to demonstrate. "What ye worship in ignorance that declare I unto you."

Lesson IV. July 23.

PAUL AT CORINTH.

Acts xviii: 1-11.

BY REV. PROFESSOR RUSH RHEES, NEWTON CENTRE, MS.

FROM Athens, where in the last lesson we found Paul waiting in loneliness the coming of Timothy and Silas from Macedonia, and while waiting giving proof of the necessity that was laid upon him to preach the gospel, Paul went on, still alone, to Corinth, the centre of Greek enterprise as Athens was of Greek learning. A place of great commerce, it had a large colony of Jews, the larger for the recent edict of Claudius expelling Jews from Rome. A place of luxury and every conceivable wickedness, it peculiarly needed the message of righteousness and peace that Paul was bringing.

But when the Apostle entered the city he seems not to have thought of its peculiar fitness for his message, or even its uncommon need of it. He came as any one of the strangers always flocking thither, and, with a sort of temporary postponement of his mission, sought out among the Jews fellow tradesmen with whom he might work and earn his bread. He found among the recent arrivals from Rome some tent-makers, Aquila and his wife Priscilla; with them he made his home and they worked together. Aquila and his wife are very frequently mentioned in Paul's letters as among the most helpful of his companions, and some have thought, because there is no record of their conversion after Paul found them, that they were already Christians when they came from Rome. Apart from the improbability of there being any christian community in Rome at the time of the expulsion of the Jews, it is not likely that Luke would have failed to mention the fact if Paul, entering a strange city, had found disciples of Jesus already there. It is most natural to count Aquila and Priscilla among Paul's early Corinthian converts, and to take the record as it stands, that similarity of trade was what drew them and Paul together.

Associated with these tent-makers, Paul worked as others worked, and with the others rested and worshiped on the Sabbath. In the synagogue, and doubtless also at his daily toil, he told the message that never was long absent from his lips. Nevertheless, through all the first part of his life in Corinth his apostolic mission recedes from view. His christian activity was like that of an earnest layman in any age. Paul the Apostle seems now to have been in heart in Macedonia, with the disciples he had left there in the midst of persecution, while Paul the tent-maker was in Corinth waiting the coming of Timothy and Silas.

When these companions came all was changed. He had been weighed down by anxiety for those whom he had left in trouble after too short teaching in the new faith. They told him of the young disciples' steadfastness, and set his heart at rest. He had been hurried from place to place, nowhere having time to see the full result of his work. They told him of its permanence and fruitfulness there, and filled him with a new enthusiasm for his mission. As he would not preach to a strange people save at his own cost, he had found it necessary to spend most of his time at Corinth in getting bread. Timothy and Silas brought him from the Macedonian disciples a contribution which freed his hands. And from the time of their coming, Paul set vigorously to work to minister salvation to the Corinthians.

The period of seeming inactivity was not without result. It got him ready to work most effectively with just the people about him. His new intensity of effort took speedy effect, partly unfavorable, partly favorable. The opposition of the Jews, which was in no place long in showing itself, became outspoken and bitter, so that Paul found it impossible to work with or for them, and turned to those who were less blinded by prejudice. There went with him to begin the little christian community some who had been convinced by his ministry, and among them no less a person than Crispus, the ruler of the synagogue.

The opposition was not content with driving the Christians from the synagogue. It took harsher forms, as when, later, on the arrival of a new governor, the Jews trumped up a charge against Paul, and brought him to the judgment seat, evidently hoping that the governor's desire to please his subjects would be stronger than his sense of justice. This was the same bitterness that Paul had met at Philippi and at Thessalonica. Similar opposition, according to all appearance, accounts for his absence now from the young church at Berœa. But when the end of his work at Corinth seemed to be coming, as it had come in other cities, an experience like that which had at first called him from Troas to Macedonia, bade him work on fearlessly, braving opposition, sure of winning many in Corinth to his Master. The promise that no hurt should come to him from Jewish hate was put to a successful test in the case just mentioned, when the Jews accused Paul before Gallio, and the governor dismissed the charge as too petty even for an answer. So, instead of removing to another place where opposition had not yet risen, Paul worked on in Corinth, making there a ministry of a year and six months, departing only when his loved cause required him to return for a time to Judæa.

This history reveals three stages in Paul's work at Corinth.

1, The period of incidental though fundamental work while his thoughts were far away with the Christians he had left in Macedonia. 2, The period of intense apostolic activity which followed on the coming of his companions with comforting reports from Macedonia and with gifts that freed his time for more continuous activity. 3, The new experience of opposition ignored and of work bravely continued until the Apostle went elsewhere of his own choice.

The significance of this experience of Paul appears more clearly if we call to mind the whole course of that missionary journey which reached its goal in Corinth. With the purpose of revisiting the churches planted on his first journey, Paul had started with Barnabas through Pisidia, Pamphylia and Lycaonia. Having done his work in Derbe, Lystra and other places, he went through the regions of Phrygia and Galatia, but was hindered from preaching there. He passed one and another place, at every turn thwarted in his purpose to make his Master known. At Troas he had the vision which called him over to Macedonia, seeming to explain and end the hindrances that had so far met him. He went to Philippi, but had just begun to gather a band of converts, when heathen opposition practically drove him from the city. This did not daunt him, for he had such experience before in Pisidia. He went on to Thessalonica. The work was opening there with promise, when the Jews with whom he had been laboring became jealous and stirred up a tumult against him. He was secretly sent to Berœa, and his heart was cheered by the readiness with which the Berœans received his message. But hardly had he begun to see results from his work when Jews from Thessalonica came and stirred up a tumult there also, and Paul was sent away alone to escape the mob's wrath. Opposition he was used to, but such hindrance as left him less and less time in successive places, and drove him away from each before he could make young disciples ready for their trials, seemed a strange commentary on that direction which had brought him to Macedonia. He was conducted by the disciples to Athens, and was left there alone while Silas and Timothy were still in the North strengthening the new churches. Of his work in Athens and of his journey to Corinth we have already made study.

Is it not clear that Corinth was God's objective point in all that journey? From place to place the Apostle was hurried, leaving each time disciples seeming to need his ministry, until he reached that great centre of life and luxury. There he was bidden to stay, let his enemies do what they would. Surely God's hand was in all that hard experience, and if so the study of it can teach us much.

We may learn from it, first, that God often directs his faithful servants to build better than they know. We, of course, always recognize that the Church's growth is, from beginning to end, God's work, and this is true. But when we see the thoughts and plans of good men over-ridden, and the success desired by them reached through their continual and almost total disappointment, we are led to bow more humbly before that august Power not ourselves that makes for righteousness. God causes to praise him not only the wrath of evil men but also the well-meant but mistaken, and therefore frustrated, efforts of good men. The Lord's people are led, often by a radical and painful contradiction of their own thoughts of his work, into lines and positions of activity where their labors will have the largest possible effect for the world's uplifting. No one of us, probably, knows how much good he is doing for the cause of his Master. Our disappointments, our apparent failures, may be the very experiences by which we shall be enabled most to glorify God and bless humanity. What a comfort this is in moments when our best endeavors, to which we have bent utmost energy and consecration, seem shipwrecked! Toil on then, brother; let not your heart sink. God is with you as he was with Paul all that disappointing way from Macedonia to

Corinth. Be your heart right, your head clear with the best light prayer will give you, and your hands busy in the work of his kingdom, and God will care for all consequences. These consequences will one day be revealed, and some of them will be so splendid as to make you glad that you lived.

We see from this part of Paul's history, secondly, that God carries forward his kingdom strategically, seizing every point of special vantage and leaving unimportant positions temporarily unoccupied. When we remember what Corinth was, its large Jewish colony offering a most natural opportunity for the beginning of a christian church, its people always changing, going to and coming from all corners of the world, making the city a promising centre for the spread of the new faith into regions as yet unvisited by it, we see the strategic significance of the divine choice which sent Paul past many other cities until he found his place in Corinth. This divine leading shows us God's far-sighted purpose in Paul's work. In Troas and the other towns of Asia Minor were thousands of souls personally as needy as any in Corinth. In Philippi and Thessalonica and Berœa lived men and women enough for the Apostle's ministry for many years. Yet God rushed him from these needy places to Corinth. Why? We can never guess until we have our eyes opened to see that God's purpose is not carried out in a haphazard way, but as great generals win campaigns.

Corinth was the place from which the new salvation could spread most widely into different regions, so affecting the world's life. Corinth had such a position in the commerce of the day that whatever wrought on men there would carry persuasive credentials to the ends of the earth. Corinth contained the intensest of the world's iniquity, of the world's need, and of the world's spiritual hunger. If the gospel proved of worth for Corinth it would be mighty for the whole world's help. This is why God sped Paul to Corinth, and kept him there until the new faith was fairly rooted and could grow and bring forth fruit for the world's health.

Notice, thirdly, the application of this thought to the missionary problem. This century has brought to God's Church a happy revival of that missionary spirit which led Paul to work in Asia Minor and Macedonia, and kept him in readiness to be sent at God's bidding to cities and regions new. The feeling of universal fellowship has deepened, and men are convinced that a gospel which is good for sons of Adam in America and Europe, is good for their brothers in Asia and Africa and the islands of the sea. We hear year after year renewed calls to go to some "Macedonia" with help for souls. As the century has passed, more and more regions have been opened to the gospel. God has thus led his people to their present opportunity, and the Church has responded with men and gifts. Now, however, as more and more are called for, there rises in many hearts an objection which sees waste in spending on the salvation of one soul in Asia men and means which might minister to the salvation of ten in America. The merely sentimental answer, that these already have a chance while the Asiatics have not, is not adequate, for sentiment is likely to reply that one soul here is worth ten there. Besides, the answer is hazardous, in that it seems to set man's solicitude for souls in contrast with a divine indifference which leaves some without a chance. The mystery of life with its various complexities is not for our solving, but it is safe to say that men's love and care will never out-do God's love and care.

In the teaching of Paul's Corinthian ministry we have the true answer to the problem. The light of Christ must be put where it can reach the uttermost corners of the earth, and in each age where it will reach as far as possible for that age. God's purpose is to save the whole world. Therefore his people cannot rest in the Philippis or the Thessalonicas; they must sweep on and on, till every Corinth on earth is reached and made a missionary centre.

We observe, in the fourth place, that the Almighty proposes not to save men as so many isolated specimens of humanity, but to save human society. Corinth did not consist of a great drove of men, such as we see at fairs or in caravans, but in an organic body of rational beings. Its importance strategically consisted largely in this. God's thought of salvation is not met by the rescue of any number of individual souls to eternal life, be the number large or small. He seeks through the salvation of individual men and women to save also the social total. For each one of us human life is a little moment of an eternity toward whose infinite unexpended part we are made to look forward. But there is a general human life which abides while individuals pass on and out from sight. Call it society, call it humanity or what you will, it is that sum of life and influence into which all of us are born, the world-life, the age, the sum-total of conscious human existence. To its health or corruption we all contribute. It preserves and hands on traditions, customs, ideals and laws, though differing from age to age and in varying climes.

This humanity is to feel the vitalizing touch of Christ, in order that the customs, laws, ideals and hopes of men may be lifted up and made heavenly; and this is to occur through the winning in earth's every corner of some souls who shall live the Christlike life and be centres of Christlike influence. Therefore it is that, through interest in the salvation of other souls, which interest can never be too large, and through the opening of the whole world to the coming of Christ's ministers, God leads his people in this day, as of old he led Paul to Corinth, each at just the right time, to the places in which their work can tell most powerfully for the salvation of the great human social body. Only when this is thoroughly renovated will MAN be saved. Only then will the Son of Man see the full travail of his soul and be satisfied.

Lesson V. July 30.

PAUL AT EPHESUS.

Acts xix: 1-12.

BY REV. W. W. EVERTS, HAVERHILL, MASS.

THIS lesson divides itself into two parts. In the first part we see how the gospel attracts those who are teachable. In the second part we see how it is repelled by those who are hardened. The teachable ones were some twelve disciples of John the Baptist, who were living at Ephesus. How disciples of John happened to be found thirty years after their master's death so far away from the river Jordan we are not told, and yet it would be a strange coincidence if the labors of Apollos, an eloquent advocate of John's baptism, whose presence in Ephesus is referred to in the preceding chapter, had no connection with the formation of this little band. Apollos was a Jew from Alexandria, a city which had been the scene of the labors of the Seventy (Septuagint), who translated the Old Testament into Greek, and was the home of Philo, the learned interpreter. In Alexandria Apollos became "mighty in the Scriptures," and he hailed with enthusiasm the reformation which John had inaugurated, with repentance for its watchword and immersion for its sign. He had a perfect understanding of the significance of this movement as a preparation of the Jews for the coming Messiah. Although thirty years had passed since the ascension of Jesus, no report of it had reached Ephesus, and though Alexandria is much nearer Mount Olivet, there is no record that any attempt had been made to evangelize Egypt. At all events Apollos, when he arrived in Ephesus, was still a disciple of John.

Many of John's disciples used to consort in Judea with the Pharisees, whose frequent fasts were more congenial to them than the free and informal life of the Apostles. "The disciple is not above his master," and they did not rise above the state of doubt expressed by John in the question which he sent to Jesus from his dungeon: "Art thou he that should come or do we look for another?" If the followers of John in Judea were not convinced that Jesus was the Messiah, it is not strange if those living, like Apollos, in Alexandria, and the twelve in Ephesus, were utterly unacquainted with the triumphs of the risen and ascended Christ and of the descending Spirit.

What Apollos taught when he came to Ephesus was the necessity of repentance and of the confession of sins. The motives he urged were the fan and the fire, the fan with which the coming Messiah would separate the wheat for his garner, and the fire with which the chaff would be burned. Those who honestly repented and forsook their evil ways made a public acknowledgement of their faith by submitting to a rite that signified complete purification. John had told the people to "believe on him that should come after him," but after his own hesitation in accepting Jesus as the Messiah it is not likely that anything more definite was demanded by his successors. We are then to understand that the disciples whom Paul found at Ephesus had been taught "the way of the Lord" as far as John knew it and no further. In other words, they were in a transition state, having accepted all the light they had seen, and were now waiting for more. Their repentance was clear but their faith was clouded. They knew little of Jesus and less of the Holy Spirit, but they were seekers after God. They needed some one to "show them the way of the Lord more perfectly." Apollos had received such help from Priscilla and Aquila, and being thus qualified for service he had gone on a missionary tour to Corinth to water the field that Paul had planted.

Thus Ephesus, the metropolis of Asia Minor, was left for Paul to labor in without building on any other man's foundation. He had been gone from Ephesus scarcely a year. In this time he had first visited Jerusalem, and then he had made a tour through Asia Minor, confirming the churches which he had established. At last he is permitted to do what he had been "forbidden of the Holy Gost" to do four years before, "speak the word in Asia," the province of which Ephesus was the capital. He finds there now a small company that need but a word from him to be formed into a christian church. As a wise master builder, the Aspostle first gave his attention to stones that were already half prepared for the foundation of the temple. He sought out "those that were worthy." There are such in every community, who are waiting for light and encouragement. A new minister in a parish is sure to find some ripe souls that his predecessor had overlooked.

The very first question put to them by Paul showed that he was an advocate who knew how to get at the root of a matter at once. The specific difference between christian baptism and the baptism of John is brought out by this question. John himself recognized the same difference when he said : "I indeed baptize you with water but he shall baptize you with the Holy Ghost and with fire." The Saviour called attention to this fundamental distinction in his last interview with his Apostles, and now Paul implies by his question that christian baptism is not complete without the gift of the Holy Spirit. He knew that these men had been immersed in water but he was not satisfied unless they were immersed at the same time in the Holy Spirit. Peter had promised the gift of the Holy Spirit to those who repented and were immersed. Paul inquired whether the promise Peter had made was fulfilled in their case. This inquiry should be made of every believer. The gospel is first of all a message to the ear and to the understanding, but it is more than that. When the word of truth is mixed with faith in the heart, then the heart is quickened by the Holy Spirit. The gospel is not an interrogation point but a dialogue, with man's questions and God's answers. One who is ever questioning without ever receiving in response a witness of the Spirit, does not know what faith is. "The elders received a good report" from heaven.

The reply given to the Apostle's question indicated plainly that these disciples knew more of repentance than of regeneration, and that they were still living under the law of works and not under the law of the spirit of life. They had not heard, no one in Ephesus had heard till Paul came, of the descent of the Holy Spirit at Pentecost. They were still shut up in the dark, not knowing that it was high noon. They acknowledged their ignorance with the utmost candor. They were well named disciples for they were ready to learn. They were not satisfied with their condition nor did they treat with contempt the "strange things" that were brought to their ears. Nothing had been said to them about the Holy Spirit when they were baptized and nothing had been said to them about this subject afterwards. Members of churches to-day who are destitute of the Holy Spirit cannot justify themselves by any such plea of ignorance.

The next question expresses surprise that any one could be baptized except into the Holy Spirit. Still the Apostle is determined to fathom this singular baptism. The only baptism he recognized was immersion into the name of the Holy Spirit and of the Father and of the Son, and he desired to know into what baptism these had been baptized. What kind of baptism is that with which the Holy Spirit is not associated? What astonishment Paul would have felt if he had heard of the baptism of an infant, to which he could not even put the question: "Did you receive the Holy Spirit when you believed?" John's baptism, any baptism, that was not accompanied by the Holy Spirit, was a matter of surprise to the great Apostle and should be to all those who follow him. One might as well seal up a letter before it is written as baptize any one who is spiritually a blank. Though John's baptism was of heavenly origin, the Apostle accorded to it no validity when it was administered to persons who were both uninstructed in the truth and unenlightened by the Spirit. He would not suffer Christianity to sink, as Judaism had already fallen, into an empty ceremony. He ascribed no magical power to water. He magnified the spiritual and moral elements in the gospel and would tolerate no substitute for them. He insisted that baptism should be administered to the right persons, to those who in baptism received the answer of a good conscience, the gift of the Holy Spirit.

Paul's question they answered as frankly as before. "Into John's baptism" Then the Apostle explained to them the true relation of the Forerunner to the Lord Jesus. Before Jesus had made himself known, John referred to him as the one "who should come after him." A few months later he added: "That he should be made manifest to Israel, for this cause came I baptizing with water." He thus summed up his whole ministry in the one object of announcing and identifying the Son of God. After recalling to the minds of these disciples of John the instructions of their master, especially his command to "believe on him who should come after him," Paul presents to them Jesus as the promised Messiah. They recognized John's authority. They found in Paul's account of Jesus just the one they were looking for, and scarcely had they heard the exhortation to obedience before they were baptized, this time "into the name of the Lord Jesus."

This is the only instance of a re-baptism recorded in the New Testament. It has caused a great deal of trouble to the opponents of the Baptists and the Anabaptists, because it gives an apostolic precedent for the repetition of baptism. The result has been that learning has been disgraced in the vain efforts that men have made to force a different meaning on this passage. The repetition of baptism in this instance proves conclusively that it is not a saving ordinance, that no virtue is imparted by the act itself. It proves also that no baptism is valid unless the recipient believes in Jesus Christ and in the Holy Spirit. Indeed "no man can say Jesus is Lord, but in the Holy Spirit." It makes obligatory the re-baptism of all those whose knowledge was fundamentally defective when they were first baptized. It transfers the emphasis of the rite from the administrator and from the material element to the believing soul.

The repetition of baptism, especially by one who declared that he was sent "not to baptize but to preach the gospel" has a further significance. It proves that the Apostle insisted on the strict observance of this ceremony. No faith or good works on the part of these twelve men could atone for their imperfect baptism. He understood the pre-eminent importance of faith, and of a spiritual life, and for that very reason he insisted on baptism, not as a constituent element of grace but as an acknowledgment of grace already received. He was as eager to see it in its proper place as an exponent of faith, as he was loath to see it where it signified nothing. The Friend who rejects baptism misunderstands Paul as truly as the Romanist who ascribes to baptism power to save. After baptizing them he laid his hands upon their heads that they might receive the Holy Spirit of whom he had spoken. They were at once qualified for christian service, for they were able to address any stranger in the city in the tongue in which he was born, and they were also gifted with an insight into the secrets of a man's heart and could reprove and judge so that he would fall down on his face and worship God, declaring "God is among you indeed."

After the Apostle had established in the faith the disciples of John, he turned his attention to the disciples of Moses. For three months he labored in the synagogue. He spoke with great confidence of the things concerning the Kingdom of God, following up his arguments from the Scriptures with persuasive appeals. Such boldness on his part aroused hostility on the part of those whom he could not persuade. The only way by which they could resist his loving entreaties was by hardening their hearts. When they had decided to disobey the command of the Lord, they sought to justify themselves by speaking evil of the Way. This they did before everybody in order to hinder the progress of the gospel. Paul was compelled to seek for the disciples he had gathered another place of meeting. He found it in a school-room, where he could reason with the Greeks as he had reasoned with the Jews in the synagogue. As the teacher was in his place every day and continued the services for two years, there was opportunity for everybody to hear him, and all who lived in Asia, the western province of Asia Minor, heard the word of the Lord from his lips.

The services were confined to certain hours of the day. At other times he was working at his trade, and mention is made of his working aprons. For his aprons were taken to the sick who could not come to hear him, and the diseases departed from them. Even the handkerchiefs with which he wiped his brow during his toil were carried away to drive out evil spirits. These are called special miracles and may be compared with those with which Aaron defeated the magicians of Egypt. Ephesus was the place where magicians herded, and to prove the superiority of the gospel to their black arts those extraordinary miracles were permitted. Touching a handkerchief was like looking at the brazen serpent. All Paul's miracles were wrought in Christ's name, and the use of his handkerchief simply certified that the cure was performed by Paul's Master. There is nothing in this account favorable to the use and worship of relics. The handkerchiefs and aprons were not relics in any sense, for a relic is something taken from one who is dead. The religious impression produced by a miracle was the same whether it was wrought by means of the Apostle's hand or by his handkerchief. But if his handkerchief had been preserved and used to effect cures after his death, it would have been idolatry. As it is these special miracles prove that Paul was endowed with more power than any other Bible worthy, for when Elisha tried to raise a dead child by sending his staff to be laid upon it, he failed.

Lesson VI. August 6.

PAUL AT MILETUS.

Acts xx: 22-25.

BY REV. JOHN R. GOW, HYDE PARK, ILL.

SELDOM even in the New Testament may one find so clear a statement of a fundamental truth joined to so compact a body of illustration, as in the meagre report of Paul's farewell to the elders of the church at Ephesus. The statement is given in language attributed by common tradition to Jesus himself, "It is more blessed to give than to receive." Two principles of action are here contrasted. Egoism makes self the centre for inflowing streams. Altruism makes self a centre, but chiefly for distribution. And Jesus declares that action according to the latter principle offers to any moral being the more satisfactory results.

We might argue this truth from the outcome of action to the contrary. The miser in his dreary counting-room, the self-lover torn with jealousy, the victim of over-weening ambition, the spoiled child of luxury yielding to vice and perishing of *ennui*, the degraded recipients of misdirected charity, business rivals cutting each other's throats in obedience to an iron law of competition, employers and employed fighting for what they call their rights, and the state estopped from its high destiny by parties intent only on the spoils of office, are not to be called blessed even by poetic license of speech. Such a law of life must be an inheritance from an ancestry either animal or in some way de-humanized. Only as intelligence and morality prevail over brute instincts do men discern common interests and seek the common well-being. If humanity ascends into the divine it must be along this pathway of self-giving. Days come when treasures, never so carefully laid up in store, slip from despairing hands. Then past deeds of love must spread their heavenly pinions to bear us to the higher realms.

If God has ever drawn near to man he has moved along the heavenly portion of the same blessed way. Was not creation itself a first step in "the royal way of the cross," as a Kempis names it? God reached his Sabbath only when he had fashioned in his own image beings upon whom he might bestow himself. Has not the whole course of revelation been a continued giving as men could understand and themselves impart what they were themselves receiving?

Note three significant incidents in the ministry of Jesus. In the wilderness, incarnate self-seeking promised, "I will give thee the kingdoms of the world and the glory of them if thou wilt fall down and worship me." Incarnate self-giving replied, "Get thee hence Satan." And angels ministered to the victor. By the lake-side his own people were ready to bestow on him a crown; but the strong Son of Man again held himself only to giving, fortifying himself in this purpose by a night alone with his Father in the mountain solitude. Soon another mountain saw him transfigured. In the garden, under the walls of the city whose rulers were about to crucify him, angel guards were waiting to rescue the Lord of heaven; and there once more the choice was made to verify, even in blood-shedding, the words, "God so loved the world that he gave his only begotten Son, that whosoever believeth in him should not perish, but have eternal life." The resurrection morning began an everlasting hymn to his praise. The streams of sacrificial blood that had flowed over the altars of religion through all the ages deposited only their crystalline matter on the summit of Calvary. The altar that bore the offering for the sins of the world was glorified to dazzling whiteness by its self-offered burden. Because of its out-pouring of love the brutal tale of the crucifixion of the Son of God may and shall be rehearsed continually in that land where sorrow and pain and tears may not intrude, enhancing even the blessedness of the Lamb upon his throne. He who is able to subdue all enemies, not by the thundering of Jehu's chariots but by the ministry of love, the travail of his own soul, may surely be allowed a final opinion on the best principles of life.

After some such fashion it is possible to argue the superiority of the rule of self-giving. But in the practical stir of daily business and pleasure, it seems little more than a vision of the beautiful, a dream of the land that is very far off. A little thin-faced girl stopped to look at a fallen rose. "You can have it," said the lady from whose hand it had slipped. But the child looked from it to the blue sky long and earnestly. "Well," said the lady, "why don't you pick up the rose? It is mine." "Oh," responded the child, drawing a long breath, "I thought it was God's rose, and that he dropped it there." "You poor child," said the lady, kindly, "it is God's rose, and yours and mine, too," and she picked it up and held it out to the little girl. But the child put her hands behind her and ran off without touching the red rose, over-awed by such rare beauty coming near her forlorn life. Just so we treat this gift of God, the bliss of self-giving, unable to think it our very own because it is divine. Yet why should those made in God's image find it hard to understand that God is the centre of all beatitude when he is its eternal source, or to believe that to us supremest happiness may come from the fleeting aroma if we pass the cup of joy to our thirsty fellows?

Paul was a bolder, loftier spirit. Both in theory and in practice he accepted the Master's opinion.

1. Paul's theology was built about this principle of self-giving. The gospel as he conceived it was a story "of the

grace of God." Every man looks at the mission of Jesus from the standpoint of his own personal experience. The vision on the road to Damascus is the clue to Paul's doctrine. That he, the violent persecutor of the followers of Jesus, should have been made to see in Jesus the perfect revelation of God's love to men was an unmerited favor for which he could find no parallel. God's treatment of him, the chief of sinners, gave him a universal message. When he came to think it all out he had to use the terms with which his training had made him familiar. But all were glorified by the thought of the divine grace. He approached the old doctrine of the election of a people and of individuals from this side and softened the harshness and battered down the exclusiveness of the popular thought. He might apply to the disciples' relation to God through Jesus all the legal formularies of Jewish councils and Roman courts. He might find in the ritual of Israel the type of Jesus' mediatorship. He might speak of the death of Jesus on the cross after the fashion of the priests who delighted in the details of their bloody sacrifices. But all such special language was intended simply to describe the self-giving of God to his needy and sinful creatures. Symbols and comparisons of every kind were seized upon to convey this idea. He could even rise to the audacity of declaring that the Ephesian church was part of "the Church of God, purchased with his own blood," yet the boldest imagery was inadequate to describe his vision of "the exceeding riches of God's grace in kindness toward us in Christ Jesus." To this same "word of his grace" he turns as the last resort after all his care and reminiscence and exhortation. God might sanctify the Church by imparting new knowledge, by providential interference, by spiritual contact. But mainly he must work by the story of grace. What the law could not do in that it was weak through the flesh God had undertaken to do by the gospel. The method of ritual had come short of the needed redemption. The inner doctrine, the philosophies of the schools, the intellectual and scientific grasp of truth alike had failed to reach the miseries of the people. It was the word of grace and this alone that gathered the Church and would be able to build it up and give Christians inheritance among all the sanctified.

2. Side by side with this self-giving of God to man, Paul maintains that this same principle must absolutely prevail in the Church. Great urgency characterizes his repetition of this exhortation to the elders. "Take heed to all the flock," he says. "The Holy Spirit hath made you overseers, to feed the church." "Watch ye." "Help the weak." "Remember the words of the Lord Jesus how he himself said, It is more blessed to give than to receive." What but a thorough-going adoption of the principle of self-giving could answer to such a charge? Doubtless those poor elders of the church felt their hearts sink again within them, if indeed they at all comprehended the meaning of his earnest words. In this day christian men are still wondering if Paul and Jesus meant the things they seem to have said. The pressure of self-seeking invades the body of Christ and paralyzes many of its best intentions. Shepherds that abuse the sheep for gain, sheep that quarrel with each other over pasturage and sheep-fold and the shepherd's care offer a strange illustration of the unity of the spirit in the bonds of perfectness. Yet to the Apostle the grace received in Jesus involved the bestowal of grace in like abundance upon all that needed grace. In his mind the Church contained apostles and prophets and evangelists and pastors and teachers "for the perfecting of the saints, unto the work of ministering, unto the building up of the body of Christ."

Shall we not say, then, that the Church exists for the manifestation of the spirit of Jesus, to be the corporate incarnation of the life of God? "This is obviously God's method. When he would bring about an elevation of the world he never effects his purpose by a pull at once at the whole dead level of humanity. He has always set to work by giving special gifts to a few elect souls, and through their means leavening the whole of humanity by degrees." The doctrine of Apollos, Paul and John was to be wrought together as the doctrine of Christianity there in Ephesus in the presence of pagan philosophy and superstition. There too the application of the doctrine was to be made to the daily life, the idolatry, the trade and the splendid vice of the city. The local church is to be the constant expression of the mind of God for the world's redemption. In it the spirit of each age articulates itself in christian speech. It is to be a centre of moral and spiritual health to the changing social organism. It is not a mutual benefit association, a moral insurance company, a religious *crèche*, or even an organization for the maintenance of public worship. It is all this by being more, a body of servants of Jesus pushing the kingdom of God's grace intensively and extensively. With such a church men may be content as "their only monument." Such a church and only such a church is worth God's dying for it.

3. Our lesson contains illustration by practice as well as by theory and exhortation. Paul could declare with full sense of his responsibility that he was "pure from the blood of all men." No person in Ephesus could rise up and say that Paul had not cared for his soul. Not many had accepted the gospel of God's grace, but to the best of his ability the Apostle had fulfilled "the ministry which he had received from the Lord Jesus." How full our passage is of reminiscences of such marvellous devotion! With lowliness of mind, with tears, with trials, coveting no man's silver or gold or apparel, but caring for himself and his companions by daily labor at his trade, he gave himself to teaching publicly and from house to house, going about preaching the kingdom. He shrank from nothing that was profitable to either Jew or Greek, declaring the whole counsel of God and admonishing everyone night and day with tears. How intense, too, the flame of his devotion still was,

that had burned so brightly in Ephesus for three years. He was going to Jerusalem under constraint of the spirit. They should see his face no more. Just what was to befall him he did not know. Only as he went on clear warning came in every city that bonds and afflictions of some sort waited for him, and yet the course marked out for him in God's grace allured him more than it frightened him. He would accomplish it at any cost. In comparison with such a mission he held his own life of no account. Nor was this empty bravado. In those memorable defences of his apostolic career which he has left us, we learn how sincere was the devotion of his heart. Here was a Jew without an itching palm. Here was a man of weak bodily presence and suffering some infirmity, whose spirit feared naught that men or Satan could oppose to his ministry. Driven from city to city, hated by his fellow-countrymen, and misunderstood by those to whom he gladly gave himself, this servant of Jesus was more than willing to "fill up on his part that which was lacking of the afflictions of Christ in his flesh for his body's sake which is the Church." The spirit of self-giving utterly triumphed in him as in his Master. He gloried in his tribulations. He rejoiced in his sufferings in behalf of the disciples. He not only put the world behind him, but he forgot his own past as he stretched forward "unto the prize of the high calling of God in Christ Jesus." His swan song was full of an unearthly blessedness: "I have finished my course, I have kept the faith; henceforth there is laid up for me the crown of righteousness, which the Lord, the righteous judge, shall give to me at that day; and not only to me, but also to all them that have loved his appearing." The Roman prison could not quench his holy joy, or the Roman sword interrupt for one instant the continuity of his blessed life.

One cannot but feel after this review of the Apostle's conception of the christian faith and practice, that the principle here commended is fundamental to Christianity. More than any other it voices the essential truth of the religion of Jesus. Herein the religions of the nations fail to stand the test. Strip them of their superstitions and falsehoods and they are powerless to control the mighty passions of mankind. Christianity alone seizes upon the hearts of men and makes appeal to grateful love, because it is neither a philosophy nor an ethical code nor a scheme of life, but a simple story how God gives himself to men, in intimate and loving ways, for the removal of their weakness and misery and rebellion. It meets the wants of individuals and of mankind in its entirety, for it calls into play all the purest social instincts along the same line as God's own self-giving. For the professed believers in Jesus to substitute for this either law, ritual, or mediatorship, or even the brotherhood of humanity, is to paganize Christianity. Paul warned the Ephesian elders against the self-seeking wolves and the men who should speak perverse things to lead away the disciples. More to be deplored than the destructive critics of our Holy Scriptures are the leaders who allow the currents of an egoistic age and the false lights of the past to carry the Church away from this great pathway. "In thy light shall we see light."

One day, the great Alexander found Diogenes bathing himself in the glories of the sun. The royal conquerer stepped up to the plain, honest old philosopher, and asked him if the conqueror of the world could do him a favor. "Yes," said the happy old man, "please step aside from between me and the sun." Oh, Christian brother, let no man or opinion or earth-mist come between you and the heavenly radiance of this principle of Jesus: "It is more blessed to give than to receive!" God has given himself to us that we may give ourselves to each other and to him. In this way only shall the happiness of the world be perfected.

Lesson VII.   August 13.

PAUL AT JERUSALEM.

Acts xxi: 22-39.

BY REV. PROFESSOR J. M. ENGLISH, D.D., NEWTON CENTRE, MS.

PAUL'S fifth and final visit to Jerusalem, a chief scene of which this passage depicts, was in the highest degree dramatic. He now saw the Jewish capital for the last time. He had come with the noble object of carrying a contribution from the gentile Christians in Macedonia and Achaia to the poor among the Jewish mother church. One of the three leading Hebrew festivals, Pentecost, was in progress. He now met James the brother of Jesus. He magnanimously took upon himself the Nazaritic vow. Four times he was rescued from instant and terrible death. He conspicuously showed his remarkable tact in addressing a frenzied mob. In a most picturesque situation he declared his Roman citizenship. He appeared before the Jewish Sanhedrim. In the night "the Lord stood by him and said, 'Be of good cheer; for as thou hast testified concerning me in Jerusalem, so must thou also bear witness at Rome.'" So far as we have clear record, this visit marked the climax of Paul's unparalleled public ministry. The scene with which we particularly have to do was the meeting place of Roman power, of Jewish bigotry, and of Christian consecration. These are elements enough, certainly, to make the event of the Apostle's last visit to the Holy City one of the most striking and significant events in all his history.

The passage that we are to study introduces us to Paul when he was about completing the seven days of the Nazaritic vow, which he had willingly entered into for the sake of mollifying the prejudice against him of the believing Jews in Jerusalem. The vow was required of him at the instigation of the Zealots for the law, a part of whom, at least, were bitterly opposed to the Apostle, and had persistently striven to cripple his labors and to bring him into reproach. Petty and superfluous as Paul must have regarded this assumption of the vow, he could yet conscientiously do it, seeing that it in no wise compromised the central principle of his ministry, justification by faith independently of the law of Moses. Indeed, his present course was but an exemplification of the rule of his apostleship: "I am become all things to all men, that I may by all means save some."

"The Jews from Asia" had, from their point of view, abundant reason for attacking Paul. Asia, in its New Testament use, was a narrow strip of Asia Minor that bordered on the Ægean Sea. Of this district Ephesus was the chief city, and in Ephesus Paul had recently closed a most astonishing three years ministry. He "turned the world upside down" there. In the best meaning of the word his preaching was sensational. With such irresistible power did he reason and persuade "as to the things concerning the kingdom of God," first for three months in the synagogue and then for two years "in the school of Tyrannus," "that all they which dwelt in Asia heard the word of the Lord, both Jews and Greeks." "And God wrought special miracles by the hands of Paul," by means of which the strolling Jewish exorcists were overwhelmed and confounded. Fear fell upon all the people. "The name of the Lord Jesus was magnified." "Mightily grew the word of the Lord and prevailed." It was no wonder, then, that the Jews from Asia, stung by the recollection of the triumphs of that Ephesian ministry from which their ranks had so seriously suffered, were swift to wreak their vengeance upon the hated offender now that they had opportunity. The moment they saw him, without stopping to notice that in his christian generosity he was observing an ordinance of their own law, "they stirred up all the multitude" then crowding the temple-area at the Pentecostal feast, "and laid hands on him, crying out, men of Israel, help." They were on the point of beating the life out of him, when the Chiliarch or colonel of the Roman cohort "took soldiers and centurions and ran down upon them," carrying him off to the barracks in the Tower of Antonia.

This experience of Paul at Jerusalem emphasizes two or three lessons of universal and permanent value, which we shall now consider:

I. An aggressive christianity encounters afflictions.

If Jesus Christ has made anything clear it is surely this, that the loyalty of his disciples to himself will provoke persecution. With a noble frankness, worthy of all admiration, he warned all would-be disciples of this inevitable fact. "I came not to send peace but a sword." "Behold, I send you forth as sheep in the midst of wolves." "If they persecuted me they will also persecute you." And they did persecute him even unto the humiliating, horrible, agonizing death by crucifixion. If his precepts were thus writ large and clear in his own example, why should his disciples expect to escape? Paul followed his Lord in both teaching and precept. He wrote: "All that would live godly in Christ Jesus shall suffer persecution." Surely Paul lived "godly in Christ Jesus" and suffered persecution, as the scenes in his life that culminated in this one at Jerusalem sufficiently witness. The severity of his afflictions can be judged somewhat from his own account of them. "We were weighed down exceedingly, beyond our power, insomuch that we despaired even of life." He in effect fought with wild beasts at Ephesus, so fierce was his conflict with brutal and ferocious men. He well knew from the outset of this journey to Jerusalem that he was walking straight into a fiery furnace of tribulation "exceedingly hot." All along the way "the Holy Ghost testified " to him " in every city " at which he stopped—Philippi, Troas, Assos, Tyre, Cæsarea—"that bonds and afflictions " awaited him.

Persecution has been the common lot of pronounced ambassadors of Christ, and, with shame be it said, that persecution has in many cases had origin with the so-called people of God themselves. Chrysostom, Savonarola, Huss, Wiclif, Luther, Wesley, Whitefield, Edwards, Hannington, the Waldenses, the Huguenots, the Covenanters, the Pilgrims : how ample was their heritage of persecution, and with what sublime heroism did they receive it !

The suffering of affliction for Christ's sake is inevitable. Why it is so Jesus clearly stated to his unbelieving brothers, as he was about to start to Jerusalem to attend the last Feast of Tabernacles in his earthly ministry. " The world cannot hate you, but me it hateth, because I testify of it that its works are evil." This was the real reason of Paul's terrible treatment at Jerusalem at the hands of the unbelieving Jews from Asia, and it has been the spring of all the persecution of Christ's followers the christian ages through.

Persecution is as irrational as it is inevitable. Those Asiatic Jews incited the multitude against Paul on wholly false charges. Listen to them. " This is the man that teacheth all men everywhere against the people, and the law, and this place : and moreover he brought Greeks also into the temple and hath defiled this holy place." Every count in this indictment was untrue. At the very moment in which they preferred it Paul's course as to the Nazarite vow proved its utter falsity. With the characteristic illogicalness of persecutors the Jews from Asia in the last item of their complaint leaped to the conclusion that Paul had desecrated the temple. " For they had before seen with him 'in the city' Trophimus the Ephesian, whom they 'supposed' that Paul had brought into the temple."

II. Afflictions manifest the depth of christian happiness.

God's people are a happy people. They sing, and singing is the expression of spiritual joy. The Psalter is the consummate flower of Jewish piety, and the Psalter, while containing many "houselike airs," as Bacon says, has its "carols" too. And the carols abound. If a psalm begins with the plaintive note of the turtle-dove it is sure to end with the cheerful song of the nightingale. And the psalmists almost to a man, be it remembered, sung out of afflicted hearts. One of them triumphantly breaks forth in his environment of sorrow: " Thou wilt compass me about with songs of deliverance."

Christ's disciples sing for joy in the night of their tribulations, since Christ himself, who is their Life, possessed a serene joy that no afflictions could ruffle. So strong was his faith in his Father and his love for him, that these yielded him a peace whose tranquil deeps the cruel and unrelenting persecution of Pharisee and Sadducee had no power to disturb. When under the very shadow of the cross, he said to his disciples in a conversation that was full of prophecy concerning the tribulations which were just ahead of him and them, " Peace I leave with you ; my peace I give unto you." "Your joy no one taketh away from you." In that appalling hour his heart had peace and joy enough for itself and plenty to spare for the disconsolate hearts of his disciples.

"The kingdom of God is joy and peace in the Holy Ghost." "Rejoice in the Lord alway ; again will I say, Rejoice." These are the words of a christian Apostle who amply verified them in a baptism of affliction beyond what all other Christians' experiences have known. In the thick of his sorrows he exultingly exclaimed, "I take pleasure in injuries, in persecutions, in distresses, for Christ's sake." "I overflow with joy in all our affliction." And who cannot feel, as he sympathetically reads the record of the Apostle's journey to Jerusalem, that, in spite of the presentiment of the churches and of their strong protest against his course, enforced by his own conviction that distress would befall him, an ineffable peace filled his heart as he prayed at Miletus and Tyre, and when, at Cæsarea, he said, "The will of the Lord be done!" Finally, at Jerusalem, when half dead by the terrible beating at the hands of the bigoted Jews, and while the frenzied mob was crying out, just as that other "multitude of the people" twenty-five years before had cried out in that same Jerusalem against Jesus, Paul's Lord, "Away with him;" and after his honor had been deeply wounded by the chief captain's identifying him with the Egyptian impostor who had led four thousand daggermen out to the Mount of Olives against the Roman government, Paul's experience of his Lord's love was yet so delightful that he yearned to tell the glad-tidings to his very murderers, saying to the commander, "I beseech thee, give me leave to speak unto the people."

III. Afflictions prove the strength of christian purpose.

They both put it to the test and make it evident. "Tribulation worketh patience, and patience approvedness or tried character, and tried character hope."

The crowning glory of Jesus was a glory of the will in the face of a relentless persecution that finally sent him to the cross. How strikingly this appears in Luke's description of him, "He set his face to go to Jerusalem." Stirred to the depth of his being by the awful issue of that last journey, he summoned to his aid his splendid reserve of will-force in an indomitable purpose to press on and meet his fate. This inimitable resolve communicated itself to his body, transfusing his face with an expression of majesty, dilating his frame into a lofty and imposing grandeur, and transforming his mien into an august dignity that awed his disciples. Mark graphically paints the scene: "And they were in the way going up to Jerusalem and Jesus was going before them; and they were amazed; and they that followed were afraid."

Jesus' reign over a human soul culminates in the will. Unless he is king there he is no king at all. The history of his influence over men has shown how splendidly he has commanded the will-energy of his true disciples in the development of such traits of character as fortitude, endurance, heroism, those virtues which are essentially martial in their temper and make their possessors "terrible as an army with banners." These soldierly qualities thrive under persecution. They seem unable to come to their best quality without it.

Paul's last journey to Jerusalem and its climax in the scene in the temple were among the most convincing evidences of will-triumph in the midst of crushing afflictions, that the annals of heroism furnish. Despite the repeated testimony of the Holy Spirit that bonds and afflictions awaited him, he pressed on undaunted, the victor's cry bursting from his lips, "I go bound in the spirit unto Jerusalem." "I hold not my life of any account so that I may accomplish my course." His determination was proof against the combined pleadings of the Cæsarean Christians and his travelling companions "not to go up to Jerusalem." His heart was breaking, but his resolution was inflexible. In the temple, when he was well-nigh dead from the violence of the fierce mob, his persistent purpose equally with his tenderest love found expression in his request to the military tribune: "May I say something unto thee?" "I beseech thee, give me leave to speak unto the people."

The real heroes of the world are not the Alexanders, the Hannibals, the Cæsars, the Napoleons, but Jesus, Paul, Ambrose, Augustine, Simeon, Brainerd, Carey, Mackay. These and such as these display the most exalted courage, confronting foes more invincible and threatening than any those great military chieftains ever faced on fields of carnage. For those christian warriors stood "against the wiles of the devil, against the principalities, against the princes, against the rulers of this world's darkness."

The lesson for us of our study of Paul at Jerusalem is this: It sounds out a clarion call to the disciples of Jesus in this generation, in all christian lands, for fidelity. In our time the love of temporal comfort is almost sovereign. Our sense-life is in sore peril of becoming insubordinate by the encouraging environment in which it passes its days. Our civilization is a selfish civilization. That huge and complex thing we call the world never before began to be as potent as it is now in benumbing spirituality. It is very easy to live a luxurious life. It is very hard to live a self-denying life for Jesus Christ's sake. His disciples must look out or the hero stuff will be quite eaten out of them, and they will degenerate into a company of mere good natured and innocent people, whom the world on the whole may like, but whose presence it will not feel. We need a resolute manhood that means to deny self till it hurts, to set itself with unflinching heroism against the enervating time-spirit, and to prosecute a robust ministry against the ingrained selfishness of human nature and the manifold wicked practices of this age.

In the palmy days of the Roman legions, had a soldier consciously disobeyed the slightest wish of his commander, though unexpressed, a blush of shame would have mantled his cheek. The Apostle Paul, that "good soldier of Jesus Christ," thus owned his loyalty to the Captain of his salvation: "I am ready to die at Jerusalem for the name of the Lord Jesus." A strong infusion into the blood of modern Christendom from the vein of such a martial purpose as that, would be the most wholesome tonic it could receive to day.

"Am *I* a soldier of the cross,
A follower of the Lamb,
And shall *I* fear to own his cause,
Or blush to speak his name?"

Lesson VIII. August 20.

PAUL BEFORE FELIX.
Acts xxiv: 10-25.

By Rev. THOMAS E. BARTLETT, Providence, R. I.

IN this straightforward narrative two characters are disclosed in sharp contrast. The outlines of each are made distinct by the presence of the other. Paul is the embodiment of moral strength. He shows the manly vigor of an ideal Christian. Though a prisoner, greatly hated and in peril of life, he is self-possessed before the representative of Roman power, boldly answers the charges of his foes, keeps back nothing of his christian faith, and at last, at a favorable opportunity, makes a strong effort to reclaim his judge to virtue. Felix is the prey of moral weakness. While at the official examination he is dignified and impartial, the private, unofficial interview, when the Apostle, allowed to speak freely as a christian preacher, forces him to look righteousness in the face, presses upon him the duty of self-control and hangs over him the solemnities of the coming judgment, though he is moved for an instant even to terror, finds him unequal to the moral effort which repentance demands, and he seeks in delay escape from the pressure of the truth. Each spectacle is valuable. The example of Paul attracts to an earnest and courageous christian life; the example of Felix repels from a career of sin.

I. PAUL, THE STRONG SERVANT OF GOD.

Paul stood before the highest tribunal in Judea. His accusers were his own countrymen, his judge was an unprincipled

Roman. According to Tacitus, Felix "exercised the power of a king with the temper of a slave." Drusilla was another man's wife whom he had enticed from her husband. Jonathan, the high priest, had ventured to remonstrate with this immoral ruler, and forthwith assassins sought out the reprover and struck him down in the sanctuary. It required fortitude for an accused Jew to be calm before Felix the unrighteous. Of justice for Paul there was no hope; a low self-interest would shape this judge's decision. Paul had no Tertullus to speak for him; he made no plea for clemency, but boldly maintained his innocence. Treading in the steps of the murdered high priest, he touched his judge's private life, even with Drusilla's eyes resting upon him, and with momentary but ominous mastery shook the judge's composure.

Here was genuine courage. Before this example of heroism all shivering cowardice in the Lord's service should loathe itself. Something braver than running to a hiding-place when threatened is expected of true Christians. Christ is not satisfied merely with our repentance and submission. He would arouse us to lofty and divine courage. "Be not afraid of them that kill the body." Such words imply that Christians can be heroes.

> Oh, to be something, something!
> Able to stand for the right,
> A faithful and valiant soldier,
> A hero girded with might.

We need to sing for a while words like these to counteract the drowsiness which has crept over us in singing our hymns of trust in God. We need some bugle-blast to break our sleep if we are not to leave our noblest tasks untouched. Lost opportunities are lost world without end, and forgiveness, having no power to make good the loss, is a poor consolation.

The example of Paul in the circumstances before us ought to impel us to the active virtues, courage, self-reliance, zeal.

We cannot but admire it, and we ought to be moved to imitate what we admire.

1. There is pressing need of such virtues. Sin is about us in force: it must be resisted and put down. Upon us sin has laid its heavy chains, and they must be broken. Are we to wait motionless for a deliverer? We do ourselves and others a deep wrong when we represent the power of sin, strong as it is, as so great that the soul is helpless before it. Never yet did a soul in alliance with God valiantly withstand temptation and not win the victory. What mockery it would be to call upon us, as the Scripture does, to strive and watch and fight and stand fast and resist, if all this effort would amount to nothing.

Besides this personal struggle against evil, there is an arduous positive work to be done for righteousness on earth. The conflict between good and evil is continually at full heat. The Son of God has interposed and checked the onset of the enemy, only that he, remaining ever at hand, may lead every soul that owns him as king to a genuine though a costly advance. Here is the gospel: it must be lived and preached. Multitudes around us wait to be won to God. Earnestness and self-sacrifice must be had for their salvation. The nations are to hear heaven's message. What labor, demanding zeal and persistency, is called for to evangelize the world! Christ has sent out his call for workers. His disciples must throw away sloth and self-depreciation and press onward to posts where crowns are won.

2. Such courage and self-reliance are not opposed to reliance on God. It is not a contradiction at all for a man to have at the same time reliance on self and reliance on God. We need reliance on God if we are to accomplish anything great. We need reliance on self if we are to accomplish anything whatever. Precisely with the men who have self-reliance God elects to work, men who count it but reasonable that they

should put their utmost exertion into effort on which they crave the blessing of heaven, who cheer their hearts with the Apostle's words, "we are God's fellow workers," workers, knowing the weariness of effort, workers, not idlers, workers with God the everlasting Worker. God will bless our efforts if there are any worthy efforts to be blessed.

Why the perpetual complaint by Christians of deficiency and weakness? Are God's people the feeblest folk on earth? Have the men with one talent changed their disposition and flocked to Christ's standard, while all better-endowed souls have gone elsewhere? And how long must that poor solitary talent take comfort in publishing its loneliness? Who is not weary of this plaintive cry of feebleness from the lips of God's saints? Of course, weakness does not flee away at the prayer for pardon. Moral strength does not come up in a night even in the heart of a saint. Some must go on crutches for a while if they have lamed themselves in the service of sin. But it is pitiable to see so many able-bodied soldiers applying for hospital beds. The flower of the host is not really disabled. The shout of courage should be oftener heard in our camp. A different ideal of true humility must grow luminous before our imagination.

The Apostle supplies this. He deemed a certain reliance on self justifiable and obligatory, because into that self God had put so much of his own power. How many holy influences, how much christian work, what unmeasured power of God's spirit have been expended upon each of us to make him what he is, acquainted with the letter and the spirit of the gospel, sensitive to the call of duty, caring somewhat for Christ's honor! Is the sacred fire burned in vain? Is there not a new hero's devotion kindled, a new conqueror fitted for achievement? Some of us are like Samson, asleep; the power to carry away a city's gates is in us and we move not. In every christian congregation there is material for scores of aggressive saints. Though disciples for years some are still babes. Possible achievements by which they might be longest remembered with gratitude are not yet seriously undertaken. In God's name I charge with folly this false humility and causeless self-distrust which hold us still or make us timid when we might be with young giants' strength and young apostles' fidelity and zeal working for God. We have a right to expect that God will help us still, but who shall deem as naught the divine help that has already come? Manly reliance on self is, for the Christian, only reliance on what God has already done to equip him for service. Oh, for the spirit that is not content simply to be blessed, but longs to impart blessings; not driven from its high purpose by frowns or jeers or pains, or discouraged by difficulty, but able to withstand sharp opposition, to convince the gainsayers, and, if need be, to face principalities and powers! "I will tarry at Ephesus . . . *for there are many adversaries,*" said this spirit in Paul, and the foe soon confessed that the immemorial enchantment of Diana was on the wane. "Weep not for me," said this heavenly heroism in the heart of Jesus as he took his way from the scourge to the cross, and the throne of iniquity trembled under his step. Such a spirit is above the contempt of earth. But though it is high we must attain unto it. If it could only become common in God's host the ancient dominion of sin would soon be shaken.

II. FELIX, BOLD ONLY IN DELAY.

The preacher had not left it uncertain that what God demands is repentance. Felix knew that just then, while Paul was speaking for God, just there where he sat by Drusilla's side, he ought to renounce sin and turn to righteousness. He trembled, but he did not repent. Sin never before seemed to him so perilous, and he decided that sometime he must leave it. He was ready to answer the preacher with real respect: "What you urge is true. I ought to live a different life, but do not press me now. The time for change will come, but not now." Felix delayed his conversion. Two years went by and he came no nearer to Christ. On leaving Judea, he chose to leave Paul in chains. In fact, there is not one hint in Scripture that Felix ever became a Christian.

Here is warning against putting off repentance. Repentance may never come. But what if a man does after awhile become a Christian, is nothing to be said against the delay? Can a man neglect submission to God for a term of years, yet when he accepts pardon say truly: I ran a great risk but it is all right now; I am safe, and it is well? Is it only the risk of being lost forever that makes delay in accepting Christ deplorable? Over the peril of impenitent lives the alarm has often been sounded; it has not been struck so often over the nearer peril. Men have been warned against the risk of delay, but they are not much moved. The danger seems remote. They do not see the injury inevitably caused by the delay.

With Felix before us, we will consider this weighty truth, too seldom urged, that *impenitence every day it lasts produces irreparable loss*. Delayed conversion means continued sin, and sin damages the sinner himself and others. The effect of sin upon the soul is not taken away instantly by repentance and pardon. We drag along into the christian life the enfeebled will, the grown-up selfishness, the impaired spiritual capacity which we acquired in the years of impenitence. We expect strength for God's work, for instant nobility. We look for fervor in the divine mission we have begun to love, and they are not forthcoming. Why this want of sustained zeal for God? The fruitful cause of it all is found in our sinful past. We bear the marks of our wandering. Forgiveness releases us from divine condemnation; it does not at once, if ever, repair the damage of a sinful course.

Again, the ill influence of the old bad life on others is not arrested. Delaying repentance, we throw the weight of our example against our friends' conversion and encourage others in sin, and our pardon does not undo what we have thus done. The stone has been dropped and it must fall. It is not often given to men to lead the same souls two opposite ways. Those who betray them into sin seldom lead them back to Christ. Saul of Tarsus could inspire in less intense souls a fierce hate for Christ's disciples. He thought, at his conversion, that he of all men was best fitted to lead them to Christ. "Haste, get thee out of Jerusalem: they will not receive thy testimony," said the divine voice. "I will send thee far hence."

Delayed conversion means lost opportunities. Along our path from childhood to age there are many occasions for heavenly deeds. The hours require a soul loyal to God, instantly ready to speak and act with firm courage, able to look sin into shame. How often, when called, have we been unprepared for such holy achievements? We could not be heroic, for we still wore captive's chains, and the opportunities were lost. The victories of to-day were prepared years ago. The precious season of preparation for future power may be wasted by daily disobedience to God's call. Some equipment for christian service can be given before conversion. But this is difficult and only partial. Great duties are duties for which only matured Christians are ready. How many to-day in God's service gave themselves no christian apprenticeship, so that they now hesitate before every exacting duty, being but half-equipped? They walk with children's steps along manhood's path. If our childhood had been given to untarnished uprightness, we should have had in youth a degree of moral strength and a clearness of vision which would have carried us safely through many of youth's temptations. Had our youth been unsullied and morally victorious, we should have brought to our maturity a stability of character and a nobleness of spirit which would have served us well in meeting the severest demands upon our moral strength.

It is clear that in secular life neglect of preparation in youth stands at many a parting of ways in later years and forbids a man's choice, saying, "You cannot take the path up the heights. You must go the lower road." Many a man in such case has bowed to the inevitable, sorrowing in vain over his loss. But men dream that in the spiritual life, under redemption, they may escape in later years the weakness resulting from youthful impenitence. We fancy that pardon will repair every injury inflicted by an evil life. Pardon arrests the condemnation of God, gives us divine help and the hope of recovery from ruin. "We are saved in hope." But pardon never restores lost character. Character is a growth; it comes in well doing and strengthens by conflict; it cannot, like forgiveness, be gotten in an instant. Late conversion! Repentance when of age! What a slight injury we imagined would be wrought by the delay. As though sin could rob us of priceless years and then send us, even after contrition, along the path to heaven with step duly firm. Look at the specimens of tardy penitence whom you know. They have renounced sin; are there no marks of the forsaken evil upon them? They are serving God, but how the consequences of their former life cling to them in their heavenly march! How the shadows of our sins dog our footsteps, obtrude themselves in our best endeavors, and oppress us with their weight as we kneel before God!

Even the redeemed soul may be barely saved, as though snatched from the burning heap of its earthly deeds. Of such a one, who yet enters heaven, Paul said, " he shall suffer loss." Ah, sad shall be the loss if a soul delays the choice of the only foundation, persists in rebellion against truth and carelessly lets years of opportunity pass away unused!

Some, it may be, will maintain that there is after all a certain incidental advantage in delaying repentance. " Let us first see the world," they say, " and then when we become Christians we shall know how to fight sin." This not uncommon plea for postponing conversion needs answer. It means that an acquaintance with sin by committing it will be a preparation for christian service. Men point to Jerry MacAuley of New York who was saved from lowest degradation, yet worked successfully for the degraded. I will not caricature this thought; it is too appalling. I will only answer that the One who can perfectly sympathize with us all and who has brought hope to all sinners considered that the preparation he needed for his task was absolute freedom from sin. Jesus was pure in heart, never required repentance; and yet publicans and sinners flocked to him as doves to their windows. Sinners need the aid of those who are above their sin yet not proud or apathetic toward them. We can learn all we need to know about sin without letting it play havoc with our lives. We can view in others its stealthy approach, its full mastery, and the destruction it makes. We require no nearer view. We do not need to see fire leaping through kitchen and parlor, mounting from floor to floor, breaking through window and roof in our own dwelling in order to feel how terrible a thing is a burning home. Behold, now is the accepted time. Let the past of our lives suffice the unfruitful works of darkness. From this moment we will wear the armor of light.

Lesson IX. August 27.

PAUL BEFORE AGRIPPA.
Acts xxvi: 19-32.

By Rev. H. M. KING, D. D., Providence, R. I.

FELIX, the Roman procurator, before whom Paul had been tried at Cæsarea, and by whom he should have been acquitted, had been recalled in disgrace. Portius Festus was his successor in office, a man of very different mould and character, of whom it is said that he "had a straightforward honesty about him, which forms a strong contrast to the mean rascality of his predecessor." Felix, having been unsuccessful in extorting a bribe from the Apostle as the price of his release, had left him a prisoner at Cæsarea in the hope of thereby appeasing the Jews enraged by his oppression and cruelty. "Paul paid the penalty of a pure conscience by wearing his chain." For two years he had been incarcerated within the walls of the prætorium, when Festus, the new governor, arrived; yet in all this time the fierce enmity of the Jews against their imprisoned fellow-countryman had not abated one jot, nor had they given up their eagerness to find some opportunity to put him to death. The change of administration and the arrival of Festus filled them with hope that they could now accomplish their murderous purpose.

Three days after Festus landed at the Roman capital, he went up to Jerusalem to put himself in friendly relations with the people over whom he was to rule. At once the new chief priest, Ishmael, successor of Ananias, and the most influential man of the Jews, sought to take advantage of his friendliness and inexperience, and secure the execution of the long imprisoned Apostle of Christ. This was the demand with which they met the new governor. But they had mistaken his spirit. His reply was a noble one. "It is not the manner of the Romans to deliver any man to die before that he which is accused have the accusers face to face, and have license to answer for himself concerning the crime laid against him." Foiled in this plan, they demanded that Paul be brought to Jerusalem for trial, intending to assassinate him on the road. Festus, possibly informed of their wicked purpose, refused to accede to their wishes. Paul should be kept at Cæsarea, and should be tried there. He himself would return shortly, and then they could bring whatever accusations they had against the prisoner. The trial was held. The charges against Paul were heresy, profanation of the temple, and offense against Cæsar. In the judgment of Festus they were frivolous or unsubstantiated, and in no way rendered the prisoner worthy of death. He would have acquitted him at once, had not the fierce opposition of the Jews constrained him to make the concession of a joint hearing at Jerusalem. Then it was that Paul asserted his right as a Roman citizen, and appealed unto Cæsar, an appeal from which there was no appeal, preferring to submit himself to the unknown mercies of a heathen emperor rather than to the well-known temper of his bigoted countrymen. To the hunted and persecuted Apostle this seemed the only way of escape from a trial in which his judges and his accusers would be one and the same party. He appealed to Cæsar, to Cæsar he must go.

While Festus was waiting for an opportunity to dispatch his prisoner to Rome, a memorable scene occurred, a scene in which the kingly greatness of the Apostle was put in striking contrast with the titled littleness of those whom men called kings, and God's prophecy had its literal fulfilment--"He is a chosen vessel unto me, to bear my name before the Gentiles, and kings, and the children of Israel." King Agrippa II, the last of the Herods, the ignoble son of ignoble sires, had come on a visit to Festus, to pay his respects and congratulations to the new Roman governor. With him he brought Bernice, his sister, the sharer of his rank and of his shame. Agrippa II was not, like his father, "the king of the Jews," but possessed only a partial empire, and that with limited authority. The inspired historian accurately calls him simply "the king." "He practically became a mere gilded instrument to keep order for the Romans, with whom it was essential that he remain on good terms. They in their turn found it desirable to flatter the harmless vanities of a phantom royalty."

Soon after the arrival of Agrippa and Bernice at Cæsarea, Festus referred to the Jewish prisoner whom he held, and about whom he was not a little perplexed. The king, who had undoubtedly heard of the Apostle and was not unacquainted with his professed faith and the charges against him, expressed a wish to see and hear him, a wish which Festus was only too willing to gratify, hoping to learn something from Paul's lips on which to base an intelligent report of his case to the emperor.

The day for the hearing was fixed. It was in no sense a trial. Paul's appeal had put an end to that. It was an exhibition designed to gratify a prurient and it may be contemptuous curiosity, and at the same time the vanity of Roman host and Jewish guests. It was a show occasion. It is expressly stated that they came together "with great pomp." The Roman procurator, clothed in scarlet and surrounded by lictors, Agrippa with all the insignia of his little royalty and his gaily dressed attendants, and Bernice flashing with jewels, the great captains and the chief citizens who had been invited—all were there, a curious, self-conscious and unsympathetic assembly. Into the presence of this thoughtless and bedizened company the humble Apostle of the new spiritual faith was ushered, upon his pale and emaciated countenance the marks of his long confinement, his only insignia the prisoner's chain which hung clanking from his empurpled wrist.

It was a most impressive scene, impressive by reason of its physical and moral contrasts, power and apparent weakness, luxury and poverty, pride and humility, pampered self-indulgence and suffering self-denial, thoughtlessness and seriousness, inhumanity and tender sympathy, licentiousness and purity, scepticism and a sublime faith in God and in spiritual things. Being permitted to speak for himself, Paul slowly stretched forth his manacled hand to arrest attention, and with marvelous skill, and great self-possession and confidence, and an audacious moral earnestness, proceeded to tell the story of his exemplary Jewish life, the supernatural call that came to him, and the divine mission on which he was sent, "to open the eyes of Jews and Gentiles, to turn them from darkness to light, and from the power of Satan unto God, that they may receive forgiveness of sins, and inheritance among them which are sanctified by faith that is in Christ." Never did an orator use more consummate art in his address. Never did a holy purpose seize an occasion more firmly or employ it with such determination to a given end. Never did a man more earnestly seek to convert an unexpected opportunity into a glorious victory. Though he spoke to all the motley company, he turned his thought and his eye especially to the king, whom again and again he addressed personally, respectfully calling him by name. It was a most eloquent defence, combined with a most adroit appeal. The appeal was based upon the assumed familiarity of the king with the Jewish faith, upon his loyal adherence to national and prophetic traditions, and upon his generous openness to conviction, assumptions which required a great stretch of charity on the part of the Apostle. The defence centered, as in his address to the mob on the castle-stairs, in his supernatural vision of the Christ and in his miraculous conversion,

How could a man who had had such an experience be any different from what he was, or do aught different from what he did? How could a man be amenable to human law who was simply carrying out the instructions of the Divine Lawgiver, as made known in the sacred writings of his people, and re-enforced, and illuminated and fulfilled in the Prophet who was to come, and who had come and been crucified and raised from the dead, and by an actual manifestation of his glorified person had conquered the opposition of his heart and enlisted him in his own blessed service?

As the Apostle was borne along on the tide of his eloquent and realistic narration, he exclaimed, "Whereupon, O King Agrippa, I was not disobedient to the heavenly vision." It was that vision that had changed him from a persecutor to a disciple, that had opened his eyes to the truth, that had turned the course of his life, that had constrained him to a new career of duty and service. God who had spoken unto the fathers by the prophets, had spoken to his heart by his Son, whose superior authority he dared not disobey. And so he became a preacher of repentance and true righteousness at Damascus, on the road to which the Lord met him, at Jerusalem where Christ died and rose again, in all Judea which was the scene of much of his earthly ministry, and then, according to explicit instruction, to the Gentiles, who were also included in Christ's redemptive plan and purpose. When Paul preached the gospel in "all the coasts of Judea," we do not know; but this was the adopted business of his life. He could cross no territory and visit no country without proclaiming the riches of God's grace in Christ. Indeed all his journeyings and all his tarryings were determined by this supreme motive. This was the innocent business in which he was engaged, and it was for this reason and no other that his countrymen hated him, and hounded him, and sought to kill him, and had finally succeeded in arresting him in the temple, God having protected and sustained him hitherto by his gracious power. Moreover, Paul declared that his testimony was in entire harmony with the sacred writings of his people, Moses and the prophets, whom they all professed to honor, having foretold distinctly the sufferings of the Messiah, his resurrection from the dead, and the dawn of a new and brighter day upon the Jewish and Gentile world. Paul was but a developed Jew, a Jew to whose mind his own scriptures had been unfolded, a Jew with a broader and truer faith, a Jew who had a vision of the promised Messiah. In the light of that vision unbelief had given place to certainty, and hatred to love, so that there came to his soul a new life and a new obedience.

What is any conversion but the soul's vision of Christ? Not in the same supernatural way in which it came to Saul of Tarsus, with the dazzling light, the prostrate form, the audible voice, and the temporary blindness; but a genuine apprehension of Jesus as the Son of God, the atoning Saviour, the divine Teacher and Lord, the one altogether lovely and chief among ten thousand. Such a vision converts doubt into personal faith, and hostility or indifference into glad obedience, and quickens the soul into a new spiritual life.

Festus had up to this time sat mute under the impassioned eloquence of his prisoner, more and more astonished, it may be, by the strange words which fell from his lips about the flashing light from heaven, the pleading voice, the distinct conversation, the marvelous transformation of character and conduct as the result of that mysterious interview, the sacred prophecies and their exact fulfilment, and above all the divine prophet who had been crucified, and was declared to have risen from the dead, and was proclaimed as the author of forgiveness and the light of the whole world, Gentile as well as Jewish. This was too much for the sceptical, practical mind of the Roman. He could restrain himself no longer. Excitedly he interrupted the Apostle, who seemed to him to have lost his mental balance amid the study of prophecy and the seeing of visions and resurrections. "Paul thou art beside thyself; much learning doth make thee mad." This is the judgment of a cold, materialistic philosophy which scouts all faith in the supernatural, and can account for the sublime facts of Christianity only as the baseless dreams of visionaries. The friends of Christ thought him beside himself, and his enemies pronounced him mad and possessed of a devil. On the day of Pentecost the multitude mistook the influence of the Holy Spirit for the effect of fermented spirits. This was not the first time that the same charge had been brought against Paul. Materialism blind, earth-bound, unspiritual, is forever relegating miracles, inspiration, conversion, Christ, Christianity and heaven to the category of hallucinations, and those who believe in them to the asylum of lunatics.

Paul with great tact and courtesy met the accusation of Festus with a simple denial, and appealed to the king in confirmation of what he had said, who must have been cognizant of the facts alleged, so great was their publicity, for they occurred at the very metropolis of the nation and in connection with a great national festival. And then the Apostle pushed home the personal appeal, but in a manner most delicate and complimentary. "King Agrippa, believest thou the prophets? I know that thou believest."

The king, confused by the turn which the hearing had taken, having received more than he bargained for at the beginning, ashamed, it may be, to confess what he honestly felt, and unwilling to be entrapped into a public discussion, met the Apostle's appeal with sarcasm and contempt. "In a little thou persuadest me to be a Christian!" Whatever may have been his inward emotions, he would turn to ridicule the purpose of the Apostle to make of the Jewish king an easy convert to the despised Nazarene. On the other hand, noble, generous, serious, pathetic was Paul's reply, as taking advantage of the king's phrase, he exclaimed with all the earnestness of his renewed soul, "I would to God that, whether 'in little' or 'in much,' not only thou, but even all who hear me this day, might become such as I am, except these bonds."

Once more the royal family of Judea had been brought testingly into relation to the christian religion. Little may Agrippa II have reflected that it was his great-grandfather Herod who had commanded the massacre of the innocents, that it was his great-uncle Antipas, who had murdered John the Baptist and mocked Christ preparatory to his crucifixion, and that it was his father Agrippa I who had executed James the Elder, and imprisoned Peter, and that death or disgrace had come to each of them in swift vengeance thereafter. No such serious reflection probably came to his vain and frivolous spirit. It was his turn now. Upon his heart fell the burning words of Paul, to melt or to sear, words of reproof, of instruction, of persuasion, closing in one last impassioned appeal to him and his companions on trial (for it was their trial, not Paul's) to acknowledge the crucified and risen Christ, and be saved forever. Will his conduct differ from that of his ancestors? Will he be melted or hardened?

To find nothing in Paul worthy of death was not to find him the Apostle of eternal life. To acquit him and wish him his liberty was not to receive through his message the liberty of the sons of God. To say "he has appealed to Cæsar, to Cæsar he must go," was not to appeal anxiously to the Apostle of Christ saying, "Sir, what must I do to be saved?" The king rose and took his place in the company of his ancestors, and of all rejectors of Jesus Christ.

The scene so impressive and suggestive was over. To Paul it was no "show occasion." He had been permitted to speak for himself. Christianity had had a hearing, which was more than it always receives. But it demands more than this. It demands not only to be heard, but to be heard patiently, candidly, seriously and without prejudice. The nature and transcendent importance of its truths give to it a claim upon the thoughtful consideration of every person, whatever his station in life.

But Paul spoke not only for himself but of himself. He spoke out of his own experience. He was no theorizer. The truths he preached had been verified in his heart and life. The truth experienced and obeyed is truth made real and positive. It gives character to preaching and teaching. Obedience gives certainty to faith and conviction to utterance. Obey the heavenly vision and it will no longer remain simply a vision. It becomes a part of life. Paul knew that Christ was a risen Christ, because himself was a risen man. No man can reason you out of what you have experienced. Experience is the best interpreter of truth, and at the same time its unanswerable argument and a mighty weapon for its propagation. Paul's greatest sermons were the recital of his personal experience.

The Apostle was undoubtedly disappointed at the result of his effort. For it was not his own defense but the conversion of his hearers to Christ that he aimed at and prayed for. The audience was a most hopeless one, but he knew God was almighty. The anxious seed-sowing was followed by no signs of harvest. The eloquence of inspiration was parried by Roman scepticism. The sword of the Spirit failed to penetrate a Jewish sneer. But the brave Apostle had done his whole duty, and must leave results with God, a thing not always easy to do.

The Apostle, acquitted in the judgment of the rulers, was left a prisoner by reason of his appeal to the emperor. Before him was the perilous voyage, the shipwreck, the imperial city. By the strange providence of God, the longing of his heart and his frequent purpose which had been as frequently hindered, were to be fulfilled, and he was to have fruit among them in Rome also, by his preaching, by his bonds, and by his martyr-blood.

Lesson X. September 3.

PAUL SHIPWRECKED.

Acts xxvii: 30-44.

BY REV. W. S. APSEY, D. D., NORTH CAMBRIDGE, MASS.

THIS lesson is a simple piece of history. We do not propose to turn it into allegory, or search in it for fanciful analogies between the material and the spiritual. It is an account of real experience, the record of a great soul in a great crisis. As such, it illustrates the dealings of God with men, and emphasizes certain fundamental truths of revelation.

I. The first impression one receives in the study of this fascinating story is that of the Apostle's unique personality, perfectly adapted to the divine purposes. From the beginning, the singular influence of his character is felt on all who surround him. He goes ashore at Sidon by express permission of the centurion having him in charge, who must answer with his own life should his prisoner escape from custody. Notice that the military officer treats his alien captive with utmost kindness, suffering him to visit his friends and refresh himself, though the ship only touches at that port. The farther he goes and the more exigent the circumstances, the more distinctly does Paul loom into prominence and leadership. Captain, owner, centurion and historian all do him obeisance.

The captive Hebrew is master of every situation. Off the Cretan coast he apprehends danger and, owing to the rising tempest and the lateness of the season, counsels against continuing the voyage then. "I perceive" he says, or "I have reason to think" [Hackett] "that the voyage will be with injury and much loss, not only of the lading and the ship, but also of our lives." He is overruled, but the unwisdom of the decision is soon apparent. The history becomes tragedy and deepens to the end. When the Apostle next speaks the storm is howling through the shrouds, and all hope of succor has fled. All superfluous gear is tossed overboard, and soon the cargo goes with it into the deep. Famished and shivering, officers, passengers and crew huddle together expecting momentary death. But "Paul stands forth in the midst of them," calm, heroic, undaunted. He no longer deals in opinions, but speaks now as one having authority. He has been into the "secret place of the Most High." He has seen the invisible. He has been in touch with "the powers of the world to come." Having received a message from God, he speaks with assurance. Be of good cheer; there shall be no loss of life. I have seen an angel of God. He said to me, "Fear not Paul, thou must stand before Cæsar. I believe God. It shall be as he hath spoken unto me; but we must be cast upon a certain island." When the sailors would stealthily take to the boat and make for the shore, leaving the rest to their fate, the Apostle again declares with authority, "except these abide in the ship, ye cannot be saved," and the soldiers at once cut the boat adrift.

This brief narrative is in some sense an epitome of the great Apostle's entire life. It was not often or ever for long that "the south wind blew softly" over the seas on which he sailed. There were many other days in his career "when neither sun nor stars appeared and no small tempest lay upon him." He weathered more than one Euroclydon. His soul entered into peace at last only through the wreck of his buffeted and broken body.

Of St. Paul's character and influence we cannot hope to say

here anything new, but his demeanor amidst the scenes described in the lesson so strikingly illustrates certain facts and truths of Scripture, that we are impelled to notice briefly two of them. The first is the reality of the spiritual world. Paul's insight reaches beyond the sensuous. His is a divine clairvoyance. "There stood by me this night an angel of God, whose I am and whom I serve." The voice of God penetrates his soul. His message from the "Holy of Holies" is no cunningly worded oracle, susceptible of many interpretations, concealing thought rather than expressing it. It is clear, terse, absolute : " I have seen an angel." "Thou must stand before Cæsar." "God hath given thee all them that sail with thee." "There shall not a hair of your heads perish." There is a holy dogmatism which befits the souls to whom God and angels and the world to come are actual entities. Of many things they speak by authority. Not arrogance moves them when they say: "We know that if the earthly house of our tabernacle be dissolved, we have a building from God, a house not made with hands, eternal, in the heavens." "We know whom we have believed and are fully persuaded that he is able to keep that which we have committed unto him against that day." In the realm of the spiritual, likeness is contact ; unlikeness is distance. "The secret of the Lord is with them that fear him." To his friends he reveals all the mysteries of his love and grace.

The second thought suggested by the part which the Apostle plays in this story is the old yet ever new one of the power of God's grace in man's heart and life. Grace loses nothing by having an inherently great nature for the basis of its work. Paul would have been a ruling spirit anywhere. His intellectuality, his enthusiasm as manifest even before his conversion, his great executive ability, his tremendous will power, his transparent sincerity whether wrong or right, his loyalty to whatever authority made good to his mind its claim to service, and his unquestioned courage, constitute a combination of traits and faculties never equalled on the plane of the merely natural. In choosing Saul of Tarsus for the accomplishment of his purposes, God chose one of the mightiest of the sons of men, yet was there on this account no less but far greater opportunity for grace to work its marvels and its triumphs. Such was the man's natural greatness that grace had in him a wider sweep than in the case of smaller mortals. In this instance divine grace touched every faculty with supernal lustre, gave to every energy a new and upward bent, poured a divine life into every affection and passion, and flooded and transfigured the whole spiritual nature with "a light that never was on land or sea."

No doubt God can utilize not only relative but absolute weakness and ignorance for the accomplishment of his plans, yet he does not prefer weakness to strength. His choice of instruments and agencies proves this. His glory does not suffer by the use of greatest talent, ripest culture, most indomitable energy. As a rule, the most powerful men in his kingdom have been men of great intellectuality, of magnanimous spirit, of high and resolute purpose. They have found and accomplished their mission because of peculiar natural adaptation thereto. God has never, either by his choice of agents or by any supernatural endowment of weakness or ignorance, put a premium on mediocrity and indolence. It was necessary for the accomplishment of the work for which he was foreordained that St. Paul should be born of Jewish parents in a Gentile city; that the culture of both Greek and Hebrew schools should mingle in his mental training; that though a Pharisee of Pharisees he should also be a Roman citizen; that while physically infirm, he should be capable of enduring prolonged hardships; that he should combine the tenderness of woman with the courage of the stoutest soldier; that he should be shrewd without trickery, steadfast without bigotry, yielding to custom and circumstance, yet never sacrificing principle, "all things to all men that he might by all means save some." These elements and many more met and mingled in the Apostle's rare and majestic personality, and their effect on his character and conduct is discernible even during the short period covered by this voyage.

II. This narrative makes it evident that the force occasioning and shaping the events which it records, was the purpose and providence of God. The keynote of the story is sounded in those words to Paul, " Thou must stand before Cæsar." The divine plan required that the foremost man in the kingdom of Christ should visit the world's capital, should plead the cause of his Master at the imperial court, should win recruits for the army of his Lord in the household of Cæsar. Apparent hindrances to that plan had no real effect in delaying its consummation. The contrary winds, the multiplied landings, the transfer from ship to ship, the boisterous seas, the utter wreck "on a stern and rock-bound coast," and the tedious wintering in Malta, were all tributary to the fulfilment of a gracious and far-reaching design. It was none the less a single and controlling purpose, because of its complexity. "God fulfils himself in many ways." The tacking ships bore the incarnate decree of heaven as successfully to its destination as a single ship would have done running all the way before the wind. The relays that were essential were at hand, so that message and messenger were carried safely into the Eternal City.

We may not be able to define the exact relation of Paul's work in Rome to the subsequent spread of the gospel and the strengthening of the kingdom of Christ. It may not be ours to trace in history the effects on the general result. The spiritual "voltage" we are not able to measure. But that the choicest spirit of the age was at the great centre of an empire's activity in a crucial period of human history; that his work, done while the bright day lasted, is still telling on the ages and telling for God, of this there can be no question. And he was there by predestination, by design, in the direct providence of God.

He kindled his fires not on the summits of the hills, like the Greeks when they announced the downfall of Troy, but in the crowded cities of the empire, from Jerusalem to Rome. Amid all the intricacies and cross activities and apparent inharmonies of his career, the purpose of God, vital, intelligent, and unconquerable, is the "spirit of life within the wheels."

III. This history also vividly illustrates the province of the human in the execution of the divine plans. The zigzag course of the vessel during much of the voyage, shows us, as in diagram, the purpose of God as affected by human action, apparently deflected, modified, halted entirely amidst the breakers in "St. Paul's Bay;" yet in reality, unchanged, unarrested and always steadily moving to its destiny at Puteoli. Within the bounds of the divine decree there is ample scope for all legitimate human action. It has been shown by competent sailors acquainted with the seas traversed by Paul, that all three of the ships which bore him were skilfully navigated; that soundest judgment was exercised from first to last in handling them. Any other management of the wrecked vessel in that fierce typhoon would have caused it either to be swallowed up in African quicksands, or to be foundered with all on board in mid-sea. When the crisis came, the rescue was accomplished in the most commonplace and human way. The swimmers struck out first for land; the rest seized boards and broken pieces of the ship, or anything within reach. They were swept upon the beach, drenched, shivering and exhausted, but all alive. God had verified his promise and had given Paul all them that sailed with him; but he did it through the ordinary use of natural powers.

God's sovereignty and the free agency of man have occasioned no end of controversy. The inner harmonies of the two defy the niceties of human speech and baffle the comprehension of finite faculties; yet that they are compatible and not antagonistic, Scripture everywhere teaches, not by formal argument indeed but by bold statement. The predestined crucifixion of Christ did not lessen the deliberate wickedness of his murderers. "The determinate counsel and fore-knowledge of God" did not lessen their responsibility, or mitigate their guilt. Their ignorance may have palliated their sin but the plan of God did not. Says Dr. Pepper, "The union of God's will and man's will is such that while in one view all can be ascribed to God, in another all can be ascribed to the creature. How God and the creature are united in operation is doubtless known and knowable only to God. Free beings are ruled but are ruled as free and in their freedom. The two co-exist, each in its integrity. Any doctrine which does not allow this is false to Scripture and destructive of religion." For practical purposes we may emphasize the function of the human. It is not irreverent to say that Paul *must* plant and Apollos *must* water if God is to give the increase. The planting and the watering are, on their plane, as necessary to the harvest as is the original creation of the life in the seed. The purpose of God embraces the volition of the man.

Three attitudes are possible in relation to that purpose. The creature may antagonize it, as the sailors unwittingly did when, under cover of casting out anchors, they would have slipped away to land, leaving the rest to go down with the ship. Man may stop short of the purpose of God, as the captain and centurion doubtless did. The aim of the captain was simply to reach port in safety and unload his ship. The controlling purpose of the centurion was to deliver his distinguished prisoner to the prætorian guard. Or, lastly, the plan of the creature may be coincident with the providence of God, as was Paul's. "After I have been to Jerusalem," he says, "I must also see Rome." In all his prayers for the Church he desired that it might be God's will that he should visit them. "I longed to see you that I might impart unto you some spiritual gift." "I purposed to come unto you but was hindered hitherto." "As much as in me is, I am ready to preach the gospel to you that are at Rome also." "Whensoever I go unto Spain I will come to you." "I know that when I come I shall come in the fulness of the blessing of Christ." Paul's purpose was God's purpose. He wished to root the gospel deeper in the teeming capital of the empire. He would give impetus to the truth, and courage to the nascent church. And whether on land or sea, he was invulnerable till the hour of his reprieve should strike.

The lesson which we have studied enforces many important and practical truths. It suggests the use and rewards of consecrated gifts. It affirms the futility of every life which is in conflict with the divine will. It teaches that the largest freedom for the soul is found within the bounds of the divine purpose. It magnifies that grace which is essential to the salvation of great and lowly alike. It reveals how God's purpose is sometimes accomplished by deliverance from trial and sometimes by its patient endurance.

To the true believer both deliverance and defeat are alike success. All things work together for good to them that love God and are called according to his purpose. The true Christian will neither fear nor falter. The God of the Apostle is the God of the humblest soul that trusts him. Faith links the human to the divine, and assures the glorious destiny of the creature. God is "timing all things in the interests of Christ's kingdom." Only those who have shared in the conflict can hope to share in the triumph.

Lesson XI. September 10.

PAUL AT ROME.

Acts xxviii: 20-31.

BY REV. JOHN H. MASON, NEW HAVEN, CONN.

AT last in Rome! No wonder that Paul, striking for the great centres of life, should have been eagar to reach the imperial city. Years before at Ephesus he had said: "I must also see Rome." From Corinth he had written to the Roman Christians of his longing to be with them.

Yonder it comes, a little band of Roman soldiers with a prisoner in the midst, on the far-famed Appian Way. The sight is not so uncommon as to attract much notice. What is it to Rome that another Jew has been seized and is being hurried on to his doom? What if he die tomorrow—who cares? The tide of life will still run as strong on the Appian Way; the prisoner will be forgotten; the lustre of Rome's glory will be undimmed. Rome, supreme and complacent, looks out over the whole world and says: It is mine. Her eyes are holden that she may not see in the prisoner coming through the city gate yonder the ambassador of a kingdom before whose splendor Rome's lights shall pale.

Of the captive himself, what? Is this then the realization of his dream, to be marched into Rome with a chain on his wrist, in the custody of a military guard? But no man in that company cares less for the chain than the prisoner who wears it. It cannot fetter his spirit. No earthly sovereign can destroy the freedom of a man who is always conscious of the Heavenly Presence.

Our study is the study of a single character. We meet him as a prisoner, but the prisoner becomes a preacher and the preacher a prophet.

I. Paul the prisoner. Captivity was to Paul nothing new. He had been "in chains oft." He had just come out of a long bondage at Cæsarea. He was familiar with the wearisome delays of law, and he knew that an appeal to Cæsar did not surely mean an immediate hearing. As a prisoner he enjoyed a certain degree of freedom. Yet it would not seem strange if an eager spirit like Paul's, burning with a desire for the world's evangelization, should have fretted and consumed itself within its narrow walls. But you find in him no sign of impatience and no trace of discouragement. He gives himself little time for rest after the rigors of the voyage and the perils of the shipwreck. In three days he calls together the chief of the Jews, tells them why he is a prisoner, and why in Rome, and sums up the whole case in a word : "For the hope of Israel I am bound with this chain." It was a pregnant sentence, for it explained, first, his attitude before the Roman ; second, his attitude before the Jew ; third, his attitude toward Christ.

We must note the unswerving faith of the prisoner. Doubt sometimes gets into the heart of the Christian. Environment will have its effect. And many, applying the inductive method to an oppressed and harassed life, conclude : No God ; or a God who is ignorant ; or a God who does not care. Others interpret obstruction as a providential closing of a chosen way, and turn aside to easier paths. But with Paul doubt had no chance. He knew that he was an apostle not of men neither by man, but by Jesus Christ and God the Father. No one could convince him that he was not called to preach the gospel of the Crucified. And in all the events of his life, however mysterious, he saw the moving of a divine hand. Had Rome shut him in a dungeon with only a single ray of light to pierce the darkness, Paul would have climbed to God by the sunbeam, as saintly George Herbert phrases it. Had the sunbeam itself been shut off, Paul, in utter darkness, would still have felt a "presence that disturbed him with the joy of elevated thoughts." There was no change in Paul after the time of his conversion except the deepening of the conviction, if that were possible, that men's previous attempts after righteousness were failures and that the lost world's only hope was Christ crucified.

For Paul the prisoner, then, there was no fainting, no failure of faith, no shifting of his convictions, no trimming of his message. The influential Jews whom he so quickly called together, themselves not Christians, meeting to learn what this stranger wanted, were likely at any minute to have the cross of Christ thrust right up before them. "For the hope of Israel I am bound with this chain." That hope, as Paul saw it, was the living and dying Jesus.

There was another chain which bound Paul. It was the invisible chain of love which linked him to his Lord. The chain on his wrist was a symbol of captivity. The chain on his heart was a token of freedom.

A second meeting of the Jews was appointed; and this brings us directly to the study of

II. The prisoner as a preacher. Doubtless his preaching began with the first guard to whom he was bound. But his public preaching seems to have begun with this appointed meeting. The substance of his message is compressed into the twenty-third verse, though we need to put with this the last two verses of the lesson.

The kingdom of God, that was his theme. He preached it, we may be sure, with all the energy of his soul. They were not abstract ideas hard to be grasped, which he put before them, but truths vitalized with the life of the incarnate God. "He expounded and testified the kingdom of God, persuading them concerning Jesus." Jesus was the Word in whom they should read of God's eternal justice and of his infinite love. Jesus was the Way through which they should find the Father.

This kingdom of God was no new invention. Its foundations had been laid long before the birth of the Babe. He had come to reveal to men the nature of God and the eternal principles on which the kingdom should be builded. It was Paul's high mission to connect old systems with new. Rather it was his mission to breathe the breath of life into the corpse which the Jews were so carefully preserving. So he goes back to Moses and the prophets. There in law and prophecy and sacrifice and type and symbol, he showed them many a finger pointing to Calvary. No time seems to have been spent on speculative questions or dogmatic controversies. It was a living gospel for living men with which Paul's soul was aflame. The cross of Christ needed no guy-ropes to steady it. And so profoundly convinced was he of the impotence of every other message and of the despair which every other message should bring to the soul, that he once with sublime audacity called down the curse of heaven even on an angel who should try to substitute any other for the one which he knew was from heaven.

His theme was the sublimest which ever gained possession of the mind of man, but it was by no means easy to overcome the prejudices which had been growing and strengthening for generations. From morning until evening the work went on. Here was the preacher, right in the heart of the Roman capital, the centre of earthly power. But the resplendent name of Rome wrought no spell on Paul. His thought was busy with the splendor of a kingdom which should be universe-wide and eternity-long. He cared not for the throne of the Cæsars, which by and by should topple and fall like an iceberg drifted into summer seas, because his eye was fixed on a throne which was built upon eternal principles and which could not be touched by any attrition of time. He was anxious above all to lead these men willing captives in the train of the Heavenly King.

Had some of the Roman philosophers strolled in with the rest, the message would have been the same. Seneca was then living in Rome. In the humble room which supplied a forum for the Christian, Seneca might have learned far more of Providence and of consolation and of constancy and of happiness than he has given us in his famous works.

When the sermon was done some had accepted the truth, but not all. There was division and strife of tongues. For some, prejudice had bribed reason at the start. For some, selfishness unconquerable had stifled all suggestion of a living sacrifice. These deluded men were at war with one another, at war with themselves, at war with God.

It is an hour of destiny. The company breaks up and many depart in anger. But Paul will not let them go without one final word. To some of his hearers it will be the last which he can ever speak. He would be likely to follow them to the door. There he stands, the man prematurely old, with the ever-present guard by his side, and probably lifting his manacled hand as he had lifted it on the stairs at Jerusalem, he flings after them that sad testimony: "Well spake the Holy Ghost by Esaias the prophet unto our fathers, saying, Go unto this people and say, Hearing ye shall hear and shall not understand; and seeing ye shall see and not perceive, for the heart of this people is waxed gross, and their ears are dull of hearing, and their eyes have they closed; lest they should see with their eyes and hear with their ears, and understand with their heart, and should be converted, and I should heal them. Be it known therefore unto you, that the salvation of God is sent unto the Gentiles, and that they will hear it."

It was a sentence which would follow them and ring in their ears and prick and rankle in their consciences. It was the scripture of their own revered prophet; it was God's word spoken through him. It was God's prediction of precisely this scene. So they went out of Paul's presence warned that the guilt could not be thrust away from themselves if they would finally resist God's message. Their own hearts they had hardened; their own eyes they had closed. Thus departing they naturally had great reasoning among themselves. The sequel is know only to God.

III. The prisoner as a prophet. Prophecy in its narrower range is foretelling; in its wider range it is teaching. To look clearly and deeply into the great principles of truth and duty and to set these principles forth with authority before men is the largest function of the prophet. Hence the true prophet and the true preacher are not far apart. Just as the curtain falls on the last dramatic scene, we hear Paul's voice, predicting the triumphant advance of the gospel among the Gentiles. Let this serve simply as our introduction to the prisoner's wider work as a prophet of the Most High.

To preach Jesus was a high privilege to Paul in prison. But he was granted a privilege infinitely higher than that. Paul thanked God for his chains. Many of his hearers thanked God for his chains. And we of to-day are blind and dumb and our heart is waxed gross if we do not thank God for the chains of Paul. Some of the sublimest truths of revelation are ours because the chains were his. Here was the mysterious Providence through which God worked out the fulfilment of his plan for a completed Revelation. Four of the immortal epistles of Paul were written at just this time. Read again that Epistle to the Philippians, which leaps and throbs with the spirit of joy, and see how unfettered was the soul of the man who wrote it. There we see Christ the life, the pattern, the inspiration, the strength of the believer. "Think not that you have already found the measure of salvation; the prizes of life are ahead of you." Such was the message.

Here, too, were written the letter to the Colossians and the letter to the Ephesians, the one telling us of Christ's universal reign, the other of the Church universal in Christ. In the one we see the Church exalted as the bride, yea as the body of Christ; in the other we see Christ the head of the body; while in both we see the final shining consummation of a life that is hid with Christ in God. Dead in sin; alive in Christ. Slaves to sin; redeemed through the precious blood. Condemned by the law; saved by grace. This is the burden of the double song. In a single chapter, we find such profound and such lofty truth as this: election; redemption; inheritance; the Spirit as seal and as pledge; the call of God; the body of Christ. Gleaming through these truths are the sovereignty of God; the love of God; the power of God; our forgiveness; our acceptance; our adoption; our union with Christ; our resurrection in him; our reign with him. These great truths which pitch their shining tents outside our walls are dimly seen in this grey dawn, but they will be manifest when the light widens into perfect day.

Then the brief letter to Philemon, "the *magna charta* of emancipation," as it has been called, must be added to the rest. Think of the prisoner of Rome dealing in such truth as this, betraying such mental and moral power! The whole fibre of his intellectual and moral nature was being subdued to what it worked in like the dyer's hand.

What a debt the Church of every age will owe to Paul's chains, for we can easily believe that but for them that fiery spirit would never in these swift late years of life have taken time for solitude and meditation, without which these truths could never have become a part of his life or of our Bible. We may go farther still and say that these truths could never have had for us the living force which they possess to-day, had they not with all their transcendent, vivifying power been first thrust into a human life which was oppressed and beaten and battered and tortured by the fierce rage of man. In a crucible like that, the divine truth was stirred and made ready for humanity's need.

Not only the Church but the world owes to Paul's chains a debt which it cannot measure and which it certainly never will pay; for the revolutions and the reformations of the centuries, many of them, have been set in motion by the fettered hand of Paul.

For two years Paul remained in Rome, a prisoner, a preacher, a prophet. He preached the kingdom of God; he taught "those things which concern the Lord Jesus Christ." We do not wonder that he preached with all confidence. We are glad that no man forbade him. Yet though a prisoner in Rome, surrounded by the symbols and trophies of Rome's power, his citizenship was in heaven. He always felt

"a larger life
Upon his own impinging."

The things which are seen are temporal and shadowy. He lived in the midst of realities unseen but eternal.

We have been busy with the last paragraph of church history as penned by the Holy Spirit. And this is the closing scene: the man who beyond all others was once persecuting Christ's followers to the death, is preaching Christ crucified, man's only hope of life. From Damascus to Rome, how far, how far!

By and by came Paul's release and after that another imprisonment. At length we know that he was led out to his death by command of the inhuman monster who sat upon the world's throne. But how swift the reverses of history. In a few months more, Nero was a terror-stricken fugitive. He would have been a suicide had he not been so base a coward, and he died detested by the world.

Nero and Paul! In this world, while they were alive, Nero wore the crown and Paul the chain. Whose is the crown now, in either world?

Lesson XII. September 17.

PERSONAL RESPONSIBILITY.
Romans xiv: 12-23.

By Rev. T. D. ANDERSON, Providence, R. I.

IN the early part of his letter to the Romans, the Apostle expounds the fundamental doctrines of the christian religion.

In this latter part he applies these doctrines to the problems and duties of daily life. In the Roman church he is confronted, as ministers of the gospel are confronted even to the present day, with two opposite and antagonistic parties, the legal and the spiritual, the conservative and the liberal, or, as he terms them, the weak and the strong. Some, with large conceptions of the truth, have correspondingly broad conceptions of conduct. Others, with restricted conceptions of truth, are correspondingly narrow in their views of conduct.

How to reconcile these two parties in the one christian church, is the problem which engages the attention of him who has the care of all the churches. With the breadth of view which always characterized him, Paul recognizes that the right is not altogether with either party. He has a word of approval for each, and a word of admonition for both. A recognition of the Lord's authority, a desire to execute the Lord's purpose, and a confession of the Lord's goodness, characterize both parties. But while there is good on both sides, there are on both sides manifestations of evil. A spirit of uncharitableness is seen in the judgments of both, and to this the Apostle directs his teaching as he urges the exhortation, "Let us not therefore judge one another any more."

The first argument against this habit of uncharitable criticism is found in the truth that judgment belongs unto God, man being incompetent to render it. "Why dost thou judge thy brother? For we shall all stand before the judgment-seat of God." The Omniscient alone is competent to judge; we cannot, because of inadequate knowledge.

We have not sufficient knowledge of the mind of the Master to determine *the standard of action.* "Who hath known the mind of the Lord, or who hath been his counsellor?" "We know but in part." Even inspired apostles "prophesy but in part." "We see in a glass darkly," not yet "face to face." My conception is my working standard. It is the Master's commission to me. His word to my brother may be different. To me the Master says "Go," and I go; but how can I deny the truth of my brother's statement: "the Master says Come, and I come." We may move in opposite directions and yet both fulfil the purpose of one controlling mind. Let me be assured that my feet are planted on the truth, but let me beware how I deny that my brother stands upon the truth because he does not occupy the same square-foot of ground on which I stand. No man has a monopoly of truth. Other truth there is, which is not of my system. It is only *"with all the saints"* that "we comprehend the breadth and the length, the height and the depth." My apprehension is partial, my judgment, therefore, liable to err; only he who knoweth all things can render judgment according to truth.

Again, we are incompetent to judge because we have not sufficient knowledge of the mind of the fellow-servant to determine *the motive with which his action is performed.* "Let not him that eateth not judge him that eateth; for the Lord hath received him." Oft-times man can look no farther than the outward appearance. God looketh upon the heart. He weighs the motive. He regards the virtue of the character as well as the rightness of the conduct. Only "the judgments of the Lord are true and righteous altogether."

Yet, spite of their incompetence, how free men are to usurp this divine prerogative of judgment! Without God's knowledge, without God's love, they are quick to condemn. The strong are ready to express their contempt for the weak. The weak are all too ready to vituperate the strong. Would that zealous reformers in the christian church would oftener heed the exhortation of the Apostle, being less zealous in judging others and more zealous in judging themselves! Before the bar of God each is responsible for himself alone.

In this solemn fact the Apostle finds his second argument against the habit of judging others. "Each one of us shall give account of himself to God; let us not, therefore, judge one another any more." The relation in which a Christian should stand to his brother, must be determined in view of what God will demand of him at the last grand assize. God does not hold us responsible for our brother's action; but he does hold us responsible for our influence upon him. We are incompetent to judge, but we are under obligation to serve. "Judge ye this, rather, that no man put a stumbling-block in his brother's way."

The large demands of the divine Judge upon the Christian, and upon the Christian in relation to his brethren, the Apostle now urges especially upon the strong. There is reason in making the application especially to the strong, for in the matters under discussion they alone have freedom of choice. The strong Christian may eat or forbear eating. He may observe the day or not observe the day. The weak, however, in his present moral condition, has no choice. He *must not* eat, he *must* observe the day. To those who have the larger opportunity, the truth is the more broadly applied.

But we are not obliged to think that the entire doctrine of the relation of the strong to the weak is set forth in this chapter. Were that the case it might seem as if Paul exalted the weak man's conscience to a place of tyranny. This surely is not his teaching.

Truth is supreme. Opinion can never usurp her throne. If the weak brother's opinion is not the truth, his position is open to attack, and in the fuller presentation of the truth it may be necessary to oppose it. Paul himself was constantly leading in such opposition. He was the great champion of the liberty wherewith Christ has made us free. Even in the passage before us he does not hesitate to give his endorsement to the view of the strong. "I know," he says, and then tracing his knowledge to a christian source, he continues, "I am persuaded *in the Lord Jesus* that nothing is unclean of itself."

Not only may the position of the weak brother be attacked; there are times when his scruples have to be disregarded. They may always be disregarded by you when they are opposed to a clear conviction of your duty. "Let each man be fully persuaded in his own mind," and he need not, he must not desist out of regard for another's conscience. If he is acting counter to the consciences of others, he may, yes, ought to consider well whether his own conception of truth or duty is correct. But if, after sufficient and candid study, he is fully assured that it is his duty to act, he must act, however his action may grieve his weaker brother.

Even in matters which may be termed indifferent, the scruples of the weak brother may deserve to be set aside. Paul himself is our example. To him circumcision is nothing. At one time, on account of the Jews, he circumcises Timothy. At another time, when certain came to spy out the Christian's liberty and to bring him into bondage, he refuses to circumcise Titus. To these he "gave place in the way of subjection, no, not for an hour, that the truth of the gospel might continue" with the christian disciples.

There are, therefore, grounds on which the position of the weak brother may be attacked and his scruples disregarded. This we need to admit, in order to put the teaching of this passage in proper relation to other teachings of the Apostle, and to a general system of ethics. Nevertheless there are grounds on which the position of the weaker brother must be respected, and his scruples receive special regard. No man who is indifferent to the influence he exerts upon his brother will be able to give a satisfactory account of himself before God; for the great, enduring, ultimate law of the kingdom of God, the law with reference to which each shall be judged, is the *law of love*. "If because of meat thy brother is grieved, thou walkest no longer *according to love*."

My act is not right simply because it does not harm me. As a child of God I must look upon the things of others. Christianity is satisfied with no standard but that of love. In their endeavor to establish a standard of justice as distinct from that of love, men have brought confusion into their theology and into their ethics. In theology men have said God *must* be just, God *may* be merciful or loving. God must be just, surely; but he must be loving also. God is just because his nature impels him to be just; God is loving because his nature impels him to be loving. Certain christian teachers have alleged that God is under no obligation to redeem those already condemned for transgression of his law. Under no obligation? Does not God's nature oblige him to love? Is he simply an intellectual calculator who is satisfied when for a certain amount of virtue or vice there is meted out an arithmetical equivalent of reward and punishment? We do not so believe. Scripture does not so teach when it declares "God loved the world," when it says that "while we were yet sinners Christ died for the ungodly." God's own nature obliges him to exercise himself to the utmost for the best good of all. "God is love," and the condition of his unfaltering justice is found in his comprehensive, unwearying love.

If this is true christian doctrine, the application in christian ethics is clear. Justice is conformity to a standard; the christian standard of life is the loving nature of God. I cannot therefore be just in the christian sense unless I have love. Not what is good for me alone, nor what is good for my brother alone, but what is best for all, is to determine my action as a child of God. Only through its relation to the blessedness of all, can my action be determined as just or unjust; as good or bad; as, in the highest sense, right or wrong. Christ acknowledged this standard when he gave up his life for your weak brother. Have you made his standard yours when you are unwilling to give up your meat? "Destroy not with thy meat, him for whom Christ died."

But the Law of Love is not satisfied with the attainment of anything less than the best good of all. There are many goods. They are of divers values. Freedom in eating and drinking is a good, but this is not the highest good which Christianity has to bestow. "For the Kingdom of God is not eating and drinking; but righteousness and peace and joy in the Holy Ghost." The man who, in his zeal to establish the right to eat and drink, or the right to the free observance of a religious day, cares not how much he disturbs the peace, diminishes the joy, and undermines the righteousness of his brethren, really places the minor above the major, the subordinate above the supreme. In seeking *a* good, he misses the best good of the Kingdom of God. "Overthrow not for meat's sake the work of God."

But the strong may say in way of defense: Inasmuch as nothing is unclean of itself, may we not encourage others to imitate us in customs which are not opposed to any law of righteousness? No, says the Apostle, not so long as the weak brother considers the thing unclean, or the act unrighteous. The end of Christianity is not right conduct, viewed apart from its motive, but virtuous character. Christianity has not attained its ideal when certain legal decrees have been obeyed, but only when certain moral experiences have been evoked. Its end is not formal obedience to the divine will, but rather participation in the divine nature. A merely legal system might be satisfied with formally correct conduct, but a vital religion demands a godly character.

The teaching is sharp and decisive. "Whatsoever is not of faith is sin." Whatsoever is done without the consent of the moral nature, whatsoever is done contrary to what one believes to be right, is sin. This is striking doctrine. A man may be sinful when his action is formally right. Surely Christianity seeks something ulterior to outward conduct. But does not our best ethics confirm this view? Do we not frequently see the unhappy results of submission to precepts which may be right, and yet are in opposition to the beliefs of the heart?

In such submission the man surrenders his freedom, the birthright of moral manhood. He submits to the rule of his fellow-man. In opposition to the teaching of Christ, "Call no man master," he yields his sovereignty and lets others lay down the law of his life. This is paternalism in morals; and if under our democratic education we believe that paternalism, however great may be its temporary advantages, is not the ideal in civil government, under our christian education we must certainly admit that paternalism in ethics is far more baneful than paternalism in civics. Whatsoever is not of faith is of foreign dictation. It is the act of the bondman, not of the freeman.

By such conformity the man benumbs his sense of obligation. It is this sense which binds him to the eternal truth. It is like the cable which holds the buoy to its moorings. It may allow the man to drift in one direction and another, according to the blowing of the wind or the setting of the tide. The lower the tide of principle the greater will be the amplitude of the oscillation. But cut the cable and the man becomes an outcast, driven of the wind and tossed. The sense of obligation is the one assuring evidence that God has not forgotten us. This binds us to the eternal throne. Like the clue which Ariadne gave to Theseus, it leads through devious ways out into the world of light, of life and of love; it leads to the throne, to the feet, to the heart of God. Lose this thread and the soul is left alone, "in wandering mazes lost." Cherish your own sense of obligation; beware how you injure another's. It is the clue which binds each wandering child to the heart of the loving Father.

More fundamentally still, the performance of an act which is contrary to the soul's belief, to which the consent of the moral nature is not given, is essentially a subordination of the impulse to live for others to the impulse to live for one's self. If conscience does not always and at once recognize that the end of life is the good of all, it usually recognizes, however obscurely, that the end of life is not found in one's self alone. But when a man casts aside these larger conceptions, and performs an action simply for prudential reasons, simply because the results of such action seem to be advantageous, even though that action may be right in itself, he has found his end only in his own good. He has restricted the scope of his life; he has sinned against his own soul.

The teachings of this chapter become intelligible in proportion as we come to understand the end which Christianity seeks to attain. Christianity aims not simply to cause our actions to conform to a certain legal standard; but rather to make us partake of the nature and thus of the blessed experiences of the ever-blessed God. All conduct finds its end in character. Character is the supreme good, the good supremely worthy to be sought. The end to be sought by all Christians, is that we may "all attain unto a full-grown man, unto the measure of the stature of the fulness of Christ, who is the effulgence of the Father's glory, the very image of his substance." For the attainment of this blessedness motive is essential as well as action. Our blessedness will be complete, not simply when our acts are the acts of God; but only when our experiences are the experiences of God. "God is love, and he that abideth in love abideth in God, and God abideth in him. Love, therefore, is the fulfilment of the law."

THE FOURTH QUARTER.

STUDIES IN THE EPISTLES.

Lesson			
I.	October	1.	"The Power of the Gospel."—Rom. i: 8-17. Rev. James T. Dickinson.
II.	"	8.	"Redemption in Christ."—Rom. iii: 19-26. The Editor.
III.	"	15.	"Justification by Faith."—Rom. v: 1-11. Rev. George B. Gow, D. D.
IV.	"	22.	"Christian Living."—Rom. xii: 1-15. Rev. Wm. M. Lawrence, D. D.
V.	"	29.	"Abstinence for the Sake of Others."—1 Cor. viii: 1-13. Rev. Professor R. S. Colwell, D. D.
VI.	November	5.	"The Resurrection."—1 Cor. xv: 12-26. Rev. Charles A. Reese.
VII.	"	12.	"The Grace of Liberality."—2 Cor. viii: 1-12. Rev. Clark M. Brink.
VIII.	"	19.	"Imitation of Christ."—Eph. iv: 20-32. Rev. C. R. Henderson, D. D.
IX.	"	26.	"The Christian Home."—Col. iii: 12-25. Rev. C. C. Brown.
X.	December	3.	"Grateful Obedience."—Jas. i: 16-27. Rev. President B. L. Whitman.
XI.	"	10.	"The Heavenly Inheritance."—1 Pet. i: 1-12. Rev. Professor Wm. N. Clarke, D. D.
XII.	"	17.	"The Glorified Saviour."—Rev. i: 9-20. Rev. J. V. Garton.
XIII.	"	24.	"The Great Invitation."—Rev. xxii: 8-21. Rev. Prescott F. Jernegan.
XIII.	"	24.	"The Birth of Jesus."—Matt. ii: 1-11. Rev. H. W. Pinkham.

Lesson I. October I.

THE POWER OF THE GOSPEL.

Romans 1: 8-17.

BY REV. JAMES T. DICKINSON, ORANGE, N. J.

THE greatest man of history, writing the earliest permanent document of the greatest religion of history, the same constituting the greatest letter of history, to a little company in the greatest city of history—this is the remarkable conjunction of circumstances presented in the Epistle to the Romans. Who can estimate the influence of this letter over human hearts, minds, and lives? The great systems of theology are built on it, the mightiest reforms and revivals of history have sprung from the spiritual study of it, the most influential christian characters of history have nourished their souls on it. Yonder shrinking disciple, painfully walking thorny paths, cries, " Let me, living or dying, sustain my heart upon this uplifting book of God."

Godet calls the Epistle to the Romans " the cathedral of the christian faith." Coleridge declared it " the profoundest book in existence." Rufus Choate was in the habit of reading it as a mental stimulus before going into any great legal controversy. Chrysostom is said to have read it twice every week. Power is the characteristic of the Epistle, power to find, convince, melt, lift, transfigure.

The letter has power, not simply or chiefly because written

by a man of power, but because it unfolds a gospel of power. Very completely is the character of the Epistle brought out in verses sixteen and seventeen: "I am not ashamed of the gospel of Christ: for it is the power of God unto salvation to everyone that believeth; to the Jew first and also to the Greek. For therein is the righteousness of God revealed from faith to faith: as it is written, The just shall live by faith." All that follows in the Epistle is simply an expansion of these two verses. But these verses look both backward and forward, and we may find an exposition and emphasis of them in our lesson for to-day. The power of the Gospel—evidences and sources of that power as given in the opening verses of Romans—let this be the subject to engage our thoughts in the present study.

The power of the gospel is seen in Paul's unconscious revelation of his own heart in these opening salutations. He refers to himself as a slave, a bond-servant of Jesus. What more touching or remarkable than such an expression from such a man as the great Apostle? This Jew who gloried in his blue Hebrew blood, this scholar whose memory was stored with the rich spoils of learning, whose brain heaved with titanic thoughts, this master of men, before the magic of whose eloquence great assemblies bow, deliberately calls himself the bond-servant of the despised and crucified Jesus. A chain is about his feet, a golden chain of love, and a yoke upon his shoulders, the yoke fashioned and imposed by the Carpenter's Son. What humility!

But Paul shows himself to be more than humble, more even than a slave. Read again the opening verses of the chapter, lingering especially over the eighth. What exultant gladness, spontaneous thanksgiving, overflowing ecstasy! Paul is a Christ-intoxicated man. His slavery is heaven to him. His fetters he kisses for very love of them. His yoke is light, bringing him joy instead of heaviness. His cross is a pair of wings, strong and swift, to bear him over moor, fen, crag, torrent, and every other obstacle. Seven times in the first eight verses he speaks of Christ. The Epistle is in every line redolent with the Apostle's love for his Lord.

We cannot but notice another proof of the change wrought in the Apostle by the gospel, in the tone of his utterances to the Roman Christians. He is ready to preach the gospel to them. He even longs to do this; while with ardent and courteous yet delicate language he intimates that they may help him as truly as he can help them. He who had gloried in his Jewish caste and thought of other nations as hardly deserving God's notice, is now freely drawn by an overmastering love to minister to men of alien blood, whom he has never seen. He who recently gloried in culture now joys in servitude; he who was zealous unto death against Christ now enthrones Christ in his heart; he who was proud, fierce, and reckless of others' feelings, is now become the most unselfish man that ever lived. The bitter waters are made sweet; the thornbush smiles with flowers.

The power of the gospel is manifested in the fact that there were Christians "in Rome, beloved by God, called to be saints." Accounts of the indescribable immorality of Rome, then the mistress of the world, are only too familiar. The city was the receptacle of nameless iniquities from all the quarters of the earth. So terrible were Roman morals and customs that Paul can only hint at them as works of darkness of which it is a shame to speak. Nearly half the inhabitants of the city were wretched slaves. Gross heathen rites, contemptuous infidelity, wild lust, unbridled cruelty, degraded womanhood, brutalized manhood—these filled alike the georgeous palaces and the miserable hovels of Rome with gloom and death.

> "In that hard Pagan world disgust
> And secret loathing fell;
> Deep weariness and sated lust
> Made human life a hell.

"In his cool hall, with haggard lips,
  The Roman noble lay ;
He drove abroad in furious guise
  Along the Appian way.

"He made a feast, drank fast and fierce,
  And crowned his hair with flowers ;
No easier nor no quicker passed
  The impracticable hours."

Yet in this Rome the gospel had reached hearts, converted lives, established a church. Through pride of intellect, wealth, fashion, and sin and shame of all sorts, the gospel had made its way, until perhaps already there were saints in Cæsar's household. Christianity came to Rome to stay, and in course of time this city, which had been the capital of the devil's kingdom, became the chief city of the faith.

Passing from these signs and manifestations of the gospel's power to study the causes thereof, we have logically before us the entire question of the superiority of the christian religion over other religions. Had we space to present so extensive a subject, we should need to treat, first, the distinctively christian doctrine of the Fatherhood of God. We should find the golden core of this in that other distinctively christian doctrine, of love as the essence of all moral goodness. Study of this grand principle would lead us to see how love works the incarnation, re-creates individual character, and also how, operating constructively, it perfects society, first locally, then on and on till all humanity is redeemed. We should see the decisive function of faith in accomplishing all this. So much ground would full discussion of the power of the gospel involve ; so much of course we cannot here traverse, yet the Apostle's thought, even in this lesson, takes us to a few mountain heights whence we can see the entire continent thus outlined.

In announcing his bond-servantship to all nations, so hinting at the brotherhood of men, Paul gives us flower instead of seed; yet flower whose seed is here and in other Scripture made perfectly obvious. The seed is love. The gospel is the expression of the divine love. Love is the mightiest principle in heaven or on earth. Who can begin to describe its breadth, length, depth, or height, as displayed even in human relations like a mother's long-suffering, a patriot's devotion, a saint's zeal!

> "The solid, solid universe
> Is pervious to love;
> With bandaged eyes he never errs.
> Around, below, above,
> His blinding light he flingeth white,
> On God's and Satan's brood,
> And reconciles
> With mystic wiles
> The evil and the good."

But the gospel is the utterance of God's love, of the divine Fatherhood and Motherhood. It is the reaching out of God after his children. It is God's most characteristic expression of feeling towards man.

Christ was and is pre-eminently the Word of God, the revelation of the divine heart. Hence the gospel's irresistible influence. As every element of the natural world, planet, continent, mountain, as well as the fleece of thistle blown by the wind, or the germ too small for the microscope, is under the law of gravity, so are all moral beings, the subjects of God's love, under a sort of divine gravitation. Heathen religions represent man seeking God. This quest is seen in ancestor-worship, bloody sacrifices, all idol cults and barbaric rites, and also in Vedic hymns and Socratic questionings. All tell of man's groping, feeling, crying for God. This is the best that heathen religions can tell us, the fact of man's search after God, his despairing calls, his trembling hands uplifted in doubt, his anxious questionings and fears. Boundless, blessed difference, the gospel assures us of God's search after man. It speaks not so much of man's hand out-reached for God as of God's hand clasping man. "Ye have not chosen me but I have chosen you."

From this unselfish love which God had and has toward the world, and bids us to have toward the world, sprang that splendid Christian product, the recognition of the universal brotherhood of man with its accompanying assurance of human interdependence and obligation. Paul says, "I am a debtor both to the Greeks and to the Barbarians, both to the wise and to the unwise. . . . I am ready to preach the gospel to you that are at Rome." Epoch-making words are these. Jews, Greeks, Romans, Barbarians had during all the past been completely separated from each other by nationality, caste, pride, and vengeful hate. To each of these all other peoples were simply outcasts, a rabble, fit subjects for plunder, bloodshed, and extermination. With Christ comes the marvellous declaration that all men are interdependent, linked together by a chain of brotherhood, of mutual indebtedness and love.

Wherein was Paul indebted to Greek, Roman, Hebrew, Barbarian? He no doubt felt a certain tenderness toward them in that all of them had helped to prepare the world for Christ and for the rapid extension of his kingdom. All these nations, either explicitly or in the way of hopes, yearnings and aspirations, were looking for some great deliverer who was to come. The gospel of Christ fulfilled these hopes. Letters of Greek and Latin and Hebrew were written over the head of the Son of Mary as on the cross of Calvary he bore the sin of the world. Greeks and Romans could not, as the Hebrew nation did, give the world a Christ; yet they helped prepare the world for its Christ, in whom their noblest longings wonderfully converged. The gospel could find a starting place in every nation, with the Jews in their prophecies and their intense desire after God, with the Barbarians in their religions of nature, with the Greeks in their sense of beauty, with the Romans in their devotion to law, order and system. Wherever the gospel goes it recognizes and rescues whatever is good in individual or nation, and from that leads souls on and up to the divine redemption of which that good is a dim shadow and prophecy.

But, more particularly, the Apostle's debt was a debt of the strong to the weak. The gospel has brought into life a new love, a new thought of responsibility, a spirit of condescension on the part of the strong to lift up the weak, a glad suffering of the holy and true to save the vile and false and shameful. That is the meaning of the incarnation, from the Bethlehem manger to Calvary with its cross and to the empty angel-watched sepulchre. This sacrificial love gives a lively sense of responsibility for the lost, and of indebtedness to all who are in need. Herein consists a mighty element of the gospel's power. Wherever there is one lost sheep, one broken life, one pain-tortured body, one fear-smitten heart, one waif of humanity surge-driven or storm-tossed, thither the gospel hastens with hope and healing. Into dungeons where prisoners languish, across Africa's sands and Siberia's snows, in the wake of red-mouthed battle, among the lepers of yonder island of the sea—goes the gospel, its bearers urged on by the same love that brought the Son of God from heaven to earth, which makes strength feel for weakness the debt of a divine, unfathomable love.

Our lesson lays great stress on the efficiency of the gospel. It is a power of God unto salvation. It consists in no mere sentiment but is a living, active and mighty force making all things new. The love through which it works is a radical and exclusive principle. Once truly lodged in a heart, it asserts itself more and more, till every influence or propensity opposed to it there is forever put down. How it changed Paul we have already seen, but Paul's case was in no sense unique. To tame rebellious hearts, to sweeten lives, to put self-denial in the place of greed—the gospel has been doing this ever since it was first revealed, and is doing it on a perfectly gigantic scale to-day. So great is its effectiveness that men have nearly ceased regarding it as a phenomenon, inexplicable save as a divine energy. They fancy that human nature has improved, and that this is the reason why men's ancient savagery has so largely disappeared. A glance at heathen nations shows that human nature has grown better only so far as divine nature has entered into it.

And this is precisely what is taking place. It is the very righteousness of God which men acquire by believing in Christ. "A righteousness of God is revealed, from faith to faith." Our character is to be—and will be if we are truly joined to Christ—just like God's and Christ's, of a piece with theirs, so that we too, like the blessed Son of Man, shall be holy, harmless, undefiled, and separate from sinners. God's image is restored in every believer so that he becomes a Christ-like man. Let us mark it well: the gospel, if it really takes possession of us, delivers from the power of sin as well as from the guilt and remorse of sin. It makes us veritably new men in Christ. It is much more concerned to bring heaven into the believer than to bring the believer into heaven hereafter. To expect heaven by merely professing religion, without character, solid, strong, godly, proof against Satan's wiles, is the most fatal of heresy. Not he who saith to Jesus, Lord, Lord, shall enter the kingdom; but he who doeth the will of his Father. This is a serious test but it is the Master's own, and woe to him, be he priest or layman, who presumes to alter it.

But it is not the whole mission of the gospel to perfect individuals: the gospel is to perfect society as well. The two things are not the same. You are not sure of a model community when every citizen is a saint. A number of cœnobites, monks, living each for himself though in the holiest way, would be no society, still less a christian society. Too much of the holy living of generations past has been cursed by such individualism. Thank God, we see the error now, and the social requirements of Christianity assert themselves more and more. What but the cross is to heal the social ailments of our time, the ill will of rich to poor and of poor to rich, the robberies perpetrated through law, the evils of our politics, the waste of wealth and of opportunity, of all which believers are almost as guilty as world's people? Thank God, the gospel will prove adequate to this task too. Otherwise it would not be in the full sense a power of God unto salvation. Society must be saved. Earth has no business to be a hell. There is to be—and it is now going on—an intensive as well as an extensive coming of God's kingdom. It will "spread from shore to shore," and it will more and more righten and chasten the relations of men to one another on every shore whither its saving health shall come.

With such a God's power as the gospel here, great hope have we for the world's future. This old earth, so dear to our hearts, theatre of so tremendous a procession of human joys and sorrows, and bearing the dust of so many departed saints —what is its destiny? We cannot doubt. The end shall be glorious. Look adown the ages and behold the gleaming walls of the city of God! Listen: a voice comes out of the far past: "He shall see of the travail of his soul and shall be satisfied." Listen again: another voice is borne from the distant future: "Death and hell are cast into the lake of fire. . . . The tabernacle of God is with men, and he will dwell with them, and they shall be his people and God himself shall be their God."

Lesson II. October 8.

REDEMPTION IN CHRIST.

Romans iii: 19-26.

By the Editor.

THIS is among the most important passages in the Bible. It is the classical proof-text for the doctrine of justification, or becoming righteous, through faith in Christ, ceaselessly appealed to by all the reformers and by every defender of Evangelical Christianity. Its very familiarity makes a correct understanding of it difficult. In most minds nearly every word of the passage has acquired a more or less defective meaning and become stereotyped therein. In examining this weighty utterance we must therefore exert ourselves to avoid prejudice and preconception, and to approach it as if for the first time.

Perhaps the chief misconception touching this portion of the New Testament connects itself with the words "justification" and "justify," very poor but it may be inevitable translations of much nobler Greek expressions. "Justification" is a lawyer's term, brought into religious or rather theological speech from the Roman law, and it imparts to the whole section a false air of legalism. The reader imagines himself in a court-room, where God sits as judge. The sinner, the prisoner at the bar, easily proved guilty, is about to receive the deserved penalty, when suddenly Jesus appears as a substitute, and the real culprit is "justified" and sent scot free from the court. This is nothing less than a travesty of Paul's conception. He has none, or but the slightest, thought of court-room processes. His meaning is moral and spiritual through and through. Not how we may escape deserved penalty is his theme, but how we may escape sin and so cease to deserve penalty; not how we may improve our technical status more or less regardless of intrinsic guilt, but how we may radically, permanently and forever change our character from depravity and vice to holiness.

The teachings of the passage may be briefly summed up as follows:

I. All men, Jews as well as Gentiles, are sinners and hence under the just condemnation of God's law.

II. The Jewish law furnishes no means or appliances able to remove this guilt and restore men to God's favor.

III. The gospel offers such means, ample, adequate, satisfactory; presenting and proclaiming a plan for the forgiveness of sins and for a renewal of men's hearts through faith, whereby they may obey and enjoy God and possess everlasting life.

IV. The atonement of Christ, through which all this becomes possible, also explains the lenient dealings of a righteous God with all past generations of sinners.

I. All men are sinners and righteously condemned. The Jews admitted the hopeless guilt of the Gentiles, but accounted themselves righteous, or at least readily capable of becoming so. The Apostle declares that Jew and Gentile are both alike in this respect. There is no distinction. Every mouth is stopped, all alike are brought under the judgment of God, condemned and bound over to certain penalty.

The Apostle comes thus in conflict with his old co-religionists because his Christianity has led him to a deeper view of moral character and obligation than they entertained. With them righteousness consisted in ordinances, the fulfilment of rules, the performance of rites. Their habitual thought of it made it an external affair. Thoroughness, heartiness, inwardness in morality—conceptions which sometimes entered their minds—they construed merely as the intense zeal which would lead one to omit no prescription, however slight, which the code laid down.

Infinitely deeper and truer is the christian idea of moral goodness. It makes everything turn on man's state of heart, nothing upon isolated ordinances. By it, love is the fulfilment of the law,—the only possible fulfilment, the only necessary fulfilment. And seeing how desperately deficient the Jews were in this sovereign requirement, Paul scruples not to place them on the very same level with those who had never known the old law. They were in some respects, he assures us, even worse. Their view of the divine requirements fatally encouraged them to try and establish their own righteousness, a thing they could never do, while heathen were in no such danger.

The world's deepest moral sense now agrees with the Apostle. All men come far short of moral perfection. None live up to their best light. Sin is in every heart. Explain it as one will, or not explain it at all, the fact is that moral evil is a ubiquitous phenomenon. We are not what we ought to be. We are alienated from God. We need redemption. This allegation of the Apostle is so universally admitted that its truth need not be dwelt upon further.

II. The law offers no remedy for sin, no power to bring man into moral union with God. By works of law no flesh can be justified in God's sight. The law can show men how sinful they are but can afford them no positive help in freeing themselves from sin.

It is our duty to inquire sharply for the Apostle's meaning here, since all sorts of ideas have been ascribed to his language. He does not tell us that do what he will man can not make himself as if he had never sinned. This is true. We believe it reverent to say that God himself can never place our characters in exactly the state where they would have been had we never transgressed. But if the Bible anywhere says this it does not say it here. Nor is it the thought of the passage that nothing whatever which man can do independently of the special grace of God can render him now or hereafter what he ought to be. That may be true but is not taught in this place. Whether or not any of us can become righteous "in his own strength" is not here declared, or whether ability and responsibility are coëxtensive, or whether the clear knowledge of moral law has a tendency to prompt rational beings to obey it.

What is alleged is, in brief, this, that no system of law as such can act remedially. Law is a rule, not a force. It can direct; it cannot amend. Through law comes the knowledge of sin. Law points out how bad we are; but, unless some positive agency, medicinal instead of directive and minatory, can be brought to bear upon us, the sin abides and the sinner dies. In saying this the writer has in mind mainly the Jewish law, but all that he lays down is equally true of the moral law. The law of God itself, as distinguished from the grace of God acting *according to law*, is not remedial. The cure of sin must be a force, not a prescription.

More particularly, the Apostle would have us understand that character can by no possibility be built up, or the favor of God secured, by any mere observance of ordinances. This was the prevailing, stubborn, deadly error of the Pharisees, among whom Paul had been educated. They asked: What has the Almightly commanded us to do? meaning particular acts. What has he forbidden? That is, what specific deeds and doings? And the Rabbis answered: The divine ordinance is so and so and so. Thou shalt offer sacrifice; thou shalt keep the Sabbath; thou shalt speak the truth; thou shalt pay tithes. Thou shalt not steal; thou shalt not bear false witness; thou shalt not travel more than so far on the sacred day. Thus do, thus abstain, and thou shalt live.

These mandates illustrate the Jew's whole code, and he had by false religious teaching been led to identify perfect obedience to God with the diligent keeping of them. Some Jews doubtless had a less superficial thought than others, as, to-day, certain heathen worship the spirit behind the idol while others think of the idol alone. But the tendency was to rest in these mere "works of the law." The Apostle wishes to warn against this danger. Righteousness is a different, an infinitely deeper thing than mere code-keeping. It is a state of heart. By those works of the law can no flesh ever be made righteous or ever be regarded righteous in the sight of God.

III. "But now a righteousness of God has been manifested apart from the law, though witnessed to by the law and also by the prophets,—a righteousness of God which comes into existence through faith in Jesus Christ and is for all who believe; for there is no difference, all having sinned and fallen short of the glory of God, so that men are made and declared righteous, if at all, gratuitously, by his grace, through the redemption that is in Christ Jesus. Him did God set forth as a propitiation, on condition of faith, in his blood, in order to exhibit his, God's, righteousness, . . . to the end that God may remain righteous and at the same time make and declare righteous him who is of faith in Jesus."

In these words is the heart of Christ's gospel. They set forth the whole essence of the plan of salvation by the Son of God. Study them carefully; read them over a hundred times. What the law could not do in that it was weak through the flesh, has after all been achieved by the life and death of Jesus. Let us consider these propositions in some detail.

1. A righteousness of God has been revealed. It is God's righteousness, hence a true righteousness, radical, deep, saving. It is not formal; it does not consist in ordinance-keeping or ceremonial. It is a renewed state of heart. The subject of it has love for his deepest motive in all things. His character is therefore, at bottom, just like God's. This is what is meant by his having God's righteousness. He has Christ's righteous-

ness too,—the same in kind. It may be at present undeveloped and so relatively feeble, but if it has really begun in any case, however faint and unpromising its action, it will surely master and sanctify the man at last. Men's knowledge of it is through revelation. The wisest teachers on earth had had no clear thought of such a possibility before Christ. That men could thus become partakers of the divine nature; that sinners could be thoroughly purged from guilt and fitted for heaven, this was new doctrine to Jew as well as to Greek. Christ "manifested" it. This is what his gospel meant, that sinners can be really saved.

2. This plan of real salvation, though witnessed to by the law and also by the prophets, for it is the deep meaning of both, is independent of law-keeping, as the Jews viewed this; it is gratuitous and free. It does not arise or take effect through legality in any form. The "works of the law" do not help it along: many of them—any of them, indeed, if performed in a legalist spirit—are a hindrance to it. It is hence as available for heathen as for the covenant people. The Jews no longer have any monopoly of salvation, for, unless they keep their law from deeper motives than they commonly enjoin, they fail of salvation, while heathen who hail the new revelation and act, however ignorantly and imperfectly, from the proper motives, are saved.

3. The new, real salvation originates in faith, faith in Jesus Christ. It actually originates in that faith. Faith is not appointed its condition arbitrarily. Salvation is based upon faith because salvation itself consists in character, and faith is or involves, inchoate, that very character. He who savingly believes in Christ possesses somewhat of Christ's likeness. He takes Christ for his model. He has a love for his Lord which must in time transform him out of his first self and make him holy. Santification is no magic process. Enraptured by the supernal beauty of Christ's character, the believer is moulded little by

little into Christ's image. Faith is the first step in the process, all-important because of what it leads to, yet not different in kind from any of those which follow. When the first step is taken the Christian begins to have that righteousness of God and of Christ. This is therefore "imputed" to him. It is not "imputed" without being there. God is no bungling book-keeper. He makes no false entries. Righteousness is "imputed" to us, if at all, because in some degree we possess it. We are "declared righteous," justified, because at heart we are so, it now remaining for any believer only to subdue the outlying parts of his nature to his renewed will.

4. Such a real salvation would have been impossible but for the atoning work of our Lord Jesus Christ. This truth, persistently iterated in Scripture, is the offence of the cross. Men dislike to think of their destiny at God's hands as affected by the conditions of God's general moral government. Somewhat thoughtful people often say: If God is love why should he not save any sinner on the simple condition of repentance? Why is an atonement required? Certainly it is no defect in God's love which necessitates an atonement; it is the imperfection, the stupidity of man. Were God to announce forgiveness without atonement, on the lone condition of repentance, men would account his offer as implying a low estimate on his part of the heinousness of moral evil. They would thus be less inclined to renounce this; God's apparent benignity turning out to be in effect cruelty and not goodness at all. There was needed some mode by which God could testify that free forgiveness of sin by him does not import any lowering of his estimate touching sin's enormity. This is effected by the life and death of Jesus, which revealed the damnableness of sin and the splendor of righteousness as thoroughly as this could have been done by the everlasting perdition of all who ever sinned. It is thus that God can remain apparently as well as really righteous, yet make and so declare righteous every one

who is of faith in Jesus. Christ does not suffer the strict and proper penalty of our sins, in such wise that we shall escape penalty whether we repent or not. He does something far better than this. He brings it about that, if we repent, our sins may be forgiven out and out and their penalty not be suffered by any one. God does not in the atonement "put to death the wrong man," as Ingersoll blasphemeously glosses the evangelical theory; he only takes occasion to display once and forever his ineffable execration of sin. This done and done effectively, free forgiveness is safe. It will not make men think sin a light affair. Now the Spirit can be sent forth with a power he never exercised under the old dispensation. Now it is graciously politic to proclaim through all the earth: Ho, every one that thirsteth, come ye to the waters of life.

IV. The atonement not only relates to the present and future; it has a deep meaning in reference to the past, explaining the leniency of God's dealing with men before Christ came. "Him did God set forth as a propitiation, on condition of faith, in his blood, in order at this present time to exhibit his, God's, righteousness in view of the fact that in his forbearance he had passed over the sins previously committed."

The above exposition makes the passage just paraphrased clear. All men ever saved or ever to be saved,—heathen, Jews or Christians, are saved through the atonement of Christ. In all his earlier dealings with our race, the Almighty kept in view what the Messiah would be and do. There were saints in the Jewish world, many of them, and a few in heathendom. They "obtained a good testimony through their faith, but did not receive the promise, God having provided something better concerning us, that apart from us they should not be made perfect."

The old dispensation was not a closed dispensation, but a preparatory one. In that period of the world God treated men with a leniency and a grace which, as pointed out under III, 4, would have endangered his moral government had the then order of things been independent of what was to come. We are led to suppose that in that case penalties would have had to be sterner than they actually were. Moral progress, the course of redemption among people anterior to Christ, must have been hindered by the lateness of his arrival. There was then, except in isolated cases, no such sense of sin's deadliness and blackness as now prevails, the consequence being that men the more readily remained under its power. There are hints that many an Old Testament worthy, like Jonah, felt this lack. God's attitude toward sin, as then revealed, was not severe enough to match their own feeling of its malignancy. The Ruler of the Universe felt this too, but he bided his time, awaiting the ministry of him whose life and death were to make clear God's true abomination of sin as the one accursed thing for which he and his universe have no use. Intelligences that were confused upon this point before the Incarnation, if not enlightened now, will one day be.

The central teaching of this lesson is that Christianity is a scheme not for obviating or suppressing or toning down moral law, but in aid of its execution and fuller play. The Gospel is not sent to save men without moral character, but to produce in them moral character so that they may be saved indeed. Proceeding upon the irrefragable principle that "without holiness no man shall see the Lord," it proposes to induce and establish holiness in all hearts. True religion makes men fit for heaven; it does not juggle them in unfit. Jesus came that men might have life. He has in store for such as obey him not a status but a state. He purposes and will accomplish for every believer a REAL SALVATION.

Lesson III.   October 15.

JUSTIFICATION BY FAITH.

Romans v: 1-11.

By Rev. GEORGE B. GOW, D. D., Glens Falls, N. Y.

JUSTIFICATION brings to the believer in Jesus blessings immeasurable. The cost of justification fortifies our assurance that the purposes of grace involved in it will be accomplished. These two truths furnish the material of our lesson.

To justify is to make righteous. In what sense and by what means does this occur? Paul's doctrine is that God in the suffering of his Son, of which "the blood of Jesus" is a comprehensive symbol, presented to mankind such an "exhibition of his righteousness" that now without sacrifice of righteousness he can make and declare righteous the believer in Jesus. (Rom. iii: 25-26.)

According to this scriptural view two things are impossible: first, to make any sinner who refuses to believe in Jesus a righteous person: second, to make believers righteous without some such display of the divine righteousness as appears in the suffering of the Son of God. These are the two co-ordinate necessities of justification. Questions of great difficulty are connected with them, but they must be held fast in all discussion of redemption.

The incarnation is incomprehensible by us, but to the thoughtful mind the Holy Lawgiver and Ruler of the universe does appear with transcendent clearness and force in Jesus. The philosophy of it is wrapped in mystery, the fact is indisputable. The suffering of the Incarnate Word is beyond finite measure. All the suffering of holy men living and dying in martyrdom, does but hint at its limitless proportions. The most impressive fact in the life of Jesus is that though sinless and because righteous "he was a man of sorrows and acquainted with grief."

However incomplete our apprehension of the righteousness that found expression in Jesus, we do know some things touching it. It is the righteousness of God, the expression of his wisdom concerning conduct, the rule by which he governs himself in the manifestation of his love. It is the righteousness that asserts itself in all normal action of man's moral character. Always essentially one in nature it takes a form in every manifestation suited to the purpose involved. For the judicial expression of the ill-desert of sin it takes the form of penalty. This is the guise which it wears in its relation to us as sinners consciously deserving penalty. It confronts us as the wrath of God, which is as true an expression of his love as of his wisdom and righteousness, though to the soul conscious of guilt, a consuming fire. For the purpose of redemption, to open to the sinner the possibility of recovering his lost righteousness, it assumes the form of propitiatory suffering—the suffering of a high priest who by the power of his holy love suffers with (Heb. iv: 15) the soul conscious of guilt and consumed by wrath. We repeat that it is the same love whether it appears as penalty or as propitiation. This is the righteousness that appears in every work, word and groan, in every active movement and in all the silent endurance of the God-man.

It would be presumption to suppose that we comprehend the entire bearing upon men's justification of the righteousness which finds voice in the suffering of Jesus Christ, but the primary and essential element in justification is simple and easily understood. The penalty of sin, wherever inflicted, exhibits the perfect and changeless righteousness of God. The propitiatory suffering of Christ exhibits the same, however much more it may show forth. Penalty as executed reveals the moral feeling of God toward a sinner. Propitiation, under given conditions, accomplishes the same purpose besides bringing out other important aspects of the divine nature. The standing of the sinner in the moral universe under the condemnation of God is hopeless. The standing of the penitent sinner, for whom the propitiatory suffering of Jesus has become efficient, is full of hope. That suffering, as vice-penal, accomplishing the purpose of penalty, has set him right. It has brought him justification. Is the wrath of God toward impenitent men just and necessary, as the expression of his righteousness? Is it truthful? Does it, where displayed, accomplish a necessary purpose in the administration of moral law? If so, it can give place only to some other expression of the divine righteousness which, under the given conditions, accomplishes the same purpose as well or better. Penalty or something that shall do the work of penalty is therefore the inevitable demand of a holy being in dealing with sin—the demand of perfect love regulated by perfect wisdom.

Such vice-penal suffering is vicarious because it is endured by another than the one for whom it avails. It is propitiatory, not because it works a change in the moral nature or eternal purpose of God, but because it grounds a changed moral state in the believer, and hence also a changed judgment on the part of God concerning such believer.

We now go on to notice that to the justification of a believer another condition is requisite besides that deed or appliance of grace which is to take the place of the execution of penalty upon him.

In Romans iii. 25, 26, Paul speaks of God as setting forth Christ in his blood to be a propitiation, that he may justify *him who is of faith* in Jesus. Faith then is necessary to justification, but faith is not the whole righteousness or right standing with God of which the Apostle speaks. God makes the believer righteous, justifies him, mainly after he has become a believer. Paul here uses the term "justify," with primary reference to a making righteous which presupposes that the sinner has become a believer. There are then two senses in which a sinner is justified or made righteous. A sinner is made righteous in his relation to law and penalty by the propitiatory work of Christ, and his justification declares this new relation. But as a justification of this justification, so to speak, he must be made righteous in his personal character. This righting up of the sinner in himself occurs through the influence of faith.

Faith in what? To this important question the answer is, Faith in Jesus. That means, comprehensively, faith in the righteousness of God set forth in Christ, that righteousenss which is revealed in penalty, but which, in the suffering of Christ, appears not merely as doing the work of penalty, but as saturated with the love from which it springs, and of which it is the highest possible expression.

But what is faith? It is not merely an opinion about Jesus. It is far more than a conviction that, since God has found a way of making known his righteousness which admits of the remission of penalty, therefore we have nothing to fear from the wrath of God, notwithstanding our guilt. The faith that puts a man right in himself is the response of the whole man to the truth, goodness and justice of that righteousness which appears in the suffering Christ, the apprehension of it as the righteousness of God under which the sinner is justly condemned, the loving acceptance of it as good and just, making it the heart's new delight, and the law of its new life. Such faith is a necessary condition of justification in the strict sense of the word, for certainly it would be impossible to accept a sinner as right before law for the sake of the work of Christ, if that righteousness of God which is present in the suffering Christ has made no impression upon him. He can be justified on account of it, only in view of the fact that he has been or is in a sure way to be transformed by it.

If this is the true thought concerning God's righteousness as seen in the blood of Jesus, that which follows in our lesson is clear and very forcible.

"Being therefore justified by faith, let us have peace with God." The hortatory form recognizes the element of freedom in religious experience. Peace for the believer is the purchase of Jesus' blood, but he enters into and abides in it by the conscious exercise of faith, as a free act and a continual experience. Let every man having believed in Jesus, watch lest through carelessness his faith lapse and tempests again cloud his life. But we need not despair as we recognize that our perseverance in the peace of the gospel is in some degree dependent upon our free choice. "For, through our Lord Jesus Christ, we have also had our access into this grace wherein we stand." The favor of God covers all our need. It abides with us, and creates a gracious condition of things in which firm footing is possible and natural. It appears in all that is covered by the terms regeneration and sanctification, in the beginning of a gracious work in the soul and in the "perfecting of that work until the day of Jesus Christ." As Frederick Faber sings:

> "Oh, wonderful! oh, passing thought,
>   The love that God hath had for thee!
> Spending on thee no less a sum
>   Than the undivided Trinity.
>
> Father, and Son, and Holy Ghost
>   Exhausted for a thing like this!
> The world's whole government disposed
>   For one ungrateful creature's bliss!"

Here is the mystery of grace. Though free, though in continual peril from the weakness of our nature and the instability of our will, we are nevertheless secure by a constant divine energy which, without impairing the freedom that makes us Godlike in nature, brings us ultimately to the perfection of Godlike character. The Apostle therefore adds, "Let us rejoice in hope of the glory of God." The Christian is not the traveler who drinks of the wayside spring and is refreshed. He is the fountain itself whose business it is to bubble and flow continually with clear, sparkling waters. Let us rejoice. The hope of sharing the eternal glory of God's holiness is ours. It will not make us ashamed. By this grace into which faith introduced us, and in which by faith we stand, the perfection of our redemption is assured.

"And not only so, but let us also rejoice in our tribulations." Not indeed that trouble is in itself a thing of joy, but we discover the fact, of infinite comfort to us, that "tribulation"— the pressure of afflictions upon us—worketh Godlike strength to endure. Such divine "patience" develops the consciousness of a "tried and proved character," the very thing at which redemption aims; and this "probation" lifts to stronger and loftier "hope" as we climb the ladder of experience. The assurance that perfected character is in store for us gives a foretaste of heaven. "Hope putteth not to shame." The consciousness of the love of God shed abroad in our hearts through the Holy Ghost given unto us at the beginning of our faith and abiding in us by the same grace, is the basis of this hope, and it should never leave us. We will rejoice. What could come to the Apostle's mind with more force than the certainty that this redemption, begun in the blood of Jesus, will be accomplished for every believer? God is behind it, is immanent in it, not as mere law but as love under law to wisdom. We were weak by reason of sin, but "in due season Christ died for the ungodly." "Scarcely for a righteous man," as men would think who know not the possibilities of divine love, "will one die." The utmost to be said is that some man, possessed in a high degree of the martyr spirit, might even dare to die for a good man. But here, sum of all grace! original of all love! fount eternal of all goodness! "God commendeth his love toward us in that, while we were yet sinners," wilful, despicable sinners, against this infinite love, Christ, God's own self incarnate, died on our behalf.

Upon the basis of this thought, by means of an argument from the less to the greater, the Apostle concludes: "Much more then, being now justified by Christ's blood, shall we be saved from the wrath of God through him." To be justified by the blood of Jesus is to be restored to favor with God so far as our relation to law and condemnation is concerned. But justification requires faith on the part of the sinner.

Faith is righteousness in living germ, the fruit of the Spirit, the new life in Christ. But this new life must be sustained. Let it lapse and the soul sinks under the wrath of God as surely as a drowning man into the depth of the sea. The sinner needs therefore something more than the initial justification that sets him right. He needs a progressive justification, called by the Apostle "sanctification," which shall keep him right, or rather make it certain that he will keep himself right, a sanctifying power which will cause the germ of righteousness, already originated in him by faith, to grow and possess the whole man. This sanctification is our complete salvation from the wrath of God. Being justified, reconciled, restored to the favor of God through faith, this blessed condition shall be maintained and perfected through Christ, "by his life."

If the rescue how much more the perfecting! "Is not the life more than food?" If he made us will he not feed us? So our Saviour reasons when on earth he addresses his timid hearers, men of little faith. So Paul reasons about the salvation which Christ offers to all who have ears to hear. If our enmity to holiness, our uncleanness and bitterness of spirit towards God, could not deter him from seeking us and suffering with us in holy endurance to redeem us, will he not love us still, now that his holiness has won our love, his beauty sweetened our temper, his righteousness cleansed and taken possession of our souls? It would be absurd in God, having put forth the matchless grace which has set us in the path of holiness, not to continue his gracious work in us till our holiness is complete.

A son, rebelling against his father's home and law, forsakes his father's altar for haunts of vice. But his father gives him no peace in his folly. From city to city and from den to den the boy seeks a hiding place from his father's uncompromising love, but in vain. One night a tempest bursts upon his vile retreat, and levels it in ruins to the earth. Himself bleeding and in peril of his life, the father, from whom he has never escaped, drags the son, half dead, from the wreck, bears him tenderly to his own bed, and patiently nurses him back to health. Released by exhaustion from the power of appetite, a new affection enters the youth's soul. He sees how great the love on which he has trampled. His father's agony gives him a new idea of what righteousness is, its stern side—for the father has not compromised with the son's depravity in the slightest—as well as its tenderness. He sees, too, how damnable a thing sin is and how worthy the sinner to be left to himself for ever. Repentance and holy resolution spring up within him. He is a new creature.

Shall he now be flung back into the world of his former choice? "I deserve to be," he says, even weeping. "I am no more worthy to be called a son." Such treatment would well exhibit what filial enmity deserves. That proper purpose of penalty it would indeed serve. But the holy suffering of his father has far more effectually compassed that end both for the son and for all others affected by the case. That suffering, therefore, is vicarious and propitiatory. So the father feels, and embracing his penitent boy he answers, "Nay, my son, you shall not go. I have suffered for you. I have kept your place in the home and it is yours as if you had never wronged us. You are my son now, purchased by agony ineffable though most freely suffered. The penitent boy is justified through faith in his father's blood.

And now, is there anything in the old home needful for the son's continuance in virtue that his father will withhold from him? And if what the father has done and suffered has been effectual to reform the son and to reconcile him to his father and his father to him, is it not certain that the same regimen of grace, so beautiful now as exhibited in a thousand daily acts of goodness, will avail to drive from the returned prodigal the last vestiges and seeds of his old life? Thus human experience may teach us the meaning of that momentous saying: "He that spared not his own Son, but delivered him up for us all, how shall he not with him freely give us all things."

Lesson IV.   October 22.

CHRISTIAN LIVING.

Romans xii: 1-15.

By Rev. Wm. M. LAWRENCE, D. D., Chicago, Ill.

AS living may be simply a struggle for existence, so christian living may be vague and ineffective, based on no clear idea of the proper relationship between christian profession and life. This is unfortunate, because the Christian's happiness and usefulness are affected by the lack. The mere professor of religion cannot feel the satisfaction which comes from accomplishing christian work, while the world cares nothing for christian theory, and knows Christ only through the lives of his followers. Christian living is broader than the nominal or real christian work with which it is often confused. It is a positive misfortune to make these public relations of the Christian synonymous with christian living. Church work necessarily covers but a small part of our life. The New Testament says surprisingly little about specific forms of christian activity; but it is full of instruction regarding christian living.

To-day's scripture is an illustration of all this. The hasty reader suffers a shock when he compares the close reasoning and the exact method pursued by the Apostle in the preceding chapters with the collection of mottoes that seem to be gathered up and thrown together in this. But when we look closer we see that this chapter is a conclusion rather than a mere set of commands. Its exhortations are the logical sequence of all that precedes. It points to a conflict, describes the foe, and indicates the tactics whereby victory is to come.

I. THE CONFLICT.

This is distinctly a christian experience. Though in a general way the principle of action and re-action, of life through strife, applies to all moral struggles, its specific application in Paul's mind is, in this verse as elsewhere in the Epistle, to believers. What is the moral position of the Christian after conversion? Godet aptly describes it when he says: "The believer is dead to sin no doubt; he has broken with that perfidious friend. But sin is not dead in him, and it strives continually to restore the broken relation." This conflict makes up the Christian's life, he growing stronger and the conflict less violent, till ultimately the victory, through Christ and the Holy Spirit, is his. This accords with our experience; not in the earlier stages of our christian life, when the joy of pardon brings ecstasy each moment, and Christ's love banishes all thought of sorrow; but as years pass by, the soul recognizes that between its life and the principles controlling it, and the life and principles of the world there is irreconcilable disharmony and combat.

No small danger lurks for the inexperienced convert while he is learning that pure and real religion is not emotion, sentiment, or feeling, but principle in action, action incessant and watchful, ofttimes anxious and painful. The real satisfaction of the christian life, and it is ineffable, comes not from emotion but from rational experience of the oneness of the soul with God. Not alone christian experience shows that the way to perfection is through trial, but also the testimony of Scripture. The sacrifice of Christ is our reconciliation, but, being reconciled, we are to present our bodies before him in living sacrifice as our reasonable service. The regenerating act of God is the seed whence renewed life is to grow. But all life is strife with adverse forms of life, with the elements, with the soul,

Christian life is no exception to this principle. We are to grow in grace, to work out, not for, our salvation. Happy the disciple of the Lord Jesus who has ceased to expect earthly joy in any cessation of conflict, but who, asking only, Lord, what wilt thou have me to do? goes steadfastly on in the path of duty, fighting the good fight and contentedly leaving to God the bestowment of reward.

II. THE GREAT FOE.

If, as some suppose, Paul in the first verse of our chapter refers to the sacrifice of reconciliation, the Christian's warfare consists not so much in joining issue with forces outside the soul as in overcoming those within. A skilful general does not deploy his army over every acre of ground between himself and the enemy. He scans the battle-field and selects the key positions both on his side and on that of the enemy, so that his attack and his defense may be conducted in the wisest way. Great generalship oftener turns on this than on bravery or dash. All depends on mastery of strategic positions, where the ablest fighters are.

So in this chapter, the Apostle views the whole field of each probationer's struggle and selects the main enemy, noting well his position, strong for both attack and defense. He sees that the sovereign foe to be overcome in our natures is selfishness, in its various forms of anger, pride, revenge, ambition and retaliation. The very best of men find that on some occasions in their lives they are called upon to battle sternly with these passions, and that surrender means slavery. Selfishness in its coarse and gross forms everyone condemns. Its subtler onsets are the ones most likely to be fatal, when it attacks in the guise of some right, virtue or christian grace. Paul guards against a perversion of his meaning by saying: " Let no man think more highly of himself than he ought to think." Every man is entitled to appreciate justly his own merits. There is, therefore, a pride which is not sinful, which may even involve virtue. But there is also a selfish pride, very different from the self-respect of a conscientious man, and into none of Satan's snares do we more easily fall.

In like manner, it is usually legitimate for each of us to defend his rights, and there may sometimes be involved in this the infliction upon any who transgress them of some penalty or other hardship to serve as a restraint for the future. But revenge, the malignant and purposeless infliction of pain, is a very different thing from this. It is always and wholly of the devil, and no temptation which ever comes to man can possibly justify it.

In a famous trial not long since, the leading counsel on one side was an able lawyer whose face an accident in his youth had much disfigured. The contest was bitter, and the opposing attorney was beaten at every point. Stung by his defeat, he so far forgot himself as to taunt his antagonist with his physical defect. Breathless was the stillness in the court-room, and hundreds of pitying eyes were bent on the scarred face of the legal gentleman, who slowly rose and addressed the court. "Your Honor," said he, "never before in all my life have I felt called upon to explain the cause of my facial deformity, but I will do so now. My mother, God bless her, said I was a pretty boy when little, but one day as I was playing round an open fire with a sister just beginning to walk, she fell into the roaring flames. I rescued her before she was hurt but fell into the fire myself. When they took me out of the coals *my face was as black as that man's heart.*" This sentence was greeted with loud applause for the speaker and contemptuous hisses for the one who had so cruelly wronged him. The retort was deserved, but was it justified? Great as was the provocation it was in the main a temptation merely to inflict pain. I cannot avoid the conviction that the great orator would have been a better man had he been able to suppress the telling comparison with which he closed.

Few people are aware how much selfishness exists within them. In the day in which we live, the tendency is uncommonly strong for men to avail themselves of all their accidental advantages and ignore the rights of their fellows. A Christian needs to be ever on his guard lest this arch enemy become intrenched in his soul, getting possession of its main strongholds and so reducing the man's Christianity to a mere lifeless profession.

III. THE MEANS OF VICTORY.

The Apostle goes on to indicate to us those principles by which our lives may be made victorious over these special foes and over all others that may assail us. What shall a man do who discovers that he has within himself this terrible enemy of selfishness, of morbid and sinful relf-regard?

The Apostle urges the cultivation of humility. Let this be understood, for the term humility is used so frequently as to be almost void of meaning. What is humility? Is it self-debasement or self-depreciation? No, humility is not the reverse of manliness, but a real and just appreciation of our sins and other limitations on the Godward side, as well as of our true relations to our fellowmen. As wicked pride takes no account of obligation to God, so it ignores the dependence of man on man. A bright boy just entering college may be very proud till he finds that the other boys know as much or more than he does. Then his pride suffers a fall, and unless the vice is peculiarly deep-seated, humility has a chance to become permanently characteristic of him. His real power now immensely increases, for as he works for others he makes others carry out his ends. "So we being many are one body in Christ." In such union is strength not only for all but for each. The isolation caused by pride and other forms of sinful self love is the great source of human weakness. The power of the christian life comes from identification of our own welfare with that of others,

The sweep of this truth is immense. Here is the solution of all the troubles now affecting the various ranks of life. Not the passage of resolutions by religious bodies, not the appointment of investigating committees or the enactment of laws by Congress, but the christian humility that shall make the rich and great identify themselves in interest with the lowliest, the application to living questions of the idea that "one is your Master, even Christ, and all ye are brethren:" this is the only means for securing peace between the different members and ranks of society.

But humility is in itself a fruit, the fruit of love. The world is being conquered by the love of God displayed in sending his Son. The impatience of men, the defiance they hurl at his laws, their plottings to defeat his will, are finally to be overcome by his long patience. We also are to possess this love, to help us to overcome in our disappointments and vexations. What the inspired writer specially insists on is that this love of ours be genuine. "Let love be without dissimulation; abhor that which is evil." Certainly no other evil could be so great as an affectation of love. If the spirit of genuine love could only prevail in commercial and social affairs, if christian men in business, instead of following the law of retaliation so much censured by them in individual relations, would act upon the law of love, there would be an exhibition of christian living whose moral power would go far toward settling the vexed questions of the day. The higher men are in the scale of intelligence and morality, the greater the obligation upon them to go according to this christian law. The christian employer owes to his ignorant employee a debt measured by the scale of his privileges and his superior light.

Let it be remembered that every effort one may make to exemplify love will result in the development of his spiritual nature. No general advance may be at once observable, but a forward movement will certainly come, a progress of different parts of the nature, just as the whole body is fitted for living by exercising different muscles at various times and is kept in health by attention to its several functions. Also it is through christian living that men gain power over others. "Ye are the light of the world." A wise old friend once said to me, "Remember that your greatest victory will be to turn the enemies of the Lord Jesus into his friends." We are to overcome by making men feel that we are their friends. We cannot do this by any worldly temper. The proud man is repelled by pride, the selfish man by selfishness, the angry man by an exhibition of anger in others. It is CHRISTIAN LIVING that is to gain us our end. It is living like Christ.

With the theories of Christianity, its doctrines and its past, all men are familiar. What men want to-day is the life of Christ actually lived over in the lives of his people. It was Christ "who for our sakes became poor, that we through his poverty might become rich." It was the Lord Jesus who turned and looked upon Peter that look of love which melted his heart. I have often striven to realize the interview after the resurrection between that impulsive, loving, blundering disciple and his Lord. It was Christ who when earth's views were fading from his sight said, "Father, forgive them." It is related of some missionaries that they lived and labored among the people to whom they had been sent for many months without success. They sought to accomplish their work by civilizing influences, but to no purpose. Finally they gathered a few natives around them and rehearsed in plain conversation the story of Christ. The effect was marvelous, and the missionaries had the satisfaction of knowing the truth of his words: "And I if I be lifted up, will draw all men unto me." What happened there will occur anywhere if men strive to realize the words of the Apostle, "For me to live is Christ." It is that story set forth simply, sympathetically and sincerely in the lives of his followers that leads a man to desire with all his heart to enter the christian path.

Lesson V. October 29.

ABSTINENCE FOR THE SAKE OF OTHERS.
I Corinthians viii: 1-13.

BY REV. PROFESSOR R. S. COLWELL, D. D., GRANVILLE, O.

THE First Epistle to the Corinthians is one of the few parts of the New Testament whose genuineness and authenticity have never been seriously assailed. It was written by Paul, probably from Ephesus, about 57 A. D., to the church at the Greek city of Corinth. This church, as we learn from the eighteenth chapter of Acts, had been founded by Paul during his second great missionary tour, and was, for the most part, composed of Gentile Christians. The city of Corinth was distinguished for its commerce, its wealth, its intellectual activity, and likewise for its wantonness and corruption. It is not strange that the church, situated in a city of such character, soon found its peace disturbed and its existence endangered by internal difficulties. Party strifes, heresies of doctrine, improprieties in the observance of the Lord's Supper, and even gross and revolting crimes were among the sins of which the members of this church seem to have been guilty. In the midst of their troubles, they applied to Paul for instruction and advice in regard to their relations with the world around them. Paul probably wrote this first Epistle to the Corinthians in response to this application. In some important particulars the epistle differs from the other epistles of Paul, but in no respect more than in the fact that, unlike the rest, it contains a minimum of what we call "doctrinal discussion." Except the single passage which treats of the great doctrine of the resurrection, there is here very little of such discussion. The letter has to do with practical affairs. But it is by no means less important on that account. On the contrary, in it we are shown how inspired wisdom applies divine truth to actual life. It gives us clear illustrations of the way in which the Apostle Paul decided just such matters as we must decide almost daily.

One of the questions submitted to the Apostle pertained to eating meat offered to idols. Corinth was filled with a mixed population, which, worshipping a great variety of deities, offered sacrifices in many temples and at many shrines. These offerings were in fact so abundant that at times a large portion of the meat used for food had been presented before the shrine of some heathen deity. Consecrated meat was presented as food both at the feasts celebrated in the temples and at private banquets. For the Corinthian Christians, therefore, whose business and social relations brought them into frequent contact with this practice, it became a question of no small importance whether partaking of this food was consistent with their vows as Christians. This is the question which occupies the Apostle's attention in the passage before us. It cannot be other than interesting to observe how he decided the matter. From his directions we may not only learn how to make similar applications under different circumstances, but we may also gain clearer conceptions of divine truth itself.

It is noteworthy that Paul first discusses the question from the basis of the fundamental principle involved (vv. 1-6). He asserts that in the case of intelligent Christians, whose minds are informed and whose consciences are properly educated, this eating of meat offered to an idol is, in itself, perfectly innocent. That is, were they the only persons in the world, the question would not exist at all. They would then, and properly, feel as free to eat this meat as they would to eat at all. Such Christians know that there is nothing in the world corresponding to those gods which the idols are supposed to represent. Such beings exist only in the imaginations of the deluded worshippers. There is in the universe no basis whatever, underlying the images which their imagination has constructed. Therefore, to one who has such knowledge, the act of offering this meat in a so-called sacrifice before an idol image is a form entirely without meaning. It has no moral significance whatever. It is a mere empty parade without any proper influence upon the believer's conscience one way or the other. In this we find the Apostle's answer from the point of view of the deepest principle involved. It is perfectly clear and distinct, namely: that the moral quality of the act of eating meat is in no way affected, in the case of those who have knowledge, those whom we may call normal Christians, by the fact that the meat has previously been offered in pretended worship to an idol. In other words, there is nothing in itself sinful in the act of eating meat which has been offered to idols.

But while giving this answer, so clear and distinct that there remains no room for doubt as to his meaning, he takes occasion to caution his readers that there is, in the knowledge of the total non-existence of such things or beings as these heathen gods, nothing " building-up," nothing " edifying." Such knowledge is merely negative. Unless guarded, it may easily lead to undue elation. If anyone dwells on such special enlightenment and thinks that there is anything in it to commend him to God, the man is deficient at the very foundation of knowledge. " He knoweth nothing as he ought to know it."

After having pronounced thus explicitly on the first principle involved, the Apostle proceeds (vv. 7-8) to call the attention of these Corinthians to two other facts which ought to be considered by them in deciding upon their duty in such cases, facts which have an important influence upon the decision which they are to make. The first of these facts is that this knowledge about the nonentity of heathen gods is something which all men do not possess. Some men, some Christians even, are in this respect uninformed and ignorant. They believe that heathen gods do exist. They have been accustomed to regard the adoration of idols as a real act of worship, and to think that to eat meat which has been consecrated in idol worship is in some sense to share in that worship. The other fact is that a man's attitude upon this matter of meat, of food, in itself considered, in no way commends the man to God. It has in, of and by itself, no moral quality at all. He who eats is no better, and he who refrains from eating is no worse. As Paul himself has expressed it in the fourteenth chapter of Romans, "The kingdom of God is not eating and drinking, but righteousness and peace and joy in the Holy Ghost." There is, therefore, no obligation either way resting upon a Christian in regard to eating meat, so long as he acts conscientiously and so long as his own relation to the act is the only thing which comes into view. In this as in many other things not in themselves morally binding or intrinsically right or wrong, the Christian is left to the exercise of his own personal judgment.

The Apostle then proceeds to discuss the influence which the knowledge of these two facts properly has upon the question submitted to him (vv. 9-12). In the estimation of the Apostle it does not settle the question of duty in regard to eating meat offered to idols to know that the act is not in itself wrong. There are other things which may determine the moral quality of an act beside the intrinsic nature of it. One of these things is the effect of such action upon others. The ignorance of others as well as one's own knowledge is an element in the problem. Although the eating of this idol meat is for those who have knowledge an innocent act, it is sinful for those who do not understand that these heathen gods have no existence.

It is possible therefore that the eating of this meat by those to whom it is not sinful, when witnessed by those to whom it is a sin, may embolden the latter to do the same thing, an act which in their case, since they have not this knowledge, would be wrong. In such a state of affairs as this, a state which seems to have existed at Corinth at the time, doing an act harmless in itself becomes a sin. In other words, on account of the ignorance of some of the Corinthians, it became wrong for those who had knowledge to do certain things intrinsically innocent. Under such circumstances, therefore, to do intrinsically innocent things is to "sin against the brethren" and to "sin against Christ." Inasmuch as he has reached this conclusion we are not at all surprised to read the sublime words with which the Apostle closes his discussion of the subject and gives his ultimate decision in regard to eating meat offered to idols, "If meat maketh my brother to stumble I will eat no flesh for evermore, that I make not my brother to stumble."

We have thus seen that the Corinthian Christians received their answer, an answer full and explicit, an answer founded on general principles and applied to the specific case, an answer which would leave no room for doubt as to either the principle or its application. But the difficulty which disturbed the Corinthian church has long since passed away. Eating meat offered to idols presents no practical difficulty in the world to-day. But the knowledge of this incident and the Apostle's words of inspired wisdom concerning it have not passed away. Nor have these words become merely an interesting record of an ancient solution to a practical difficulty. Far from it. This passage in this ancient letter remains to-day unsurpassed as a clear setting forth of an eternal principle, a principle forever binding upon all moral beings associating with those who are weaker,—the principle of *abstinence for the sake of others.* Or, to put it in different and perhaps plainer words, this passage teaches that it is a Christian's duty to refrain from the use or enjoyment of even innocent and lawful things, when such use or enjoyment tends to lead a fellow-mortal into sin. This truth will not commend itself to those whose chief object in what they call religious living is merely "to be saved," for it is set forth with no formal "thus saith the Lord," nor is it followed by any threatened penalty of "wrath and fiery indignation" in case of disobedience. Throughout the discussion Paul appeals to no sense of fear, and presents no line of action as a requisite of salvation. His severest language merely reminds his readers that to neglect this duty is "to sin against a brother," and to "sin against Christ." That is, he appeals to their love to their brethren and to Christ, and thus builds upon the foundation on which, as our Lord declared, "hang all the law and the prophets."

In the complicated relations of life at the present time there is continual occasion to exercise this duty of abstinence for the sake of others. On every hand are these "weaker brethren," men without knowledge, men to whom the influence of other, stronger men becomes an occasion for virtue or sin, men whose judgment is not clear and true, whose will is not firm and steady; in short, men who have not sufficient intellectual and moral stamina to stand alone. They drift. They move in masses. They attach themselves to others. Their life is largely determined by what others do and say and think. As it was in the days of the Corinthian church so it is now, though we may hope that the proportion of the strong to the weak has steadily increased. Inasmuch as all of us live in the presence of these "weaker brethren" and constantly have an influence upon their thought and life in very many ways, it is not at all sufficient for us to ask if a proposed line of conduct be right in itself. It is also necessary to ask whether it will have a right and helpful influence upon the lives of others; and, if no moral obligation is involved, the answer to this last question must, for those who have both knowledge and love, be decisive.

It would be impossible, as it is undesirable, to enumerate or classify the many applications of this principle pertinent at the present time, but there are two which are sufficiently prominent to deserve mention here. The first of these concerns the "Temperance Question," the use of alcoholic liquors as beverages. Following the same order of reasoning which is observed by the Apostle, we may note that there is not necessarily any moral quality involved in the act of drinking an alcoholic beverage. It can be said of it, in some cases at least, as Paul said of meat. "Neither if we drink not are we the worse; nor if we drink are we the better." That is to say, the act in itself may be entirely innocent. If it be sinful at all it must be because of some such reason as that it is a violation of the laws of health, a principle which would at times make the eating or drinking of anything wrong. On the other hand is the fact that the use of alcoholic drinks is the most terrible force for evil that the world has ever seen. It is a curse more powerful for misery and death than all the wars that have been waged since history began. It is possible to construct truthful statements showing that by it millions on millions of dollars have been wasted, millions on millions of homes hopelessly ruined, untold millions of mortals sent down to untimely death, millions more made criminals, and millions of innocent victims plunged into wretchedness and misery. But although we may construct statements of this sort which must appal every thoughtful man, it is utterly impossible for any combination of statements to describe adequately the enormous evil wrought by this habit. The figures pass the limits of human comprehension long before an adequate statement is reached. It is impossible for a finite mind to comprehend the full extent of this tremendous curse. In view of such unquestioned facts, while we may admit that the act of drinking alcoholic liquor is in itself a harmless one, must we not say of him who refuses to give up the habit, "Through thy knowledge he that is weak perisheth, the brother for whose sake Christ died; and thus, sinning against the brethren and wounding their conscience when it is weak, ye sin against Christ?" Can the attitude of any one who hates evil and loves good be other than that expressed in those noble words of Paul, "If meat maketh my brother to stumble, I will eat no flesh for evermore, that I make not my brother to stumble"?

The other prominent and general occasion for the application of this principle of abstinence for the sake of others is found in the matter of amusement a subject closely connected with the spiritual life of very many. The question what amusements are to be indulged in should be decided in the light of the truth taught in this passage. There are very few amusements which can be said to be sinful in themselves. Even those which have been associated with sin in the minds of many Christians for generations seldom necessarily involve anything evil. With very few exceptions they are intrinsically harmless, innocent. In the case of any well balanced person, of good judgment, firm self-control, and strong will, their use and enjoyment is not attended by any harmful result. They may be decidedly beneficial. But, as we have already seen, this is not enough to decide the matter finally. That consideration is important, since it lies at the foundation, but it is not all. Nothing should be done which is in itself wrong, but not every thing is allowable which is in itself good. It is never right to neglect the "weaker brethren." Legitimately the first test to apply to any amusement is, "Is it right?" But to any amusement which successfully meets this test a second is to be applied, viz: "Is its influence right?" Many amusements which successfully bear the first test fail under the second. There are a number of amusements, exceedingly attractive and popular, whose whole history shows that their influence is in a great majority of instances injurious. They tend to absorb thought and attention which belong to more important affairs.

They develop and stimulate unnatural tastes and desires. They check spiritual aspirations, and thus retard or destroy spiritual life. They establish and strengthen mental and moral conditions unfriendly to the best interests of the soul. This is seen in the fact that they who indulge in and support them are very seldom found among the earnest and zealous servants of God. They do not live hearty, wholesome, christian lives. They belong to that large class of people who constantly hover about the line separating the servants of God from those of the devil. A few stalwart souls are able to resist these tendencies and maintain their spiritual life, but the many are overcome by them, and thus the "liberty of the strong becomes the stumbling-block of the weak." In regard to these and all such amusements the teaching of the Apostle is clear. They must be abandoned. To continue them is inconsistent with duty to God and duty to man.

He who is willing to be controlled not only by the expressed and positive commands of Christ, but also by the slightest indications of his will and pleasure, will put to his lips no cup which contains death for others, nor will he delight himself with pleasures which by his example will be made fatal to the welfare of many of his fellow-men. Remembering, as it is expressed in the fourteenth chapter of Romans, "that it is not good to eat flesh, or drink wine, or any thing whereby a brother stumbleth, or is offended, or is made weak," he will appropriate the spirit, if not the words of Paul, and joyfully deny himself the use of even lawful things, whenever that enjoyment becomes the occasion of stumbling to his fellows.

Lesson VI. November 5.

THE RESURRECTION.

I Corinthians xv: 12-26.

BY REV. CHARLES A. REESE, MINNEAPOLIS, MINN.

A FEW months ago an iron bridge was building over the Mississippi. From the east bank it advanced across the stream, pier by pier, stretching out its girders like long arms toward the western bluff. The chasm grew narrower by degrees, then disappeared. As we travel backward to assure ourselves of the truth of the gospel history, we come to the date 300 A. D., beyond which unbelief says we cannot go. "The difficulty," it is alleged, "is not to prove that Christ was believed to be an historical personage after the fourth century, but to bridge over the years between 1 and 300 A. D. You cannot carry the history of Christ and the history of the gospel over that terrible chasm of three centuries." By his words in this chapter Paul puts us in a way to build an iron bridge over this gulf of time. The first pier is the fact, not disputed by the most hostile, that Paul wrote the first Epistle to the Corinthians. The second pier is the established date of his writing: A. D. 57. The third pier is the short space of time between his writing and the event to which he bears testimony—less than the time between Gettysburg and the present year of grace. The fourth pier is his appeal to living witnesses of the risen Christ, as we might ask for the story of Gettysburg. We thus see that the gulf is much narrower than is asserted, that the Christ of the four gospels was certified to by credible witnesses before the year 60. In fact a highway as solid as truth itself has been constructed across the alleged abyss. "Nothing stands more certain, historically, than that Jesus rose from the dead and appeared to his followers."

The Corinthians had accepted the evidence of the resurrection, but had not apprehended the place and value of the doctrine. They had given it a local, a personal, or a creedal application. These historical piers, "unshaken as the eternal hills," did not suggest to them that God had laid the foundation of a bridge, broad and strong enough for humanity to march over to firm faith in all the truths of Christianity. In the passage before us the Apostle shows how the resurrection unifies all doctrines. Without it other parts of the circle of revelation are fragments, isolated, disconnected, unsubstantial. He presents the consequences of denying and those of believing that Christ has risen.

He begins with the attempt to harmonize the preaching of the resurrection with the notion that there is no resurrection from the dead. Paul indignantly rejects such a union of contradictories. "If there is no resurrection of the dead then is Christ not risen." If unbelievers state a universal negative they cannot modify it by holding to a positive case of resurrection. Either admit the resurrection in principle, or deny the instance of Christ's resurrection which falls under that principle. We need not spend time in the unprofitable search for the exact form of doubt which Paul was combating; whether or not the "some" denied natural immortality as well as the general resurrection. Paul is not discussing the subtler doctrine of immortality. He is meeting current thought, to the effect that the resurrection is scarcely more than a vague figure.

Then, as now, this truth was refined and spiritualized until it was practically denied. Pagan philosophy stood opposed to it.

The ancient idea of the opposition of matter to spirit did not accord with it. And there was the question which still troubles so many: How can it be? Paul answers the last further on. Here he strongly asserts the difference between the "saying" of "some" and the preaching of the Apostles. A rugged doctrine of Scripture is often toned down to conform to human speculation; but with revelation before us the line between the true and the false may be clearly traced. Human reason falls into confusion the moment it refuses credence to the resurrection. Reason may define the doctrine and test its proofs, but it cannot produce any modification of it or substitute for it. It is idle to admit, as certain Corinthians appear to have done, that Christ rose from the dead, unless the resurrection of men in general be admitted. The absolute identification of Christ here with the body of humanity is most comforting. If man's resurrection is a mere figure of speech, "then is Christ not risen."

This necessitates a second step. The Corinthians denying the resurrection must regard as empty words all the other truths that they had heard Paul zealously proclaim. He had urged them to believe on the ground that Christ had proved himself the Son of God by rising from the dead. Christ himself had predicted that his resurrection would give validity to his teaching and effect to his character and work as the Son of God. His qualifications as the Redeemer were conditioned upon his victory over death. If Christ was conquered by death, the Apostle's arguments, persuasions, promises in Christ's name were only sound, signifying nothing. This would afflict Paul personally as a preacher, but the hearer would suffer too. "Your faith is also vain." As it is a conscious joy to preach divine truth, so it is a joy, on suitable evidence, to believe, to add truth to truth till it forms a system and becomes in the mind a a circle of blazing light, with Christ, the Light of men, as the centre. But if the resurrection were denied all this study and acceptance of truth would be like the electric wiring of a chandelier when the current has failed. The whole is formal, "dead," without the risen Christ to surcharge it.

Following to its conclusion this assumption of "no resurrection," Paul proceeds: "Yea, on that supposition we are found false witnesses of God." To one who felt the responsibility of preaching as Paul did, it was more than a mistake to teach wrongly on this or any subject. It was false witnessing, forbidden by the law hoary with the veneration of centuries. However easily other men excuse themselves for superficial teaching, Paul sternly held himself to strict honor in proclaiming the truth. People speak of the apostles as either deceived on the subject of the resurrection or wilfully deceiving others. Paul asserts that it is perfectly easy, by questioning living witnesses, to ascertain what the truth touching the resurrection is. There is no chance for honest self-deception. That horn of the dilemma is destroyed by full evidence just at hand. Now if he and his associates testify to this cardinal doctrine, provided "some" are right in denying that Christ has risen, the apostles are not deluded but deliberate deceivers. Either they preach the truth on the subject or they are liars. The falsehood appears in a specially dreadful light, in that it is committed against God, putting the Supreme Being himself in a wrong light. Well might one shrink with horror from being found a false witness of God. And, as before, the deadly consequence of the untrue hypothesis does not end with the apostles. "Ye are yet in your sins." "If Christ hath not been raised your faith is vain." And since faith is vain, all the work that Christ is supposed to have accomplished through faith is unaccomplished. Unless Christ rose he cannot be the Saviour, and the sins of men still rest upon them.

Those who deny the resurrection are driven on again like the wandering Jew. If we are deceived here the lot of the dead is as desperate as that of the living. The earthly believer, mistaken in the object of his trust, still has his sins upon him; the departed believer, clinging to the same false faith, must be receiving the punishment of his sins. A groundless faith can save no man. If Christ does not avail, the sinner perishes. He is lost like the coin in Christ's parable when it had slipped from the neck of its possessor, and like the sheep upon the mountains when it had strayed from the shepherd. He has less hope than the prodigal son when he was in the far country in sin, for he could return, while, if Christ is naught, no "way" is open for us to our Father's house. What a fearful thing to fall asleep in Jesus, trusting him as the all-sufficient Saviour, and just beyond the veil to wake to the sad certainty that our sins are still upon us with all their penalty because we were mistaken in the object of our faith. If Christ is not master over death, "then they also which are fallen asleep in Christ have perished." It is, bless God, a supposition that will never come true; but it should arouse us to see how terrible the awakening if we die in any false trust, whether in ourselves, the world or some kind of sophistry, instead of in the risen Christ.

One more dreadful consequence is suggested, which brings the inspired writer to his limit. "If in this life only we have hope in Christ, we are of all men most miserable." His assumption thus far has been that a Christ not risen would be the same as any other illusory object of hope. It would be pitiable to believe in anything that deceives. How sad is the lot of many who, in the realm of the temporal, are trusting in things more unsubstantial than dreams! But more wretched than other deceived persons, more miserable even than the lost who never cherished faith at all, would be the lot of those who believed on Christ, provided the resurrection were discredited. By as much as their expectations rose higher than the unbelievers', so much deeper and darker would be their misery when the wing of hope, paralyzed in the keen light of truth, dropped useless and heavy. Christian hope leads a man to let go this world for the more goodly and glorious world of the future. If the Christian misses what he staked his all for, he loses both worlds, one by default, the other by delusion.

Thus are enumerated and canvassed the dire implications of the thesis "No risen Christ," supposing this true. The considerations adduced bring before us several important lessons.

I. We should beware of holding contradictory views, made up of God's truth and men's mistakes. There are other doctrines and sayings that do not fit together any better than those which Paul has been discussing. An unbalanced, inconsistent system of belief constantly exposes its holder to the shipwreck of faith. Sooner or later some crafty disputant will seize upon the false part of your system, and lead you down a logical incline like this one, away from the cross, the resurrection and your hope of a mansion in the Father's house.

II. We see the fate to which doubt leads. Doubt upon one essential point exposes the doubter to a second doubt. Doubts, like cormorants, fly in flocks. It is easier to believe the whole system of revealed truth than to believe all its propositions but one, having doubt upon that one; for if you deny one point you must accept all the consequences of such denial. The down grade in this region is easy if you once enter upon it. The steps to the abyss of unfaith are just as plain as the steps up to the triumph of faith. Eight such steps are noticed in to-day's scripture, forming a stairway which lands in blank infidelity. Note these steps so as forever to avoid such a gloomy passage-way. They are graves locked never to open, meaningless preaching, empty faith, dishonest witnesses, unforgiven sins, hopeless believers dead, still more hopeless ones living. God be praised that we can say with Paul: "Now hath Christ been raised from the dead."

III. The resurrection of the human race is involved in that of Jesus. Christ is the first fruits of them that sleep. Here is a field of waving grain. A portion is ripe earlier than the rest, yellow as gold, perfect as wheat ever was. The owner joyfully cuts and binds these first sheaves, confidently predicting that a rich harvest will follow. He knows that the ripening will progress till all the broad acres are harvested, because he is sure that seed and soil were the same over all the field. So Christ Jesus is but a sheaf of the great human harvest, early ripened. He is bone of our bone and flesh of our flesh. If he is raised up surely we shall be. We cannot affirm the resurrection of Christ and deny that of men. He is so vitally related to us that whatever you predicate of his lot after death you predicate of ours. Lifted up out of the grave, he will draw all his brothers after him. The dead "sleep" only as grain sleeps in the ground, soon to rise up where the sun is, aspiring higher and higher to greet the skies. Death is called in common speech a reaper. He is rather a sower. The angels are the reapers; may they harvest us, not to be burned as tares but as good seed for the heavenly granary.

The whole harvest follows the first sheaf because the first sheaf is the same grain as the rest of the sowing. Christ was man as really as Adam was. His resurrection affects men as widely as Adam's death did. This is one of the deeps of God's wisdom, but its sides are studded with flowers. Out of it grow splendid truths: Christ's representativeness of the race, his sinlessness, his oneness with us in death, his inherent power to make alive all who are in their graves. From the broad fields of the-dead shall arise a mighty army. Each man shall be in his own company. Christ leads. The first division after him will be the redeemed, roused by the trumpet which announces his second coming. Those who are not Christ's will complete the infinite array. Even the rejectors of Christ are to rise through him, though refusing the greater gift of salvation.

IV. The raising of men from their graves is a demonstration of Christ's kingship. The demonstration began with his ministry, and will end with the complete subjugation of every enemy to righteousness and to divine authority. "He must reign." It is a necessity growing out of the fitness of things. Before his universal power, organized and unorganized opposition shall bow; personal and physical resistance shall cease; open and private hostility shall vanish. As a proof that the crucified and risen Christ has established his specific reign, a survey of the fields of death's former dominion shall reveal not one undespoiled sepulchre or one unopened grave. When the archangel shall have declared "there is no more death," perfect authority will be in Christ's hands, and the long battle with sin and death will have been won. Then, in exercise of rulership over himself, greatest of all kingship, Christ shall deliver up the kingdom to God, even the Father. The crowning of his work with success leaves nothing more for authority to contend with. The office of king expires when all subjects have learned self-government. Christ's establishment of righteousness in the hearts of men is itself a completion of the work which God gave him to do. "The fear of the Lord is swallowed up in the love of the Father." So we ascend with the Apostle to a consummation of Christ's glory, the boundary of human thought, where imagination fades into eternity.

The theme of to-day has been called the Sphinx of God's word. The Sphinx, though you fail to solve its riddle, is a fact. So these great truths are none the less truths though mysterious. They are put with this chapter, which has been the artery of life to millions of souls, as the Sphinx is stationed by the Nile. "A hundred difficulties," says J. H. Newman, "do not make one doubt." When the light of "the day of Jesus Christ" falls upon this Sphinx it will open its stony lips and speak so that the universe shall hear them the glories of the Son of God.

Lesson VII. November 12.

THE GRACE OF LIBERALITY.
II Corinthians, viii: 1-12.

BY REV. CLARK M. BRINK, NEWARK, N. J.

THE people of Palestine are suffering from famine. The christian church at Jerusalem shares the common distress. Paul, touched with compassion, importunes the Gentile churches to contribute for their relief. In a letter to the church at Corinth he has taken occasion to present the matter and to give explicit directions for making the offering. In a second letter he urges the Corinthians to complete their contribution and advances reasons for making it a large one.

This incident brings before us the entire question of christian liberality. Vital to a right understanding of this question are certain truths that I desire briefly to emphasize.

I. LIBERALITY IS A CHRISTIAN DUTY.

If a soul is a branch of the true vine, the fruit of liberality will inevitably appear. It is not a matter of choice. Sin is selfishness. The great mission of Christianity is to destroy selfishness. When, therefore, a man professes to be a Christian and yet cherishes a penurious disposition, we deny the genuineness of his conversion. There is one circle in which the parsimonious man cannot sit,—the christian church. His name may be on the church roll, but he is not in the church.

Spirituality and stinginess are mutually exclusive. The gospel and parsimony cannot dominate the same heart. When one is enthroned the other must be dethroned. A man says he is a Christian, very well! What does he mean by the assertion? Does he mean that he professes to be a Christian for the sake of what he can get out of religion, claiming all privileges but recognizing no obligations? Simply this? Then what right has he to bear the name of Christ? To be sure, salvation is a free gift. It cannot be purchased with money; but unless one is willing to give of his money, we may be certain that the free gift has not come to him. The life of Christ in the heart is sure to loosen the grip on the pocket-book. A man does not love God at all, unless he loves him to the last dollar.

A Christian is not to be a barrel, into which water is poured to stagnate, to be drawn thence, insipid and lifeless, only through a rusty faucet, that gives forth a creaking protest every time it is turned; he is to be, rather, a fountain, into which the waters of life flow with a benediction and from which they leap with a song, to carry refreshment and gladness to others. Christians need to cultivate the grace of liberality. They should practice giving according to their means, not according to their meanness. The christian virtues cannot thrive on a diet of niggardliness. It is only "the liberal soul that shall be made fat," and "he that watereth" is the one who "shall be watered also himself."

The need of emphasizing this duty did not perish with that generation. In these afternoon hours of our wonderful century, when the high tides of life sweep and surge around us with such terrific force; when great fortunes are accumulated; when multitudes are falling down to worship the great god Mammon who rules this modern Babylon; there is danger that even christian men will become so absorbed by the feverish struggle for wealth as to grow sordid and grasping. There is still many a Shylock—and I fear he sometimes pretends to be pious and joins the Church—who will not fail to demand his "pound of flesh" nor to mourn for his "ducats" if he happen to lose any of them. To guard against this spirit and subdue it altogether we need to cultivate the opposite virtue.

II. CHRISTIAN LIBERALITY IS BASED ON DEFINITE PRINCIPLES.

The word "principles" implies, at the outset, that giving is not, in itself, a virtue. "Though I bestow all my goods to feed the poor, ... and have not love, it profiteth me nothing." We may go further, and say that indiscriminate and large giving to individuals may be a curse and almost a crime, ruinous to his confidence in human nature on the part of the giver, and degrading to the character of the recipient, promoting shiftlessness and destroying self-respect. That some one asks you to give is not a sufficient reason why you should give. To be poor is not necessarily a virtue, or to be rich a crime. And should the rich man give until he, too, shall become poor, that fact alone would possess no merit.

Again, the basis of true liberality is not impulse. Too many Christians, even of those who give largely, are spasmodic in their giving. They give, not according to a well-considered plan, but as controlled by their uncertain feelings.

It is a method without method. In it is no satisfaction, and upon it can be placed no dependence. It is just about as rational, as would be the attempt to obtain a liberal education by ignoring systematic and persistent study, and by superficially reading whatever "happened" to come in one's way, whenever one "happened to feel" like reading. By such giving, the chief end of christian beneficence, as an act of worship and a means of developing character, is entirely lost. To be governed by feeling is as objectionable in this matter as it is in the exercise of any other christian duty.

Better than this hysterical way of giving, spasmodic and

impulsive, is the system of Paul. With all our nineteenth-century wisdom we have not improved on his method. And this is largely because it *is a method*, and because it embodies the best conclusions of "sanctified common sense."

In his earlier letter to the Corinthians, the Apostle gives specific directions for making the offering for the relief of the famine-stricken Christians at Jerusalem. " Upon the first day of the week let every one of you lay by him in store, as God hath prospered him.". Here is the whole matter in a nutshell.

The first thing we notice about it is that it is universal in its application. "Every one." Upon this thought we need not tarry. We have already seen that liberality is a duty, from which no christian man can be exempt.

We notice further that this system demands regularity and frequency. The offerings are to be laid by "every week," not once a month, not quarterly, not yearly, still less when the mood is right. Who can suggest a more common-sense way of raising money? It fits the wage-earner as well as the millionaire, and implies that those in moderate circumstances no less truly than the wealthy are to share in the responsibilities and privileges of sustaining christian enterprises. As the majority of wage-earners receive their pay weekly, what method so easy, so likely to secure large results, or so helpful to the giver, as for each one, when pay day comes, to deposit a fixed portion of his receipts in the Lord's treasury? How, moreover, can each so certainly be kept in touch with the various objects of christian beneficence? One cannot forget or be indifferent to that for the sustenance of which he frequently and regularly contributes.

Still further, this plan requires equity in its operation. "Let every one . . . . as God hath prospered him." And again : " If there be first a willing mind, it is accepted according to that a man hath, and not according to that he hath not." According to ability, no less, no more ! That is the rule. The rich man, much; the poor man, a little; the pauper, nothing. But each one according to all the circumstances. God would not unduly burden his people. There is a limit to what even the rich man should be asked to give.

For, while emphasizing the duty of liberality, we must know that it is possible to give more than one ought. To be sure, there may come extraordinary conditions, when a man must give to his last dollar. God has a right to say: "The silver and the gold are mine," and to demand his own to the uttermost. But until these extraordinary exigencies arise, God requires a wise as well as a generous use of money. To some he has given responsibilities different from if not greater than those bestowed on others. The relative demands of these various responsibilities must be weighed before a right decision can be reached as to the amount to be given for what we ordinarily term benevolence. For example, a man is responsible for the education of his children as well as for the conversion of the heathen. If, therefore, he give so largely for missions as to deprive his children of the opportunities they have a right to demand, he is not giving "according to his ability" as God requires, but more than his ability. It is not a virtue to give for the purpose of converting the heathen into christians, if thereby he allow his own children to be converted into heathen.

Again, true liberality requires wisdom in its exercise. It does not bid all men of equal means to give equally for benevolence. God's moral laws harmonize with his economic laws. Mr. A. may be rich, keeping a thousand men in his service. He might give a million dollars to some charity and still be rich; but if he should, by the act, withdraw so much capital from productive channels as seriously to cripple his business and thus materially diminish his subsequent power to give, or as to compel the discharge of a hundred workmen, or necessitate a reduction of ten per cent. in the wages of a thousand, the gift is obviously larger than he ought then to make. As things are, he is morally responsible for keeping that regiment of men employed. In meeting this responsibility he is really doing a work of beneficence that should be reckoned as a part of his obligation, whether he or the world look upon it in that light or not. On the other hand, if his wealth be all invested in interest-bearing stocks or in rented houses, his "ability" will be greatly enhanced, and consequently his responsibility. It is admitted that Mr. A. is not likely to step forward and introduce himself as the rich man who is about to withdraw so much capital from productive channels as to cripple his business and injure labor, for the sake of giving to some charity. The case is purely hypothetical, yet it will serve to illustrate one of the basal principles of the New Testament plan of beneficence, namely: that you can not absolutely determine how much one ought to give, solely on the basis of his possessions or income.

Finally, christian giving is to be voluntary. It is to be an offering, not a tax. I know that for saying this I may be branded as a heretic. Many good men assert that the Mosaic requirement of one-tenth of the income has passed over into the gospel dispensation. But I am not convinced that the assertion is well-founded. I do not object to it because of the proportion. Many men ought, doubtless, to give more than a tenth, while some may properly give less. The chief objection rests in the fact that the theory annuls a fundamental principle of Christianity—the voluntary element. A prime distinction between the old dispensation and the new is that the old was a system of legal requirements, while the new is a system of free choice. The old drove, the new draws; the old rested on the love of law, the other exalts the law of love; the old thundered from Sinai, the new pleads from Calvary. Christ's death broke the bondage of the law, and introduced the liberty of the gospel. No exception was made in the case of benevolent offerings. The Mosaic exaction of one-tenth went with the rest. And it is well; otherwise, giving would become mere formalism, burdensome and lifeless, instead of, as intended, an act of love and worship. That the law was abolished, Paul plainly teaches in this second letter to the Corinthians: "Every man according as he purposeth in his heart, so let him give; not grudgingly or of necessity." So he would have us bring our gifts; not because giving, as such, is a virtue, or from impulse; but to bring them as a universal duty, regularly, according to ability, wisely, voluntarily, and lay them at Christ's feet, because love prompts us to "bring an offering, and come into his courts."

III. CHRISTIAN LIBERALITY IS BENEFICENT IN ITS RESULTS.

To the giver it signifies the development of his spiritual nature. For we must remember that the christian virtues are not to be segregated one from another. You cannot elevate or degrade one, without exerting a corresponding influence upon others. When a Christian practices true liberality, thus lifting his giving up to the high plane of free and joyful service and worship, he is, likewise, elevating and imparting culture to all the finer qualities of his soul. The exercise of this grace quickens his conscience and his judgment, by compelling him to study his obligations, and to give on the basis of duty, as measured by the relative claims of those obligations on the one hand, and by his ability on the other. It promotes love for his fellow-men and enlarges his sense of responsibility for them, by giving him a new and personal interest in the christian enterprises which his benefactions help sustain. By lifting him above the narrow valley of selfishness, it broadens his horizon, so that he may catch the vision of remote need, as well as of that on his own street.

The Germans have a motto: "Over the mountains are people also." The practice of true liberality puts the spirit of this proverb into the Christian's heart. It gives him a conviction of the brotherhood of man, and makes him realize that there are other people for whom Christ died beyond the mountains that shut in his own dwelling-place. So it teaches him to look at life in a large way, as sweeping from the past into the future in one great whole, in which each individual and each moment of time possesses vital relations to all the race and to all time.

To the church this system, if adopted, is, likewise, a blessing. It promotes unity and equalizes burdens. The poor are not oppressed by it, nor can the rich enjoy a monopoly of its advantages. All have a share in the burden and the blessing. It brings in more money than to proceed planlessly or by any other plan. Should it be generally adopted, how the Lord's work would prosper! The thought of such a condition brings a vision of church debts abolished, of pastors' salaries promptly paid, of church work strengthened and extended, and of the missionary societies enabled to press forward to make new conquests and subdue new territory for the King.

Since liberality is a christian duty, based on definite and simple principles, and beneficent in its results to the individual and to the church, may we not hope that there will come a time when this grace will be universally exemplified?

To the world at large, the results of its general adoption would be equally glorious. Should all Christians put it into operation to-day, the work of conquering the world for Christ would receive a tremendous impulse. The missionary hosts thus put in the field would be invincible.

> "Like a mighty army,
> Marching as for war,"

they would make such progress, that, by the close of this century, the missionary drum-beat would be heard around the world. With the sun-rise of the new century would appear at least the faint dawn of that day for which we wait:

> "When wealth no more shall rest in mounded heaps,
> But smit with freer light shall slowly melt
> In many streams to fatten lower lands,
> And light shall spread and man be liker man
> Through all the season of the Golden Year."

Lesson VIII.   November 19.

IMITATION OF CHRIST.

Ephesians iv: 20-32.

By Rev. C. R. HENDERSON, D. D., Detroit, Mich.

THE greatest devotional work of the christian centuries was written by a Romanist monk, and bears the title, "The Imitation of Christ." Four gospel writers have left on record as many pictures of Jesus, differing but harmonious. This enables us to know what Jesus himself taught as the vital law of his religion: "Follow me." This phrase sums up all the forces and rules and graces of our holy faith.

I. The divine principle and source of christian life is thus declared: "Even as God in Christ forgave you." There is a natural and instinctive bond of sympathy between most of the higher animals, especially those of a gregarious nature. Even a tigress exhibits toward her young an affection which hints at the moral bond of humanity. As one mind created all conscious beings it would be strange if there were not some common elements between the lower and the higher which might serve as parables for the spirit of man. And that more conscious and purposed morality which is manifested even where gospel light does not shine, is connected with a feeling of kinship. The ancient tribe recognized certain rights as belonging to those who are of one race and who worship one deity. Savages who scruple not to rob and kill members of other tribes will hold sacred the welfare of their kindred. But when God revealed himself incarnate in Christ the deeper meaning of all unconscious and narrow sympathies become apparent. In God the Father all men are of one kindred. The historical critic may doubt or deny that all men are descendents by physical lines from one ancestor, as Adam. The devout man of science, Agassiz, thought there must have been several centres of human life at the beginning. But while christian men of science may think the common origin of man from one human ancestor to be questionable, the common relation to God the Father cannot be denied. Here is a truth that does not wait upon the slow process of historical investigation. From this incarnation of God in Christ there is a transition of love. By the Mediator, Son of man and Son of God, we receive forgiveness. The same outflow of mercy which forgives, regenerates. That eternal love of God in Christ is the cause of the new man "which after God hath been created in righteousness and holiness of truth."

This revelation is the foundation of christian ethics. Duty as viewed by a Christian is more than an animal instinct of sympathy or a local feeling of clan fellowship. It is a distinct recognition of universal brotherhood in God. Its argument is this: "Be ye holy, for I am holy," spoken by God. And no other argument addressed to self-interest, to conscience, to aspiration for noble life, to gratitude or hope could be so powerful and convincing as this. The argument becomes a motive. "I beseech you by the mercies of God." "The love of Christ constraineth us." The impulse to act uprightly and kindly starts with the personal influence of the Lord, the Image of the Father. As the body of plant or animal is formed by its vital principle more than by its environment or food, so the chief forming law of our conduct is this "life in Christ Jesus." As the source of duty in Christianity is the highest, purest and divinest, so the morality that grows out of it is superior to all others. The moral philosophy and the civilization of christianized cummunities both manifest the presence of the supernatural christian energy. The inherited tribal morality of earlier times based the right to hold black men slave property on a denial of kinship. These words of the eminent politician, Mr. Stephen A. Douglas, shock and startle us now by their awful blasphemy. "I do not question Mr. Lincoln's conscientious belief that the negro was made his equal and hence his brother, but for my own part, I do not regard the negro as my equal, and positively deny that he is my brother or any kin to me whatever." The mental and moral confusion of that last sentence would be impossible now in a youth; not long ago it was regarded by many as political wisdom. Even yet the pride of wealth and the envy of poverty and the strife of industrial war blind men to the fact of their kinship. Only in a genuine realization of such kinship as a divine fact can society ever come to be at one.

II. The Apostle expects from this christian source of goodness, this influence of the divine image, and the accompanying energy of the regenerating spirit, christian dispositions. "Be ye kind one to another." In our language the word kindness is closely related to the word kinship. And kinship is given here as a reason for veracity and for all holy graces: "For we are members one of another." In God the Creator, in Christ the Redeemer, in the Holy Spirit, the regenerating agent, we are one by a bond of faith and love.

Would we know the breadth and compass of the required kindness? See how great: "Even as God." Here the disciple merely repeats what the Master had said: "He maketh his sun to rise on the evil and the good, and sendeth rain on the just and the unjust." "While we were yet sinners Christ died for us." Let us not look for "worthy" objects of our charity, but even seek the unworthy to transform them. Here is no pinched morality of the tribe or sect or province. It is wide as the arch of heaven and deep as divine pity. "Be ye perfect even as your father who is in heaven is perfect."

And this kindness is to reach the degree of "tenderness." Jesus was not stoical. He was not a frosty philosopher who could stand unmoved and tearless by the sepulchre of a friend that had often shown him hospitality (John xi. 35). Let others boast of a wisdom that makes their hearts marble to misery and sin; Jesus wept over Jerusalem. This sensitiveness of heart is contrasted with that blindness and hardening which results from gross and selfish sin, as well as from a false doctrine of God (v. 18). Burns, in giving advice to a young friend, selects for special remark this effect of sensual vice: "It hardens all within, and petrifies the feeling." The cruelty and lust of Nero were not connected by mere accident. As fire and oil make hotter fire by mingling, so vice and cruelty react upon each other to augment the fury of destruction in each. Kindness reaches its climax in that disposition which demands the most self-denying, Christ-like love,—forgiveness. It is with this word Jesus sums up his doctrine of prayer (Mat. vi. 14). "If ye forgive men their trespasses, your heavenly Father will also forgive you." The gift for the very altar of God must wait until the last trace of malice and revenge has been washed away in a sincere effort at reconciliation with an estranged brother. If there is any other grace that is lovely and of good report it will arise out of kindness. As all the branches and limbs and leaves of a tree grow from its root and trunk, so all forms of goodness will spring from moral union by faith with God in Christ.

III. But the Apostle shows in this passage that it is not enough to have good dispositions hidden in the heart. God became incarnate in Christ, and the divine disposition must become embodied in outward form and institution. Music is not fully music so long as it remains an unheard dream of melody in the mind of the artist. It must find material instrument and voice. The architect is never sure that his plan is beautiful and conformed to the laws of strength until it is embodied in the frozen music of marble and metal. Now the order and institutions of society are the divine ordinances (Rom. xiii: 1-7) for manifesting and cultivating right dispositions. In this chapter, the writer selects several of the outward social forms and invests them with the sanctity of christian motives and ideals. In doing this he does not attempt a complete code of laws for all times, but shows the way to apply Christianity to life everywhere and always. Here are germinal notions of a christian science of society to whose genial expansion all modern knowledge and experience may be made tributary.

Human life is made sacred. While the command, "Do no murder," is implied rather than expressed, it certainly is involved in the words: "Let not the sun go down upon your wrath. . . . . Let all bitterness, and wrath, and anger, and clamor and railing, be put away from you, with all malice." As the very steps of a noble temple are made of shining marble, protected with walls and towers, and adorned with carved work, so the approaches to the sanctuary of human life are defended and beautified. Jesus had taught that to hate a brother in the heart was to kill. The Apostle does not seem to think it necessary to forbid Christians to kill each other. But he knew too well that malicious thoughts lead to cruel words and these to mortal blows.

Human chastity is protected in the same way (v. 19).

Marriage is the source of life and must be kept pure. Lust and greed are its foes. The safeguard of the family is this law of kindness which keeps unlawful thoughts at a distance and refuses to enslave or be enslaved.

Human property, as the material basis of life, is made sacred by the kindness of Christ. That love of God infused into the soul, would make the origin of property holy. "Let him that stole, steal no more; but rather let him labor, working with his hands the thing that is good." We are not only to work, but to work for ends, for uses. The thief is often very industrious. The burglar busily turns night into day. The dishonest clerk, the speculator in the savings of widows and orphans, the railroad wrecker, the saloon keeper, the distiller are often very industrious men. They rise early and sit up late to cheat and injure other men. We are bound by christian law to work at something honorable and socially useful. Paul set the example himself. He was a tent-maker.

Property must be kept sacred in its uses, when once acquired by upright means: "that he may have to give to him that hath need." This is the highest end of business and agriculture and manufacture, to give. The needy are God's altar. Christian character finds its supreme test, in our mercantile age, in the use of money. As a man gives so is he. We talk of the "sacredness" of property. Honest acquisition and humane use make it "sacred." But when it is gained by injustice and employed in wasteful extravagance or in oppression, it is then, as Proudhon said, "robbery."

Human speech is made sacred by Christian kindness. The bond of social fraternity requires entire veracity. "Putting away falsehood, speak ye truth each one with his neighbor; for we are members one of another." "It is mean to lie to your kindred; but then all men are brothers." So the Sweet Voice said. Language is the symbolic bond of spiritual fellowship; he who lies cuts that bond and isolates men. Domestic, social, industrial, commercial welfare is built on veracity. Speech is the current coin of social interchange of thought and feeling and purposes. To debase it with alloy of deception, exaggeration, obscenity, profanity, is a crime condemned by the law of love.

In the same spirit a Christian will guard with justice and kindness the good name of his brothers. This is that jewel whose loss makes one poor indeed. "Thou shalt not bear false witness against thy neighbor." So said the old covenant law. The new covenant teaches us that all men are our neighbors.

Whatever new conditions may arise in the course of history, whatever may be the relations of business or of state, this method of christian charity will suffice to solve the problems and point the way. An agnostic or atheistic sociology must ever fail to comprehend and compass all the elementary forces of humanity, and must ever come short of suggesting all the available agencies of redemption and progress.

Christian kindness is manifested in outward conduct, but it is also affected by conduct, according to the law of reciprocity between act and inward state. As the flying shuttle weaves warp and woof in cloth, so the actions of life weave together right dispositions and worthy conduct into one strong fabric of character. The root is supposed to feed the leaves, but it is often forgotten that leaves nourish the roots. A life of piety leads men to deeds of justice and mercy, but deeds of goodness send the man of God back to his meditations and prayers with a truer insight and a deeper purpose of holiness. Prayer, meditation and temptation form the theologian. The eye shows the hand the food, and the stomach nourishes both hand and eye. The interplay of these external and internal elements of christian life is well shown in the passage before us for study. The world has no need of an atheistic morality, for that omits the highest ideals, the most sacred duties, and the most powerful motives. Nor do we need a mere unmoral religiosity, a sentiment of dependence and gratitude. Such are without corresponding devotion to duty. The supreme need is a religious, a christian righteousness. A righteousness apart from God is a cut flower stuck in a vase, and it soon withers. An emotional worship that expends itself in shouting, without purity, honesty, veracity, is a cloud that sweeps before the wind over a parched soil and yields no fruitful showers. We must seek to attain earnestness of faith in the invisible together with an intelligent apprehension of the right ways of the holy Lord.

Lesson IX. November 26.

THE CHRISTIAN HOME.

Colossians iii: 12-25.

BY REV. C. C. BROWN, SUMTER, S. C.

THE ideas that present themselves in these verses may be grouped as :
I. Directions for a godly life, vv. 12-17.
II. Directions for a godly home, vv. 18 ; iv : 1.
The two sets of reflections are not sharply contrasted, but the first leads up to the second.

I. Directions for a godly life.
"Put on therefore," the lesson begins. The costume of a saint is here described, made up of compassion, kindness, humility, meekness, long-suffering, "and over all the silken sash of love." The Christian could surely have no more fitting uniform than this.

"Forbearing one another." Forbearance is a wonderful virtue, rarely appreciated or possessed. It has reference to our treatment of those from whom we have a right to expect something, but in whom we have been disappointed. The forbearing man is he who knows how to surrender at times and for good purposes even his rights. Forbearance is a greater virtue than forgiveness. We are to forgive when one repents ; we ought often to forbear whether there is repentance or not, so passing over the infirmities of our fellows.

"And forgiving each other." To forgive is to forth-give, to

send out clean from you—to dismiss from mind and heart. Revenge is mean and little; forgiveness is divine. To win a fight with sword and gun is not of necessity great, but to subdue your enemy after God's way, using the one weapon of forgiveness, is the greatest of victories. Forgiveness is a distinctively christian virtue. A Roman considered himself happy who, on his death-bed, could say, in reviewing his past life, that no man had done more good to his friends or more mischief to his foes. Our Lord's teachings subverted and supplanted such a creed, and gave to the world the doctrine of the skies. Alas that so few of us have really gotten hold of his idea. A great deal that is taken for forgiveness is just a passing over of offenses without forgiving them, with no removal of the bad feeling from the heart. Hence it is that there is so much bitterness among men.

A traveler saw, in the south of France, a row of beggars sitting on the side of a bridge, day by day, winter and summer, showing sores on their arms and legs. These sores were never allowed to heal, but were kept continually raw, in order to excite compassion and obtain alms. The man with only an inflamed knee would envy him whose whole leg was sore. Some persons nurse their grievances as these beggars their sores. They seem proud of them, loving to expose what they call their wrongs. Thus life is kept in continual ferment. The doctrine of the Bible is, you must forgive. To what extent? one asks. "Even as the Lord forgave you," is the answer.

"'Teaching and admonishing one another," sets forth the idea of mutual helpfulness. This is not to be an *ex cathedra* impartation of instruction, but rather an interchange of spiritual help, in a purely religious spirit, as a religious exercise, by the use of "psalms and hymns and spiritual songs." Song, jest and wine formed the pastime of the ancients. Paul urges that we seize upon and use the best of these, the song, as a means of helping each other to heaven. The counsel of the

Apostle is that we use a regular service of song for our spiritual benefit, and the fact that he names three sorts of songs indicates that he did not expect us to confine ourselves to Psalms alone.

Song is a wonderful agency. Our song makers largely make our theology. Some modern doctrines found in our hymns are rather foreign to the Bible. But God has surely approved the service of song. It should be used in such a way as to help not only those who sing but as well such as only listen. No merely mechanical or perfunctory service ought it to be, but performed "with grace in our hearts unto the Lord"—not that you must sing with great skill or precision, with exact time or pleasing rythm; but that the graces of the heart, and all its affections that remind of God, must be brought into play. Then singing becomes service, and heaven comes down to earth.

It is worthy of notice that great revivals of song have always accompanied great revivals of religion. To these revivals we owe many of the mediæval hymns, the hymns of Luther, of Watts and of Wesley, and in later days the hymns of Bliss, Sankey and McGranahan. The history of hymns and of the victories they have won over men's hearts makes up a library of volumes. There are chords of music whose mystic tenderness defies all explanation. Our dearest memories are apt to cluster around some song. When President Garfield lay dying, he was permitted one day, feeling a little better, to sit at the window. His wife was in the next room, faith, hope, love and prayer all mingled in her christian heart. Softly and plaintively she began, "Guide me, O thou great Jehovah!" As the words floated into the chamber, the sick president turned and said, "Quick! Open the door a little!" After listening a few moments, Mr. Garfield exclaimed, as the tears coursed down his sunken cheeks, "Glorious, isn't it?"

Dr. Pentecost tells of a boy who came to one of the New

York city missionaries, holding out a dirty and well-worn bit of printed paper, and said, " Please, sir, father sent me to get a clean paper like that." Taking it from his hand, the missionary found it to be a bill with the hymn, " Just as I am," printed on it. Asked where he got it and why he wanted a clean copy, the boy answered, " We found it in sister's pocket after she died, and she used to sing it all the time when she was sick, and she loved it so much that father wanted to get a clean one to put in a frame to hang up." O the hymns! the hymns! Let us fill the world with them, singing them with true grace in our hearts, that we may praise God, teaching and admonishing men that they may turn to him and be saved.

II. Directions for a godly home.

Parents, children and servants are mentioned in these admonitions, the weaker, the subordinate, being in each case placed first. Wife comes before husband, child before parent, servant before master.

" Wife " means " weaver." Before the erection of our great factories, all clothing was woven at home by the wife. The girls spun the thread, hence were called spinsters. No doubt woman's position in the world has greatly changed since the Apostle's day, and will change more yet. So full is the air of declamation about woman's rights, some think a preacher out of his senses who dares to speak of women's " subjection." Yet the right kind of woman never hesitates to be in subjection to the right kind of a man; for it is no base subjection that the Apostle has in mind, but a sort of loving and voluntary bondage like the subjection of the Church to her heavenly Lord. The wife is subject, not because she has a master, but because her heart has found a rest. She takes a second place out of deference to her heart's idol, as every worshipper would fain be lower than the object worshipped. This relation places upon the husband a most solemn trust. In him we ought to find " pure religion breathing household laws."

Wrong as the Bible may appear to some in this, it cannot be denied that God, fate, government or custom has placed immense power in the hands of the husband and father in every house. He is expected to be its head. Every family requires a centre of authority, and men are so constituted as, commonly, to play this part better than women could. Women themselves nearly always defend this position. Those among them who are masculine and love to rule, find their severest critics among their own sisters. Nor does the subjection required involve any loss of power on the whole. The surest way for woman to gain her rights and to exercise an absolute and queenly reign, is lovingly to fill her God-ordained place as a help meet. Love conquers all things.

But husbands on their part have responsibilities. They must love their wives "and be not bitter against them." This is an important point. "Husband" means "house-band." The husband is the agent who keeps the house together. The word here used for "love" is a very strong one. It expresses the highest and most spiritual affection. Where the wife finds love like this she can endure much. The old adage, "when poverty comes in at the door, love flies out at the window," is base and false.

Note, Paul does not say, "Wives, love your husbands." Failure in this respect on the wife's side is comparatively rare, but the man, often absent and pre-occupied, is apt to fall into some disloyalty of heart. Other society takes up his time; he is led into amusements intended only for men; the wife loses her place as the confidante and sharer of his secrets; and home becomes to him only a sort of selfish convenience. Then he grows irritable, chafing under every domestic care, making no allowance for any human infirmity, magnifying every trifling mistake, and at last ignoring the wife's patient affection and untiring efforts to please. Bachelor though he was, the Apostle shows wonderful insight when he adds, "Be not bitter against them." How many there are who, while cross, churlish and spiteful at home, still pass for saints abroad, and who seem to have forgotten, or never to have known, that bitterness toward any one at home is not compatible with christian love!

Children next come in for an admonition. In this age of insubordination, when children are the masters of the home, it is well for us to hear again the precepts of the old time religion concerning parental rule, the command that children obey their parents in all things, and the assurance that this is well-pleasing to the Lord. Many a child has "come to himself" in the course of years, when it was too late, to discover that life's great mistake was made in despising the warnings and teachings of those at home who loved him and knew what was best for him. Not once in a thousand times do fathers or mothers teach children to go wrong. The testimony of multitudes who have won high places in the world is that they were greatly helped upward by obeying the voices of love at home. Thos. H. Benton, a United States Senator for many years, once said: "My mother asked me never to use tobacco, and I have never touched it from that day to this. She asked me never to gamble, and I never learned to gamble. When I was seven years old, she asked me not to drink. I made a resolution of total abstinence. That resolution I have never broken. And now, whatsoever honor I may have gained, I owe it to my mother." That such a man should become a senator is no wonder. The world has no place too high for such.

But the Apostle knows full well that children's failure is not always due to their own depravity. He therefore warns parents, and especially fathers, not needlessly to provoke children, so as to discourage them. In the hands of some persons authority is always out of place. Especially is this so in the case of a father who uses his parental power only to censure and abuse. Even parents are sometimes mean and exacting just because they have no one over them. Thus the child comes to regard his father as a tyrant, and loses heart. I have seen many children cowed and broken in spirit because of abuse; whose sense of justice had been violated until they wondered if there were such a thing as justice, and who, at last, became sneaks and sulks, without will or purpose to seek good things.

Dr. Bushnell has given us some wise words on this subject, showing parents how children's spirits are broken. 1. By too much prohibition,—a sort of monotonous "Don't," that does not stop with ten words, like the words of Sinai, but keeps up an everlasting thunder. 2. By unfeeling and absolute government. If a christian father is felt to be a tyrant, he will seem to his child to be a tyrant in God's name, and that will be enough to create a sullen prejudice against all sacred things. 3. By an over-exacting manner and a difficulty of being pleased. Children love approbation, and are disappointed when they fail in their meritorious endeavors. 4. By holding displeasure too long, as if to make the child think the parent entertains a grudge, thus turning the child's repentance into a stubborn aversion. 5. By hasty and false accusation. When children are put under the ban of dishonor, they are very likely to show that they are no better than they are taken to be. 6. By keeping them in a continual torment of suppression. Only to be in a room with an over-anxious person is enough to make one unhappy. What, then, is the woe put upon a hapless little one who is shut up day by day to the fearing look and deprecating whine and supercautionary keeping of a nervously anxious mother. 7. By giving them tests of character that are inappropriate to their age, such as requiring the boy to retire to pray because he has given way to a fit of passion. The rule destroys itself which says a child must not play at all on Sunday, while the father interests himself, even in the church, with his secular concerns.

The Apostle's attention now naturally turns to servants or slaves, who are to "obey in all things them that are their masters according to the flesh." The Bible does not teach the doctrine of race-superiority; but history shows that, in nearly all ages and lands, some men have been masters and some slaves. Servants not legal slaves are not seldom slaves in effect. Often the most abject slaves are found among people who are the most blatant about human freedom. It being true that some human beings are to be slaves or servants for others, the Bible, doing ever the wise thing, seeks to show these how to make the best out of their circumstances. The master's will, says the Apostle to the slave, is to be your will, and you are to obey heartily, not only when watched, or when doing such things as will catch and please the master's eye, but in all things. In doing your duty, try to please both your earthly and your heavenly master. Your faithfulness God will reward. He will ultimately right all your wrongs. If your master wrongs you, leave vengeance with God. For a slave to be an heir was a paradox, but here is promise of an inheritance even to slaves provided they serve in the spirit of Christ.

As parents are under obligation to children, so are masters to such as serve them. "Masters, render unto your servants that which is just and equal, knowing that ye also have a Master in heaven." This is the Apostle's noble, manly plea for truth, justice and mercy to every toiler and bondsman under the sun. The fact that one is a slave does not give another any right to abuse him. The master has his rights but he has his duties also. He is dealing with human beings, not with machines. The iron laws of political and domestic economy are not safe guides here. They may teach how to get rich, though gospel rules will aid even this, but will never show how to get to heaven. "Just dealing and fairness must rule in the relations of master and man, if they are to be on a moral and righteous footing. He must not take a hard advantage of his servant's necessity, or allow their dealings together to degenerate into a mere struggle between capital and labor for every inch of vantage. Cruel greed that grasps at immediate gain at whatever cost of toil and poverty to others, and that 'grinds the faces of the poor,' may enrich the individual, but in the long run will prove fatal. Political economy itself teaches that ill-paid labor is the most expensive and wasteful. The man who has want and fear gnawing at his heart cannot be a good workman, even if he be an honest one. Christ's golden rule of equity is the only safe, as it is the only righteous, basis for the dealing of man with man, of class with class, of nation with nation in the world's great polity. 'As ye would that men should do unto you, do ye also to them likewise.' "

Combine, now, all these virtues which the Apostle urges, and what a home have we not—the wife and children dutiful, the husband gentle, the father tender, the master considerate, the servants willing and honestly anxious to please—a veritable heaven on earth! Yet precisely that is the christian ideal of domestic society, an ideal realized just so fast and far as the gospel of our Lord Jesus spreads.

Lesson X. December 3.

GRATEFUL OBEDIENCE.
James 1: 16-27.

BY REV. PRESIDENT B. L. WHITMAN, WATERVILLE, ME.

THIS Epistle was written to persons already Christians, whose character was defective, whose conduct wrong. It quite subordinates doctrine, never discussing it out of any speculative interest, but abounds in precepts of a practical nature. It names Christ only twice, though there is in it nothing at variance with the most exalted conception of his character and work. Christ is, indeed, the source and subject of its thought. No book of the New Testament is more pervaded with his moral teaching. Ever since this Epistle was written men have found it in spirit if not in word, a true echo of the Sermon on the Mount. It is the message of an intensely earnest and clear-headed man who, not neglecting christian doctrine, exalts life as against all mere theory and speculation.

In the section forming the lesson of to-day are set before us two great and rich thoughts, God's goodness and man's consequent obligations, the one having to do rather with doctrine, the other more conversant about duty.

I. GOD HELPS BUT DOES NOT TEMPT.

The section is introduced by discourse concerning temptation. Running through that introductory matter and the first few verses with which we have particularly to do is a line of instruction and exhortation in which we find a common misconception corrected.

Outward and inward trials then pressed hard upon the Jewish-christian flock. They seem to have mistaken both the purpose of their suffering and the source of the evils from which some of them were in danger. They overlooked the revealing work of trial. They failed to see how affliction is adapted to draw out the graces of life. They saw in free moral agency only the possibility of sin, disregarding the fact that through freedom alone are virtue and piety possible, and that freedom was given for virtue and piety, not for sin. They thus missed the most important of all the truth concerning trial, that men are tested not to allure them to sin but to lead them to triumph over sin and so become morally strong.

They still more seriously mistook the source of moral evil. They did what men are forever doing in their attempt to find excuse for wrong actions. They said, "This temptation is of God. As he is the author of it he must assume the responsibility for it." James tells them that such a suggestion is from the devil. Sin is not of God. Permission is not compulsion. Moral evil is due to voluntary disorder in the being in whom it is found. The strength of temptation is not from without but from within. The responsible agent is neither God nor the devil, but the man's own self. When a man goes wrong it is his own lust that has led him astray. We must not give this word "lust" too narrow a meaning. It does not imply mere sensuality, as common use might suggest. Any ungoverned desire is lust; any propensity however innocent in itself, when it has gotten the upper hand. We are to see to it that every inclination of our nature is kept perfectly under the control of reason and religion. "Evil concupiscence," says a Jewish writer, "is at the beginning like the thread of a spider's web; afterwards it is like a cart rope." But at every step vicious desire is a man's own belonging, not another's. This is what James alleges and maintains. He clears God of all responsibility in the matter. He repudiates utterly the principle of of fatalism. He sweeps away his brethren's misconception and assures them that when they sin they alone are to blame.

A better thought is then given, for it is never enough merely to refute error. Positive truth must be put in its place. What does come from God—and he is continually active in our lives—is the good impulses and suggestions which assist us to overcome when we are tempted. What James says is, in effect, that "Good gifts and no other come from God; good gifts come from God and [ultimately] from no other." For the idea of "good gift" James has a double expression, one form suggesting a thing not proceeding from man himself, the other emphasizing the gratuity of the gift as a free present. In both senses the gift is declared good.

The writer gives us to understand that this is precisely the kind of dealing which we should expect from God, as indicated, first, by his nature. The word evil has no meaning as applied to God's acts or character. Used in such a connection it introduces a contradiction of thought. Moral evil has in him no part or lot. He is not even tempted to it. What is more, his nature is such that he cannot be tempted to it. Evil has no hold on him whatever. How then can we think of God as dealing with men with any purpose to lead them wrong?

The absurdity of such a thought is further evinced by viewing God's work in the physical world. We should have to search far for a better description of God than that given here, "the Father of lights." The very words are opposed to the suggestion of evil. Darkness is everywhere a hint of evil. Here the light of the heavenly bodies is regarded as simply a reflection of the essential character of God. The author of light can have no fellowship with evil, and his gifts to men will be like himself.

His work in spiritual creation is additional confirmation of this. His redemptive activity is peculiarly significant, as it reveals God in a sphere peculiarly his own. It is at bottom a work resting immediately on the divine will. It declares at once the author, the nature, the means, and the purpose of regeneration, and all these are alike good. Regeneration is simply God's crowning work and gift. From the goodness of this know the goodness of all that he does for us.

Such, then, is our lesson's first helpful thought. God is good. So far from wishing to lead men into evil, he is doing all he can to bring them through spiritual generation into goodness like his own.

Our scripture goes on to set before us also:

II. MAN'S DUTY IN VIEW OF GOD'S GOODNESS.

Regeneration is the crowning proof of the goodness of God. Attention is at once fixed by the writer upon the means blessed to that end. The gift of life comes to the believer from the grace of God through the gospel preached or read. "The new life is conceived of as having its source in God, but as brought into conscious being by the word of truth," "word" here meaning not "the Scriptures" of the Old Testament or the New, but rather the spirit or essence of all revelation. And, important as this christian truth is in the communication of the new life, it is no less important in the maintenance of that life. Continuance in the word means salvation. What duties in this matter do the claims of gratitude and safety lay upon the believer? They are many, but James specially emphasizes two.

Ready hearing of the truth is one of these. Maliciousness, stubbornness, opposition are out of place against any utterance of the word of truth. Even in earthly schooling hardness and reserve prevent the learner from getting the best that his teacher has to offer. A hypocritical attitude in a pupil is fatal to progress.

It is suggestive that the admonition to receive the word with meekness is addressed to believers. Christian men and women are to take heed how they hear. Upon them above others is laid the duty of teachableness. Those early believers were saved not for themselves only but as a kind of first-fruits, the beginning of an organic kingdom of righteousness. They were saved in consequence of God's love for the race. From that moment they were charged with a mission to the race. The same is true of all who are ever saved. As part of the fruit of Christ's work and as the pledge of a greater work, we stand in the place of the disciples when the Lord expounded to them the parable of the sower and bade them hear carefully because they were to be in their turn teachers. The best knowledge of divine truth that we can get is the least we ought to have. Whether through teaching, preaching or private effort, we are to make the word our own. An unread Bible is useless. Hasty, careless recognition of the truth hardens the soul.

Let a man just casually glance at his image in a mirror and then go away; how soon he loses all but the most general impression of what he is like. If the figure is suggestive now, how much more so when the mirror was only the polished metal with which James was familiar. The mirror shows one what otherwise remains unseen. It is intended to give detailed knowledge of one's appearance, especially of blemishes, and to show what improvements are desirable. This suggests a right use of God's word. A man is to look into it deeply, bend close over it, searching long and earnestly. He is to keep doing this. He will thus find out what manner of man he is. At the same time he will learn a good deal more. He will see where betterment is possible. He will learn to his profit how he may advance in the divine likeness and become in larger measure what he has already begun to be. Only the foolish man will be slow to use or careless in hearing the word of life.

Faithful doing of the word is of equal importance. This is

in fact the really vital matter. It begins to be so as soon as hearing begins. Evil in the heart is a bar to learning. So the hearer must at once lay aside all his evil thoughts and purposes. And when the word has been received, it profits only as it is used. Indolent contemplation avails nothing. The mere hearer, however satisfied he may feel that he is getting all he needs, is simply cheating himself. He deludes and robs his own soul. We need to beware of this, because religious truth has an immense speculative interest. One must get beyond a passion for mere hearing or idle contemplation. He must press learning to its issue in life. We are to know in order to do.

The believer's course in the discharge of the obligation thus propounded is clear enough. He is to follow the word as the law of his life. What is law? Speaking generally, law is a rule which must be observed in order to bring about a certain end or certain ends. That expresses exactly what is meant when we speak of the word as the law of life. It is the rule which we are to carry out that we may obtain the blessedness promised by God. Like every other law it is an expression of will. The word expresses the will of God. The New Testament is at one with the Old in this. They confront man with the same demand of submission. But the new is more perfect than the old. The Old was good, for its time the best available or applicable. But it had always upon it the stamp of immaturity. It was a code, a register of details, of prescriptions and ordinances, which inevitably failed by reason of men's weakness. In the New the same will is declared, but with what a difference! The Old discouraged men and added to their bondage by requiring obedience to an apparently infinite number of details, with comparatively little stress upon the spirit in which they were to be kept. The New requires obedience none the less, but gives life and ability therefor by revealing the unity and inspiring rationality of the moral law as identical with love. Love fulfils the law, itself fixing the code, the details thereof, by bending reason to its service for this purpose. Love being in the heart, obedience to God's law is rational, voluntary, and unconstrained.

This is why the law as set forth by Christ is "perfect." It is complete for the life whose conduct it directs and it fully and directly attains its object. It is also the law of liberty, because it does not burden with a yoke and enslave with enactments, but simply expresses what, by virtue of regeneration, it is the soul's tendency to do spontaneously. Thus the word appeals to the believer in two senses. It declares what he must do in order to fulfil the divine will; it declares what he is doing so far as he is in Christ. Hence the paradox of every day life, doing the will of God as the natural thing and ever submitting to the will of God anew. The law by which we accomplish this is perfect. Perfection of knowledge and obedience on our part should answer to the perfection of the law as divinely given.

However, even the believer, having still a double nature and so subject to carnal impulses, is exhorted to hold himself to practical righteousness. The man who does the work is the man who gets the blessing. The word of truth genuinely lodged in a man is no mere word, but a vital power, creative and life-giving, manifesting itself in all holy ways. Life shaped by the word is a life of activity. This is the point where many fail. They mistake desire for attainment. Knowledge is counted sufficient. Sometimes the mistake is unconsciously made. Oftener consciousness of mistake is betrayed by half-confession that there is in us something wrong, or by efforts to appear more than one is. When a man is satisfied with profession, or, on the other hand, goes out of his way to seem religious, it is a sure sign that there is weakness either in his heart or in his head. All such James rebukes and corrects. Mere appearance is nothing. Talking is vain. Self-deception cannot save. That which saves is regeneration by the will of God through the word. Man's part is to believe and do.

The "doing" required is partly within ourselves and partly without. True religion involves both an unspotted life and practical service for mankind. The world is godless. Its spirit is evil. The lust of the flesh, the lust of the eyes, the vain glory of life are like the world. They must be left to it. Sin is to be banished from desire, word, and work. The life is to be made clean and kept clean.

But there is an outward requirement. It takes an active hand as well as a holy heart to do all that religion commands. Life has its outer as well as its inner mission. The unspotted life is to bring something to pass in the world. Right effort is to be the evidence of right disposition. The direction effort ought specially to take is indicated by the specification "fatherless and widows." These words convey no exhaustive definition, but they do suggest a very prominent class of the righteous man's duties. Fatherless and widows stand for all the needy and sorrowing ones in the world. There is no better test of one's real state of heart, as graceless or in grace, than one's attitude toward the woes of the unfortunate. A pious spirit is sure to be a philanthropic spirit. What pure religion requires is not gush and tears over the unfortunate, but actual intervention, toil, generosity on their behalf, such as is indicated by "visiting" them. Off-hand and desultory benevolence is also not the thing. Intended kindness of that order is often a curse. "Visit" them; ascertain what they need, whether counsel, management, or alms, and minister accordingly.

It is true that according to the christian idea, the service of God consists not in any given specific acts, but in the offering of the whole life to him. But every man must remember that only through specific acts can the reality of the offering be judged. So we come to the thought of James that performance must pass judgment upon profession and that faith shows itself faith only as it finds issue in works.

He greatly mistakes who thinks he reads in all this a polemic against Paul's doctrine of justification by faith. We know from Peter that Paul's idea was early misunderstood, to the detriment of many. James doubtless intended by his Epistle to aid in correcting this abuse. But he will interpret Paul, not contradict him. Any one who has had practical experience of faith will not find it hard to see how James and Paul agree. Each has his own problem. James corrects the old Jewish error of trusting to a knowledge of the law without effort to do the law. But he everywhere assumes regeneration by the will of God as a thing indispensable to the production of good works, so that the doing of the law is simply the working out of that faith on the part of the Christian, of which Paul makes so much. Paul deals with those who cannot or will not break away from the habit of trusting forms and ordinances, as if salvation were to be earned and not gained through the grace of God. To these he says, "By grace have ye been saved through faith; and that not of yourselves; it is the gift of God." But Paul everywhere insists that the faith which saves is a living faith, doing as well as believing. Nowhere does Scripture hint that a mere intellectual faith is by itself of the slightest avail toward salvation. The problems of the two inspired writers are different, but when worked out the results are the same. The proof of spirit is life.

The message of James greatly deserves heeding. This is no "Epistle of straw," as so famous and good a man as Luther foolishly called it. Christian life is no mere matter of words, but a strenuous effort to do the will of God. It is forever the glory of the gospel that it makes men free, but our freedom is freedom for service. The law of our life is a law of liberty, but its obligations are more imperative than any decree of bondage. We must be diligent to accomplish good. Only so can we do God's will. Only so can we exhibit a love responding to God's love. Only so can we render grateful obedience.

Lesson XI. December 10.

THE HEAVENLY INHERITANCE.

I Peter i: 3-12.

BY REV. PROFESSOR WM. N. CLARKE, D.D., HAMILTON, N. Y.

WHOEVER desires to breathe the air of the Delectable Mountains, let him come hither. This whole passage is vocal with praise to God and aglow with joy. The high things of God are here. God himself is here, Father, Son and Holy Spirit. The trinity of graces is here, faith, hope and love. The heavenly glory is here, incorruptible, undefiled, unfading. Heaven on earth is here, a present salvation, joy that conquers sorrow, gladness unspeakable in him whom the eye sees not but whom the heart loves well. How great a gift of God it is that men are able to attain to these sober ecstasies of reasonable joy, and sing such strains of praise as this to God who has begotten us again unto a living hope!

1. The living hope is first the theme of rejoicing and of gratitude. Unto a living hope, a hope that throbs with divine vitality, God, the Father of Jesus Christ, has begotten us again. By a new birth it has become ours, even by that birth in which we became his full and genuine children; and so the hope is the filial hope, the expectation of possessing that which belongs to us as sons in God's own family. It is the hope of obtaining our inheritance, the hope of coming to our own. For we are heirs; heirs of God, and joint-heirs with Christ.

The First-born has many brethren, and to each of them as a child of God belongs the heavenly inheritance. To that inheritance therefore we lift up our eyes in living hope.

What a vision greets us as we look! The heavenly portion that we call our own is incorruptible, undefiled, and one that fadeth not away. Imperishable, no changes can destroy it; spotless, no marks of sin or shame are upon it; unfading, always divinely bright, its glory is never dimmed, its blessedness knows no alternations. "Incorruptible, undefiled and that fadeth not away:" how divinely such words about the unseen future sound, in this corruptible, defiled and fading world! How the vision shines, above the brightness of the sun! How it cheers our hearts as we lift our eyes to its glory! Yet this is no vision of mere fancy, no dream of the impossible: this is a glimpse of our inheritance as sons of God. What hope sees is the real. God has all this for his children. It has not still to be created, for it exists unseen; it is awaiting us, reserved in heaven, ready to be revealed in the last time. Our heavenly portion has not to be provided, but only to be manifested. When our eyes are closed, and opened, we shall behold it as it is.

But shall we, even we? Is it indeed for us? Shall we come thither? We know ourselves to be far from it as yet, and the uncertainties of the way seem great. How shall we know that it is possible for us to attain to the heavenly inheritance which so delights and fascinates our hope? These two are the agencies by which we are to be brought thither, power, and faith; power on God's part, and faith on ours. By the power of God, made effective for our help by means of faith in us appropriating it, we are guarded from the perils through which we must pass, until we come to that full salvation which is reserved in heaven and ready to be revealed. Is it enough? The strength is God's part, the trust is ours. He guards us all our journey through, and we, like children whom their father is bringing home, gladly accept his guardianship and loyally commit ourselves to his keeping. We know that he desires to bring us home, far more surely than that we desire to come thither. Is it enough? Is not he almighty? Is a hope that rests on such assurances from him a lifeless and decaying hope? No, this is a living hope, strong, vital, deathlessly alive. Because he lives, it lives also. It binds us by a link of living certainty to that holy future to which our best desires look forward, but upon which, otherwise, humanity has no certain hold. If we are born children of God whom he is guarding through power of his and faith of ours until the crowning-day, surely we have a living hope, glowing with divine reality.

Blessed be God for this, for his is indeed the glory. It was of his great mercy that he wrought all this grace in us, and him will we praise forever. And we will gratefully reckon this living hope as among the christian gifts, for it came to us by the resurrection of Jesus Christ from the dead. Christ came, and wakened spiritual hope in those who knew him, but when he was slain, hope was slain with him. What hour so dark as that in which the hope that he had nourished was turned to desolation and despair? But he arose from among the dead, and showed himself to his friends as one who could be trusted, not in this world only, but beyond this world; and thus he quickened again the hope that had died with him and been buried in his grave. Thenceforth men knew that they had a living Saviour, whose power not only took hold upon their inmost souls, but reached over to the unseen eternity; and thenceforth it was possible for the hope that was built on him to be a living hope, imperishable, undefiled and fadeless as the inheritance to which it looked. Yes, his living triumph brought into this earthly life the possession of the heavenly realities. It not only gave assurance that the city of our hope is the city that hath foundations, but it further justified our highest praise by bringing in, even here and now, a present salvation.

2. The present salvation is next the theme of gratitude.

Hope is not the whole. Faith already receives the fulfilment of its aspiration and its hope, and we possess as a present reality, incomplete, indeed, but genuine, the salvation of our souls. Salvation is not wholly a matter of the coming periods, ready to be revealed in the last time. Faith brings it near; nor is it merely seen as if it were here already,—it is here already. We possess it. Its transforming power is already manifested. The substance of heaven is upon the earth, and the divine inheritance is possessed here and now.

The present salvation is manifested in the glow of such a joy as this world knows nothing of. This is a world of sorrow; but when the Master went away he said to his friends, "I will see you again, and your sorrow shall be turned into joy." In the fulfilment of that omnipotent word we have our present salvation. Trouble is not to us what it was. Once we simply knew that we were suffering, that manifold trials were heaped upon us, that grief was our inalienable portion. But now we see these things in altered light. Now we know that it is but for a little while that we are put to grief through manifold trials, and this not without necessity. The conflict will soon be ended, and while it lasts it is not without its purpose, which is not hidden from us while we endure. Faith is our one thing needful, for by means of it God's power guards us to the end; and by the manifold trials our faith is tested, strengthened and approved. Men try gold by fire, and count exceeding precious the metal that is thus proved genuine; but the proving of our faith is in reality more precious far than the gold that men so highly prize. When we stand before our Lord and Master Jesus Christ, and the full fruit of this testing is apparent, the attestation of our faith will stand out glorious as bringing honor, praise and glory to our Lord. Our troubles thus confirm our faith and glorify our Saviour; and viewing them thus we glory in our tribulations also, aud are helped by them, not hindered, in holding our living hope of the pure inheritance.

Herein is indeed salvation even now. Christ has transformed us, when he has transformed our relation to our troubles. Only men of a new citizenship can see their troubles in this light. Thus to be lifted above the depression of our pains by a holy hope is to be saved out of the very heart of this world's evil.

But the present salvation is manifested even more richly in the new joy of love. Jesus Christ in whose resurrection our new hope was born, Jesus Christ whom we are to meet in the day of his revelation, Jesus Christ we love. It is true that we have never seen him, but not less therefore do we love him. We do not need to see him in order to love him, for we believe on him. We do not merely believe in him, as one who really exists: we believe on him, trusting soul and welfare to his gracious keeping; we believe on him as the Saviour whose power extends through all realms and ages, and who is able to keep forever that which we commit to his hands. Believing on him thus, we love him. Why should we not? He is worthy. He is the living justification of our living hope: for since such a friend as Jesus ever lives to save us, no hope that rests on him need ever tremble into disappointment. He will accomplish the work that he has begun, and fulfil to us the highest expectation that he has awakened. Such a friend we love, and our love toward him gladdens us with a joy already like the joy that is glorified in heaven. We do not merely rejoice because we have been delivered from the burden of our troubles; even more do we rejoice because we have a Saviour who is worthy of all our love, who bears the weight of all our faith, and who justifies our highest and divinest hope. Thus our joy is greater than we can express. It is joy unspeakable, and full of glory. Thus to receive, though incompletely, that end for which our faith is waiting, and to know our souls saved because we love the unseen Friend who saves us, is indeed to have unutterable reason for rejoicing, and to glow with a joy that transcends all songs of praise. Our heavenly inheritance has begun to come to us already, and our hope has begun to be fulfilled. Salvation is not a matter of time and of worlds, but of experience and reality.

> "Farewell, ye phantoms, day and year;
> Eternity is round us here,
> When, Lord, we dwell in thee."

No wonder that we would gladly call the attention of all creatures to so great an experience. We call upon all that is within us to bless the holy name of our Saviour God, and we invite all beings to rejoice with us in our high blessedness. We do not wonder when we learn that converging interest gathers to our little field of heaven on earth, for it is meet and right that all should acknowledge grace so great and joy so unspeakable.

3. The converging interest next arrests our notice. From before, and from above, the eyes of God's own have turned hither. Prophets have forseen this grace, and angels look wondering on, desiring to gaze more deeply into it. We have a sense of eyes upon us, and we joyfully consent, because they are the eyes of the holy, converging upon the wonders of grace.

Prophets, enlightened in former days, saw the gift of salvation coming to bless the world, but it still hung in dim outline before their eyes, and only by thoughtful study could they at all make clear to themselves the form of the future blessing. They discerned the coming Christ, the messenger of grace. They made out in the distance the sufferings that were appointed unto him, the way of pain through which he was destined to pass, and they saw the dawn, the day after darkness, the glories that must follow the sufferings of Christ. All this was shown them by that Spirit whom we know as the Spirit of Christ, testifying beforehand what God would do. But when? Was all this to come soon? Was it to bless their own age? This they sought to know, longing for speedy fulfilment of so divine a possibility. But they were taught by him who enlightened them that it was not for them or for their time. For us of later ages was this gift to be. The things that our heralds of grace, helped by the heavenly Spirit, have caused to be known as household words to us, they dimly knew as future; hoping, wondering and rejoicing, therefore, they bent their gaze toward this blessing which is now our portion, intent in thought upon Christ, the sufferings, the glories and the saving grace.

The prophets are not alone in their attention. Higher intelligences, wise with a heavenly wisdom, watch with living interest this introduction upon earth of a heavenly inheritance. Into these things angels desire to look, and we do not wonder. This is a world that holy beings cannot keep their eyes away from. The purer the spirit, the surer the hitherward look: for in this raising of men from sin to the undefiled inheritance, this actual springing-up of God's holy life in us his children, this planting of earth with heaven, the holy ones must all be interested. We know that Christ our Saviour watches it with joy, satisfied with this fruit of his pains, and that God our Father never loses sight of his children, in whom his own likeness is growing. Therefore we are not surprised if we are told that all holy interest converges upon our christian life. We are content to feel that we are compassed about with a cloud of witnesses. We are glad the heavens care. We are willing to live our life in the sight, and sing our songs in the hearing, of all who love our God, and to be his witnesses before all creatures, illustrating the glorious work of the grace which is in Christ Jesus. Watch us, ye holy ones, and cheer us with your eyes, and help us to keep our hearts intent upon loving Christ and being transformed into the likeness of our undefiled inheritance.

And now unto God let us sing our psalm of praise. Blessed, our hearts cry within us, blessed be the Lord God of grace, who is pleased for his mercy's sake to make new creatures of sinful men. Blessed be he who wakens within us the spirit of faith, that we may see him and trust him. Blessed be he who breathes into our life the breath of love, so that we become loving souls. Blessed be he who gives to us the strength and glory of a living hope. Thanks be to God, who found us living unto this world and lifeless unto the world above, and who made us alive together with Christ unto the realities that are incorruptible, undefiled, unfading. To him who has removed the home of our souls from this fading world to his own eternal habitation; to him who is transforming us into souls that care for holiness; to him who enables us to live the life of heaven upon earthly ground, and is making his very heaven in us here; to him in Jesus Christ, and to Jesus Christ in him, be gratitude, and trust, and love, and loyalty, to-day, and to-morrow, and all the days of the eternal life. Amen.

Lesson XII. December 17.

THE GLORIFIED SAVIOUR.

Revelation i: 9-20.

BY REV. J. V. GARTON, CAMBRIDGE, MASS.

TWO false and antipodal methods of interpretation have been applied to the book of Revelation with harmful results. The first is the prophetic, regarding the Apocalypse as prophecy pure and simple. The Saviour is supposed to have revealed to John an outline history of the Church and the world until the end of time. Some even believe that the chief events are given, in figurative form, with chronological accuracy. Interpreters of this class have made the book a theological skirmishing ground, prejudicing the minds of honest Christians and leading them to regard it as a repository of enigmas. The second school of interpreters is the rationalistic. These go to the other extreme. They eliminate the prophetic element and regard the treatise as contemporary history.

A third system of interpreting the Apocalypse combines what is true in each of the foregoing and yields the most satisfactory results. We may designate it as the historic-prophetic. According to this method the Book of Revelation is viewed as history, dealing with passing events. The aim of the book is practical; it is a message for the times, comforting and inspiring outraged and persecuted Christians. But the Book of Revelation is not only historic, it is prophetic as well. It rooted itself in its age but sent its branches into future ages,

It is history; this makes it a real book. It is prophecy; this renders it a continuously living book. To ignore either of these elements gives a false and narrow view of this scripture.

Let us now proceed to study the lesson of the day. It comprises an introduction to the epistles addressed to the seven churches of Asia. This initial revelation assumes the form of a vision, and it is our purpose to discover the contents and the signification of this.

I. PREPARATION FOR THE VISION.

The manner in which John introduces himself is noteworthy, and in striking similarity to that repeatedly used in the Book of Daniel. In his Epistles John addresses those to whom he wrote as "little children." Here he addresses them as brethren. In the Epistles he speaks with apostolic authority; now he is simply "a fellow partaker in their tribulation and kingdom and endurance in Jesus." In common with his brethren he is beneath the harrow of prosecution, enduring hardness as a good soldier of Jesus Christ. It is fitting that he should refer to himself as a brother rather than as a father.

"The island called Patmos" was a rugged, rocky crest, little more than a huge boulder projecting out of the water. It was situated in the Ægean Sea near the coast, south of Ephesus, and is about thirty Roman miles in circumference. In John's time it was probably uninhabited except by prisoners and their keepers. A cave is still shown where John is said to have received this revelation. How came John here? Some allege that it was not as an exile but as an Apostle engaged in christian work. Others believe that he visited Patmos by special divine order, for the specific purpose of receiving this important message. We prefer the traditional and generally accepted view, that John was a prisoner, a religious exile. The expression in the ninth verse indicates that it was a season of persecution, and that John was suffering with his brethren. He was there, he says, " because of," " in consequence of the word of God and the testimony of Jesus." The most natural meaning of this is that he was banished because of his love for the gospel.

John was in a state of spiritual ecstacy, induced by divine influence. Connection with surrounding objects through the senses seems to have been more or less completely suspended, and some special connection with the invisible world established. This occurred on the Lord's day. The evident reference here is to the first day of the week, kept by the christian Church as the festival of the Lord's resurrection. The evident familiarity of this expression indicates that "The Lord's Day" was a common designation of the christian day of worship and would be readily understood. So circumstanced and so prepared, the favored servant of God hears a great voice : the real voice of a real person, yet a person belonging to that spiritual world beyond the sphere of the senses and present only to one who, like John, was in the spirit. In loudness and clearness the voice resembled a trumpet. John is informed that he is to be the recipient of a divine message which he is to transcribe and remit to the churches of Asia. Only seven specific churches are mentioned, but there were other churches in the vicinity and they were, no doubt, all included. The number seven was selected, as is so often the case in the Book of Revelation, to express perfection, universality, completeness. The number of churches chosen here is representative, not exhaustive. Ephesus being the home of John, and the field of his labors, as well as the chief city of the province, heads the list.

II. THE VISION.

Having heard the trumpet-toned voice behind him, John turns to see from whom it comes, when a magnificent and extraordinary spectacle appears, the first feature of which consists in seven golden lamp-stands. The seven-branched lightholders in the tabernacle and temple from which the imagery is here derived, was for holding lamps. Reference is not made to the light but to the light-holders. The candelabrum of the Jewish sanctuary, described in Exodus and referred to in Zechariah iv. 2, consisted of a single seven-branched lamp-stand. In John's vision seven candelabra appear, each having seven branches or light-holders,—and these we are informed represented christian churches. In the Jewish system there is organic unity, one complex lamp-stand; in the christian system there is organic multiplicity, seven complex lamp-stands. Each is perfect in itself, while all are unified by a common life and a single purpose.

In the midst of the golden lamp-stands John saw a striking figure, "like unto the Son of Man," none other than the exalted and glorified Christ. The appearance of the Christ whom John had known so intimately and loved so tenderly was striking and significant. His long robe fastened about the chest with a golden girdle bespoke his priestly dignity and princely power. The transparent whiteness of his head and hair, as white as wool and snow, reminds us of his glory upon the mount of transfiguration and symbolizes his purity and majestic splendor. The brightness of his eyes resembled a flame of fire and gave force and expression to his face and perhaps indicated his omniscience. His feet were like fine brass, bright even as molten brass refined and glowing in the furnace. We can only conjecture what this imagery means. Possibly it refers to his swiftness in serving and ministering to his churches. We are reminded of Miss Havergal's couplet: "Take my feet and let them be swift and beautiful for thee." Or the glowing brass feet may refer to his power to trample upon his foes and crush the serpent's head with his now invulnerable heel. His voice was as the sound of many waters. An attendant angel apparently announced the vision and his voice was compared to a trumpet. John is now listening to the majestic voice of the exalted, glorified Son of Man himself, and while it is sonorous and impressive, it is also musical and soothing, like the sound of many waters.

This majestic, awe-inspiring personage holds in his right hand seven stars. They are arranged possibly upon his extended palm, in a circle like a wreath or garland. In the last verse of the chapter John is informed that the stars represent the angels of the churches. But who were intended by the angels? The term was doubtless clear to John's early readers, to-day the explanation needs explaining. Do the angels stand for the churches themselves? This would complicate and confuse the symbolism. Or shall we accept the phrase, "angel of the church," with the usual signification of the word "angel," as a heavenly genius or guardian spirit of the church? There are strong objections to this view also. The angels of the churches are held subject to condemnation and liable to blame as representing the churches. This could hardly apply to angelic beings. The angels of the churches are certainly none other than their authorized christian teachers, their pastors. Bishops in the modern sense can not be intended, for Episcopacy had not yet assumed sufficient development to render possible the use of such a title. But we know that even the earliest churches had each its quota of overseers, elders or pastors.

Out of the mouth of him who held the stars in his hand proceeded a double-edged sword. It is difficult to get a clear image of what is here presented. "We may think of a shining appearance, like a sword, as if it might be visible breath, proceeding from the mouth." The meaning, however, is obvious from other references. In II Thessalonians ii. 8, Paul says, referring to the lawless ones: "whom the Lord shall consume with the spirit of his mouth and shall destroy with the brightness of his coming." Revelation ii. 16 is of kindred import. In Ephesians vi. 17, the word of God is spoken of as the sword of the spirit, and in Hebrews iv. 12 it is declared to be sharper than a two-edged sword. The symbolism of the sword proceeding from the mouth therefore indicates the power of Christ's word and truth, which is destined to further whatever is good among men and to overthrow all evil.

Following the detailed description, the vision concludes by indicating the general effect of Christ's appearance. "His countenance was as the sun shineth in his strength." The sight was more than John could bear. Dazed and trembling he "fell at his feet as dead." When Moses came down from the mountain where he had met God, the people could not look upon his shining face and he was forced to wear a veil. We need not wonder that a view of Christ in glory should have so powerfully affected John. But he is soon reassurred. "He placed his right hand upon me," says the narrator. Up to this point possibly John was ignorant who this being was, though it was none other than "the Son of Man" whom he had known so intimately and between "whom and himself the tie had been so peculiarly tender." "Fear not." Voice is added to touch and John's trepidation is wholly dispelled. "I am the First and the Last."

The lesson ends with two mighty notes of triumph from the exalted Nazarene. "I was dead, I am alive." He was the living one, having life in himself, who had once tasted death for sinful man. Now he is alive forever more. Death hath no more dominion over him. Yea, he hath the "keys of death and of Hades." Christ's death and resurrection were representative. He is now Master of Death. He is alive from the dead, and all who live in him are destined to rise from the dead as he did, and to reign forever with him.

For suggestiveness, sublimity, and tender pathos this account of Jesus in glory appearing to John in solitary exile, is not surpassed in the whole Bible. How deep the emotion and intense the joy when John recognized in this majestic and glorious being the unmistakable features of his divine friend! He was exalted and clothed with power, but was John's loving Saviour still, still Son of Man as well as Lord of heaven and hell.

This lesson introduces us to three objects very important as seen from a heavenly view-point: the exalted Christ, the militant Church, and the gospel minister. Let us hastily review them.

1. The Apocalyptic conception of Christ.

On earth Christ was known as the humblest of mortals. He was despised and rejected of men. When men saw him there was no beauty in him that they should desire him. He had voluntarily laid aside his glory, that he might redeem sinful man. In his last intercessory prayer, Jesus besought, "O Father, glorify thou me with thine own self, with the glory which I had with thee before the world was."

John's vision shows this prayer answered. Christ is glorified. His countenance shines as the sun. But he is still the same loving, compassionate Christ that once trod the earth. He tenderly lays his pierced hand upon John, and banishes his fear with reassuring words. The human-divine Christ exalted, clothed with majesty and power, still retains his brotherly love and sympathy toward men and seeks their salvation. John sees him walking in the midst of the golden lamp-stands, viz., the churches. He is enthroned, yet abides with his militant people. "Lo, I am with you always." And he is in the midst of the churches not as an idle observer, but an active helper, familiar with the history and work of each, and ready to aid and guide.

2. The apocalyptic conception of the Church.

The individuality of the local church is emphasized. Each church is complete in itself, as illustrated by the seven-branched lamp-stand. In the epistles which follow the vision, each is addressed separately and held individually responsible for its own work and conduct. Such churches make up the Church.

Every church is set before John under the figure of a lamp-stand or light-holder. Sin is darkness, Christ's gospel is the true light. The church is the divinely ordained medium for communicating the light, and illuminating the dark, sinful world. Paul speaks of the Philippian Christians as "children of God, in the midst of a crooked and perverse generation, among whom ye shine as lights in the world, holding forth the word of life." "Ye are the light of the world." Sinful and dark our world is. Many are groping. "Let the lower lights be burning." Trim your flickering lamps; look well to the supply of oil; bear aloft the gospel light, until the darkness of sin is banished, and the full orbed day appears.

3. The apocalyptic conception of the ministry.

John saw seven stars. These were the angels or ministers of the churches,—the pastors. The stars were in the hand of the glorified Redeemer. They were his possession. A true minister is God's man. He has placed himself in God's hands to obey and serve and be used as God shall dictate. Paul spoke of himself as the bond-servant of Christ, who was his Master and Owner. But the conception includes more than this. Isaiah employs the same imagery to express God's love and interest. "I have graven thee upon the palms of my hands." Christ holds his ministers as jewels in his right hand; a position of safety and honor. They are not only his posession, but also his beloved.

In the epistles which follow the vision, the angels of the churches act as interpreters of the divine message to the churches. This was the chief function of the Old Testament prophet. He doubtless foretold future events, but his real office was to reveal to the people the mind and will of God as discovered in passing events. According to John's vision, the pastor is still a prophet, in the same sense. God still speaks to his Church through his ministers. It is still the duty of the christian minister, as a modern prophet, to live close to the throbbing heart of the exalted Christ, and having discovered his will, to deliver it warm and living to his people.

Lesson XIII. December 24.

[MISSIONARY LESSON.]

THE GREAT INVITATION.

Revelation xxii : 8-21.

BY REV. PRESCOTT F. JERNEGAN, MIDDLETOWN, CONN.

THE Alps are best viewed not from either extremity of the range, from the cloud-veiled summit of the highest peak, or from the hill-encircled base of the lowest, but from Mount Righi, near their centre. Thus the seventeenth verse of this chapter is the best point of view from which to interpret the whole. The preceding verses anticipate its approach; the following justify its presence. The morning and the evening twilight are best explained by the noon-day Sun. "Worship God" is the heralding note of the Great Invitation; "surely I come quickly" is the significant postscript to the King's call. In the study of this noble passage, note

I. THE FREENESS OF THE GOSPEL INVITATION.

Herein is the marvel of the gospel. Not that it is an invitation; invitations are common. Not so much that it is promiscuous; whole nations have been invited to advantageous alliances. The chief wonder of this summons is not even that its promise is life; life was offered before, but on very arduous conditions. "This do," viz., every detail of the law, "and thou shalt live." Evangelical salvation is the first world-wide gift that costs only the taking.

Ever since the gospel interpreted Isaiah's foreshadowing of this promise it has been an axiom that the water of life is without money and without price. Ever since Peter said to Simon Magus: "Thy money perish with thee because thou hast thought that the gift of God may be purchased with money," wealth has been regarded as a hindrance rather than a help to the acquisition of a Christian's hope. It is free or it is nothing. No debt of purchase-price is outstanding. "Jesus paid it all."

But, strangely enough, the gospel is hindered less by those who still strive to pay a price for salvation than by those who accept this as free but mistake the nature of its freeness. The remark, "It costs nothing to become a Christian," indicates almost infallibly that its author entirely misconceives the colossal gratuity of which he speaks.

To say that the gospel is free is to say, first, that it is not purchased, does not come in the way of any commercial return whether for money or for hard and taxing deeds. But it is the wildest defiance of reason to infer from this that only a tenth of our income and a seventh of our time ought to be at the disposal of the Master. The gospel is free in that its value cannot be measured in gold or its blessings gotten in a mercantile way. But the possession of it does not free the possessor from the obligation to devote both himself and his substance to God's cause.

A New York City club makes it an essential condition of membership that the applicant's ancestors shall have resided in the city for at least a century. Money cannot buy admission to that company, yet he who joins will freely spend money therefor. It costs nothing to enter, but much to stay.

Entrance to Victoria's court is granted freely if at all. The queen's favors are not for sale, but he who sees her pays his penny often over. Money is not the qualifying condition, though the fees amount to five hundred dollars.

So the gospel costs nothing, not because nothing is to be spent in its service, but because nothing can be an equivalent for the benefit it brings. Its price is beyond rubies, but he who embraces it cannot thereafter hoard his jewels. The chapter that bids us "take the water of life freely" offers the right to the tree of life to those who "do Christ's commandments."

The gospel is a free gift, calling for a free gift in return. In this sense it costs everything. The idea of payment whether of wealth or of personal service involves the thought of giving a portion of our substance or ourselves to obtain something less valuable than we because purchased with a part only of what we have or are. But to give the whole of wealth and of self, as one must to be a Christian, is not to purchase; it is absolute surrender. We cannot buy the water of life; we must "take" it if we have it at all. A man is more than his wealth; the gospel is greater than self. It costs nothing because it costs all.

Still is salvation free, because its price, in this only sense in which it bears a price, is in every man's possession. Were the price something external to the soul the gospel would be far from free. The external has neither unity nor universality. The endless catalogue of "things that are seen" embraces not one that is within the reach of all. If any gift of civilization were required in order to salvation the heathen world would at once be excluded. To ask a man to give for the water of life what he cannot get, however small the consideration, were to place a prohibitory tariff on the gospel. Better ask all of every man than to ask inferior but unacquirable gifts of any. In no other fortune or estate are human beings so alike, so equally well off, as in simple selfhood. A man's fellow-being may have a mortgage on his property, but not on the man himself. A man may have given his goods for other treasures than those of the gospel, but he has himself left. He may have abused himself till he is a battered fragment of what he once was; he has an immortal soul with all its stores of affection still in his keeping. He needs but to give himself, whether he be much or little, and the water of life is his.

It is his "freely," because more valuable than himself; "freely" because given for his easiest obtained possession; "freely," last and best, because in giving himself he finds himself. To give other things than self we must part with them. To give one's self to Jesus is to find one's self. "Whosoever will save his life shall lose it, and whosoever will lose his life for my sake shall find it." That the water of life is free because it costs all is a paradox. That in giving self we regain self, saved, bettered and enlarged, is the paradox explained.

Here is a strong missionary incentive. The freeness of the gospel is the reason why there need be no waiting for the heathen to secure preliminary equipment of wealth, learning, or rectitude before we bear them our message. Their need is their qualification. Observe

II. THE UNIVERSALITY OF THE INVITATION.

"Come," is its unqualified bidding. Other commands have been to individuals or at most to nations; this command traverses the globe and the centuries, encountering no limitation of nation, sex, color, condition or time to turn its welcome to rebuke.

"Let the Spirit say, Come," gives the invitation a very broad sweep. But the question of the Spirit's "effectual calling" suggests a possible limitation. Hence the "bride," too, is to say, Come; the Church gives its world-wide call. But the Church has not always welcomed every one. Its missionary zeal is but kindling after nineteen centuries. The invitation must be more widely heralded. So the hearer, whoever he may be, is to say, Come, whether the Church sanctions his preaching or not. William Carey is to say, Come, even if

Ryland snarls, "You are a miserable enthusiast." Mr. Moody is to say, Come, even if regularly ordained clergymen would dissuade him. The Church may object to audience or to preacher; never mind. Every hearer's mission is to say, Come. Every agency that can be enlisted is to assist in the proclamation of this universal invitation.

But as Church and hearer both may be unfaithful, an added message issues, addressed directly to its objects. "Let him that is athirst come." Any one's thirst for salvation proves that salvation is meant for him. They at least are elect who elect. And if there is one yonder on the margin of the crowd who is not exactly thirsty yet would rather drink than not, with some desire, some will in the matter, he too is asked and urged. "Whosoever will, let him come." Not a soul on earth is left out. "Whosoever will." There is no exclusiveness about that invitation. If any are excluded it is because they exclude the invitation.

If doubt could still linger whether "whosoever" means all or only a few, the character and work of him who issues the invitation would silence the last possible query. These words are the testimony of Jesus, whose reward is with him to give to *every* man according as his work shall be. He who judges all must invite all; he who tests the work of each by an exalted standard cannot refuse to any the possibility of conformity to that standard. He is the "Alpha and Omega, the beginning and the end, the first and the last." Such a one will be far-seeing enough to view the whole race in his prevision, powerful enough to include all in his provision. His vision is not so piercing as to see a want which his strength cannot supply. He is the first and the last; every son and daughter of Adam falls under his eye. He is the "root and the offspring of David," our brother; all the interests of humanity are precious to his heart. He is the "bright and morning star;" all the resources of the Godhead his hand wields. By nature and by work he is qualified and he is prompted to welcome the entire race to drink from the living stream that all Humanity's thirsty sons cannot drain. Blessed be God, the face of Jesus is not that of a clique's master. All will not follow him, but all may if they will. He sounds forth a universal invitation.

Here is a second urgent missionary motive. The universality of the Lord's invitation should cut the nerve of all dispute about the condition of the heathen, past or present, living or dead. The invitation is universal in our Master's intent; let us make it so in fact. Whether the freedom from responsibility which the heathen enjoy through absence of light, will make their destiny darker or brighter than ours it is hard to say certainly, but of one thing we are sure: they lack the knowledge of the Great Invitation which we have, and which they may have if he that heareth will say, Come.

We have still to consider

III. THE RESULT OF ACCEPTING THE INVITATION.

"Life" is the word in which crystallize man's dearest hopes. Nor ought we to think that by "life" the gospel means less than the deepest and most real content which we attribute to life. Not physical life is offered, if regeneration of body be meant, but life as a divine power, participation in God's likeness, purity, knowledge, self-mastery, spiritual insight, the incorporation in ourselves of all that is true and beautiful and good. These qualities equip one for all the storm and stress that assail mortals here below, and fit him for a residence eternal in the heavens. Taking the word in this profound and true sense, man can have no deeper need than life. Age and pain are crowding inch by inch limbs feeble at their prime into the narrow house. With one foot in the grave and the other on crumbling sands, man baffles, through the hope of eternal life, the woes of the present brief span of existence,

Other remedies serve only to prove that here death is mightier than life. The gospel has a surer efficacy. It robs our earthly sojourn of half its terrors by bidding us expect them, and draws the sting of the other half by the promise of a perfect and painless life when He shall come who is himself the Life. The gospel does not assure us of freedom from pain here, but of ability to bear it. The gospel does not offer India or Africa "silver or gold," but it does bid their children enter into spiritual life. Life is man's true fortune, not painless limbs or exhaustless treasure. Life is substance indeed, the eternal gold. Life is what man most deeply needs: the gospel fills this need.

The necessity which the gift of life satisfies is as general as it is deep. America has more light than Asia, but not equally as much more life. The spread of civilization is not by itself life; the progress of education is not life; mere knowledge of the gospel is not life. Only the personal knowledge of God is life. Differences of race, social advancement, intellectual discernment and religious knowledge are not perceptible beneath the shadow of the one pre-eminent need. Our different estimates and treatment of the Anglo-Saxon and the African are not justified in view of their fundamental common destitution, which places them on practically the same level before God. The boast of the American over the Asiatic is like boast of butterfly over caterpillar. One flies where the other walks, but they are alike frail and transitory, and neither can raise itself to the sky.

The need of life is as permanent as it is deep and universal. Here more than before the equality of men appears. Satisfy permanently this requirement, endow a man with immortality, and, were the difference what it seems, the start one gets of another in this bit of eternity called life is not worth mentioning. A ship's length is not a large lead for a vessel that is to race another around the globe. The man born the day before his cousin does not always surpass him at fifty. The threshold of the other life will hardly be crossed before many a Telegu or Karen has equalled or surpassed the European or American who counts himself worth in all respects a thousand fold the savage. None can say whether Judson's first convert may not in the light of eternity outshine even that wise and good man from whom he first learned of Christ. The gifts of civilization that conceal for a day the essentially equivalent values of the Western and the Oriental, will pass away when the spirit becomes homeless and souls awake in a rational world.

Here is a third stimulus to missionary endeavor. The promise of life answering the one deepest universal and permanent want of man makes the heathen so our brothers in equality of distress and possibility of development that all distinctions of race and culture between them and ourselves should be forgotten. If the dark horde of the unevangelized were white, cultivated and intimately related to us, what an exodus of men and money there would be on their behalf. But the differences in color, culture and blood are more insignificant in God's sight, compared with our fellowship in the lack of spiritual life, than to the aëronaut the variant hues and sizes of lichen and oak miles below. All are the children of God, though far from him. All have some sense of this distance, and desire to lessen it. All must perish if the chasm is not bridged. For all a living way of access to the Father has been provided in the atonement of Christ. In this community of poverty and of possibility is the motive that should give impetus to work among the distant, the degraded, the hard to win. Canon Taylor may mock at small results among so-called worthless tribes; but among God's children, for whom Jesus died, there are no worthless tribes. The value of the heathen is to be judged in view of the possibilities of their development in another world. To them, too, as well as to the more favored children of our race, be the heavenly message rung forth, "Whosoever will, let him take the water of life freely."

Alternative Lesson XIII. December 24.

[CHRISTMAS LESSON.]

THE BIRTH OF JESUS.
Matthew ii: 1-11.

BY REV. H. W. PINKHAM, BRIDGEPORT, CONN.

BEAUTIFUL and instructive is the story of the wise men who came to do honor to the infant Messiah. The evangelist outlines a picture which well repays patient, sympathetic study. The center of the picture is the Christ. A light from heaven seems to shine upon him. The wise men worship him. In the dark background appears Herod's evil face.

THE WISE MEN.

Imagination has delighted to add to the sacred narrative. Tradition makes the wise men three in number, representative of the periods of life; one a ruddy, beardless youth, another in the prime of life, the third hoary with age. Real knowledge, however, is limited to this, that they were "Magi from the East." Magi was the name given by the Babylonians, Persians, and others, to the learned, priestly class. "Astrologers" is its best equivalent here. The wise men believed that human affairs are controlled by the heavenly bodies. An extraordinary appearance in the sky was supposed to indicate some remarkable event in human history.

Ancient historians declare that the Jewish Messianic expectation was widespread and shared by many peoples,

Throughout the East there prevailed a strong conviction that a powerful monarch would arise in Judea and gain dominion over the whole world. The wise men thought that the "star" announced the birth of this expected king of the Jews. They journeyed westward to do homage even in his infancy to one whose career was to be so glorious.

Did they have any clear conception of the real nature of the Messiah's kingdom? The text affords no decisive answer to the question. But one cannot think that it was to no purpose that God put it into their hearts to make their long journey. Doubtless they were granted the privilege which the devout Simeon enjoyed because, like him, they had come to recognize the need of humanity for some new and mighty uplifting force. Simeon was "looking for the consolation of Israel." The wise men represented the Gentile world which, no less than Israel, was in need of a great Deliverer. They are to be numbered with those nobler souls of heathendom who, spite of false religious systems, rise into a recognition of the living God. By astrology they sought to discover the divine purposes. Astrology was falsehood and superstition. But God graciously speaks to men in a language they can understand though it be but an imperfect medium of expression. The wise men studied the stars. God brought them to the Light of the world. He satisfied their half-conscious desires and permitted them to behold him who was to bring salvation to the Gentiles. Their experience illustrates God's method of imparting fuller truth to those who are seeking truth. And their worship of Jesus and their gifts to him seem prophetic of the triumphs he was to win in the Gentile world.

HEROD.

Even across the Saviour's infancy fell the black shadow of human sin. Herod's guilty heart was troubled by the inquiry of the wise men. He himself, an alien, had no right to the throne of David, and he was ever haunted by fear lest he be overthrown. His jealousy of possible rivals had already made his palace crimson with the blood of his own kindred. This is the penalty every sinner suffers: God gives him up to further sin. Herod's life had been a series of appalling crimes. Now, in his old age, he would if possible anticipate the fury of the Jewish mob that cried, "Crucify him!" Crucify him!"

But in order to accomplish his wicked purpose he hides it and feigns sympathy with the wise men. He helps them to discover the object of their search, intending to use them as his tools. "Bring me word, that I also may come and worship him." Not seldom a mask of devoutness covers a face distorted with evil. Herod has his disciples. They are those who make religious professions in order to further their business or social interests. They are the politicians that avow a profound regard for the public welfare and then barter that welfare for their own gain. They are the scholars that loudly proclaim their zeal for truth while all the time they seek to blind men's eyes to truth.

Christ is the touchstone of human character. In one his presence kindles lofty purpose and brings to light latent nobility. In another his presence intensifies evil desire and reveals a hidden depth of malignity. The wise men welcomed the new king and gave him homage and gifts. Herod was troubled by his advent and sought to slay him. None understood him then as we may now. When one recognizes his true character, to refuse allegiance to him is to acknowledge spiritual kinship with Herod.

THE STAR.

Kepler's calculations show that at about the time of Jesus' birth there was a very unusual planetary conjunction, sure to attract the attention of men given to astrology. It was, moreover, in a region of the heavens supposed to be especially connected with the fortunes of Israel. When the same conjunction occurred in 1604, there appeared a brilliant temporary star. After shining for about a year it gradually disappeared. Was this the " Star of Bethlehem ?" And is its appearance periodic? So some have thought. Perhaps the "star" was a comet. It is asserted, though hardly established, that the Chinese astronomical records show that a comet appeared at this very time. Whatever the phenomenon, whether natural or miraculous, it was the means which God used for the guidance of the Magi.

In the East they had seen the star. It had seemed to speak to them with more than human authority, impelling them to travel to Judea to see for themselves what great thing had come to pass. Night after night of their journey they had welcomed its appearance. It seemed to them a great, superhuman friend, and they loved to look upon it. Now, following Herod's direction, they leave Jerusalem for Bethlehem. Night comes on and once more the friendly light begins to beam upon them. It seems to go before them and to point out Bethlehem as their journey's end. "The star!" "The star!" they cried, and " rejoiced with exceeding great joy." So may we rejoice as we recognize God's presence in our lives. There is a great, heavenly Friend who guides our steps. Light from the star of Bethlehem falls upon our way.

THE CHRIST.

It was only a helpless babe in his mother's arms that met the wise men's gaze. What was he that they should bow in reverence before him? And why do we celebrate his birthday?

Wordsworth expresses the poetic fancy that the human soul enters the earthly life, passing through the gateway of birth from a pre-ëxistent state of heavenly glory.

"Not in entire forgetfulness,
And not in utter nakedness,
But trailing clouds of glory do we come
From God, who is our home."

The poetry is at least suggestive of a real truth. Every new human soul is a messenger from heaven, a fresh inlet of divine love, another medium through which God reveals himself. Who can see the innocence, the joyful trust, the sweet simplicity of early childhood without recognizing the truth that "Of such is the kingdom of heaven." Alas, that ever the heavenly glory which encircles the child-life should be darkened by the earth-clouds of sin!

Natural and fitting is it that we observe the birthdays of our loved ones. To give them presents is to say, "I am glad you are here. This is a token of my gratitude because I have you." There are birthdays which whole nations celebrate. We in America are grateful that God gave to our country Washington, and the day when his life began seems to us a great day. But there is one birthday whose celebration is wider than the limits of any family, nation or race. The world around there are those who rejoice upon Christmas Day and call to mind the beginning of his human life who was indeed a messenger from heaven as no other human being ever was, who came to earth indeed, "trailing clouds of glory." He was "the effulgence of God's glory and the very image of his substance."

Christ expresses God in terms of human experience. Thus He is Mediator and Saviour. Man is made in the image of God. Something of divine light shines out from every human soul. But, alas, that light only feebly struggles through the dim and dingy windows of imperfect, sinful lives. Men refused to have God in their knowledge and "God gave them up unto a reprobate mind." From the beginning of history until Christ came, the faithful historian must paint the experience of the race in sombre colors. And the darkest hour was just before the dawn. When the wise men made their journey the world was "effete with the drunkenness of crime." Even in Israel, the chosen nation so highly honored of God, while there were some righteous and devout, the most were Pharisaical, their religion hardened into certain forms, or Sadducean, sharing with the heathen their scepticism. The fulness of the time came at last. Men were feeling the despair of those "without God and without hope in the world." And Christ came. God who of old time had spoken unto the fathers in the prophets by divers portions and in divers manners, then spoke to men in his Son.

> "The Word had breath and wrought
> With human hands the creed of creeds,
> In loveliness of perfect deeds,
> More strong than all poetic thought.
>
> Which he may read that binds the sheaf,
> Or builds the house, or digs the grave,
> And those wild eyes that watch the wave
> In roarings round the coral reef."

In Jesus the consciousness of God, which the world had seemed to be losing, was clear and strong. His fellowship with the Father was unbroken. He did perfectly the Father's will. Sincere souls coming within his influence found God through him. And this was no accident. God had indeed entered into a human life and filled it to the full with himself. They who looked on Jesus saw in him more than a Galilean peasant. They saw God. Jesus is the most complete revelation God has made of himself, and we look for no higher. "The Father is greater than I," he said indeed. Always the manifestation falls short of the fulness of that which is manifested. But it is the most perfect revelation possible for human beings to receive. Our conception of God must be in forms of human thought. God must come to man, if at all, with his glory veiled in human limitations. And thus "God was in Christ reconciling the world unto himself."

Christ is prophetic of redeemed and perfected humanity. That man is made in the image of God renders possible an incarnation. The historical incarnation reveals the possibilities of humanity. In Christ we see that ideal toward which we are bound ever to strive. He is the prophecy of that which his disciples may become—aye, and by God's grace sometime will become. He came not alone that men might know what kind of a being God is, namely a Christ-like Being, but also that men might themselves be Christ-like. To the degree in which any man is Christ-like, God has entered into his life. Men looking at him see God, not clearly as in Christ, but dimly, though, it may be, with increasing clearness. Are there many incarnations then? Shall Christs be multiplied? It is enough to say that God came to earth in Christ that through him he might come to many, and so Christ be "the first-born among many brethren."

This is the great lesson of the Incarnation, that God is in humanity. He is in your life and mine. According as we let him work and work with him, as Jesus did, he works in us and through us, restoring in us his own image which sin has marred, by our lives revealing himself to those around us, making us the channels along which his love may flow to others of his children.

All this we know because of him whose birthday Christmas celebrates. Well may the Christmas season be filled with rejoicing. When Christ was born the angel-choir burst forth in song. Shall not our hearts echo that song at every Christmas anniversary? "Glory to God in the highest!"

We honor the birthdays of our friends by gifts to them. They are the tokens of our love. The heart goes with them, else they are meaningless. "The gift without the giver is bare." What shall we give to Christ on his birthday? The wise men opened their treasures and offered unto him gold and frankincense and myrrh. Shall we set apart for him a portion of our money? Yes, but only as a sign that all our money is his, and that we will use it all for him. Shall we devote to him a portion of our time? Yes, but only as a sign that all our time is his, and that we will spend it all in his service. This is the gift we will bring him on his birthday—even ourselves, the gold of all our possessions and talents, the frankincense of our hearts' richest devotion, the myrrh of our self-sacrificing toils and pains. This is the best celebration of Christmas, to give to Christ ourselves. This is the birthday gift he desires from us, even ourselves.

www.ingramcontent.com/pod-product-compliance
Lightning Source LLC
Chambersburg PA
CBHW032000300426
44117CB00008B/842